WHEN HARRY MET CUBBY

WHEN HARRY MET CUBBY

The Story of the James Bond Producers

Robert Sellers

First published 2019

The History Press
97 St George's Place, Cheltenham,
Gloucestershire, GL50 3QB
www.thehistorypress.co.uk

British Library Cataloguing in Publication Data.
A catalogue record for this book is available from the British Library.

ISBN 978 0 7509 9042 4

Typesetting and origination by The History Press
Printed and bound in Great Britain by TJ International Ltd.

Contents

Acknowledgements

I am indebted to all of the following who spoke to me for this book and over the years on the subject of Broccoli and Saltzman and the world of James Bond:

Sir Ken Adam, Nick Alder, Vic Armstrong, Robert S. Baker, Keith Baxter, Michael Billington, Lord Birkett, Andrew Birkin, Honor Blackman, Earl Cameron, William P. Cartlidge, Chris Coppel, Michael Craig, Len Deighton, Shirley Eaton, Britt Ekland, Anthony Field, Sir Ranulph Fiennes, Cyril Frankel, Sidney J. Furie, Lewis Gilbert, Julian Glover, Ron Goodwin, Roger Green, Adrian Hall, Guy Hamilton, Graham Hartstone, Johanna Harwood, Cherry Hughes, Richard Jenkins, Burt Kwouk, Peter Lamont, Walter Lassally, Sir Christopher Lee, George Leech, Euan Lloyd, Sue Lloyd, Dyson Lovell, Joanna Lumley, Tom Mankiewicz, Tania Mallett, Sir Roger Moore, Monty Norman, Simon Oates, Luciana Paluzzi, Mollie Peters, David Picker, Eric Pleskow, Gary Raymond, John Ronane, Ken Russell, Philip Saville, Robert J. Sherman, Paul Tucker, Jeremy Vaughan, Norman Wanstall.

Special thanks go to: Mark Cerulli, Ajay Chowdhury, Matthew Field, Edward Gross, Sylvan Mason, Gareth Owen, Lee Pfieffer, Luis Abbou Planisi, Graham Rye and Dave Worrall.

Harry and Cubby: An Introduction

They are two of the most extraordinary filmmakers the movie business has ever known, responsible for the most successful movie franchise in history, and yet they were two men of such vastly different personalities, ambitions and desires, that it was a remarkable feat in itself that their partnership lasted as long as it did. Cubby the large, warm, Italian New Yorker, and Harry, a tough pugnacious Canadian; together they created fireworks. 'We have a kind of chemistry that gels,' Saltzman once said. 'We fight with the distributors, we fight with the agents and we fight with each other.'[1]

Even with all the bickering and disagreements, they did complement one another because each of them brought something completely unique to Bond, as screenwriter Tom Mankiewicz observed: 'Harry was such a volatile guy, all the time moving, going, things happening. And I always thought privately that Harry was never happier than when he was either suing somebody or getting sued. So much of the pizazz that went in Bond belonged to Harry, and much of the essence and soul of Bond was Cubby.'[2]

Cubby was the calmer of the two, the diplomat, as Michael Caine observed: 'They're like two policemen. Cubby gives you the cigarette and Harry knocks it out of your mouth.'[3] Harry and Cubby worked as a double act, in the sense – and this often happens in partnerships – that Cubby was the nice guy, while Harry did most of the dirty work, laying down the law. This probably didn't help Harry's reputation with the crew, although that was probably his natural disposition anyway. As Honor Blackman observed on the set of *Goldfinger*, 'Harry was the one who put the pressure on. Cubby was acting like a teddy bear.'[4]

Cubby was the practical one; problems in shooting or personal relationships, he would sort those out. He believed in people who worked hard and delivered the goods, not temperamental geniuses. 'A genius is someone who costs you money,' he once said.[5] He was the one that would spend more time on the set, chatting with the crew, telling stories to the prop guys. 'Cubby was more one of the boys,' said Ken Adam.[6] One of the things he loved to do was to arrive on a location very early in the morning and watch, as he put it, for the 'circus' to arrive, the camera and lighting trucks, the catering vans, the actors, and everything else that made up a crew on the road. 'That was his big thrill,' Barbara Broccoli remembered.[7] Yet he could be just as tough as Harry and equally ruthless in business, while retaining unwavering loyalty from those around him.

Harry was a dreamer, a showman, a whirligig and a great salesman, a throwback almost to the old-style Hollywood package-promoter type of producer. Full of energy and ideas, he was constantly flitting from one project to the next. 'I think probably his greatest strength was his greatest weakness,' claimed Michael G. Wilson, 'which is that he could talk anybody into anything, including himself.'[8]

He had an incredibly low boredom threshold. Where Cubby was a very steady kind of producer, focused on the job in hand, Harry's mind was always racing. 'His concentration was appalling,' said his assistant Sue St John.[9] In meetings he might suddenly grow restless and begin talking about something completely unrelated.

As people they were chalk and cheese, with scarcely anything in common, including their outside pursuits and social circles, as Tom Mankiewicz observed: 'If one went to Harry's house for dinner, or you went to Cubby's, even if there were twenty people at dinner there was no overlap, Cubby's friends were completely different to Harry's.'[10]

Their attitude to work was different, how they operated as producers. Paul Tucker, who worked as production accountant on the early Roger Moore Bonds, saw this first hand. 'Harry would be around, but you wouldn't know he was there. He might be in his trailer or having meetings somewhere. Whereas Cubby was always very visual, always around.'[11]

Most significant of all, their attitude to Bond contrasted markedly. Harry was always busy on other ventures, buying up companies, signing up talent or movie properties; he had so many other strings to his bow, other balls in the air. 'That was part of his nature,' said Guy Hamilton. 'Harry was a big entrepreneur. He loved the idea of being busy. Cubby meanwhile knew that Bond was like the goose that laid the golden egg and was intent on preserving it and to make sure that nobody tarnished it.'[12]

In spite of their differences, both men were creative, innovative and good businessmen. Both backed talent and followed their hunches. Roald Dahl called them 'perfectionists'.[13] George Lazenby preferred to label them as 'good hustlers'.[14] That's why the partnership worked so well, at least at the beginning: they represented, in the words of publicity guru Jerry Juroe, 'a relationship that was based on two opposing points of view reaching the same objective.'[15] Yes, they used to have fights, with Harry the instigator and Cubby the leveller, according to effects man John Stears, but what kept them together at first was the success of the films; they needed each other, and it suited both of them to stay together. It was only when the films grew in size and immense popularity that, what had always been, in the words of art director Syd Cain, 'an uneasy alliance',[16] began to fracture and ultimately fall apart.

This, then, is their story, a remarkable story that left the world with one of the greatest cultural legacies of the twentieth century.

1

Cubby

On the morning of 20 May 1927, the young Cubby Broccoli's outlook on life changed forever. He'd read in the papers about the aviator Charles Lindbergh's plan to fly the Atlantic solo, a course of action ridiculed by many since it had already claimed a number of capable pilots. To Cubby, Lindbergh wasn't a fool; he was a hero, and sitting on a tractor about to plough the fields on the family farm in Long Island, his heart started racing as the unmistakable drone of an aircraft's engine approached. Screenwriter Tom Mankiewicz recalled Cubby telling him what happened next:

> He said, 'Lindbergh flew over my farm, and everyone knew the *Spirit of St Louis*, and there it was on the side of the plane. It was so loaded with fuel it was flying very low, and I jumped up and down and I waved at the plane, and I can't tell you for sure but it seemed to me he waggled his wings at me. That was the most thrilling moment of my life.'[1]

That night Cubby listened intently on the radio as news of Lindbergh's historic flight was relayed back to a captivated nation. Cubby's hero had beaten the odds; he'd made it in spite of all the naysayers. It was an event that proved to Cubby that anything was possible, just so long as you believed in yourself and aimed at the big horizon.

★

Cubby's maternal grandmother Marietta, a widow, and her three children came to America from Calabria in Southern Italy in 1897, full of hopes and dreams, arriving by ocean liner at Ellis Island, the disembarkation point for all immigrants into New York. From there the family made their way by train to Astoria, Queens and settled into two small rooms at the top of a tenement block on Hoyt Avenue, packed with Polish, Jewish and German families. A tenacious woman, whose attitude to hard work inspired not only Cubby but the rest of the family, Marietta set herself up as a midwife and became a valuable asset to the neighbourhood.[2]

Marietta's eldest daughter, Cristina, had met and fallen in love with another Italian immigrant, Giovanni Broccoli, a construction worker twice her age. They married in the spring of 1902 and within a year Cristina gave birth to a son, John. Six years later another son arrived, Albert Romolo Broccoli, on 5 April 1909, born in those same tenement rooms on Hoyt Avenue. Family legend has it that it was a breech birth and the baby had trouble breathing. Marietta resorted to a traditional Calabrian remedy – shoving the head of a black chicken into the mouth. The treatment worked and the boy started to breathe again.[3]

Kids grew up fast in Queens and Cubby was no different; he even learnt to tolerate the taunts of other kids when they called him 'Dago'. One escape route was the picture house, where he went as often as he could, sometimes with his brother John or his cousin Pat de Cicco. Home was a warm and loving environment cultivated by his mother. His father worked at any construction job he could find, which sometimes took him away from the family for months at a time.[4]

For a while Cristina landed a job as a live-in cook and housekeeper with a rich family before Cubby's uncle invited them to come live with him. Pasquale de Cicco had managed to scrape together enough cash to rent a farm outside Astoria and try his luck planting vegetables, especially broccoli. According to Cubby, Pasquale brought the very first broccoli seeds to America, taken from a particularly fine strain back home in Calabria. It would form the basis of a successful family enterprise.[5]

The Broccolis happily earned their keep on the farm, with Cubby helping to wash and crate the produce for delivery to Harlem market on carts drawn by horses; 'beautiful big bay horses with feathers on their legs'.[6] It was on the farm that Cubby and de Cicco's son Pat grew even closer; there were just nine months separating them, forging a friendship that lasted until Pat's death in 1978. It was Pat who came up with the now famous nickname of 'Cubby' that in time replaced his given name of Romolo. Pat said his cousin reminded him of a little fat, roly-poly comic strip character called Abie Kabible and that's what he went around calling him. Over time, Kabible was shortened to 'Kubbie' and finally 'Cubby'.[7]

Just like Pasquale, Giovanni Broccoli dreamed of buying a farm, and after years of hard graft and putting as much money as he could afford to one side, that dream became a reality when he purchased a modest 25-acre piece of land close to Lake Ronkonkoma on Long Island. It came complete with a couple of tractors and a farmhouse, and the idea was to follow Pasquale's example and grow vegetables to sell in Harlem market. Unable to afford any labourers at first, the whole family lent a hand; it was backbreaking work. Cubby's shift started early in the morning before school, a 2-mile walk away. He'd plough the fields in a tractor, having learnt to drive at the age of 12, or crawl along the ground weeding out the crops.[8] It was also his job to drive the produce to market and sell it. 'It was hard times,' he admitted. 'If nobody would buy the stuff, instead of hauling it back again we'd dump it in the river.'[9]

Doing as well as he could at school, Cubby had no real idea what he wanted to do in life, 'just a fascination for painting and sculpting, trying to create things'.[10] Then he made an important decision: to quit school early to work on the farm full-time and help out his parents, who were toiling in the fields and not getting any younger. As writer and family friend Donald Zec would recall, 'The thing that kept turning in Cubby's narrative would be his memory of his mother on her knees in appalling heat pulling out the weeds between the furrows of the crops.'[11] The family finally persuaded Cristina to give up physical chores and instead concentrate on feeding the increasing number of migrant labourers who had been taken on. Tragically, it was too late for Giovanni. One hot summer's day working out in the fields with his two sons he suffered a massive heart attack and died within minutes.[12]

After the death of their father, Cubby and John embarked on a farming venture out in Florida, with disastrous results. Blight and a hurricane decimated two successive crops and left them both cash-strapped.[13] Calling it quits in 1933, Cubby went to work for a distant relative, Agostino d'Orta, who owned the Long Island Casket Company.[14] The morbidity of working around funeral parlours and undertakers soon depressed him and he was looking for another avenue of employment, but those months with the company certainly stayed with Cubby and are the reason why coffins pop up periodically throughout the 007 series, from Bond being menaced by a hearse in *Dr No*, to almost being cremated in *Diamonds Are Forever*, avoiding a coffin full of snakes in *Live and Let Die* and threatened by a knife-wielding killer emerging from a floating coffin in *Moonraker*.

While he was thinking what to do with his life next, Cubby decided to take a short break in Hollywood, where his cousin Pat was now living. Pat became a rich man when his father Pasquale died. Ditching farming altogether, his dark good looks and sartorial elegance made an indelible impression on New York's social scene, where Cubby was sometimes asked to tag along, his first taste of an exciting new world that was a million miles away from clawing at the earth with your bare hands.

Now making a name for himself as an agent and business manager for actors in Hollywood, Cubby had been urged by his cousin to fly over and see him. Pat had married comedy actress Thelma Todd, then under contract to producer Hal Roach, working for the likes of Laurel and Hardy, along with being loaned out to star opposite the Marx Brothers and Buster Keaton. By the time Cubby landed in Hollywood the union had dissolved, but Pat still appeared to be very much a fixture about town, having cultivated friendships with the great and the good, including Cary Grant and Howard Hughes.

It didn't take long for Hollywood to rub off on Cubby; the glamour and excitement of the place was intoxicating. Renting a tuxedo, he went to his first movie premiere, mixing with the stars. What left the biggest impression, though, was the fact that all these movie tycoons who ran the studios were immigrants themselves, all hailing from his father's generation. From humble beginnings the Goldwyns, the Mayers and the Cohns had risen to the top, commanding absolute power over their empires.

With Pat keen for his cousin to stay in Los Angeles and try to find work, Cubby landed a job selling hair products door to door, then as a salesman in an exclusive Beverly Hills jeweller. But what he really hankered after was to get into the film business somehow. It was another immigrant tycoon, this one from Russia, Joe Schenck, who provided that invaluable first leg-up. Schenck, along with Darryl F. Zanuck, had established 20th Century Fox, and through Pat's contacts Cubby got a job there as a third assistant. 'If the director wanted a cup of coffee, or needed an actor to be called onto the set, I arranged it.'[15]

Sharing a house with Pat, the two men were often seen together at the Trocadero, an upscale nightclub that had only just opened on the Sunset Strip and immediately become the place where a lot of stars went to be seen and photographed. It was owned by Billy Wilkerson, who ran the *Hollywood Reporter*, the town's most-read trade paper. Going there wasn't cheap so Cubby asked the manager, Tom Seward, if there were any jobs going. As luck would have it the club needed a bouncer, and Cubby's larger than life frame fitted the bill. The hours he worked paid for his food and bar bill. Seward recalled

Cubby as an excellent doorman, certainly one not to mess with; 'Cubby never backed down from a fight.'[16]

It wasn't only at the Trocadero that Cubby spent his leisure time. One August evening in 1938, he was seen out on the town with a young glamorous socialite by the name of Nancy 'Slim' Gross. Making up a threesome was *King Kong* actor Bruce Cabot, whom Nancy uncharitably labelled 'seriously dumb', as opposed to the 'truly intelligent' Cubby. After going to watch a prize fight, the cosy group called into the Clover Club, a private gambling nightspot on the Sunset Strip. As Cubby and Nancy danced to the soft, lilting music, a pair of eyes couldn't stop staring at them. They belonged to maverick film director Howard Hawks, whose picture *Bringing Up Baby* had recently opened. Hawks took Cubby aside to casually enquire, 'Who's the girl you're with? I'd like to meet her.' Hawks was pushing 42, Nancy was 20, but that didn't seem to matter. Nancy went on to become Hawks's wife and self-confessed muse, exerting a huge influence over his career.[17]

Slowly but surely Cubby was rising up the Hollywood ladder, perhaps not from a professional point of view, but he was certainly mixing in the right circles. Most weekends, along with Pat, Cubby was invited round to Joe Schenck's house for a barbecue, and he had cultivated the friendship of businessman, filmmaker and aviator Howard Hughes. Often Hughes picked Cubby up and they'd fly out for a couple of days at the gaming tables of Las Vegas. Hughes also knew that if he needed help, Cubby was always there for him at the end of a telephone. 'He and I got along, I suppose, because I understood and respected his craving for privacy,' said Cubby. 'Also, we agreed on most things, and I liked him.'[18]

Then there was Gloria Blondell, the younger sister of actress Joan who had starred alongside the likes of James Cagney and John Wayne. Gloria was an actress too, though not in Joan's class. She had met Cubby and fallen in love with him. So fast was their romance that Pat tried to talk his cousin out of it when news reached him of their intended plan to marry. It went ahead anyway, in July 1940 in Las Vegas.[19]

Thanks to his connection with the two Howards – Hughes and Hawks – Cubby landed the role of assistant director on a Western picture the pair of them were making about Billy the Kid called *The Outlaw*. Hughes took personal charge of casting duties and snapped up at $50 a week a stunning 19-year-old girl that he was going to launch as a star. Her name was Jane Russell and she currently worked as a receptionist to a chiropodist.

About to travel with the crew to Flagstaff, Arizona, Hughes phoned Cubby the night before to ask if he could personally escort his starlet on the train to the location. 'Make sure she has everything she needs,' he ordered. 'Oh … and Cubby. Keep all the characters away from her.' From that moment on, Cubby acted as Miss Russell's unofficial bodyguard.[20]

Another responsibility was to wake the Native Americans who were working as extras. Out he would go every morning into the wilderness to find them all covered in frost having slept outside in the desert.[21]

After just two weeks the film was in chaos. Hughes had the rushes flown to Los Angeles daily and was soon complaining of Hawks's method, that he was economising too much and not 'taking enough time' with the filming.[22] Fine, said Hawks, and quit. Hughes brought the entire cast and crew back to Hollywood to take personal charge of the filming on the Samuel Goldwyn lot. A renowned perfectionist, requiring twenty-four takes for some scenes, Hughes completed *The Outlaw* in February 1941, although it didn't reach the nation's screens for another two years, in part due to censorship problems surrounding the natural assets of Miss Russell. The country's top censor, Joseph Breen, had seen nothing like them, according to a March 1941 interoffice memo: 'in my more than ten years of critical examination of motion pictures, I have never seen anything quite so unacceptable as the shots of the breasts of the character of Rio … Throughout almost half the picture the girl's breasts, which are quite large and prominent, are shockingly emphasized'.[23] Maybe Mr Breen should have got out more.

By the time *The Outlaw* opened across the US, Cubby had joined the navy in light of America's entry into the Second World War. His post was the Eleventh Naval District, which booked stars like Bing Crosby, Bob Hope, Danny Kaye and Dinah Shore to perform in shows for servicemen in camps and military hospitals across the States.[24]

Cubby was discharged from the navy in late 1945. Going in as a yeoman First Class, he'd ended up an ensign and considered his three years in the services a life experience, and in many ways a privilege. Back in Hollywood, though, he was just an unemployment statistic, trying to get another break in the industry. He had worked briefly as production manager for his cousin Pat on a film he was producing called *Avalanche*, directed by Irving Allen, but this was strictly B-movie territory and didn't lead anywhere. The critic of the *New York Times* decried it as 'A painful hodgepodge', and that the most articulate member of the cast was a talking raven, 'whose comments are crisply put and mercifully brief'.[25]

Things were no better at home, either. He and Gloria had decided they just weren't compatible and sought an amicable divorce. Already in his mid-30s, Cubby found himself at something of a crossroads.[26]

In the winter of 1947, Cubby went into business with a friend of his called Bert Friedlob, a wealthy liquour salesman married to the actress Eleanor Parker. The idea was to sell Christmas trees and that's exactly what Cubby had to do, standing in the freezing cold on the north-west corner of Wilshire Boulevard. It wasn't very glamorous. 'Now and again I began thinking, I have a multimillion-dollar friend, Howard Hughes: I'm the former naval ensign who took Lana Turner out to dinner, and now I'm hustling trees on a street corner.'[27]

The Christmas tree business lasted just the one season, after which Friedlob and Cubby tried their hand at the motor racing game. Along with another friend, Bob Topping, a millionaire socialite and the current husband of Lana Turner, they started promoting midget car racing, then a popular sport in the US. The idea was to take these cars and drivers over to Europe and race them there, but the whole thing turned into a financial disaster when crowds in London didn't take to it and the whole tour collapsed.[28]

This was Cubby's first trip over to Britain and he fell in love with the place and its people. 'Where's the King's Arms?' he asked a passer-by one evening as he searched for a pub to meet some friends. 'Around the Queen's arse,' came the reply, which endeared him to the country instantly.[29]

This was 1948 and Britain was still in the grip of austerity, so soon after the war. Staying at the Savoy, Cubby was politely told that due to rationing his breakfast order of bacon and eggs and a pot of coffee would not be possible. A couple of days later, the same waiter came over to his table and proudly unveiled two boiled eggs. When Cubby asked how he'd got them, the waiter answered, 'I brought them from home, sir.'[30]

Back in Los Angeles, Cubby went to work for Charlie Feldman, who ran the Famous Artists Agency, which had some of the biggest stars in Hollywood signed to it. Cubby liked Feldman, he was suave and personable, and learnt a great deal from him, not just about making money, but how to use it the right way. Feldman was amongst the first in Hollywood to put together 'package deals', choosing the right story, the right director and stars, and sometimes even financing and producing the films himself.

Cubby did well at the agency, bringing in Lana Turner to swell their star ranks and representing the likes of Ava Gardner, along with up-and-coming actors such as Robert Wagner. With his career on the turn, he decided to settle down and marry again. Her name was Nedra Clark, a former model and occasional actress. Nedra was attractive, with an easy-going charm that belied a life of heartbreaking tragedy. Born in Missouri in 1919, Nedra married at the age of 18, but the union quickly soured and when she sought a divorce her husband went wild, slashed her with a knife and stabbed to death their 2-year-old son and Nedra's mother. Going to Hollywood, Nedra married the popular American singer Buddy Clark and they had a daughter together. In October 1949, Buddy was flying back from San Francisco when the small plane he was in developed a fault and had to make an emergency landing. The only passenger not wearing a seat belt, Buddy was thrown from the plane and died of his injuries.[31] Less than a year later Nedra's beloved daughter Penny, then just 7 years old, was struck by a car and killed on her way to a friend's house. It was Cubby himself who had to break the devastating news to Nedra and drive her to the hospital.[32] When the couple tied the knot in February 1951 in a Las Vegas chapel, Cubby must have hoped that he could bring some stability and happiness into Nedra's life.

Facing the responsibilities of being a husband for the second time, one would have thought Cubby might knuckle down at his job at Famous Artists; after all, it had good prospects and was great security. Instead, this was the moment he decided to leave the company and strike out on his own as a producer. He believed that he had found the right story material for a film in Hilary St George Saunders's book *The Red Beret*, published in 1950. Within its account of the British Parachute Regiment's exploits during the Second World War, Cubby saw vast scope for a stirring tale of derring-do. With little or no spare money, he approached Irving Allen, not exactly flush himself, with the idea of going into partnership and pooling their meagre resources to buy a short option on Saunders's book.

Cubby had got quite pally with Allen when they worked together on *Avalanche* and thought he might make an ideal partner. Born in Poland in 1905, Allen was still a child when his family emigrated to America. Educated at New York public schools, he attended Georgetown University and Brooklyn Law School before quitting to enter showbusiness. Moving to California, his big break arrived when he landed a job at Universal as an apprentice in the studio's cutting rooms. Rising through the ranks from editor, to second unit director, Allen finally made it as a director in his own right, specialising largely in B-pictures. He also shot a number of well-received short films and documentaries, including *Climbing the Matterhorn* (1947), which earned him an Oscar for Best Short Subject.

Allen agreed to Broccoli's proposal of joining forces and it was hoped that Saunders himself, who had served in the Welsh Guards during the First World

War and been awarded the Military Cross, might adapt his own novel to the screen. When he died suddenly towards the end of 1951, Cubby and Irving brought in two experienced Hollywood screenwriters, Frank Nugent, a regular collaborator with John Ford, and Sy Bartlett.

Rejecting any idea of shooting the film in America, the producers decided to set up operations over in England. For one thing, they would be able to exert more creative control based outside of Hollywood, as well as taking advantage of what were cheaper production facilities and technicians. There was also the added inducement of something called the Eady Levy, a production fund established by the British government a little over a year before. This fund, accumulated from a tax on cinema tickets, was an absolute boon for producers working in the British film industry. What made it especially attractive to people like Cubby and Irving, and for the large number of American filmmakers who followed in their wake, was that even if a film was backed by a US studio, as long as the crew and actors were predominantly British then the production qualified for the subsidy.

Attention quickly turned to finding the right actor to play their paratrooper hero, with Richard Todd approached early on. As a member of the 7th Parachute Battalion and part of the D-Day landings, Todd didn't much care for the script, 'probably because I was still rather serious-minded about anything to do with the Airborne Forces and thought it an over-fictionalised treatment', so he passed.[33] Other names like Ray Milland and Trevor Howard were touted in the Hollywood trade journals before Cubby and Irving set their sights on Alan Ladd.

Their timing couldn't have been any better. Ladd had just quit Paramount over a dispute about money and was looking for a fresh challenge. By chance, Cubby had a mutual friend, Billy Wilkerson of the *Hollywood Reporter*, and a meeting was set up. 'As I drove out to his house,' Broccoli later wrote, 'I started thinking, here am I, going out to try and hire the biggest box-office star of the day, and I can just about pay my rent!'[34]

Ladd lived on a 5,000-acre ranch in Hidden Valley, a retreat tucked away in the Santa Monica mountains 50 miles outside Los Angeles, and when the producers arrived, he was up on the roof carrying out some repairs. Invited inside, the men talked about the project over a Jack Daniels. While Ladd expressed interest, the producers knew the one person they really needed to convince was the actor's wife, Sue Carol, who essentially worked as his manager and was known as a tough operator. In the end, the offer on the table was too sweet to resist: $200,000 plus 10 per cent of the profits. In addition, Sue asked for $50,000 in expenses and for the producers to provide a house conveniently close to the studio, so Ladd could bring over his family for the duration of his stay in England.[35]

Not only did Cubby and Allen agree to all this, probably wondering how the hell they were going to pay for it, they also cannily broached the idea of Ladd signing up for a total of three pictures. Sue knew how advantageous it would be for Ladd's tax situation to live and work outside the United States for something like eighteen months, and agreed the deal. It was an auspicious deal in so many ways, not just in launching Cubby as an independent producer, but also Ladd's insistence that his personal friend and collaborator Richard Maibaum join him in England to rewrite the script.

Having bagged Alan Ladd, all Cubby and Allen needed now was a studio to back them. Together they approached Cubby's old pal Howard Hughes, who had gained control of RKO Pictures. Enquiries were made and favourable noises came back, enough for Cubby to draw up the relevant paperwork, only the mercurial Hughes started avoiding him and not returning his calls. Finally, Broccoli tracked Hughes down at the home of one of his associates, Walter Kane, where the tycoon was on the phone in the toilet, a not unusual occurrence since Hughes often locked himself in a bathroom to conduct business; it was one of the few places he was never likely to be disturbed. There was the occasion, for example, when Cubby ran up debts with a local florist sending flowers on behalf of Hughes to his numerous girlfriends. When it came time for Cubby to tentatively broach the outstanding bill, Hughes locked himself in his toilet denying all knowledge. Cubby was made to wait sweating outside the bathroom, until there was a peal of laughter from inside and dollar bills came sliding under the door, one by one.[36] This time he was in no mood to wait, and rapped hard on the door saying he wasn't leaving until the contract was signed. 'Pass it under the door,' said Hughes. After a little while the signed document re-emerged. This might have been an unorthodox method to tie up a deal, but it meant Cubby and Allen were in business.[37]

Then disaster. C.J. Devlin, the man Hughes had put in charge of the day-to-day running of his studio, voiced a dislike for the project and the financing was pulled. In the end it didn't matter; *The Red Beret* was gathering its own momentum around town and Leo Jaffe over at Columbia was happy to step into the breach and provide backing. Final negotiations took place at the Warwick Hotel in New York; a good omen, thought Cubby and Allen, who named their fledgling company Warwick Films.

Cubby and Nedra, along with Allen and his wife Nita, arrived in London full of excitement and expectation about what the future might hold for them in this new country. The Broccolis took over a large apartment in an old building in Portland Place, a short walk from the BBC's Broadcasting House. A few months later, Ladd and his family arrived via boat, and eager to maximise publicity the producers leaked the arrival time of their train into Paddington station to ensure a large crowd of fans and journalists were there to greet him. They needed all the positive press they could get, since a controversy was brewing in the newspapers as to why a Hollywood star rather than a homegrown one had been chosen to play the lead in a film about British paratroopers. Eager not to offend the sensibilities of war veterans or the military establishment, Cubby stressed that Ladd's character was in fact a Canadian who enlists in the Parachute Regiment to learn from them, and not another example of Americans believing they had won the war singlehandedly. Such assurances seemed to do the trick and what might have been harmful criticism of the film was avoided.

Shooting itself, which began late in September 1952 in North Wales and at the Royal Air Force's Abingdon Parachute School in Oxfordshire, with interiors at Shepperton Studios, passed relatively smoothly. Cubby found Ladd to be a total professional; if he had any gripes or problems they were usually left to the formidable Sue to sort out. The producers were also fortunate in their choice of Terence Young as director, having admired his work on a recent British war picture called *They Were Not Divided*. Young had been an intelligence officer attached to the Guard's Armoured Division during the war and saw heavy fighting at Normandy and Arnhem. He stayed with Warwick off and on for the rest of the decade, establishing himself as a director of transatlantic action movies.

A couple of things stand out about *The Red Beret*. Firstly, the decision to use Technicolor; most British war pictures of this period were made in black and white, largely as a cost-cutting measure so that newsreel battle footage could be used. When Cubby first approached Technicolor, he was told the company was booked up solid and nothing could be done. Not giving up, Cubby once again approached his friend Billy Wilkerson, who personally knew Herbert Kalmus, co-founder of Technicolor, and managed to persuade them to change their minds. As a token of gratitude, Cubby bought the parking lot next door to the *Hollywood Reporter* offices that Wilkerson was currently renting and handed him the deed.[38]

The producers also surrounded Alan Ladd with a supporting cast of consummate British actors: Harry Andrews, Stanley Baker, Donald Houston and Leo Genn. At one stage Genn, as the unit's commander, enters an office and casually tosses his beret across the room onto a hat rack. It's a little bit of business that Terence Young later remembered and had Sean Connery do in

Dr No. What lets the film down is the all-too-hackneyed plot of watching a group of disparate individuals go through training and following them onto the battlefield, although the action set pieces are competently handled.

Someone who got an early break on the picture was a young greenhorn stuntman called Bob Simmons. At the end of one stunt, that saw Simmons blown up on a staircase and fall 16ft, he landed with a crunch on the floor, obviously in distress. Cubby was the first one over to see if everything was all right and noticed he wasn't wearing any protective clothing or stunt pads. Simmons asked in all innocence what stunt pads were. 'If you want to go on working,' said Cubby, 'you're going to have to wear pads – as of now.' With that, he beckoned Alan Ladd over. 'Just look at this kid, will ya? No pads. Not even a back pad. Jesus.' Ladd brought over a set of his own stunt pads and gave them to Simmons, telling him if he didn't wear them, he'd personally throw him off the picture. Simmons kept those pads for the rest of his career.[39]

Simmons went on to work on a number of pictures for Warwick. Already Broccoli was beginning to earn a reputation for employing the same technicians and crew members. 'If Cubby liked your work, chances are you would be employed on his future productions,' said art director Syd Cain, who also landed his big break at Warwick.[40]

By the time *The Red Beret* opened in cinemas to a lukewarm reception from critics, but solid activity at the international box office, Warwick had already begun their second picture with Alan Ladd, *Hell Below Zero*. It was based on a book by popular author Hammond Innes about whaling ships in the Antarctic and directed by Mark Robson, who replaced the original choice Raoul Walsh. Although the film's melodramatics would be criticised, the producers showed real ambition by sending a film crew out to capture the work of real whaling ships operating in the frozen wastes near the South Pole. It was Cubby who drew the short straw and went out with the second unit while his partner stayed behind in London. This turned out to be a general pattern in their relationship, according to production supervisor Adrian Worker. 'Cubby always had the dirty end. When we went out to Africa, Cubby's the one who had to come out there, not Irving. Irving wouldn't move outside a hotel if he could help it.'[41]

Worker made five pictures for Warwick, and at the beginning saw Broccoli as probably the minor partner in the relationship: 'Irving certainly was the go-ahead one. But Cubby was always a nice man. He never got flustered, ever.'[42]

Cubby never forgot his experience at sea. Hiring an icebreaker out of Cape Town the film crew rendezvoused with the whaling fleet and stayed with them for six weeks capturing the grisly business of harpooning and then eviscerating whales. As a parting gift the crew presented Broccoli with two whale penises.[43]

Some of the cast made the trip out there, too, including Stanley Baker, who Cubby recalled was great company aboard ship, and it was the start of a close and lifelong friendship. Ladd wasn't required, with the crew making use of a double for long shots. Even so, Ladd was pretty miserable on the film according to Mark Robson.

> We all knew we were working on a stinker. Alan did the best he could, under the circumstances. Alan frequently remarked that he was fed up with Europe, that he had made a mistake in tying himself up for so long and felt he was serving a prison term. He was a very, very unhappy man.[44]

If *Hell Below Zero* was tough to bear, Ladd reached an absolute nadir with his third and final picture for Warwick. *The Black Knight* was a historically muddled attempt to cash in on the sudden popularity of medieval epics, and cast Ladd as an unlikely swordsmith who heroically defends King Arthur's throne against a coup led by a villainous Peter Cushing. At first Ladd wanted nothing to do with the project, running around in tights à la Errol Flynn was just not his scene at all. It was only the intervention of a young publicist called Euan Lloyd that saved the day. Euan had become friendly with Ladd and was invited to join the actor and his family on a brief holiday in the South of France. Within days Cubby and Allen arrived to start negotiations. 'But Alan hated the script of *The Black Knight*,' recalled Lloyd:

> [He]swore never to play in it. Cubby used all his persuasive powers to change his mind, all to no effect. Cubby would not give up. Finally, Alan relented, on one amazing condition. He would do the picture if Cubby and Irving would employ me, not as a publicist, but in the production itself. I was speechless.[45]

For the next five years Euan Lloyd served as personal assistant to the two producers. 'Being alongside these two great men on a daily basis was unquestionably the education any student of film production could only dream of.'[46] Watching Cubby, especially at close quarters, Lloyd learned how to deal with stars, getting that little extra out of them through sheer good manners and courtesy rather than aggravation and implacableness, and how he took a calm approach to matters: 'A desperately needed skill in producing, especially large budget films.'[47] Something else Lloyd took from Cubby was how to choose his material carefully, 'and when focusing on a particular property to examine it from every angle and ask yourself before proceeding, would I pay good money to see this film?'[48] Lloyd did later carve out a successful career as an independent producer, responsible for teaming Sean Connery with Brigitte Bardot in the western *Shalako* (1968), and testosterone-charged action films such as *The Wild Geese* (1978) and *Who Dares Wins* (1980).

Ladd was right about the script: it stank. The writer was Alec Coppel, who'd worked on *Hell Below Zero*. He was an odd choice for a medieval story since he normally specialised in thrillers, and according to his son Chris regarded his time working on *The Black Knight* as:

> A living hell. He always wished he had never had a credit on that one. He was not that happy working on writing projects where it was dictated how it was to be written and felt 'caged' doing re-writes and adaptations. He, however, liked the money. He did used to come home disheartened while working on *The Black Knight*. I remember his referring to the producers as cigar smoking tasteless hacks.[49]

With shooting due to start in a few days under the stewardship of Tay Garnett, Cubby felt the script still required another quick touch-up and brought in a young actor by the name of Bryan Forbes, whose recently published collection of short stories had caught his eye. Forbes was also beginning to win a reputation as a script doctor, usually called in, as he put it, to perform 'emergency surgery on terminal cases'. So, Cubby gave him a call. 'I gather you're a fast man with the pen. Can you provide some pages?'[50]

It was Forbes's presence on *The Black Knight* set at Pinewood that led to one of the most amusing anecdotes to come out of any Warwick production. It concerned a scene in which Ladd was required to steal a horse in order to escape from the villain's lair. Sue, who carefully vetted all of her husband's scripts, was having none of it: such an act would do harm to Ladd's clean-cut image back in the States. Told to find a compromise, the producers quite frankly couldn't see how else the action could unfold; Ladd had to get out of the place.

'Not on a stolen horse,' insisted Sue.

'You want him to take a taxi,' said Allen.

It was Forbes who made the suggestion that perhaps after Ladd jumps from the battlements into a hay wagon, a kindly Saracen could appear saying, 'Sire, this is the horse you ordered.'

Amazingly, this seemed to placate Sue and the scene went ahead. Cubby certainly saw the funny side of it as Forbes watched him laugh all the way back to his office.[51]

While the three films with Alan Ladd were hardly artistic triumphs, they put Warwick on its fiscal feet and established Broccoli and Allen as producers who could churn out saleable products on time and on budget. Both men firmly believed in making entertainment for the masses; their films were supposed to make profits, not win awards. It was commerce they were interested in, not art. 'If somebody sends me a literate script do you know what I do with it?' Allen told one journalist. 'I throw it in the waste paper basket, that's what I do with it. It's no use making intelligent films. There aren't enough intelligent people to fill the cinemas.'[52] In the same interview, Allen made the confession that he would never watch one of his own films. 'I've got more taste than that. Does Barbara Hutton buy her jewellery at Woolworths?'

Warwick had set up their business in a plush set of offices in South Audley Street in London's Mayfair. In a 1959 *Evening Standard* profile, it was reported that Warwick had a staff of twenty-six, 'including a company secretary who used to be at the Bank of England – round the clock chauffeurs, a private cinema done up in red leather, and a Turkish bath.'

Euan Lloyd recalled that the two men shared the same office, facing each other across a vast desk, and yet were of vastly conflicting personalities. 'Irving was abrasive, quick-tempered, and sometimes downright rude. Cubby was patient and kind. When Irving created a tempest, Cubby would quickly pour oil on the waters. In fact, during my years with Warwick, I can recall only one occasion when Cubby lost his temper.'[53] Even Broccoli himself had to admit that Allen was 'a cantankerous associate, though with a bark much worse than his bite'.[54]

Thanks to a close relationship with Mike Frankovich, who was in charge of Columbia's British office, Warwick continued to have the backing of the Hollywood studio and sought out fresh story material. They bought the film rights to Robert Graves's exciting historical novel about the Greek myth of Jason and his crew of Argonauts, *The Golden Fleece*, but the project never went beyond the pre-production stage, probably because of the inherent high cost involved.[55] Columbia obviously found merit in the material since it would later finance the famous 1963 Ray Harryhausen version of the story.

Instead, the producers turned to a novel called *Prize of Gold*, about a US military officer stationed in Berlin who steals a cargo of gold to help a refugee's bid to repatriate European war orphans. Feeling confident, they approached one of the most respected writers in the country to adapt it to the screen. R.C. Sherriff, whose screen credits included *The Invisible Man* (1933),

Goodbye, Mr Chips (1939) and *Odd Man Out* (1947), is best remembered for his enduring play *Journey's End*, set in the British trenches of the First World War. Sherriff agreed to the offer and accepted a fee of £4,500 to write a first draft. If this was a move on the producers' part to gain a little bit of respectability, it backfired when they ended up using none of Sherriff's work when the script was rewritten and his name left off the credits.[56]

With the departure of Alan Ladd, the producers brought over another American star, Richard Widmark, who had just been released from a seven-year contract at 20th Century Fox. This was to remain Warwick's policy for the rest of its existence, to import an American 'name' to maximise the international appeal of their product, as Broccoli stated in a 1954 interview:

> We're not making British pictures, but American pictures in Britain. We're trying to Americanize the actors' speech in order to make the Englishman understood down in Texas and Oklahoma – in other words, break down a natural resistance and get our pictures out of the art houses and into the regular theatres.[57]

Widmark was teamed with the Swedish actress Mai Zetterling, but under the direction of Mark Robson *Prize of Gold* remained fairly routine stuff, with a 'leaden and synthetic plot', according to the unimpressed critic of the *New York Times*. It was only enlivened by a top-notch supporting cast that included Nigel Patrick, George Cole and Donald Wolfit, and some atmospheric location photography amongst the bombed-out ruins of Berlin courtesy of Ted Moore, a camera operator on Warwick's first three productions who had been promoted to Director of Photography.

★

Cubby had arrived in Estoril, the resort town on the Portuguese Riviera, to begin work on Warwick's next production, *Cockleshell Heroes*. All relevant permits had been obtained and he was looking forward to a straightforward shoot. Then came the phone call. It was a senior government official: permission to film in their country had been rescinded. As Cubby struggled to comprehend what might have gone wrong, the conversation continued and he realised what was happening: blackmail. Cubby was incensed, but it was too late now to make alternative plans.

Driving all the way from Britain, Euan Lloyd scarcely had time to unpack when Cubby and Allen accosted him in the hotel lobby with the news. 'They want a short documentary about Portugal to expand the tourist trade,' said Cubby. 'That's the deal. I don't like blackmail of any kind, but there it is. Our hands are tied.'

Allen took over. 'As of this moment, Euan, you are the writer, director and producer of this documentary. Keep the costs down, but do a good job.' When word reached the authorities that the documentary was under way, they immediately restored permission to make *Cockleshell Heroes*.[58]

The producers approached the subject of this picture with great care, since it was based on true events in which a team of Royal Marines canoed almost 100 miles behind enemy lines to blow up ships in the German-occupied French port of Bordeaux during the Second World War. Like *The Red Beret*, the story focused mainly on the meticulous training leading up to the raid and the producers were given the full cooperation of the military. Major Hasler, the man who planned and personally led the operation, acted as technical adviser and sundry other Royal Marine personnel were seconded to the production, along with the use of barracks and army facilities.

Cubby had already come to appreciate the writing skills of Richard Maibaum and thought he was the ideal choice for the film. While Maibaum delivered a tightly constructed first draft, Cubby thought it lacked an authentic British flavour, especially in the servicemen's dialogue, so he turned again to Bryan Forbes to do a rewrite. *Cockleshell Heroes* became Forbes's first credit as a screenwriter.

Although a wholly British operation, the producers' rigid policy on imported American stars meant that a miscast Jose Ferrer was the Commando leader. Much better was Trevor Howard as his second-in-command, and there was the usual fine supporting cast, including an early role for Christopher Lee. Whilst screening the rushes every night on location in a local cinema, Cubby noticed that Ferrer, who was also directing, had an interminable number of close-ups paddling his boat earnestly towards the enemy. Allen had noticed, too, and wasn't one to keep his own counsel. 'Jesus Christ!' his voice boomed out into the darkness one night. 'If there are any more of these shots, we'll have to change the title from *Cockleshell Heroes* to *Rowing up the River*!' There was a commotion at the back of the auditorium. Cubby looked and saw the figure of Ferrer dart out of the door. Not only had Ferrer not seen the funny side of Allen's comments, he later informed Cubby that he didn't want the man anywhere near the set from now on.[59] According to the film's focus puller, Ronnie Maasz, Ferrer and Allen never spoke to each other again.[60]

In order to give the film added gravitas, Broccoli and Allen mounted an impressive premiere in November 1955 at the Empire Leicester Square, with both Earl Mountbatten and Prince Philip in attendance. When the prince suggested some inaccuracies in the plot at a drinks reception after the performance, Cubby decided to incorporate his advice and hurriedly shot additional scenes to be added to the release print at a cost of almost $6,000.[61] It was money well spent, as *Cockleshell Heroes* made the top ten list of UK box office champions for 1956 and won critical plaudits; 'A very worthy member of a long line of distinguished war films made in this country,' said the *Manchester Guardian*. 'It is extraordinary though that an American company should have made it – and should be the first to honour the Royal Marines.'

It was whilst riding high on the success of *Cockleshell Heroes* that Broccoli and Allen negotiated a new contract with Columbia to produce a total of nine films over the next three years at an overall cost of £6 million.[62] It was a deal that showed just how much faith Columbia had in the two producers to deliver the right product.

There was another reason for Cubby to feel in a happy mood. Early in his marriage, doctors had broken the news that Nedra was unable to have children, a heartrending revelation that led to the adoption of a newborn child in 1954, christened Tony Broccoli. Imagine the couple's delight, especially given the traumas of Nedra's past, when she announced an unexpected pregnancy and later gave birth to a healthy baby girl, which they called Tina, after Cubby's mother.[63]

Warwick's next production was by far the company's strangest. *The Gamma People* was a real oddball of a film combining elements of horror, science fiction, political thriller and comedy. The story is of two journalists who find themselves stranded in a fictional European bloc country ruled over by a Nazi-like scientist performing sinister gamma ray experiments on children. Evolved from a script written in the early 1950s by Robert Aldrich, future director of *What Ever Happened to Baby Jane?* (1962) and *The Dirty Dozen* (1967), the film is a weak commentary on the Cold War climate of the time, though Leslie Phillips and Paul Douglas, a former New York sportswriter, make an endearing team and the Austrian backdrop is nicely captured by Ted Moore's camera. Director John Gilling would later become noted for his work at the famous horror studios of Hammer.

As work commenced on *The Gamma People*, Cubby and Allen were tying up a two-picture deal with Victor Mature, the star of such biblical epics as *Samson and Delilah* (1949) and *The Robe* (1953). Mature was a little strapped for cash at the time, which might explain his readiness to leave Hollywood and work in England. Arriving in London, Mature told a journalist about his financial plight and within days fan letters arrived at the studio containing money, which the grateful star sent back.[64]

Mature's first film for Warwick was *Safari*, directed by Terence Young, an adventure-melodrama in which he played a big game hunter in Kenya opposite a pre-*Psycho* Janet Leigh. Another big game hunter film, *Odongo*, starring Rhonda Fleming, was scripted and cast in five weeks by Cubby and Allen in order for it to be shot back-to-back with *Safari* on the same African locations during late autumn 1955.[65] Africa presented itself as an ideal 'exotic' location for Warwick, since the producers could take advantage of an Empire development scheme that provided British grants to filmmakers working in Commonwealth nations.

The story of *Safari* took place against the backdrop of the Mau Mau uprising, which was still going on when Cubby and his crew touched down at Nairobi airport. Sometimes the troubles got a little too close for comfort, such as when a crude bomb exploded outside Mature's hotel room. According to Janet Leigh, the second unit was actually attacked by the Mau Mau and several of the crew were robbed, including Janet herself.[66]

There were other discomforts, too, like dysentery, understandable in such a far-flung location. Terence Young suffered so badly from heat exhaustion it brought on a fever; gamely, he carried on. Then the plane carrying the film's wardrobe and props crashed in Khartoum and everything had to be replaced.[67]

Mature had confessed to Cubby that he was 'a devout coward', although no one blamed him when he asked for two armed guards to protect him round the clock. When the crew moved out into the bush, Mature insisted on sharing a tent with Cubby. 'He reasoned that if anybody was going to be safe, it would be the producer.'[68] As for being asked to wade through a crocodile-infested river in order to rescue his leading lady, Mature would only do it if Cubby went in first. To placate a star, these are the kinds of things a producer often finds himself doing.

Once in the water, Cubby felt something brush past his leg and he flinched. Luckily it was only a catfish. Looking across at Mature gingerly treading water, it was obvious his star was still not fully committed to what he was supposed to be doing and needed a bit of gentle encouragement. 'For chrissakes, Vic,' Cubby yelled. 'Go out there, pick up Janet in your arms and put her on the beach.' Before too long there was another disturbance in the water and something brushed past Mature's leg, only this time it was much bigger. 'Screw this!' he shouted and jumped back onto the riverbank.[69]

Safari is an interesting film in regard to Warwick's relationship with an organisation called Film Finances, which began on *The Red Beret* and continued until their final picture. Film Finances was the world's leading completion guarantor since its formation in 1950. Its function was to guarantee delivery of a film to the distributor. To this end, it acted as both mediator and production consultant. It required the independent producer, in this case Broccoli and Allen, to undertake the most rigorous preparation before a film went on the floor and continued to monitor the progress of the production closely. If a production exceeded its budget, they would then step in and provide the extra finance necessary to complete the film.

Warwick's seven-year relationship with Film Finances was fraught to say the least, since their films tended to go over schedule and over budget due to excessively tight schedules. John Croydon, formerly a production manager at Ealing Studios, who acted as an independent assessor for Film Finances, was prone to bouts of exasperation whenever a Warwick project passed his desk. By their fourth picture, *Prize of Gold*, he'd already had enough, writing, 'I can safely say we have now had too much of this unit and I do not want to be "persuaded" into the acceptance of any more of their papers.'[70]

With *Safari*, Croydon was faced with the old Warwick fault in regard to scheduling and budgeting. 'The entire thing seems out of proportion, having a very long script with a very short and tight schedule, a director we know to be very difficult and budgets that are not all that they could be. The whole thing leaves me with a very uneasy feeling.'[71]

It's interesting to note that Terence Young already had a reputation as a director of some extravagance in the way he spent money and the leisurely manner he kept to schedule, especially on location. In one letter to Film Finances from the set of *Safari*, associate producer Adrian Worker claimed that, 'Terence is going along quite fast, particularly when I am able to stand by his side.'[72]

As expected, *Safari* did go over budget and Film Finances were required to supply further funds in order to complete it. In the end, Warwick came to an arrangement to cross-collateralise three or perhaps four films, so that if a couple failed to get their money back the more successful one would bail them out. It's obvious that Broccoli came to depend heavily on Film Finances in his early producing career; indeed, he sought their services on the first Bond picture, *Dr No*.

Mature's second picture for Warwick saw him playing an Afghan bandit in a 'Boy's own' adventure called *Zarak*, a role originally earmarked for Errol Flynn when Irving Allen first optioned the property in 1953.[73] Filmed on location in Morocco, with the acclaimed stuntman Yakima Canutt in charge of the second unit, the cast also included a pre-*La Dolce Vita* Anita Ekberg and Michael Wilding, then married to Elizabeth Taylor, who was a regular and charming visitor to the set. She certainly ingratiated herself to the crew, carrying out little errands for them, including bringing cups of tea.[74]

All of the female members of the cast and crew were warned that if they intended visiting the local kasbah, appropriate clothing was essential and never to go alone. These instructions were rigorously adhered to, save for the wild Anita Ekberg who not only went unsupervised but wore shorts and a clinging top. Bedlam ensued. Word quickly reached the unit that Anita was in some trouble and sure enough, when help arrived she was cornered by a mob of men brandishing swords and sticks shouting, 'Whore!' Terence Young bravely stepped into the breach and using all his military bearing, plus a few bribes, managed to disperse the crowd. Panic over. Anita was later reprimanded but the repercussions carried on, as her co-star Eunice Gayson recalled: 'Cubby and Irving were informed by the local crew that her behaviour was "totally unacceptable" and, if she didn't leave, they feared it might be difficult for the film to continue.'[75] The producers were in a real quandary. They'd only been shooting for two weeks but Young assured them he could finish off Anita's scenes in the studio, and the actress was asked to take the first available flight out of the country.

Miss Ekberg's physical attributes caused problems of another kind during the film's marketing campaign in Britain, when the poster, featuring as it did a goodly portion of Miss Ekberg's torso, was criticised in the House of Lords as 'bordering on the obscene'. It was subsequently banned.[76]

Zarak turned out to be quite an exciting picture, and one of Cubby's favourites from his Warwick days. Way down the billing, playing the thankless role of second-in-command to Wilding's army hero, was Patrick McGoohan in one of his earliest film roles. It was a performance that particularly caught the eye of *Picturegoer*'s respected critic Margaret Hinxman, who singled him out as someone to watch out for in the future: 'In the fantastic hodgepodge of *Zarak*, there's only one acting performance worthy of the name, from Patrick McGoohan.'

After a string of real potboilers, *Fire Down Below* was an attempt by Warwick to hit the big time, employing not one but two major American stars in Robert Mitchum and Rita Hayworth, making her screen return after a four-year absence. Added to the mix was a young rising star called Jack Lemmon. Robert Parrish was put in charge and there was a script from noted American novelist Irwin Shaw. With a budget of $2.5m, substantially more than any previous Warwick film, and location shooting in Trinidad and Tobago,

Fire Down Below had pedigree and ambition, only it turned into a real headache for Cubby.

First off, Parrish had to hunt down Rita Hayworth, who was lying low in Paris after walking out on her fourth husband. If she refused to do the picture Columbia weren't going to offer any finance. After several phone calls, Parrish found out which hotel she was staying in and managed to persuade her to read the script. An admirer of Irwin Shaw's work, the actress agreed to play the role of a mystery woman who comes between two friends when they agree to take her on board their boat across the West Indies.

Flying into London together, Rita asked Parrish what the producers were like. 'They're okay,' he replied. 'Hardworking. Hustling. Cubby is a very nice guy and Irving is a bit on the crude side. He makes a lot of noise, gets everyone riled up, then Cubby moves in and calms things down.'

'And what does Irving do then?'

'Oh, he usually lies low for a while, then remembers he's a co-producer and starts kicking and screaming again.'[77]

Rita was certainly relieved to hear that it was Broccoli, rather than Allen, who was going to be out with them all on location. But it was Mitchum who caused a stir on his arrival at the airport in Trinidad. Asked what he had in his flight bag, the maverick actor promptly announced, 'Two kilos of marijuana.' It was meant as a joke, but given his reputation the comments quickly reached the ears of the local authorities. 'He damned near caused a riot,' recalled Jack Lemmon. 'We were practically barricaded in our rooms for three days and there was talk of throwing us off the island.'[78] No doubt Cubby had a lot of fun calming that one down, drawing on his previous friendship with Mitchum back in Hollywood. It was a friendship sturdy enough to survive the moment when Cubby arrived on the set one morning to be told that his star was lying on the deck of the boat drunk. When Parrish refused to wake him up, Cubby calmly picked up a bucket, filled it with sea water and poured it over the unconscious Mitchum. As Cubby later observed, it was scarcely something out of the producer's handbook, 'but it's as good a trick as any to get a hungover actor on his feet'.[79]

Returning to England, where filming resumed at MGM's Elstree Studios, Parrish instructed cameraman Desmond Dickinson to take his time over lighting Rita Hayworth's close-ups. Having been away from the screen so long and approaching her forties, the star was understandably sensitive about how she was going to be presented. Allen wasn't having any of it, scathingly asserting, 'No matter how long you take, Hayworth ain't gonna look any younger.' The actress burst into tears and ran off the set, locking herself in her dressing room. It was Cubby, of course, who went over to try and persuade her to return to work, only to get a bottle of acetone thrown at him because she thought it was Allen. The result was the film closed down for two days. Rita simply refused to appear until Cubby guaranteed her that Allen would not show up on the set when she was working.[80]

Adding to the creative tempest was a fractious relationship between the producers and their director, according to Euan Lloyd. 'Parrish, a charming and very capable director, insisted on making changes to the script as production progressed. Inevitably, this created budget and schedule over-runs, which caused Harry Cohn, head of Columbia, to intervene. He sent his senior VP Leo Jaffe to London to sort things out.'[81]

Lloyd was asked to accompany Cubby to welcome Leo Jaffe to Claridge's hotel before taking him to the set. Lunch was ordered and Cubby began his charm offensive. 'But when the telephone rang in Leo Jaffe's suite,' said Lloyd,

> it was as if lightning had struck the hotel. Mr Jaffe's face turned white and Cubby rose quickly to enquire why, spilling cushions to the floor. 'Leo, what's up?' he asked. A spluttering response proclaimed, 'That's it, that's all I need. Your madman Irving Allen has fired the director!' Cubby, never stuck for words, couldn't contain him. With a powerful kick Jaffe sent two cushions flying across the suite, just as the door opened and a waiter, carrying a silver tray with drinks, glasses and sandwiches, entered. The cushions found their target and glass etc went flying around the room. It was a scene worthy of a Keystone Cops comedy.[82]

Fire Down Below fell flat with critics and audiences, its losses of a cool million dollars almost put Cubby and Allen out of business. It certainly soured their relationship with Columbia and necessitated a rethink on their part to keep budgets under control. There were compensations for Cubby, though, such as working for the first time with Bernard Lee, who would become a stalwart of the Bond series as 007's crabby boss M. It was also the start of a lifelong friendship between the two men and while Lee had his inner demons when it came to alcohol, Cubby always respected his authority and professionalism.

With *Fire Down Below* haemorrhaging Warwick's funds, faring slightly better with the public and critics was *How to Murder a Rich Uncle*, a black comedy based on a French stage farce that starred Nigel Patrick, who also directed, as a destitute baronet planning to bump off his rich uncle, played by that amiable and constantly monocled comedy character actor Charles Coburn. It has to be said that the cast is the best thing about this movie: we have a scene-stealing turn from Katie Johnson in her last ever movie role, just a couple of years after finding fame as the kindly Mrs Wilburforce in *The Ladykillers*; the always reliable Wendy Hiller; and Anthony Newley, who was starting to pop up with alarming regularity in Warwick pictures. Then in his mid-twenties, Newley had played the Artful Dodger in David Lean's *Oliver Twist* (1948), then had trouble creating a career for himself as an adult actor. Signed to Warwick, Newley ended up appearing in an impressive eleven of their productions.

Those with a keen eye will also spot a very young Michael Caine. With just one screen credit to his name, Caine was sent by his agent to Broccoli's Mayfair office and saw that he was up against a fellow out-of-work actor and former bodybuilder he'd met a couple of years before at a party. With only the one role on offer and two candidates, Caine started to sweat. Cubby walked in and one by one interviewed the actors, before finally making his choice – Caine. 'No hard feelings,' said Caine, shaking the other actor's hand. Not at all, it was all part of the game. The actor who didn't get the part was Sean Connery.[83]

Another rising star that slipped through Warwick's fingers around this time was Peter O'Toole. After his success in the hit West End play *The Long and the Short and the Tall*, O'Toole began to receive movie offers, but even in those early days his wild behaviour and drinking had become legendary within the business and who knows how many potential film roles went down the plughole because of it. On this occasion O'Toole went to see Broccoli, who was looking, irony of ironies, to replace an actor who had a drink problem. Alas, O'Toole stumbled into Broccoli's office and a bottle of whisky fell out of his overcoat pocket, and that was that.[84]

Cubby and Allen were keen to do a picture that celebrated the present-day RAF and asked English writer John Davies to visit RAF bases around the country to come up with a suitable story idea. Davies came away from the experience with huge admiration for what he called 'The flower of our youth', risking their lives flying at supersonic speeds.[85] The story Davies came up with centred on a group of flight cadets beginning a three-year training course to become RAF pilots. In *High Flight*, Ray Milland plays their commanding officer, a neat piece of casting since Milland had worked as a civilian flight instructor for the Army Air Forces in the Second World War. Again, there is a score of familiar faces in the supporting cast including Bernard Lee, Leslie Phillips, Anthony Newley and Kenneth Haigh playing a headstrong cadet, a role that very much traded on his image at the time, having been the original angry young man, Jimmy Porter, in John Osborne's play *Look Back in Anger*.

Warwick received the full cooperation of the Air Ministry and were allowed to film on real RAF bases and given the use of a variety of planes, from Hawker Hunters to the de Havilland Vampire, which makes this a real treat for aviation enthusiasts. Indeed, the best thing about the film are the aerial sequences which are brilliantly handled.

Sticking with contemporary themes, Warwick's next production, *Interpol*, was a fast-paced globe-trotting thriller starring Victor Mature as a US narcotics officer on the trail of a drug baron, brilliantly played by Trevor Howard, very much against type. Howard was also involved in a PR stunt to coincide with the film's opening in Frankfurt that very nearly cost him his life. The idea was to demonstrate to the local press that a getaway car, even with a ten-minute head start, could be apprehended by the police. With Howard in the back seat, off sped this car with a professional driver making a series of dramatic manoeuvres in heavy traffic. Unfortunately, one particular policeman had not been notified about the stunt, and even worse the car with Howard inside matched the description of a vehicle that had been involved in a recent bank robbery. Taking out his pistol, the policeman fired several shots at the speeding car, which stopped abruptly. A panicked Howard bolted out of the door and ran across an electrified railway line to get away. By a miracle he emerged unscathed.[86]

Mature returned in Warwick's next picture, only he was by no means their first choice. Broccoli and Allen had purchased the rights to Ronald Kemp's World War Two novel *No Time to Die* with the hope of persuading Montgomery Clift to star.[87] When that proved difficult Alan Ladd was considered, as was Van Johnson when director Terence Young made a casting trip to Hollywood in the spring of 1957. It was also reported that Jeff Chandler turned the role down and a proposed fee of $200,000.[88]

In the end, Kemp's novel was pretty much jettisoned by Richard Maibaum who concocted an entertaining 'boy's own' adventure yarn in which Mature played an American tank commander in North Africa seconded to the British Tank corps. The film, known in America as *Tank Force*, benefited greatly from a six-week shoot in the Libyan Desert, near Tripoli.

Mature's fifth and final picture for Warwick saw him back on the north-west frontier as yet another heathen brigand, or as the title refers to him, *The Bandit of Zhobe*. The film only really came about after Terence Young shot so much footage during the making of *Zarak* that Broccoli and Allen didn't want to see it go to waste, so asked John Gilling to concoct a story to incorporate it all.[89] The end result was forgettable, as was *The Man Inside*, which had Jack Palance as a private detective on the trail of diamond thief Nigel Patrick.

★

According to his stepson Michael G. Wilson, Cubby had been interested in the James Bond novels of Ian Fleming from the moment they were first published[90] and yet he didn't make an approach until the early summer of 1958. Maybe he felt that his initial lack of a track record would have scuppered any potential deal. What captivated Broccoli about the books was a feeling that here were all the right ingredients to make a successful film franchise: a resourceful hero, colourful and exotic locales, espionage and action, plus lashings of sex; in other words, not a million miles away from the sort of stuff Warwick had been churning out. As Barbara Broccoli was to later observe: 'When you look at the Warwick films, most of them are big exciting action-adventure films with all the elements that later on worked so incredibly well within the James Bond franchise.'[91]

Contacting Fleming's agent, Robert Fenn, a meeting was arranged between both parties at Les Ambassadeurs, an exclusive gambling club and restaurant off Park Lane. There was just one small problem. Irving Allen did not share his partner's enthusiasm for the Bond books. He couldn't understand what Cubby saw in them and when he was asked to read a few in preparation for the meeting, barely gave the type more than a cursory glance.

Then out of the blue, just days before the meeting with Fleming, Cubby heard the devastating news that Nedra needed to go into hospital. She had cancer of the bladder which was going to require surgery as soon as possible if there was to be any chance of survival.[92] Calling Allen, Cubby told him that he was going to have to discuss the Bond deal with Fleming on his own and report back any news. The meeting turned out to be an unmitigated disaster. Allen did not hold back his views, telling Fleming to his face that in his honest opinion the books were not even good enough for television.[93] Tact was never Allen's strong suit, and as he excused himself from the table, any potential deal to make the Bond films was dead in the water.

Neither were Columbia that interested either, when Cubby approached them about possibly financing this new venture. One morning in the office, Cubby gave Euan Lloyd a brown paper shopping bag holding several items, instructing him to go and ask Mike Frankovitch for a formal decision on its content. Arriving at Columbia's Wardour Street office, Lloyd up-ended the shopping bag and seven Ian Fleming paperback books fell onto the executive's desk. 'Mike, not moving a centimetre, rolled his Churchill cigar in concentrated thought. Then, edging slightly forward to read the titles, paused awhile and eventually said, "Tell Cubby Columbia is no longer interested in making second features!"'[94]

Disappointed with these setbacks to his Bond plans, Cubby's priorities lay elsewhere. It had been decided that Nedra was best treated by specialist doctors they knew and trusted in New York, and the family flew there without delay. Tragically, when the doctors carried out an exploratory operation it was clear the cancer had spread too far and it was only a matter of time before the inevitable. It was now just a case of keeping Nedra as comfortable as possible.[95] Nedra bore her fate with stoic bravery. She died that September. She was only 39. The body was flown back to California and laid to rest at Forest Lawn Memorial Park, Glendale.[96]

As the weeks and months passed following Nedra's death, Cubby wasn't too concerned about making movies, rather he was more preoccupied with putting his own life back together and looking after Tony and Tina. Friends played a huge part in that, none more so than his cousin Pat, who always seemed to be there when he was needed.

That new life began to assemble on New Year's Eve when Cubby, accompanied by Cary Grant, flew out to spend the festivities in Las Vegas. At a party, Cubby was struck by 'an exquisite beauty'. Her name was Dana Wilson and by the end of the evening Cubby had her phone number carefully stored in his wallet.[97]

Born Dana Natol to a well-to-do New York family of mixed Irish/Italian heritage in 1922, Dana decided at an early age to become an actress and studied at the celebrated Cecil Clovelly's Academy of Dramatic Arts at Carnegie Hall in New York. Starting her stage career on the New York and Boston stage, and in summer stock, Dana met and married Lewis Wilson, a struggling actor, and in 1942 gave birth to a son, Michael. A year later, when Wilson was just 23 years old and a complete unknown, he made history by becoming the screen's first Batman, starring in a fifteen-chapter serial for Columbia.

Wilson's fame as Batman proved fleeting and his career stalled, as did his marriage to Dana. When the couple divorced, Dana moved to Beverly Hills where she took a few acting jobs in film and television but concentrated largely on a writing career. Filmmaker Andre de Toth, who later worked for Saltzman in the 1960s, knew Dana in those early Hollywood days and liked her enormously. 'She was a budding writer with a promising future, a single parent bringing up a son. In the '40s that took guts. She always was a strong lady.'[98]

After their chance encounter, Cubby saw Dana whenever he could and out of that grew genuine affection and then a deep love. The pair married in Las Vegas on 21 June 1959. Fittingly, Cary Grant was best man.[99] The night before the ceremony, Broccoli and his new stepson, Michael, went gambling and drinking and by morning it was Cary Grant's duty to inform Dana that both men were suffering stinging hangovers. 'I did a film once,' he said, 'where the best man ran off with the bride. How about it?'

Dana laughed. 'As tempting as it may sound, I don't think it's going to happen this time.'[100]

*

Specialising mostly in adventure stories, thrillers and war pictures, Warwick had rarely ventured into the realm of comedy. However, with the current renaissance in British film humour, thanks largely to the Boulting brothers and the emergence of the *Carry On* series, Cubby and Allen saw dollar signs in going with a comedy venture and found inspiration in the recent real-life drafting of Elvis Presley into the US Army.

Realising that none of their stable of writers would be up for the job, the producers turned to Associated London Scripts, a writers' agency that worked as a cooperative and included amongst its number Spike Milligan, Eric Sykes, Galton and Simpson and Johnny Speight. Another member was a young writer by the name of John Antrobus, who had recently co-written a couple of *Goon Shows* with Milligan and contributed material to the first *Carry On* film, *Carry on Sergeant* (1958). Although he'd never written a full screenplay before, Cubby and Allen took a chance and hired him to write *Idol on Parade*.

The story turned out to be quite simple: a young rock 'n' roll singer, on the crest of fame, must undergo two years of compulsory National Service in the British military. Cast in the lead role, Anthony Newley was disappointed to learn that he would not be required to sing on screen. Since it had long been an ambition to pursue some kind of singing career, Newley managed to persuade Cubby and Allen to include five tunes on the soundtrack, two of which Newley co-wrote himself.[101] Released to coincide with the film's opening, it was the song 'I've Waited So Long' that unexpectedly became a top three hit on the UK charts in May 1959. Even more unexpectedly, it turned Newley from a British supporting actor into a singing matinee idol almost overnight and was to ultimately propel him to international fame. Broccoli would later approach Newley to write the lyrics to the *Goldfinger* theme song. The two men obviously had a good relationship, though Newley was rather less predisposed towards Allen. 'Cubby's job was to walk behind Irving saying, "I'm terribly sorry, he didn't mean that, I'm terribly sorry," because Irving was a tough, very wild, old style American producer.'[102]

Having created an unlikely pop idol out of Anthony Newley, Cubby and Allen set about making not one but two star vehicles for him, shot back-to-back by director Ken Hughes. *In the Nick* was a prison comedy, while *Jazz Boat* was an unsophisticated musical. Newley's leading lady in both films was Anne Aubrey, a contract artist at Warwick that Cubby and Allen hoped to personally groom for stardom. Shooting one scene in *Jazz Boat*, Anne was required to climb on top of Newley lying prostrate on a cramped bunk bed. After the first take she jumped up and rushed off the set, complaining to Cubby that Newley appeared to be enjoying their love scene a little bit too much. It turned out to be a practical joke, of course, when Newley revealed he'd placed a Coca-Cola bottle down his pants.[103]

Both of these films never amounted to very much, save for one significant appointment. Ken Adam was a young and extremely gifted art director who had been hired ostensibly to do preparatory work on a Viking picture Warwick proposed to make called *The Long Ships*.[104] When that film was cancelled, Cubby found him work on *In the Nick* and the two men immediately warmed to each other. Adam was less enthused about his partner. 'Irving was enormously abrasive. A monster in a way. Very explosive. But he was a good showman. In a way, Irving was the nasty guy and Cubby was the nice guy. Irving was very tough and vulgar; Cubby was none of these things.'[105]

Killers of Kilimanjaro was Warwick's fourth picture shot in Africa and perfectly complemented the company's previous colonial adventures, taking inspiration from a novel about white explorers in East Africa called *African Bush Adventures* by Dan P. Mannix and J.A. Hunter. However, by the time the picture opened late in 1959 these empire-building boy's own yarns looked dated and cliché-ridden in the light of so many African nations winning their independence. As the critic of the *Monthly Film Bulletin* observed of *Killers of Kilimanjaro*: 'Anyone who has a conscience about Africa and takes the preposterous story seriously will be appalled.'

The 'preposterous' story saw Robert Taylor as a rugged American engineer out to finish the construction of an African railroad and to find his predecessor, who has mysteriously disappeared. Along the way he encounters all manner of treacherous obstacles. As the US poster put it: 'See! The furious bull elephant attack flame-haired beauty! See! Sinister assault of the killer crocodiles! See! History's most barbaric slave traders!' Were cinema audiences ever really that naive to be taken in by such Barnum and Bailey baloney?

An astute professional, Cubby realised pictures like *Killers of Kilimanjaro* just weren't going to cut it any more with audiences that were becoming more sophisticated and critical in their tastes. This recognition coincided with a decision both Cubby and Irving made to reduce Warwick's output, which had seen the company churn out an astonishing seventeen films since *The Red Beret* in 1953. With falling cinema attendances, combined with rising production costs, the producers were looking to make savings by concentrating on just one picture a year, as Allen explained: 'In five years costs have doubled and earnings have halved. When those two graphs meet, you're out of business.'[106]

Another significant decision was to sever links completely with Columbia, a relationship that had been worsening over the last couple of years. Indeed, according to Euan Lloyd, Columbia's London representative, Mike Frankovich, had broken off personal contact with both Cubby and Allen. 'I was elected to represent them at daily morning briefings in Wardour Street to report on the previous day's shooting, budget matters and so on.'[107]

The producers also believed Columbia were taking too large a share of their revenues and so set out to establish themselves as independent distributors. To this end they purchased Eros Films, a company founded by three brothers, Philip, Sydney and Michael Hyams, all former cinema owners. Eros had been in operation since 1947, financing independent British productions along with reissuing old Hollywood favourites. But as Cubby later admitted, the distribution side of the business was something neither he nor Allen knew anything about, 'and the result was a disaster'.[108] The company was eventually dissolved in 1961 with loses of over a million dollars.[109]

To set them on their way as masters of their own destiny, Warwick required a prestige picture, and Cubby believed he'd found the ideal subject: a dramatisation of the libel and subsequent criminal cases involving Oscar Wilde and the Marquess of Queensberry, which brought about the downfall of the celebrated playwright. It wasn't going to be cheap, and much of the £269,000 budget came from their own coffers.[110] It was going to be a case of win or bust. But no sooner was pre-production under way, than Cubby learnt of a rival outfit making their own version of the Wilde scandal. Lawsuits flew backwards and forwards without effect. In the end, it was going to be a straight race to see who could get their picture into cinemas first.

After doing a good job on *Jazz Boat*, Ken Hughes was hired to write and direct *The Trials of Oscar Wilde* and given a punishing shooting schedule of just six weeks, starting in March 1960. To speed things up even further, the producers set up four cutting rooms at the ABPC Studios in Elstree with a team of editors working round the clock.[111]

It wasn't just speed that concerned Cubby, he was after quality, too, and drew upon the best actors and technicians available. Australian-born Peter Finch was known to be a great admirer of Wilde and was the producers' first choice. Waving in front of him the not inconsiderable fee of £35,000, Finch accepted and went on to give one of the finest performances of his career. Up against the naturally portly Robert Morley in the rival film, Finch underwent a weight-gaining diet consisting of bread, potatoes and six double whiskies a day to put on the required 14lbs.[112] Cubby had never known an actor prepare himself for a part with such dedication. Everything Wilde had ever written or had written about him Finch digested. Once at the studio in between set-ups Cubby saw Finch reading a Wilde poem, then suddenly break down in tears. 'Somehow Wilde's personal agony, the scandalous self-destruction of a genius, had got to him.'[113]

In the end, both Wilde films opened in British cinemas within a week of each other,[114] and neither did very well at the box office. Cubby was justifiably proud of his picture and it was rewarded with fine notices; the *Evening Standard* wrote, 'Here is a tragedy laid bare to the heart, given heroic stature.' A clutch of well-deserved awards followed, including a BAFTA for Finch's performance.

When the time came to open in America, the film's depiction of homosexual issues caused consternation in some quarters. Fearing a backlash from religious organisations and moral pressure groups, the US distributor demanded that one particular exchange in the courtroom scene be excised, when Wilde admits he didn't kiss a male valet on the grounds he was too ugly. With the picture having already failed financially in Britain, Broccoli showed considerable balls by refusing to kowtow to censorship. Without that key exchange, he insisted, the entire prosecution case made no sense. 'The result was, the Protestant, the Catholic and the Jewish organisations all came out publicly against the film.'[115]

With a general release out of the question, all the producers could hope for now was to get onto the arthouse circuit, along with a few isolated bookings in major cities. It played in New York to little fanfare, despite an excellent review from the noted critic of the *New York Times*, Bosley Crowther, who wrote: 'Mr Wilde himself could not have expected his rare personality or his unfortunate encounters with British justice on a morals charge to have been more sympathetically or affectingly dramatized.'

It was hoped the film's West Coast debut would resonate more fully with cinemagoers. The venue chosen was the Paramount Theatre in Los Angeles, but the date turned out to be a catastrophe, falling on the eve of Yom Kippur, the holiest time of the year in Judaism. Cubby was to recall that barely fifteen people showed up. 'We sat there, Dana and I, holding hands, and I don't mind confessing, we wept.'[116]

The failure of *Oscar Wilde* proved to be the death knell in Cubby's partnership with Irving. In truth, their relationship had been sticky for the past few years. They had begun to disagree about what film subjects to make, and there had of course been the Fleming debacle. Cubby was ready to go solo. Ken Adam saw how Irving had even begun to disrupt the making of pictures, recalling an incident during the *Oscar Wilde* shoot when the producer appeared on set one day and Ken Hughes, with whom he did not have a good relationship, ordered everyone to stop work. 'Irving thought better of it and disappeared.'[117]

While they had begun to disagree on professional matters, both men always managed to maintain what Broccoli considered to be 'a good, indeed very warm relationship. We were able to shake hands and go our separate ways without hard feelings.'[118]

What these two Americans managed to achieve with Warwick has never truly been given the critical kudos it deserved. According to Euan Lloyd, Cubby and Irving Allen changed the face of British cinema. 'They were the first American producers to set up shop in Britain after World War Two with the full financial backing of a Hollywood studio. Their success soon attracted some notable filmmakers to follow in their footsteps, including Carl Foreman, Sam Spiegel and, later on, Stanley Kubrick.'[119]

A couple of major projects did slip through their fingers. In 1956, Cubby and Irving purchased the film rights to John Wyndham's science fiction novel *The Day of the Triffids* and hired Jimmy Sangster, who had written the screenplay for Hammer's breakthrough horror movie *The Curse of Frankenstein*, to adapt it for the screen.[120] Sangster was a big admirer of Wyndham and felt both honoured and 'a little bit intimidated' that he was about to 'start messing' with Wyndham's novel. While he was paid for the job, Sangster never heard anything back from the producers and his script was never filmed.[121]

Then in 1960, Stanley Baker was looking for finance to produce his pet project, about the heroic exploits at the battle of Rorke's Drift in 1879 entitled *Zulu*. Cubby and Allen's interest was piqued enough for them to assign one of their associate producers, Harold Huth, to the project and a budget of 2 million rand was agreed with location shooting taking place in South Africa.[122] The dissolution of Warwick obviously put paid to their interest in the project.

Irving Allen continued to make movies with his own independent production company for the next ten years and his track record was quite impressive.

He resurrected his Viking project *The Long Ships* in 1964, starring Richard Widmark and Sidney Poitier, and produced the underrated historical drama *Cromwell* (1970) with Richard Harris. Allen was also responsible for bringing Matt Helm to the screen, Donald Hamilton's killer agent from a series of pulp novels, who was played by crooner Dean Martin. Allen produced all four Helm movies: *The Silencers*, *Murderers Row*, both 1966, *The Ambushers* (1967) and *The Wrecking Crew* (1969).

Euan Lloyd worked on one of the Matt Helm films and was pleasantly surprised to see that Allen had somewhat mellowed. 'Gone were the days of angst with Warwick, when every day was a battleground.'[123] Although the gruff, no-nonsense businessman was never very far away, as Ken Adam discovered when he and Maurice Binder went to see him about an idea for a film and he threw them both out. 'I've got enough geniuses around me I don't need you two,' he blasted.[124]

Strangely enough, throughout this time Allen continued to operate from the same office he shared with Broccoli at South Audley Street. It was quite disconcerting, according to art director Peter Lamont. 'If we had a meeting and we went into Cubby's office, Irving Allen was down the other end ear-wigging.'[125] Lamont recalled a meeting during pre-production for *On Her Majesty's Secret Service* when a particular gimmick was being discussed, which in the end was never used: 'It cropped up later in one of the Matt Helm movies.'[126]

For much of those Warwick years, Cubby felt that he was living under the shadow of his more flamboyant partner. Allen was always more at ease with the public relations aspect of the film business. The time had come to establish his own credentials. But how and with what? Warwick had almost bankrupted Cubby and battered his self-confidence. There were several projects in his head he wanted to pursue, but no money to back them up. He even contemplated packing up and returning to America, a tricky proposition since Dana had become pregnant, later giving birth to a daughter, Barbara.

Then one night, after pacing up and down the living room in their apartment for hours on end, Dana sat him down in the kitchen. Yes, things might look bad now, but Cubby had proven his worth as a filmmaker and as a hard worker. And if it was purely a matter of money, Dana could rent out her Californian home or sell her jewellery. 'You're not alone,' she stressed. 'I have the strongest feeling that this is just the beginning for you. Something will happen.'[127]

2

Harry

There was always something of the showman about Harry Saltzman, the spit and sawdust of the circuses he worked in during his early days in show-business and the thrill of the greasepaint of the variety halls and theatres where he learnt his trade, elements that he later brought to bear upon his film work, especially the Bond movies. As Ken Hughes claimed, 'Only a Harry Saltzman could make a Bond picture. He's a modern-day Barnum.'[1]

There is a story that perfectly illustrates this point from Harry's youth, when he was travelling around selling soap from the back of a wagon. He'd stop somewhere, and as a crowd began to gather round him the wheel from his wagon would fall off and he'd hastily fix it, covering himself in black axle grease. Taking one of his soap bars he'd wash the grease off in an instant, to gasps of amazement from the assembled who'd rush to relieve him of his stock. But it was all a trick, the grease was in fact just black soap. It was nothing more than a performance, Harry putting on a show.[2]

Harry Saltzman was born Herschel Saltzman on 27 October 1915 to Jewish immigrants living in Sherbrooke, a city in southern Quebec, Canada.[3] The family soon moved to Saint John, a port city in the Canadian province of New Brunswick[4] where Harry spent the first seven years of his life. His father was a horticulturist, but virtually nothing is known about his mother. 'He never told us anything about his own mother,' said his daughter Hilary. 'But I know that she died young.'[5]

The family moved to Cleveland, Ohio,[6] where as a young boy he used to sweep floors at a vaudeville house after school. 'That's what started his love for show business,' said Hilary Saltzman.[7] There certainly wasn't anything for him at school. 'Unfortunately for him, he was left-handed, which was very frowned upon at the time,' recalled Hilary. 'So, he was not allowed to use his left hand and, because of that, he failed at school.'[8]

Harry had two elder sisters and two younger brothers, and as the one in the middle always felt he got the rough end of things. When he was young his eldest sister was given a bicycle as a present. Forbidden to borrow it, Harry often sneaked it out of the house and went riding, but every time his father found out he took a beating.

> Then one day when everyone was out and I was sure no one was looking, I took the bike and went for a ride. When I got back there was still no one around, I was safe. I put the bike back where I found it. But that night I got a beating from the old man, just the same. My sister had put a pencil mark on the wall exactly where she'd leaned the handlebars, and I hadn't noticed. I think that was the time I decided I'd better clear out.[9]

Harry was around 15 years old when he ran away from home and joined a circus, enjoying a long spell on the road. Sometime in the early 1930s he moved to Paris, ostensibly to study political science and economics, but within a year carved a niche for himself as a talent scout supplying performers to music halls and circuses all over Europe.[10] In 1937, Harry helped get a whole circus troupe out of Barcelona just ahead of Franco's armies during the Spanish civil war. Everyone was put to sea in a dilapidated boat and were luckily picked up by a passing liner.[11]

By 1938, Harry was working for one of the biggest variety agencies in Paris, with forty theatres scattered across the continent, constantly shuttling acts from one to the other. But the growing threat of war raised a number of concerns, not least the fact that the agency's 2 million marks held in banks in Berlin had been blocked by the German government and couldn't be taken out of the country. Harry volunteered to be the one to go to Germany and try to do something about it; a brave thing to do given his Jewish heritage.[12]

No sooner did Harry arrive in Berlin than he began purchasing as many railway tickets and steamship tickets as he could, all through that summer of 1938, wherever there was a means of getting an act, a chorus, a company of acrobats and their families, or a circus out of the country across any border. Pretty soon he had whittled down the agency's holdings to a nominal sum. With the rest of the cash he bribed minor Nazi officials to provide *Ausweise* (identity cards) for Jewish variety artistes trapped in Germany. Then, early one morning, he was awoken by a loud rap on his hotel room door. The men outside looked menacing and official. Saltzman was sure it was the Gestapo and that his only hope was to bluster his way out of trouble. Demanding to know why he, as a foreign visitor, had been disturbed at such an ungodly hour, he refused to come out until he had bathed and got dressed. To his amazement, the ruse worked and the men said they would wait for him in the lobby. Hearing their departing footsteps, Harry dived for the telephone and called the Canadian and the French embassies. By the time he walked down at eight o'clock, there was a vice consul from each embassy waiting for him. As it turned out, the mystery men weren't Gestapo but police officers sent to warn him over his ticket-buying activities.[13]

That evening Harry paid a visit to a vaudeville theatre and was wandering about backstage when he was stopped by the manager and asked what he was doing. Harry told him he was hoping to chat to a couple of the acts. 'What do you want to see them for?' asked the manager. 'They aren't Jewish. That's all you're interested in – getting Jews out of the country.'

'If you know that much, you must be a member of the Gestapo,' asked Harry.

'I've been a member for seven years,' the manager said proudly. 'And it's time you got out of Germany, Harry. This morning it was only railway tickets. But next time, it will be *Ausweise* – and that's different.' Saltzman left for Paris the very next morning.[14]

When war eventually broke out, Harry enlisted in the Royal Canadian Air Force in Vancouver. Attached to the supply depot, director Tony Richardson recalled Harry telling him that he was involved in various scams including smuggling jukeboxes, then impossible to get hold of, inside crates of Red Cross bandages to sell in Europe.[15] There's also a story of him organising unauthorised flights to Vichy, France, to buy wine.[16]

Whatever the validity of these tales, what is certain is that a lot of Harry's war activities were shrouded in mystery and sleight of hand. After being medically discharged from the Air Force, Harry was recruited by the psychological warfare division of the OSS, the Office of Strategic Services, a wartime intelligence agency and predecessor of the CIA. This was 1942, and Harry spent the majority of the rest of the war in Europe.[17] Harry's fluency in French and a decent command of Spanish and German, picked up from circus stagehands and acts, along with his first-hand knowledge of Europe, made him a perfect candidate.

Sworn to secrecy, Harry never talked about his exploits or experiences with the OSS, not even to his family, and it was only in the early 2000s that his children got to learn something of what he did. When his daughter Hilary relocated from Los Angeles to Quebec, the Canadian government required some documentation about when her late father became an American citizen. Putting in a request to the US State Department, Hilary faced a wall of bureaucracy when she learnt that Harry's papers were classified. After much pressing and petitioning the documents were finally released, revealing that Harry's oath of allegiance to the US took place in March 1939. Many of the papers, however, were heavily redacted, meaning that after more than fifty years her father's role in the OSS remained a highly sensitive issue.[18]

One document revealed that in the summer of 1943, Saltzman was assigned to Algiers to serve on the staff of C.D. Jackson, an expert on psychological warfare and propaganda. At the time Jackson was deputy chief of the psychological warfare branch of the OSS in North Africa while Eisenhower was supreme commander of the Allied forces there. When Eisenhower moved to England at the beginning of 1944 and set up headquarters in London to prepare for the Allied invasion of Normandy, he took Jackson with him. Jackson's assignment there was to rouse the conquered peoples of Europe, by radio and leaflet, to active support for D-Day. Towards the end of this campaign his organisation was sending the French underground after specific targets, like bridges and railroad switches.[19]

It's interesting to see that in January 1944 there was a formal request for Harry to join Jackson in London, where his 'services are more urgently needed'. Harry was to operate out of the American embassy. It's no surprise, given that Ian Fleming was serving in British naval intelligence at the time in London, that speculation has grown in recent years as to whether the two men ever crossed paths.[20]

While there is no evidence suggesting Harry actually met Fleming during the war, there is no doubt that something resonated with him when he read the Bond books. And when discussions began about a potential film deal, Hilary Saltzman believed there was almost certainly an 'unspoken connection, bond and understanding' between them.[21]

At some time towards the end of hostilities, Harry was back in France, since Tom Mankiewicz recalled the producer telling him once that when a city was liberated his job was to go in there and pick out accommodation for the officers who were about to arrive; General so-and-so will get the bridal suite, while Colonel whatsit is down the hall. 'Can you imagine Harry doing this, organizing all these Top Brass?'[22]

After the war Harry remained in France carrying out reconstruction work for the French government and then took a communications role with UNESCO.

> I had a misguided idea, after six years of war, that my generation had mucked up the world and we were going to have a better one. In 1946 through 1949, I thought it was my generation's task to make a better world, and that we would have a better world. And after three and a half years I realised I was wasting my time.[23]

So he went back into showbiz, basing himself in Paris. Here he came into contact with Mitty Goldin, a famous pre-war theatrical agent, then trying to put the theatrical business in Europe back on its feet. One of the things Goldin got Saltzman to do was return to the kind of big travelling circuses he'd been with before and get them back to a healthy state. 'Harry was forever telling me that he was always going to bail out some circus that was in trouble,' recalled Guy Hamilton:

> Mainly because the elephants cost a fortune to ship around in train carriages, and they ate everybody out of their profits. But once the elephants had been sold the circus very shortly thereafter went broke because the public only really came to see the elephants. And this led on to Harry's great philosophy, that films were a show; give the public what they want, give them their elephants. When the first Bond film went over budget Harry didn't care because he wanted to put everything up there on the screen. The bigger the better.[24]

By the end of 1950, Harry was back in the States as partner in a firm that specialised in coin-operated hobby horses. Within just a few months Harry had forty-three of these installed in department stores across the country, including Macys in New York.[25] He then worked for a time in the advertising business at Procter & Gamble but it didn't suit him. 'I was sitting in some building in Rockefeller Centre in the middle of a meeting of 40 people when I decided to get up and go for a walk. I spent the rest of the day in Central Park and then came back and quit.'[26]

For a short time, Harry worked as production manager on the popular NBC anthology series *Robert Montgomery Presents*, which showcased live drama introduced by the veteran MGM star. In his private life Harry began what was to be a brief relationship with a New York magazine journalist by the name of Judith Krantz, later a bestselling author. She remembered Harry as, 'a wonderful companion, with a fantastic imagination. He resembled a giant panda as much as a human can.'[27] She also revealed that her father liked him enormously, finding him to be an entertaining conversationalist, but that she refused his proposal of marriage.[28]

Gaining invaluable television experience on *Robert Montgomery Presents*, Harry's ambitious nature took over and in 1954 he formed his own television production company, Frantel Inc., with the intention of making his own programmes. The unlikely candidate to star in his inaugural production was former Olympic swimmer turned movie serial actor Buster Crabbe, who back in the 1930s played three of the top syndicated comic strip heroes: Tarzan, Flash Gordon and Buck Rogers. Harry had watched Crabbe hosting his own kid's variety show that played weekday evenings on a New York television station. After it was cancelled, he asked the actor to come over to see him at his office. 'I'm going to raise some French money and do a Foreign Legion thing,' Harry proposed. 'I think that you could play the captain.'[29]

Both men talked at length about the show, and when it came time to leave Crabbe asked if he could take a few scripts home to read before making a decision. Crabbe liked them well enough and also noticed that one of the recurring characters was a young boy whom the captain takes under his wing after his parents are killed. Returning to Harry's office, Crabbe asked if the role of the boy had been cast yet, since his own son, Cullen, might fit it perfectly. Harry wasn't stupid, he knew having a father and son team on the show made for good publicity, so he immediately agreed to the idea.[30]

Captain Gallant of the Foreign Legion was shot on location out in Southern Morocco and was one of the first US television series made overseas. Harry also boasted that the show incorporated actual members of the Foreign Legion. Making the show in Morocco was cheaper than doing it in Hollywood, although there were drawbacks as well as advantages, as Crabbe explained: 'The crew was slower, it took us four days to make an episode instead of wrapping it up in two. But the workers were cheaper, and there was the benefit of *really* getting the feel of the desert and sand in your boots.'[31] Interior shooting took place at Neuilly Studios in Paris, where Harry installed $60,000 worth of equipment and hired nine American crew members along with four writers on permanent standby.[32]

It was during this period that Harry met the love of his life. Jacqueline Colin had been living in Paris ever since fleeing her native Romania with her family after the war.[33] The couple later married and had three children together – Steven, Hilary and Christopher. Like Dana Broccoli, Jacqueline was Harry's rock and together they made a formidable team. Michael Caine remembered her as 'a very attractive and vivacious woman'.[34]

No sooner had *Captain Gallant* premiered on NBC in February 1955, than Harry was telling the press about his plans to produce more television series, thanks largely to a deal he had made with the New York Trust company, a large trust and wholesale banking business. This involved a $500,000 revolving fund for future television/film production. It was understood that the collateral on the loan was the negatives of the first series of *Captain Gallant* episodes.[35]

One of these TV projects was to be a romantic drama called *Jill Gardner*, a character Harry created along with film publicist and writer Dick Condon, who a few years later wrote the controversial novel *The Manchurian Candidate*. Jill, as the synopsis explained, was a Women's Army Corps officer attached to NATO, who helps her young friends out of all sorts of romantic entanglements. Harry hoped to entice a 'name' actress to play the role. Two other projects were a supernatural anthology series called *The Evil That Men Do* and a medieval adventure show. All three were to be produced at the Neuilly Studios.[36] None of them came to fruition.

Captain Gallant quickly proved a ratings winner, successful enough to spawn its own comic book and action figure play fort. By the time work was due to begin on a second season, the political climate in Morocco, which was fighting for home rule against the French government, was so bad Saltzman feared for his crew and relocated the entire production to Italy. 'Harry imported three moth-eaten camels from Algeria or somewhere and stuck a palm tree on the beach and that sort of made the desert,' recalled Guy Hamilton. 'It was really B-picture stuff but I think Harry learnt an awful lot about production working on that show.'[37]

It wasn't quite as haphazard as that. Harry took over Pisorno film studios in Tirrenia, dubbed by many who worked there as 'Hollywood on the beach', to shoot a further twenty-six episodes.[38] There was also talk of making another television series there comprising thirty-nine half-hour episodes entitled *GI* depicting events in the lives of US army infantrymen. Harry had obtained the cooperation of the Department of Defense and planned to start work on a pilot early in 1957. Just like his other TV ideas, *GI* went nowhere.[39]

Captain Gallant was a show Harry was especially proud of, making sixty-five episodes in total. When *Ipcress File* author Len Deighton first met the producer, he was told a story about a visit to the studio by a group of businessmen who sponsored the show. They were shown round the sets and saw a bit of the filming before being sat down in a viewing theatre with a glass of champagne to watch the latest episode. Harry said that as they were watching it, one of these wise guys called out, 'Wait a minute, it's out of sync. In fact, I think that's been post-synced.'

'Hold on,' said Harry and picked up the phone to the projectionist. 'Just give us that again will ya, roll it back.' The screen flickered into life again. 'You're absolutely right,' went Harry. 'Just because on this episode I wasn't there. This is what happens when you let things go and you allow other people to take over.' Harry turned to his guests. 'I'm so angry about this,' he said. 'I feel so bad about it that I'm not going to charge you for this episode.'

'That was wonderful of you Harry,' said Deighton.

'Yeah, because they were all post-synced.'[40]

Even before the first series of *Captain Gallant* had been completed, Harry was keen to get into movies, making a trip to Rome to try and set up a film with Vittorio De Sica and Sophia Loren.[41] When nothing came of that, he developed his own story idea. Well, not wholly his own, since it borrowed elements liberally from the famous 1939 MGM comedy *Ninotchka*, starring Greta Garbo as a stone-faced Soviet envoy won over to Western democracy by the charms of a Parisian playboy. Harry's version used the same basic plot device of clashing ideologies, only this time the woman was a Soviet military pilot who landed her plane in West Germany and fell for an American Air Force officer.

Looking for a suitable writer to turn his idea into a script, Harry turned to one of the most talented people in Hollywood, Ben Hecht, an Academy Award-winning screenwriter, director, producer, playwright, journalist and novelist. Forming their own company, Benhar Productions Inc., the plan was to cooperate on a number of projects. For a time, Harry was interested in financing a play Hecht had written about his late literary friend the poet and novelist Maxwell Bodenheim, known as the King of Greenwich Village Bohemians during the Jazz Age of the 1920s. The hope was to put it on Broadway.

Theirs was a clearly delineated partnership, with Hecht in charge of all script and creative matters and Harry handling, in his words, 'business administration'.[42] Hecht's agent at the time, Ray Stark, later a successful independent Hollywood producer, was also brought in, ostensibly to look after his client's interests but also to tout the film project around the studios. It's obvious from his dealings with Harry that Stark was excited about Hecht's partnership with the producer, despite his lack of film experience. In a letter dated 25 October 1954, Stark wrote: 'I am so very happy that you like Saltzman. He is a tough businessman and this is good. Also, I think he is a very honest guy – as well as a very good promoter.'[43]

As work began on the screenplay, with the working title of *Not for Money*, later changed to *The Iron Petticoat*, Harry and Hecht agreed that the 'Garbo' role would be a perfect vehicle for the formidable talent of Katherine Hepburn. Intrigued by both the role and Hecht's script, Hepburn signed up in the autumn of 1955 and personally selected Ralph Thomas as director, after his recent success with the first of the Dirk Bogarde *Doctor* films, *Doctor in the House* (1954). In turn, Thomas brought in his wife and regular collaborator Betty Box to act as co-producer with Harry.

Betty and Ralph Thomas had never heard of their new producing partner before; indeed, according to Betty, 'When Harry arrived in London to meet us he was quite unknown in the film world.'[44] Betty also stated that she was to handle the 'creative' end of the picture while Harry returned to LA to deal with contracts and lawyers.

With finance raised through distribution deals with MGM and the British-based company Remus Films, run by one of Britain's most important producers, John Woolf, it was hoped Cary Grant might agree to play opposite Hepburn, rekindling a dynamic double act that had already worked so well in four previous pictures. Grant would have been perfect as the romantic hero, but when he proved unavailable and Bob Hope was cast instead, the actress privately baulked at the idea. As she later confessed, Hope was not exactly her idea of a heartthrob. 'I'm sure I wasn't his, either.'[45]

It didn't take very long for things to turn sour. Making his first picture outside of America, no sooner did Hope land in England to begin work at Pinewood Studios than he declared a dissatisfaction with the script. Bringing along his own entourage of gag writers, Hope wanted the material tailored to suit his trademark wisecracking persona. 'Frankly, Ralph Thomas and Betty Box are aghast at the idea,' Harry wrote to Hecht. 'They are perfectly happy if the writers would submit to you a gag line, but they feel, as I do – and I am sure you do – that we do not need nor want to use Hope's expression, "the script punched up"'.[46]

In the end, though, this is exactly what happened, as Hepburn ruefully observed: 'He really wanted to play Bob Hope, and he did.'[47] This had the effect of throwing the whole film off-balance with the inevitable result that Hepburn and Hope appear to be performing in two quite separate films. Even Thomas later confessed that he didn't direct the picture so much as referee it. 'Each star would come on the set each day with a different piece of script. Each was happy with the scene – until they compared notes!'[48]

Miss Hepburn could be quite the diva herself when she wanted to get her own way. About halfway through the shoot she wanted to take a week off to be in America with her married lover Spencer Tracy. 'At first I said no, she couldn't go,' Harry later recalled. 'Then she said, "I may not be very well next week." And I knew exactly what she meant. So, I gave her permission to fly to New York the next day.'[49]

Hecht reacted to Hope's rewrites a little differently by walking off the picture, anticipating it was headed for disaster. He was still smarting eight months later when MGM granted his request to have his name removed from the credits on the US release prints. Prior to the film's New York opening, Hecht took out a full-page advertisement in the *Hollywood Reporter* to bemoan the fact that Miss Hepburn's 'magnificent comic performance' had been 'blow-torched' out of the film.[50]

Meanwhile, Harry had asked for a special screen credit that was to read: 'Based on a story idea by Harry Saltzman.' Under his agreement as screenwriter, Hecht had to give his approval, and in characteristic style suggested an alternative – 'Despite a story idea by Harry Saltzman.' The idea was hastily dropped.[51]

Harry could only watch from the wings as his first foray into film production began to unravel and fall apart in front of his eyes. He later joked that his was the only Bob Hope film that flopped at the box office. Indeed, so personally did Hope take the film's failure he took sole possession of the property, steadfastly refusing to allow it to be exhibited again. *The Iron Petticoat* didn't receive an American television airing until forty-six years after it opened in theatres, following Hope's death.[52]

Actually, looking at it today the film isn't as bad as its reputation suggests. It's fun to watch Hepburn's lively performance, even if her Russian accent often has a life of its own, and there's an appealing supporting cast of familiar British character actors, from James Robertson Justice as a barking, grumpy Russian bigwig, to Sid James and Richard Wattis. There's also a neat turn from renowned dancer and choreographer Robert Helpmann as Hepburn's former Russian lover, a role Harry thought he'd talked Alec Guinness into playing until negotiations fell through.[53]

As for Harry's partnership with Hecht, it didn't last much past the film's release. There was talk of them adapting *The Imaginary Invalid*, Molière's comedic attack on the medical profession, and the last play he wrote before his death. Robert Helpmann was set to play the lead. Nothing came of it.[54] There was also to have been a venture into television variety with a series of thirty-nine half-hour shows featuring the famous tenor Mario Lanza. In a package worth a reported $1 million, the series was to have been shot in England and feature big name symphony and opera performers. In the end the pair couldn't raise sufficient finance.[55]

Still smarting from the failure of *The Iron Petticoat*, Harry was keen to find a successful screen vehicle. He hired noted Canadian screenwriter Ben Barzman to write an original script called *The Ceremony*, a declaration against capital punishment. Anthony Mann, noted for his work in the film noir and Western genres, was attached as director.[56] The project fell through, later being made in 1963 with Laurence Harvey both starring and directing.

At the time Harry was using the London office of the Famous Artists Agency as his base, ironically the same company Broccoli cut his teeth at as an agent over in Hollywood. The agency's London representative was a charming Hungarian by the name of John Shepridge. Harry and Shepridge were pals, so when Shepridge left to work for 20th Century Fox in Paris, he let the offices to him. Along with all the fixtures and fittings, Harry also inherited Shepridge's assistant, a young and ambitious woman by the name of Johanna Harwood. Less than pleased with the prospect of being a mere secretary for Harry, when asked what she wanted to do, Johanna replied, 'I want to write film scripts.' Harry thought about it and answered, 'I'll let you write film scripts if you stay on.' So began a productive association that was to last several years.[57]

As an employer, Johanna found Harry pleasant enough, 'if a bit uncouth. He didn't have a lot of social polish. And he was very tactless. That was his main problem, really, he rubbed people up the wrong way very easily.'[58] There was something else about him that Johanna found interesting, the fact that with his rotund shape and cherub-like features he resembled a baby. 'I always used to think he must have looked exactly like he looked in the pram. Which helped him because he looked as if you could trust him, and of course you couldn't, not really.'[59]

Johanna had never heard of Saltzman before, like a lot of people in the movie industry they were a bit hazy about his background, all she knew was he was looking for something to latch onto, something that would make his name and, of course, make him money. He found that special something in a motley group of young radicals who had revolutionised British theatre and were now determined to do the same thing about the moribund state of British cinema.

Since the war, London's West End had remained stiflingly highbrow, its productions designed largely to please a middle-class audience who still came to the theatre dressed in dinner jackets and cocktail dresses. One only had to look across the Atlantic at Broadway and the plays of Tennessee Williams and Arthur Miller to see a theatre culture that dealt with real social issues. Where was the voice of the common man in the West End? As theatre critic Kenneth Tynan bemoaned in 1954: 'The bare fact is, that apart from revivals and imports, there is nothing in the London theatre that one dares discuss with an intelligent man for more than five minutes.'[60]

The instrument of change came from a very unlikely source: the Oxford-educated George Devine, who had run the Old Vic theatre school, directed at Stratford and acted with Olivier. Devine had been caught by the brilliant energy of a young BBC director called Tony Richardson, the son of a chemist from Shipley in Yorkshire. Richardson also studied at Oxford, where he wrote film essays for the university's highbrow cinema magazine with his friend Lindsay Anderson. Accepted on a BBC director trainee course, Richardson quickly rose through the ranks to become the corporation's 'hot' new talent. His bisexuality was also an open secret to his friends.

Devine and Richardson shared the same passion about making English theatre more relevant in the life of the nation, and with financial backing from Lord Harewood, cousin to the Queen, along with theatre producer and member of the Communist party Oscar Lewenstein, no lover of West End middle-class dirge, the English Stage Company was born. Its home was the Royal Court theatre, situated next door to Sloane Square underground station, both a physical and metaphorical distance away from the glitz of theatreland.

Placing an ad in the *Stage* newspaper looking for new plays, Devine's office was inundated with some 700 submissions. Amongst a pile of largely unproducible material, one play stood out. It was called *Look Back in Anger* and was written by a 27-year-old struggling actor and son of an advertisement copywriter and barmaid, John Osborne.

With Kenneth Haigh cast as Osborne's anti-hero Jimmy Porter, venting his spleen on everything from religion to sex, Mary Ure (soon to be Mrs John Osborne) as his put-upon wife Alison and Alan Bates as his friend Cliff, *Look Back in Anger* went into rehearsals under the direction of Richardson. But as opening night loomed, Devine's confidence in the play began to slip. Lord Harewood had given the play to a friend and got this response: 'People won't stand for being shouted at like that, it's not what they go to the theatre for.'[61] Even the company's own press officer doubted he could interest any journalists in it and told Osborne to his face, 'I suppose you're really an angry young man.'[62] It was the first time the playwright recalled that phrase ever being used.

Nobody who was there on opening night, 8 May 1956, came away from the experience unaware they had not borne witness to a piece of British theatre history. 'It really knocked you for six,' recalled Anthony Field, then just starting out as a producer in the West End. 'It was certainly a new style of theatre, people were suddenly standing on stage and being you, and thinking like you and talking like you. I remember there was enormous applause at the end.'[63]

Most of the critics, however, were appalled by Osborne's creation, but Kenneth Tynan gave the play a rave review in the *Observer*, ending it with his now famous observation, 'I doubt if I could love anyone who did not wish to see *Look Back in Anger*.' Tynan's words had an almost immediate effect, turning the Royal Court into the theatre of the moment. 'It changed everything for the working-class actor in the British theatre,' is Michael Caine's view on the play's impact.[64]

It's no surprise to learn, being an avid theatregoer and alive to new trends and happenings, that Harry was among the first people to see *Look Back in Anger* and, duly impressed, put a call through to Osborne. They met for tea at the Dorchester, where Harry was staying. Osborne recalls Harry saying how his play could be a hit on Broadway if handled properly. 'He had more flair than to suggest it be translated to Greenwich village.'[65]

When the play did transfer to Broadway in the fall of 1957, where it was to enjoy a healthy year-long run, Harry made his move, ingratiating himself with both Devine and Osborne; Richardson had left the production by then to run things at the Royal Court. Very much the toast of Broadway, Devine and Osborne were courted by all types, invited to the best parties and mixed in privileged circles. When it came to playing the perfect host, however, nobody could beat Harry. They went to iconic jazz clubs like the Five Spot, out in the Bowery district, and Birdland on Broadway. There was even a trip out to Harlem for the Wednesday Amateur Night at the Apollo Theatre, already a showbusiness institution, famous not only for the talent but also for its tough partisan audiences and the individual known as 'the executioner', who literally swept failing acts off the stage with a broom.

While Devine, given his nature, was more cautious, Osborne allowed himself to be totally won over by Harry.

> He had an amazing profligacy in his enthusiasms, whether it was restaurants, girls or hot properties. 'What do you want to eat tonight?' he'd ask. 'French, German, Italian, Jewish? I know the best Finnish restaurant in town.' One always, rightly, chose the best in town. A week later he might ask the same question. 'Well, that Finnish place was terrific. Why don't we…' He would cut you off like some blundering toddler. 'Forget it. I know a much better place.' I don't think we ever went back to a best-restaurant-in-town.[66]

More importantly, Harry had begun making business overtures. 'He dropped ideas for films like restaurants,' said Osborne. 'He talked engagingly of his wild intentions.'[67] Osborne's solicitor, Oscar Beuselinck, had quite the opposite view of Saltzman, regarding him as a parody of a movie producer –

'D'ya wanna make a movie?' Beuselinck would mimic, spreading his arms wide, 'Or d'ya wanna make a movie.'[68]

Osborne paid no heed. He had fallen for Harry's charms, later calling him 'a natural courier to my anarchy', and allowed himself to be whisked off to Paris with him that Christmas, leaving his new wife behind in London. They stayed at the Hotel Napoleon off the Champs Elysees and dined out in grand style every night. Osborne wondered quite what he was going to tell poor Mary Ure. 'Hell, we'll send her a cable,' was Harry's answer. 'As if that settled everything,' said Osborne. 'Bemused, I watched him dash it off. "We love Paris, Paris, Paris. Happy Christmas. See you for New Year. Love John and Harry." It did not go down well.'[69]

Devine was certainly of the opinion that teaming up with Harry would bring a measure of financial solidity to the Royal Court, and Richardson was given the job of going out to New York to finalise things. It was Harry who personally picked Richardson up from the airport in a limo, an obvious attempt to make a good first impression. Over the next few days Richardson was able to assess this potential benefactor and form a solid opinion of him, one that never really changed over the next few years they would know each other.

> He had a perfect mogul's figure – stocky, tubby – crinkly grey hair and the face of an eager coarse cherub. He bubbled with plans, and he had great charm. He was a splendid raconteur. By his generosity in big and in small things – he always loved to give – he radiated affluence.[70]

At the time, Harry was living in a large apartment in Alwyn Court, a twelve-storey apartment building located on the corner of Seventh Avenue in Midtown Manhattan, one block south of Central Park. Richardson remembered it as 'dark and dingy', and looking as if it hadn't been cleaned. 'There was an old Latino crone who baked in some hidden kitchen.'[71] Richardson moved in and found the place to be a hive of activity, everyone and a dog seemed to have their own key and people would be coming in and out at all hours.

The location soon switched to Los Angeles and Richardson found himself sharing a huge bungalow in the grounds of the Beverly Hills hotel with both Osborne and Saltzman. They frequented the Polo Lounge, where Osborne observed that Harry 'exuded a feeling of tetchy over-familiarity towards the praetorian waiters',[72] and buzzed in and out of expensive shops up and down Wilshire Boulevard. At night, Harry retired to his room with a copy of *Variety* and spent the next few hours shouting down the line to various world cities.

'His fluent French,' said Osborne, 'sounded like a union leader addressing a rioting mob.'[73]

Work on a potential partnership deal between Harry and the Royal Court hadn't gone very far before Richardson began to sense that there was nothing very concrete behind it. These concerns only grew louder upon the discovery that Harry had very little capital to draw on. What was on the table wasn't very appealing anyway; the creation of a company that got a free option on any of the Court shows, something Richardson and Devine had not the slightest intention of sanctioning. A secondary idea of a company that would handle all their affairs in the States was a non-starter from the get-go, as there was evidently no significant money available. 'So, it all fizzled out,' said Richardson. 'And George (Devine) himself, although he still liked Harry and was often charmed by him, realized he'd been led up the garden path.'[74]

At the conclusion of the negotiations, Richardson had formed another opinion of Harry: that he was a hustler, 'but a sublime hustler'.[75] Why then, after reaching such a conclusion, did Richardson stick around and not get the first flight back to London? Like Devine, he was fascinated and intrigued by this 'hustler' and what he might be able to accomplish. Harry had all these wild schemes and fantasies, many of them with not a chance of bearing fruit, and yet he had this boundless energy that might be able to get things done. 'What Harry was able to exude in abundance was potential,' said Richardson,[76] and this was something the budding filmmaker felt he could tap into in order to realise his ambition to make a film of *Look Back in Anger*. Maybe Harry's knowhow about the movie business could be invaluable.

Harry reacted with enthusiasm about this new proposal, and together with Richardson and Osborne it was agreed to set up their own film production company. It was named Woodfall after the street in Chelsea where Osborne lived with Mary Ure, and the trio took offices in Mayfair's Curzon Street.

Woodfall Films' policy ran parallel to that of the Royal Court, a basically naturalistic style, a sort of writer's cinema. 'To prove that good films, ones that showed British life as it really is, could be made,' in Osborne's words.[77] To some extent, this policy had already found expression with the Free Cinema movement of the mid 1950s that consisted of Richardson himself, Lindsay Anderson and Karel Reisz, a Czechoslovakian who had come to Britain as a child refugee. For years all three men had felt excluded by the established British studio system.

Taking their cameras out onto the streets, these budding filmmakers captured a new naturalistic and unscripted look at England in a series of groundbreaking short films and documentaries. 'Free Cinema had a manifesto,' stated Walter Lassally, who worked on them as a cameraman:

> It pointed out that the films were free in the sense that their authors were free to do what they liked, there weren't any pressures, either from front office or backers or anything of that kind. These films were made outside of the system, it was true independence and very unusual because there weren't many films of that kind being made in Britain or elsewhere in the world either.[78]

Harry was certainly intrigued by the Free Cinema movement, but thought that he could be the one to bring in some commercial perspective. As he sought to raise the necessary finance, however, obstacles were being placed in his way. It was clear to Richardson that in the hands of a British studio such as Rank, Osborne's play would be emasculated. Osborne had also insisted that Richardson be installed as director in spite his never having directed a feature before. 'You would never believe the trouble we had to get Tony Richardson accepted by the distributors and financiers,' Harry was to complain. 'You see the structure of most of our biggest producing companies is such that they will not accommodate new creative ideas. They have an almost pathological fear of them.'[79] In the end the £250,000 budget was raised by Harry through Warner Brothers and Associated British-Pathe, a feat of monumental persuasion that Osborne would be forever grateful for.

As for the script, Osborne must have been reluctant to adapt his own play, since on the advice of Kenneth Tynan television writer Nigel Kneale, famous for his spine-tingling BBC chiller *Quatermass*, was hired to do the job,[80] only to run into censorship troubles over a forthright use of language. Harry was hoping for an A certificate and was dismayed when John Trevelyan, the chief censor, insisted the film carry an X certificate. Worried about the likely effect this would have on the box office, Harry asked for a face-to-face meeting. Determined not to back down, Trevelyan explained his objection to words like 'bitch', 'virgin' and 'bastard', along with the portrayal of Porter's sadomasochistic affair with Alison. It was Trevelyan's contention that if an A certificate was sought, there would have to be some considerable pruning to the script. At the meeting Harry did agree to omit 'Christ', a word Trevelyan preferred not to have even in the X category, but *Look Back in Anger* was ultimately released as an 'adults only' feature.[81]

In terms of casting, there weren't a whole lot of high-profile British actors around able to competently play Osborne's working-class hero. Dirk Bogarde had already expressed a desire to play Jimmy Porter but Rank's managing director John Davis, who held Bogarde under contract, returned the script to him with a note saying that there was altogether too much dialogue. Finally, Richard Burton was chosen, and seized by the pioneering spirit of the enterprise waived his usual Hollywood salary, although it still amounted to almost a quarter of the budget.

With filming due to start in the autumn of 1958, Harry made the permanent move to London and Woodfall requisitioned a place for him and Jacqueline to live, paying the rent into the bargain. Lowndes Cottage was located in the heart of Belgravia and was the former home of composer Sir William Walton. Here, according to Richardson, Harry installed a mini-empire: 'Secretaries, chauffeurs, multilingual cooks arrived from wherever; international hookers rotated in the guest rooms.'[82]

Richardson moved in too, using the place rather like an office, as he had done at Harry's New York apartment, to the occasional irritation of Jacqueline, as the budding director made a habit of sometimes bursting into their bedroom early in the morning to talk to her husband. Stars like Kirk Douglas and Burt Lancaster, along with top Hollywood producer Charles Feldman, came visiting as Lowndes Cottage hosted all manner of exclusive parties and dinners. 'It was a heady, crazy world,' noted Richardson. 'We never questioned it – how it happened; who paid – Harry was totally in charge of the business side. Harry created a wonderful atmosphere and I – and John too – enjoyed every minute of it.'[83]

Work on *Look Back in Anger* progressed smoothly on locations around London including Kensal Rise cemetery, a disused railway junction in Dalston and Romford market; interiors were shot at Elstree Studios. Richardson certainly took to his role of director like a natural, according to actor Gary Raymond, who played Cliff in the film. 'He was wonderful. He had power business breakfasts before anybody else, it seemed to me. He just loved it all. There was no sense from him of, oh God, what am I doing here, none at all. It was just something to be enjoyed.'[84]

According to cinematographer Oswald Morris, Richardson barred Harry from the set,[85] although that didn't stop the producer from mixing Richardson a cocktail in a thermos and putting it in the limo that took him to work every morning.

Burton, too, was in fine form, believing that he was giving one of his best performances and in a letter to a former teacher declared: 'I am for the first time *ever* looking forward to seeing a film in which I play.'[86]

Once completed, Osborne and Richardson took a print of the film over to Los Angeles where Harry had arranged a private showing of it to Jack Warner, head of the Warner studio. Not long into the screening, Warner asked what language the actors were speaking. 'English,' replied Harry. 'This is America,' Warner stated and promptly walked out.[87]

Far from disconsolate, Harry whisked the pair off to Las Vegas for a lads' outing that Richardson never forgot:

> We were comped at some hotel and comped also with one gargantuan hooker between the two of us (Harry disappearing with someone much more attractive). Each tried to unload the poor girl on the other till, not succeeding, we made a quick escape together when she disappeared into the Ladies room. It was all part of Harry's magic carpet.[88]

In spite of the pulling power of Burton's name and an ABC circuit release, *Look Back in Anger* did poorly at the box office. Even a clutch of encouraging notices couldn't save it; Penelope Houston in the *Monthly Film Bulletin* considered Richardson's tough, vital style as, 'something new in British cinema', and while the *Manchester Guardian* admitted it wasn't a great film, 'in the prevailing dreariness of recent British film-making it could be a beacon'.

As Harry later conceded, 'It got good reviews everywhere and died in 51 countries. In Finland they took the picture off and the cinema owner said he didn't care if we sued. The ushers were getting lonely.'[89] While Harry laid some of the commercial failure of the picture at Burton's door, saying that at 33 he was too old to play Osborne's protagonist, he also believed the burden of an X certificate played its part, too, despite the fact that another 'angry young man' X film, Jack Clayton's *Room at the Top*, had cleaned up in British cinemas just a few months before. Harry even blamed the weather, that the picture had the misfortune to open 'in a heat wave that turned London into an outdoor city for at least a fortnight, people sleeping in the parks at night'.[90]

Maybe out of desperation, Harry employed bribery, according to Osborne, to get the picture accepted as the official British entry for the Cannes Film Festival. 'He hosted an elaborate dinner for the French dignitaries, and afterwards dealt out pound notes like a croupier to the gaiety of a circle of outstretched hands.'[91] In the end, *Room at the Top* got the nod. As compensation, Harry was thrown the measly crumb of competing as Britain's entry in a film festival in Acapulco: 'A banana-republic fiesta with no cultural pretensions,' disparaged Osborne.[92]

In America, *Look Back in Anger* was dealt a poor hand by the critics and box office numbers were correspondingly bad. This was something of a blow to Harry's contention that Woodfall's films would find an international audience.

After all, the company wasn't formed, he noted, 'from an arty-crafty point of view. We are extremely commercial-minded and we regard the properties we have as commercial properties.'[93] Indeed, despite the bitter disappointment over the reception towards their first film, work had already begun on Woodfall's second.

Osborne's highly anticipated follow-up to *Look Back in Anger* had been a huge smash at the Royal Court when it opened there in the spring of 1957. *The Entertainer* told the story of a clapped-out variety star called Archie Rice who plays to half-empty theatres in dreary seaside resorts. The crumbling music hall setting was a clear metaphor for a Britain in decline post-Suez.

Osborne had written the part especially for Laurence Olivier, at his request, in spite of the actor's revulsion over *Look Back in Anger*. Olivier's change of heart wasn't so much artistic as highly intuitive, a keen sense of where the wind was blowing, and at 50 years of age a calculated attempt to place himself at the heart of this new drama movement.

Olivier turned Archie Rice into one of his greatest stage triumphs and there wasn't any question of him not recreating his role in the screen version. However, after the failure of *Look Back in Anger* Harry found it a tough sell to investors, even with Olivier's name attached. Another reason may have been Woodfall's insistence on having artistic control over their pictures. 'We want to make them honestly,' said Harry. 'In other words, we control the script, the cast, the shooting and the completion of the picture. We won't allow the distributors or the people who back us to tell us how to make a picture.'[94] According to Saltzman, Woodfall were the only company doing that in England, 'and it is a battle all the time'.[95]

Knowing he had a fight on his hands, Harry looked into alternative financing and approached the brewers Bass to put money into the film, seeing that in the play Archie Rice was permanently pouring the stuff down his neck. Instead, the modest budget of £192,000 was provided by British Lion, the National Film Finance Corporation (NFFC) and Bryanston, a newly formed independent production company headed by Sir Michael Balcon, ex-head of Ealing Studios. To keep costs down, Olivier, Osborne and Richardson, returning as director, all took reduced fees. Harry took a producing fee of just $5,000.[96]

With money at a premium, Harry persisted in doing some kind of deal with Bass and had a 20ft cut-out of a bottle of their beer specially made. During a rehearsal at Shepperton Studios, he sneakily placed it behind the actors in order to tempt the brewers with this early example of product placement.

'How he imagined that this construction would go unnoticed is unimaginable,' queried Richardson. 'Olivier was not amused.'[97]

Neither was Olivier much amused by the suggestion that Vivien Leigh play Archie's wife, an idea swiftly abandoned due to the terminal nature of their marriage by this stage. Instead, Brenda de Banzie revived her role from the original Royal Court production. Other cast members included veterans Roger Livesey as Archie's father, and Thora Hird. For the pivotal role of Archie's daughter, two actresses were tested: Geraldine McEwan and Joan Plowright, a 28-year-old actress who had appeared on tour with the play and was currently in a not very secret love affair with Olivier. Both tests were screened in the viewing room of Harry's office, and as the lights went up it was patently clear that Michael Balcon preferred McEwan. 'That other girl simply won't do.' While the makers were determined to follow their artistic conscience, as one of the main backers of the film Balcon's voice clearly had some influence and it was going to be a brave person to argue against it. Stand up Jocelyn Rickards. 'Why are you against her, Sir Michael?' she boomed. 'She's a marvellous actress, will play well with Olivier and won't be intimidated by him. Why don't you settle for her?'

Fearing what might happen next, Osborne led Jocelyn out of the room. Balcon turned red-faced to Harry. 'Who is that girl? I won't be spoken to like that by anyone.'

'Jesus Christ, Michael,' answered Harry. 'She's the costume designer. And it's not just that – she's the author's mistress.'[98] Plowright got the role, making her screen debut. *The Entertainer* turned out to be a film notable for its debuts, as Richardson also gave first screen opportunities to Alan Bates, as Archie's cynical son Frank, and Albert Finney as Rice's other son, seen briefly going off to fight at Suez, a conflict from which he will not return. It only took a single night to shoot, at Liverpool Street station.

Other filming took place in the Lancashire coastal town of Morecambe, whose fading Victorian grandeur and naff seaside cafés made it ideal. For Osborne it was a nostalgic return, having spent days there as an actor in repertory theatre, and putting the finishing touches to *Look Back in Anger* reclining in a deckchair. Harry made a point of visiting the crew in Morecambe to see how things were progressing, especially since the production manager had given the London-based crew a dire foretaste of what to expect: 'Reports from the north are that it is inclined to be a bit crisp from time to time in October, so members should take suitable clothing.'[99]

While Harry tried to cut corners, it was clear the film was running over budget and he had no choice but to spend his own money to keep cameras rolling. Returning to Bryanston for additional funds of £6,000, Harry was blankly refused at first, but there was a change of heart and £4,000 was made available. By the close of shooting the film had gone £9,000 over budget, largely due to unexpected legal fees, costs incurred having to re-dub most of the actor's dialogue on location, and Harry's extravagant telephone bill.[100] Indeed, the producer's phone bill was so exorbitant, somewhere around the figure of £700, that an accountant working for the NFFC called Charles Wilder refused to pay it and got a fearsome call from Harry ordering him down the line to, 'Sign that bloody cheque!' When Wilder refused, unless more details were provided, Harry caught the next train down from Morecambe and had a blazing row with him at his office in Soho Square.[101]

Once again, Harry found himself in a headlong fight with the censors over the film's liberal sprinkling of colourful expressions such as 'bloody', 'Christ', 'bastard', 'whore' and 'arse', along with society-imploding lines of dialogue like 'take me to bed', which, according to one of the readers at the censor's office, exemplified, 'The enfant terrible language to which Mr Osborne is much addicted.'[102]

Trevelyan offered Harry much the same choice as before, an X certificate without cuts or face substantial alterations, which Trevelyan saw would only weaken the film. But Harry wasn't going to play ball this time. Having put much of the blame on the failure of *Look Back in Anger* due to its certification, he held out for an A. Negotiations dragged on for three months, since neither Harry nor Trevelyan were willing to relent. Ultimately, Trevelyan triumphed. 'He hobbled us with an X certificate,' said Osborne, 'which insured that it would be turned down as an entry for the Royal film performance which might have helped its general release.'[103] And so it proved. Despite some decent reviews, *The Entertainer* failed at the box office. Even the venerable critic of the *Observer*, C.A. Lejeune, recommended it: 'The film is gloomy. Gloom is not my favourite cup of tea. Osborne is not my favourite plate of biscuits. But I think *The Entertainer* is a film that should be seen.' It's a shame so few punters took his advice.

After barely two years in existence, Woodfall was dangerously close to collapse.

Woodfall's first two pictures had made a strong critical impact and established the company as a true independent working outside of the mainstream. As filmmakers they believed there was a place in Britain for realistic, hard-hitting films which took chances and gambled with new faces, new writers and untried directors. But they had not been commercial successes. 'And there's a big difference between critical success and financial success,' explained

Johanna Harwood. 'And what Harry was interested in was financial. What he wanted was money, and power, which comes obviously through the money.'[104]

Someone who fit easily into the Woodfall ethos was Joan Littlewood, a visionary stage director whose socialist principles fuelled her ambitions for a theatre that served the community. Her Theatre Workshop stood in a run-down area of the East End and was just as big a two-finger salute to the West End as the Royal Court. Joan showed up one day in Harry's office with a copy of a play she wanted to film. *The Lion and the Jewel* was a comedy set in a small remote African village and written by the Nigerian playwright Wole Soyinka. Harry promised Joan that he would read it by the time she returned that evening. When she came back, Harry said he liked it so much he was prepared to try and raise some finance. The only problem was Joan's determination to shoot the film out in Nigeria; she had already been to a London store to buy thick rubber boots due to her fear of snakes. In the end, it was the logistics of shooting out in Africa that proved too much of an economic risk and the project collapsed. Harry, however, remained interested in working with Joan and when she co-wrote a screenplay for a musical set in the East End called *Sparrows Can't Sing*, he declared an interest in producing, only to later pull out.[105]

Meanwhile, Woodfall were wondering what to do next. There was talk of bringing in the emerging playwright Arnold Wesker to write a screenplay, and Harry also asked Johanna Harwood to produce a number of scripts. These included an adaptation of Colin MacInnes's 1957 novel *City of Spades*, which focused on London's emerging black community and culture. Harry would produce and it was hoped the American actor Sidney Poitier might play the lead. 'I liked that a lot,' said Johanna, 'but Tony Richardson didn't want to do it.'[106]

And there was an ambitious trilogy of films under the collective title *Articles of War*, which Johanna seemed to recall was an original Harry idea. Each film dealt with a different facet of conflict and the hope was to hire three different directors, one British, one German and one Japanese.[107]

None of these projects got off the ground. That was the trouble with Harry. He was always looking to make things happen. 'That's what he did best,' said Johanna. 'He was great at setting up deals and selling ideas. He was a great salesman. But he didn't have much critical judgement.'[108] Harry did have this habit of overworking a script, thinking it could be improved, bringing in writer after writer, and often running the whole thing into the ground. 'He wasn't good at grasping what needed to be changed and what was ok,' viewed Johanna.[109]

Then, a project was found that would turn around the fortunes of the company – and Harry.

Alan Sillitoe spent much of his youth in a council house in Nottingham and his literary hero, Arthur Seaton, a boozy, rebellious factory worker who shags and boozes his weekends away, was inspired by a tale his brother told him about a young guy in a pub falling down the stairs one Saturday night after drinking eleven pints and seven gins.[110] Rejected by publishers, 'because it didn't fit into the pre-conceived romantic notions that people had about the so-called working class',[111] Sillitoe's debut novel was eventually published in 1958 to great acclaim. It was called *Saturday Night and Sunday Morning*.

After the failures of *Look Back in Anger* and *The Entertainer*, Woodfall was almost on its knees financially but managed to scramble together £4,500 to buy the film rights.[112] Jeffrey Simmons, who dealt with film rights at Sillitoe's publisher, recalled an extraordinary meeting he had with Saltzman at Lowndes Cottage:

> When I entered, I was reminded of that scene in Chaplin's *The Great Dictator* with the autocrat seated at the massive desk. The carpet between the door and Saltzman's desk was the length of a cricket pitch. Also, he had at least four telephones in different colours and as I discussed the deal for the film, I was regularly interrupted by one of these, with Saltzman enunciating his replies to make sure that I knew who was calling. 'Hello Lauren,' he'd say, and whisper to me, 'Lauren Bacall.' Clark Gable, Marilyn Monroe, Greta Garbo, all seemed desperate for his attention during the hour or so I was there.[113]

Simmons was not taken in at all, estimating that when Harry was speaking to these luminaries it was probably four o'clock in the morning in Los Angeles.

In spite of his behaviour at the meeting, Simmons was delighted that Harry wanted his client to write the screenplay, even though Sillitoe had never written or even attempted one before. Keeping faithful to his own book and the realistic scenario it represented, it came as no surprise that censor Trevelyan took offence at the number of expletives in Sillitoe's script, a profusion of bloody, bleedings, bastards and buggers. As Trevelyan wrote to Harry: 'I appreciate that words of this kind are normal in the speech of the type of people that the film is about but I have always found, strange though it may seem, that these are the very people who most object to this kind of thing on the screen.'[114]

Harry later sent a revised script to the censor's office which met with better approval, but a letter from Trevelyan to the producer outlined a few remaining problems: 'The love scenes can be passionate but should not go too far. The director should use discretion in shooting them… The line, "get down in bed," is perhaps rather direct.'[115] Also, on page 50, Trevelyan took issue with the use of 'sod' – 'a word that we are trying to keep out of films.'[116] Even with these and other revisions, Trevelyan still considered it to be an X, though added, 'but with a good film this should be no handicap'.[117]

It had been agreed that Karel Reisz, one of the founder members of the Free Cinema group, be given the chance to make his directorial debut with *Saturday Night and Sunday Morning*, with Richardson co-producing this time with Harry. But when Reisz and Richardson wanted their Free Cinema colleague Walter Lasally to photograph the film, Harry put his foot down and made arrangements to bring in Freddie Francis. Harry felt that as it was Reisz's first feature, he needed someone more experienced.

The choice of Albert Finney to play Seaton was certainly made by Reisz and Richardson, ignoring Harry's suggestion of Peter O'Toole. Richardson had directed Finney in the theatre, as well as giving him his screen debut in *The Entertainer*, and there was a feeling that here was an actor ready to explode on the scene at any moment.

With an unknown in the lead there was pressure to cast Diana Dors as Brenda, the married woman Seaton has an affair with and gets pregnant. When she turned it down, Reisz gave a huge sigh of relief and went with his first choice Rachel Roberts, who ended up winning a BAFTA award for Best Actress. The rest of the cast was filled out by fellow working-class actors Norman Rossington and Finney's old RADA drama school colleague Bryan Pringle, along with Shirley Anne Field.

Meanwhile, Harry was facing severe difficulties raising the finance, roughly £114,000. 'Many of the financial people, on reading the screen treatment, said that cinema-goers wanted to see comedy, adventure and musicals,' said Sillitoe, 'and not a story set in conditions with which they were too familiar, and from which if they had any sense they would only want to escape.'[118] Eventually, Harry managed to raise the finance with loans from Lloyd's Bank, with the rest coming courtesy of the National Film Finance Corporation.[119] Sillitoe was to remain personally beholden to Harry: 'Without someone as hardworking, knowledgeable and dedicated the project would have been dead-stopped.'[120]

As with Broccoli over at Warwick, Woodfall also took advantage of the services of Film Finances, first on *The Entertainer* and now on this film, given the small budget. Indeed, there were some at Film Finances who didn't believe the film could be made with such financial restraints and was thus a risk for the company, as their assessor John Croydon wrote: 'This is a matter of the producer convincing us that he has been able to make suitable arrangements for his picture within the limitations he is imposing upon himself.'[121] Indeed, Harry was scrimping and saving and cutting so many corners that Croydon was moved to say, 'If ever there were an effort to pour a quart into a pint pot, this is it.'[122]

Croydon also pointed out the inexperience of Karel Reisz, though mentioned that Harry had told him, 'If Reisz slipped by a day he would be taken off the picture.' Brutal perhaps, but it did help convince Film Finances to take on the film, and when it did indeed go slightly over budget step in to supply the funds to complete it.[123]

Filming began in the spring of 1960 on location around the Nottingham streets of Sillitoe's youth; 'My mother enjoyed making tea for the stars as they came and went.'[124] Harry employed a gentleman whose job it was to knock on people's doors to see if they would allow their backyard to be used in the film or if they would like to be an extra. Everyone was paid a fee from a large suitcase he carried stuffed with money; in this way, Harry avoided tax liabilities for registered employees.[125]

As filming continued, it became obvious that Harry's time at Woodfall was drawing to a close. Over these past two years Richardson had grown savvy to how films operated from a business point of view, largely thanks to watching Harry operate at close quarters, but had also grown wise to his partner's bluff and bluster. The simple fact was there wasn't very much money around, and what there was appeared to be being poured into things like Harry's operation over at Lowndes Cottage.

The more Richardson expressed his concerns about the financial state of the company, the more Harry refused to face the reality of it. 'A certain amount of bluff is very much part of all show business,' said Richardson. 'But when you're bluffing your own partners, you're in bad trouble.'[126] All Richardson and Osborne were after was the truth; instead Harry, in Richardson's words, 'rushed from one impossible scheme to another. Deals of more and more dubious kinds were being proposed, or some transaction about which we knew nothing.'[127]

Things reached a head after Richardson purchased an option on Shelagh Delaney's play *A Taste of Honey*, which had been originally staged by Joan Littlewood at her Theatre Workshop in 1958. Without his knowledge Harry tried to flog the property to Hollywood producer Charles Feldman, despite the fact he'd earlier declared it, 'too provincial and too English'.[128] An incensed Richardson was forced into contacting Feldman to explain that Harry had no right to carry out such a deal.[129]

Things weren't going so well between Harry and Karel Reisz, either. The director found Saltzman, 'A very charming, exuberant sort of rascal, really. He had any amount of energy and cheek.'[130] Betsy Blair, an American actress who later married Reiz, saw first hand the contrasting ways in which Karel and Richardson dealt with Saltzman. 'Harry liked to wander round the sets offering advice. Karel indulged him, without taking him too seriously, but Tony was more calculating. He would stop everything and say, "Harry, please make any suggestions you feel will help," and Harry would withdraw, embarrassed.'[131]

Perhaps because Richardson could only see further difficulties ahead, with a widening artistic incompatibility, with Harry attaching himself to projects that neither Richardson nor Osborne wanted to make or felt were right for Woodfall, the decision was taken to vote him out of the company. Richardson took over full producing reins on *Saturday Night*, though Harry did retain a credit. Paid off with the limited funds still available to the company, Harry was asked to leave Lowndes Cottage and his business affairs there were terminated.[132]

The staff at Lowndes Cottage were given the choice of either going with Harry or staying at Woodfall. Given how Harry used to bully and harangue them, Richardson thought he would win the popularity contest hands down. Not at all. They all voted for Harry – except one, a Polish chauffeur who went to work for Richardson.[133]

Interestingly, Osborne offers up a different take on why Harry left Woodfall, that the producer took the decision himself that the time was right to end his association and take up new challenges: 'Tony and I had become like last week's greatest restaurants.'[134]

Whatever the truth, Harry's legacy at Woodfall cannot be overlooked. The three 'kitchen sink' dramas he helped make with the company – *Look Back in Anger*, *The Entertainer* and *Saturday Night and Sunday Morning* – were at the forefront of British New Wave cinema and landmarks in our nation's cultural history.

Certainly, Osborne was sad to see him go. 'I had enjoyed Harry's company when he was at his effervescent best, before marriage tamed his bravado. Without him Woodfall would never have got started. He had fairground flair and uncanny taste.'[135]

It's ironic that Harry left the company at the moment of its greatest triumph, when *Saturday Night and Sunday Morning* became an unexpected hit at the British box office and made Albert Finney a star overnight. Harry was in Paris at the time, trying to raise finance for several projects in a city he knew well, certain that his final Woodfall production would flop. 'He was convinced it was as bad as the others and that it wasn't going to make any money,' said Johanna Harwood. 'He was very surprised when the film turned out to be a hit.'[136]

The huge success of *Saturday Night and Sunday Morning* was significant in two ways. Firstly, it enabled Woodfall to continue in production for the rest of the decade, churning out a diverse output that included *The Loneliness of the Long Distance Runner* (1962), which introduced Tom Courtenay to film audiences, a postmodern adaptation of Henry Fielding's novel *Tom Jones* (1963), which was an international hit, and Richard Lester's comedy *The Knack… And How To Get It* (1965).

And secondly, Harry was entitled to a share in the not-inconsiderable profits, 'As he well deserved to do,' said Sillitoe. Indeed, Sillitoe maintained that it was Harry's profit dividend from *Saturday Night* that enabled him to go out and purchase an option on the Ian Fleming Bond books, and seal his own place in film history.[137]

3

Everything or Nothing

While the Woodfall films gave Saltzman immense personal satisfaction, he knew the writing was on the wall for the 'kitchen sink' genre they had helped to bring in, that the public would soon tire of seeing their own lives depicted on the screen with blunt realism. 'What people wanted after the "kitchen sink," I felt, was something different – strong plots with excitement, fast cars, bizarre situations, drink and women.'[1] He found all that in the novels of Ian Fleming, but what exactly drew him to the literary world of James Bond in the first place? Betty Box, who co-produced *The Iron Petticoat* with Harry back in 1956, offered up one interesting story. Whilst making the film in London, Katherine Hepburn had stipulated no publicity interviews. Nancy Spain, respected columnist on the *Daily Express*, was a friend of Betty and asked as a favour if an interview could be arranged. Betty went ahead and organised it. As a thank you, Nancy sent Betty a proof copy of Fleming's latest Bond novel. 'The book lay on my desk when Harry Saltzman came to see me. When he'd gone the book had gone, too.'[2] Was this when Harry first came into contact with Fleming's work?

By a stroke of good fortune, Saltzman shared the same London lawyer as Fleming, Brian Lewis, and through him contact with the author was made. A lunch meeting in December 1960 was arranged at Les Ambassadeurs. Before Harry arrived, Lewis had already laid much of the groundwork, advising Fleming that he really ought to sell the film rights to his books sooner rather than later. Far from a healthy man, Fleming was in the process of setting up a trust fund for his family; the worst possible thing would be for him to pop his clogs at a time when the trust value of his books was skewed at a low rate based on the 1954 sale of *Casino Royale* to the Russian-born director Gregory Ratoff for just $6,000.[3]

Saltzman began his pitch by discussing his involvement with Woodfall. Fleming confessed to never going to the cinema, but requested to see his last film. 'Not my best but my *last*, which happened to be *Saturday Night and Sunday Morning*, my last and my best.'[4]

It's never been established whether the two men discussed their shared wartime experiences. As their conversation must have revolved around the character of James Bond and the world of espionage that he inhabited, it seems unlikely the subject didn't merit at least a mention. Hilary Saltzman believes that her father's spy past did play a crucial role in cementing the deal. 'Because they had a similar background during the war, which was in confidential missions, they had a mutual understanding. Even though they couldn't publicize it, I really think Ian felt that this series was safe in my father's hands.'[5]

Fleming was still after the best possible deal and wanted to know what Saltzman was prepared to pay. The offer proposed was $50,000 for a six-month option.[6] Fleming was agreeable and Saltzman was told to get in touch with Bob Fenn of MCA, who handled all the author's TV and film enquiries.

The deal that ended up being fixed was a real coup for Harry, but also a financial risk. The producer was granted the movie rights to all of Fleming's published works, save for *Casino Royale* and *Thunderball*, then tied up in litigation. Part of the deal required him to option any new Bond book within an eighteen-month period or the rights would revert back to the author. Significantly, part of the deal stated that if the Bond series became so successful it exhausted all of Fleming's published works, Saltzman had the right to make original Bond movies.[7]

In obtaining the rights to the Bond novels, Saltzman's timing was immaculate. Just a couple of months into the option, the 17 March 1961 edition of *Life* magazine published an article on the voracious reading habits of President Kennedy. While the president confined himself to mostly political and historical non-fiction, he did admit to a hankering after the literary exploits of James Bond and placed *From Russia With Love* as his ninth favourite book. Amusingly, the article went on to say that CIA director Allen Dulles had informed Fleming about this and promised to invite the author to the White House for dinner on his next trip over to the States.

Not even the best publicist in the world could have dreamt up a better piece of PR. Practically overnight, Fleming's works became something of an American literary sensation. Saltzman must have been ecstatic when he heard the news; surely this was going to make his job simpler, studios and distributors would be pounding on his door. Not a bit. The appetite for a film of

Fleming's hero remained inert and by June, Harry was no nearer making any kind of deal. Time was running out.

★

Meanwhile, Cubby was still coming to terms with the failure of his *Oscar Wilde* film and was determined to learn the lessons from it. The picture had recently won a prize at the Moscow Film Festival, but that did nothing to alter the fact that he had lost a considerable amount of money on the venture. 'I decided I wasn't a philanthropist. You can win prizes but you can't eat them.'[8]

Cubby looked to other projects to make, and for a while considered bringing some of Charles Dickens's novels to television. He asked one of his associates from Warwick, Harold Huth, a former actor turned producer, to carry out some preparatory work. Huth was in his late sixties, and since the collapse of Warwick feared that his working days were over, so Broccoli's offer to re-read the Dickens novels and to make notes and suggestions as to how they could be adapted for television was a welcome tonic, according to his daughter Angela. 'Cubby paid him well for this enjoyable "work" and my father regained a sense of being useful.'[9]

Cubby had also teamed up with the novelist and playwright Wolf Mankowitz to fashion a script out of the *Arabian Nights* stories. However, by the time Mankowitz presented his first draft Broccoli had lost all enthusiasm for the project, he just didn't feel it was the right thing for him at that time. 'What exactly do you want to do?' asked Mankowitz. Cubby explained his desire to turn the novels of Ian Fleming into movies, and how his former partner had blown the deal in extraordinary circumstances. 'Then do them,' said Mankowitz. 'Call his agent and find out where the film rights lie.'[10]

Making enquiries, Cubby learnt that a certain Harry Saltzman, whom he had never met, held the option, but it only had twenty-eight days left to run. Cubby faced something of a dilemma: should he wait for the option to expire and then make his move, or get the ball rolling straightaway? Maybe it was the fact that Mankowitz knew Saltzman and would be able to make an introduction that forced his hand. Mankowitz certainly worked fast. By the time Broccoli arrived home, Wolf was on the phone with the message that Saltzman would be coming to see him in his office the following morning.[11]

There is another version to this story, one that was told to Bond production designer Peter Lamont by Saltzman's driver Frank, who used to chauffeur the producer all over the place in the 1960s. Frank was driving Harry up Audley Street one morning and there was Wolf Mankowitz walking along, so he stopped the car. 'Hi Harry,' said Wolf, recognising him. 'Are you still trying to peddle those Bond books?' And Harry said, 'Yeah, I've got a goldmine but I can't dig it up.' Wolf wrote a name down on a business card and passed it to Harry, 'Well, talk to this fella and take him out to lunch.' It was Cubby.[12]

Whatever the truth of the matter is, Mankowitz can certainly lay claim to bringing the two producers together. They were men he liked and admired in equal measure. 'They were both very easy to get on with. Saltzman was very intense, an extrovert, post-Mike Todd producer type. Cubby was very quiet with a solid, money background.'[13] Mankowitz must have been sure their combined qualities would make an ideal pairing.

At the meeting, the one thing that surprised Broccoli the most was that the subject of James Bond didn't appear to be on the agenda. Instead, Saltzman was pitching an idea for a film they could make called *Streets of Gold*, about getting rich in New York. When that didn't stir any interest, he mentioned another project, this one bizarrely about a scarecrow that comes to life.[14]

Growing impatient, Broccoli told Saltzman that it was Bond and only Bond he was interested in. 'Don't bother,' said Harry. 'Nobody's interested in backing the Bond films.'[15] In that case, Broccoli asked what he wanted for the rights. Saltzman wasn't in the market to sell them, instead the suggestion was they go into business together and he would get the contracts drawn up then and there. Reluctant to form another alliance so quickly after his experiences with Irving Allen, Broccoli's desperation not to let Bond get away from him again was so strong he agreed to go into partnership with a man he had only just met and knew next to nothing about.

Crucially, then, the Saltzman and Broccoli partnership was formed out of necessity. Normally, when partners get together it's because they like each other and they want to work together. A good example of this would be two people working on a picture together suddenly discovering they have a lot in common and decide to become partners. Cubby and Harry got together for business reasons and not personal reasons. 'They were chalk and cheese as people with one common goal,' said Tom Mankiewicz. 'They were not remotely built the same way. They were not the same human being. But somehow they made it work.'[16] Jerry Juroe, who handled publicity for the Bond films, believed their contrasting personalities actually made for a compelling combination. 'The oh-so steady and always in control Broccoli was a perfect match for Saltzman, who could be dazzlingly brilliant with his wild ideas and ingenuity. They really were a potent pair.'[17]

As for the terms of this new arrangement, Saltzman cheekily proposed a 51 per cent, 49 per cent split, in his favour. No, Broccoli insisted, it had to be

50/50 or not at all. Harry relented without much of a fight and the two men shook hands. Broccoli left the meeting, 'with the distinct feeling that this was going to be an interesting partnership'.[18]

With Saltzman having got nowhere these past few months – even Rank films had turned him down – it was Broccoli that took charge. The first person on his list to call was his old friend at Columbia, Mike Frankovich, with whom he had enjoyed a long business relationship during those Warwick years. But the verdict of the studio's story editor was blunt and not at all favourable: Bond was just a poor man's Mike Hammer, and as a character would simply not translate to American audiences.[19] Out of respect to Cubby, Frankovich did call a board meeting to discuss the project but in the end couldn't talk his fellow executives into making an offer, unless the picture could be made for a bargain $400,000. Clearly the kind of film the producers were hoping to make out of James Bond couldn't be realised on such meagre funds.[20]

Next, Cubby called another acquaintance, Arthur Krim, the powerful chief executive of United Artists. The mood music was encouraging enough for Harry and Cubby to both fly over to New York, accompanied by their wives. 'Harry, never short on chutzpah, when finding out that Cubby was bringing his wife insisted that Cubby pay for his wife as well,' revealed David Picker, then vice president of United Artists. 'Maybe that was the first clue that this partnership was destined for eventual wreckage.'[21]

The first Picker heard that Saltzman and Broccoli were on their way was when Bud Ornstein, who ran UA's operation in London, called to tell him to set up a meeting. 'Don't ask what it's about because they want to tell you themselves,' he said.[22] Ornstein had called Picker rather than anyone else because he knew of his particular interest in British film production. Maybe he also knew that Picker had personally tried to buy the Bond rights some months before, having been put onto the books by the husband of one of his cousins, a Wall Street broker. After reading a couple of them Picker realised their cinematic potential, but when he called UA's Los Angeles office to learn the rights were not for sale, he'd dropped the idea.[23]

United Artists headquarters were at 729 Seventh Avenue, and when Broccoli and Saltzman arrived at Krim's office they were slightly taken aback. Instead of a small meeting, most of the top brass were there sat round a table: Krim himself, along with his long-time friend and partner Robert Benjamin, with whom he had taken over United Artists in 1951; there was Picker, at 30 years old one of the youngest executives in the movie business, and a whole raft of other executives and publicity chiefs. Far from overawed, Cubby felt a surge of excitement pass through his body; someone was taking them very seriously indeed.[24]

After the usual pleasantries, it was Saltzman who announced that they owned the rights to James Bond. That got Picker's attention straightaway. 'I didn't even try to hide my excitement. This was a deal I felt we had to make right then and there.'[25] As his colleagues hadn't read any of the books it was Picker who took the lead in the discussion, talking to the producers about the merits of the Bond stories and what it was going to take to bring them to life on the screen. 'As we talked, it was clear we had a mutual creative vision.'[26]

Picker certainly believed that he could do business with these two men. He felt Broccoli had by far a better understanding of the ways of the film business, having worked in Hollywood for many years. 'Personal contacts and relationships count for a lot in Hollywood and Cubby had made many friends and had a personal style that fit in the ways of Hollywood. He was, in other words, accepted.'[27]

Harry, thought Picker, was different, more of an outsider. 'In meeting with him it was hard to feel totally comfortable. His limited experience made him awkward and he was often forced to rely on Cubby, whose experience was so much more grounded.'[28]

At Picker's urging, everyone round that table was happy to give the project a green light and a budget of $1 million was approved for the first of what was hoped would be a series of pictures. Other details were quickly ironed out, such as producers' fees and a 50/50 equal share of the profits, after UA had recovered their investment.[29] The deal was done and everyone shook hands. It hadn't taken more than forty minutes.

Broccoli was elated, bursting to tell Dana the good news, but Saltzman looked less in the mood to celebrate. 'We haven't got a deal,' he said. 'We don't have anything on paper.' Broccoli turned to Saltzman, 'When you shake hands with Arthur Krim you *have* a deal.'[30]

Saltzman remained unconvinced and wouldn't budge on the matter. Broccoli had no choice but to walk back into Krim's office and face the embarrassing task of asking him to put something on paper outlining what had just been agreed in the meeting. Krim understood the situation and promised a letter of intent would be delivered to their hotel by the end of the day. Now Cubby could celebrate, and together with Dana went to the famous El Morocco club in Manhattan. The date was 21 June 1961, and Cubby was too busy toasting the success of the Bond deal to realise it was also his second wedding anniversary. Hurriedly, he got the kitchen staff to bring out a special cake and all was forgiven.[31]

Back in London, the producers pressed ahead with formalising a deal with Fleming to buy the Bond books outright. Certainly, the author was delighted, after years of false starts and having very little faith left in the movie business and the people in it. Saltzman and Broccoli were different, he said. 'I'd seen *Saturday Night and Sunday Morning* and *The Trials of Oscar Wilde* and was very impressed. We discussed the project and I found them to be very intelligent chaps. I put my faith in them.'[32]

However, according to Len Deighton, who was told this by Saltzman, the purchasing of the Bond film rights turned out to be a legal quagmire, since Fleming had distributed those rights across an array of family trusts. 'Ian had decided that he would give the rights of each book to a different member of his family, so Cubby and Harry weren't just dealing with Ian, they were facing something like ten people, and all of those people had their own lawyers.'[33] The producers ended up renting several rooms in a London hotel, and after splitting everyone up went from room to room striking deals. At the end of it all, Fleming would earn a gratifying $100,000 per film and 2.5 per cent of the net profits.[34]

The print was hardly dry on the contract when Saltzman began work, particularly in the way he valued the books and how they could tie-in with the movies, that each could help the other. This is evidenced in a letter Fleming wrote that July to his publisher Michael Howard:

> Saltzman has most grandiose ideas about book sales to be co-ordinated with the film, and he is blasting hell out of Pan because he can't find my titles even in Foyles or Hatchards... He is talking of subsiding a print order in Pan's running literally into millions of copies of my titles.[35]

Indeed, in the run-up to the release of *Dr No*, Saltzman personally approached Pan, who published the paperback editions, suggesting they print an extra 500,000 copies. 'They laughed at me,' he admitted. Over the next twelve months, sales of that individual title reached over a million.[36]

Behind the scenes things were moving fast. For tax purposes, the producers set up a company called Danjaq, named after their respective wives, which was based in Lausanne, Switzerland, and would control their commercial and legal interests in the Bond films. It was a 50/50 split, with both Dana and Jacqueline holding non-voting minority shares.[37]

In order to physically make the films, an independent production company was formed by the name of Eon Productions, set up at Cubby's old Warwick HQ in South Audley Street. Within days of Eon going into operation, one of the first calls Cubby made was to Stanley Sopel, an accountant by profession who had worked on a number of Warwick pictures. Sopel was at home, having just returned from working on a film abroad, when the call from Cubby came through. 'Stanley, what the hell are you doing?' Nothing much, was the answer. 'Start work for me on Monday,' said Cubby.[38] When Sopel arrived at Eon's office, he noticed it was just the three of them and one secretary.[39]

Both producers took separate offices, with Cubby's on the first floor and Harry's at the top. Journalist Leonard Mosley visited Saltzman's office in the late 1960s and reported it to be:

> a brown panelled room with a leather sofa and armchairs, a few shelves crammed with books and scripts, a café au lait carpet, no pictures on the walls, small tables with telephones on them, and a desk also covered with telephones. I counted six altogether, and they rang at regular intervals for the next sixty minutes with calls from all over the world.[40]

Cubby's office was by far the more spacious with two identical antique partners' desks facing each other, a relic of his time with Irving Allen, and it was here where the important meetings took place. William P. Cartlidge, who worked on several Bonds, recalled that Cubby's office was set up like a gentleman's club. 'It was rather distinguished, with deep purples and greens and mahogany furniture, and bay windows overlooking a garden.'[41]

The plan of action was quite simple. Stanley Sopel recalled Cubby telling him that he wanted the crew on the Bonds to be all the people, as far as possible, that he had used on the old Warwick pictures.[42] While most of the Warwick output had been potboilers, nearly all of them boasted a high degree of technical excellence. The question remained: which of Fleming's Bond novels would kick off the series?

4

Just Another Movie

The producers' original intention was to make *Thunderball* first, but with that book currently in litigation after Irish filmmaker Kevin McClory accused Fleming of plagiarising story material from an unfilmed Bond script he owned, the lawyers at United Artists told them not to touch it until matters were resolved. This was a blessing in disguise, as surely *Thunderball*, with its tricky underwater action, would have been almost impossible to realise on so meagre a budget. Instead, *Dr No* was chosen, with its cinematically lush Jamaican setting and topical story of an unknown power destroying American space rockets.

Without delay, Saltzman gave Johanna Harwood a copy of the book and told her to do a first draft screenplay. Johanna hadn't read all the Fleming novels, but those she had she'd enjoyed and she got to work. Next, Cubby brought in his old Warwick collaborator Richard Maibaum, along with Wolf Mankowitz, to do a rewrite. Quickly the writers encountered what they perceived to be a huge problem, that of the character of Dr No himself, which they judged to be a second-rate Fu Manchu-type. Their solution was to install a villain who kept a Marmoset monkey perpetually perched on his shoulder, and the monkey was called Dr No. Thinking they'd been jolly clever, the writers attended a script conference with the producers only to be rebuked in no uncertain fashion. Cubby was especially incensed. 'You've got to throw the whole damn thing out. No monkey, d'ya hear.' Poor Maibaum was never to live it down. Over the course of his relationship with Cubby, working together on a further thirteen Bonds, whenever there was a creative argument or stalemate Cubby would simply say, 'Dr No is a monkey!'[1] As for Mankowitz, he called Cubby saying he did not want a screen credit. 'I don't want my name on a piece of crap, and that's a piece of crap!' He changed his mind after watching the finished film and asked for his credit to be reinstated, but by then it was too late.[2]

While all this was going on Saltzman approached Nigel Kneale, with whom he had worked on two Woodfall films, to see if he was available. 'I'd read one of Ian Fleming's books and not liked it,' recalled Kneale, 'so I said really I'd prefer not to.'[3]

As work continued on the script, Broccoli and Saltzman set about finding a director and drew up a list of names. Broccoli personally approached Guy Hamilton and sent him the script. Hamilton had known Cubby for years:

> He'd asked me to direct *Cockleshell Heroes* but I'd passed on it. Harry had also wanted me for *The Iron Petticoat*; I didn't fancy that particularly either. But we'd had very civilised conversations and got on well and I was asked to do *Dr No*. However, for family reasons I couldn't leave the UK for six weeks in Jamaica so wished them all good luck.[4]

Cubby next considered Bryan Forbes, who since getting his writing break at Warwick had carried on with a successful acting career and also made his directorial debut with *Whistle Down the Wind*, which had just opened to considerable acclaim. The approach took place at the White Elephant restaurant where Forbes and his wife Nanette Newman were enjoying dinner. Cubby spotted him and came over to ask if he was interested in directing his latest project. 'It's a sort of thriller,' he said. 'Lots of action, shooting and pretty girls. It's called *Dr No*.' Not particularly enamoured of the Fleming novels, Forbes gave some excuse that he was committed elsewhere and couldn't do it. Forbes was to wonder, several hundred million dollars later, whether Broccoli ever remembered that little chat; 'I certainly have,' he once wrote. 'It haunts me still.'[5] Others who perhaps had similar cause to regret the chance to make the first Bond movie included Guy Green, Ken Hughes and Val Guest. Cubby later admitted that some directors were actually insulted to have been approached, 'that we would even think of them in connection with such a project'.[6]

After a slew of rejections, the producers finally ended up with exactly the right man for the job: Terence Young. Not without a fight, though. Young was very much Cubby's choice; they'd worked on four Warwick pictures together, with Young also acting as an uncredited story editor for the company. Saltzman wasn't so sure and United Artists even less so, given his habit for going over schedule and over budget. In the end, Cubby won the argument and was to be proven right in his belief that Young's urbane manner and establishment credentials was ideal in bringing Fleming's world to vivid life on screen. 'Cubby knew that he would bring a lot of style to the film,' agreed Dana.[7]

The most crucial question of all, though, was who would play James Bond. The famous story that Cubby offered the role to his friend Cary Grant is true, confirmed by Broccoli himself and by Dana: 'Cubby would have loved to have Cary play Bond,' she claimed in 2000.[8] By then in his late fifties, Grant had the cool sophistication and light comedic touch to play 007 but probably realised himself he was too old, especially if there was going to be a series. So, in spite of some interest in the project, and being a fan of the Fleming books, Grant declined.

Back in 1958, when Broccoli first toyed with the idea of making Bond films, he'd contacted Peter Lawford, a former MGM contract player and part of Frank Sinatra's notorious Rat Pack, along with Dean Martin, Joey Bishop and Sammy Davis Jnr. At the time the prospect of playing a British spy just didn't appeal to the London-born Lawford, and he told Broccoli that even if he did manage to raise the finance he wasn't interested. It was a missed opportunity that remained one of Lawford's deepest regrets.[9]

Someone else who had cause to regret a similarly dismissive attitude was Australian-born Rod Taylor. Macho, suave and ruggedly handsome, Taylor had just finished making an American TV series called *Hong Kong*, playing a two-fisted journalist. Broccoli was keen for Taylor to screen test but the actor declined.

> I thought it was beneath me. I didn't think Bond would be successful in the movies. That was one of the greatest mistakes of my career! Every time a new Bond picture became a smash hit, I tore out my hair. Cubby and I have laughed about it ever since.[10]

Two more 'name' choices were Steve Reeves and Stanley Baker. Ex-bodybuilder Steve Reeves had come to prominence in a series of Italian *Hercules* movies and apparently said no to Broccoli's Bond offer because he was earning far more per picture in Italy. According to Stanley Baker's widow, Lady Ellen, the Welsh star also refused the Bond producer's overtures as he didn't want to be tied down to a multi-film deal. Like fellow Welshman and friend Richard Burton, Baker's screen presence was gritty and combustible, possessing an aura of dark, even menacing power. You can quite easily visualise Baker cracking skulls with Robert Shaw aboard the Orient Express in *From Russia With Love*.

Another popular British actor on the list was Michael Craig. With his Rank contract expiring, Craig was being wooed by Hollywood, and the producers contacted Craig's agent about setting up a meeting. He recalled what happened next:

> At the time, Saltzman and Broccoli were more or less joke figures in the film business in England, responsible for some real pot boiling stinkers and notoriously bad payers. No one knew quite how they had managed to get the rights to the 007 franchise, but everyone expected them to really screw up if their past record was anything to go by. The money on offer was £5,000, I think, not great even then, and they'd want an option for further films at a slightly higher fee. My agent and I agreed that it wasn't much of a proposition and I turned down the interview. I later found out that a number of actors of my age and experience had likewise turned it down.[11]

Because of the impact he'd made as John Drake in the TV spy series *Danger Man*, Patrick McGoohan was approached by Broccoli and Saltzman, only to turn them down flat no less than three times, according to the actor himself. Unlike Drake, who McGoohan had tried to ground in reality, Bond was in his view a cartoon strip fantasy with morals the actor found questionable.

Other TV stars that made it onto the shortlist were Roger Moore, although his involvement in the upcoming *The Saint* television show ruled him out almost immediately, and Ian Hendry, who had appeared alongside Patrick Macnee in the first series of *The Avengers*. Indeed, it was his reluctance to be tied down to another long contract, having just finished a year on *The Avengers*, that Hendry gave as his reason for rejecting the Bond role. There is, however, a tale told that Hendry arrived drunk for his screen test and was swiftly rejected by the producers.[12]

With no luck bagging a star, Broccoli and Saltzman turned their sights instead upon either a complete unknown or an actor yet to make it big. In that way, audiences would automatically accept him as the character and the producers would also be able to exert absolute control by tying them to an exclusive contract.

At the instigation of Terence Young, Broccoli and Saltzman approached Richard Johnson, a Royal Academy of Dramatic Art graduate with a growing reputation as a Shakespearean actor. Johnson didn't see himself as James Bond, and the fact he was currently tied to a contract with MGM for several more years gave him a reasonable excuse to say no.

Meanwhile, Saltzman was making overtures towards a young actor then primarily known for his roles in Hammer horror movies, Oliver Reed.

'When Harry Saltzman started his 007 search, I was 22,' the actor explained. 'He had me in mind for some time; spent ages trying methods of making me look older!'[13]

It was around this time that the name of Sean Connery began to be bandied around the Eon office. Broccoli had of course almost cast Connery in one of the Warwick pictures, and also recalled meeting him in London at a cocktail party thrown by Lana Turner, 'And he appealed to me as a very natural type.'[14] But Terence Young was the only one out of the assembled team who had actually worked with the actor, back in 1957 on a crude B-movie action melodrama called *Action of the Tiger*, only the Scot's third ever film role. Oddly enough, it was French starlet Martine Carol who spotted his potential first, sauntering over to Young one day on location with the suggestion that he ought to be playing the lead rather than Van Johnson. Not a surprise since Van Johnson had all the sex appeal of a haddock. Young would later recall the young Connery as something of a rough diamond, possessing 'a sort of crude animal force', like the young Burt Lancaster or Kirk Douglas.[15]

Meanwhile, Saltzman had been pointed in the direction of Connery by Peter Hunt, then carrying out editing duties on a low-budget comedy film starring the Scot about two wideboys in the RAF that nobody gave much hope for, *On the Fiddle*. One evening, Hunt was invited to dinner by its producer Benjamin Fisz at the Polish Club in Kensington. Halfway through the meal both men were joined by Saltzman and Jacqueline, and by the time coffee was served discussions turned to how things were going finding a suitable Bond. 'What about that Sean Connery,' Fisz announced. 'Don't you think he might make a good James Bond?'[16]

This represented a remarkable turnaround, since Fisz had been fervently against casting him in *On the Fiddle* when director Cyril Frankel first made the suggestion. 'He can't act,' Fisz complained. 'He's just sitting around at the Pinewood canteen doing nothing and nobody will work with him.' But Frankel wanted Connery. 'I've tested him,' he told Fisz. 'And I know I can get a performance out of him.'[17]

Hunt thought Connery as Bond was a great idea and offered to send Saltzman a couple of reels of *On the Fiddle*. The result was that Saltzman called Cyril Frankel up one day wanting to know, 'You've just worked with Sean Connery. Do you think he could play James Bond?' Frankel thought about it for the briefest of moments before answering, 'Standing on his head and reading a newspaper.'[18]

Almost at the same time, in Hollywood Broccoli was organising a screening at the Goldwyn Studios of a Walt Disney picture Connery made in 1959, a charming Irish fantasy called *Darby O'Gill and the Little People*. It wasn't the ideal vehicle to show off Connery's potential as 007, so Broccoli wanted a second opinion. He called his wife Dana. 'Could you come down and look at this Disney leprechaun film. I don't know if this Sean Connery guy has any sex appeal.' Dana caught a cab and arrived at the screening room. The lights dimmed and the movie began and when Connery appeared, 'I saw that face, and the way he moved and talked and I said, "Cubby, he's fabulous." He was just perfect; he had such presence. I thought he was star material right there.'[19]

So, a meeting with the actor was arranged at South Audley Street. It's difficult to see how Connery could have approached this interview, one that he must have known had the potential to change his life, in a manner so deliberately set out to antagonise. First, there was his scruffy casual appearance of baggy, unpressed trousers, a nasty brown shirt, no tie, a lumber jacket and suede shoes. Stanley Sopel thought Connery the most appallingly dressed man he'd ever seen. 'He looked as though he'd just come in off the street to ask for the price of a cup of tea.'[20]

Then there was his demeanour. Throughout the meeting Connery behaved with bloody-minded arrogance, repeatedly pounding on the desk with his fists, swearing and telling the producers in no uncertain terms how he intended to play Bond. It was all an audacious act; Connery had no intention of leaving the impression of a starving actor desperate for work. 'I think that's what impressed us,' Broccoli remembered. 'The fact that he'd got balls.'[21] He also felt Connery had 'a strength and energy about him which I found riveting'.[22] For Saltzman, that interview convinced him they'd found the actor with the requisite masculinity the part needed. He was later to refer to Connery as the perfect marriage between actor and film role.

Next came the thorny question of a screen test. Connery shook his head. He was past all that, it was take me or leave me. Connery recalled that Broccoli's face turned purple, 'but he composed himself and said he'd think it over and let me know'.[23]

No sooner was Connery out of the room than both men rushed to the window to watch him leave the building and cross the street. It was the way Connery moved that clinched it, for a big man he was light on his feet, like a big jungle cat. Broccoli said, 'The difference with this guy is the difference between a still photograph and film. When he starts to move, he comes alive.'[24] A lot of this was natural, of course, but much had been picked up over the course of several years attending movement classes given by the Swedish dancer and acting coach Yat Malmgeren. 'One of the chief qualities, I think, that made Sean such a big star in those early Bonds, was his movement,' observed acclaimed television director Philip Saville. 'His hand movement, his agility, he was an altogether organic man. It's a very important quality if you're making action movies. Steve McQueen had it, he had that natural sense of forward movement and all his body coordinated. Connery had it, too, in spades.'[25]

The producers had found their Bond at last. Barring falling under a double-decker bus, Connery was it from that moment. 'We'd never seen a surer guy,' said Saltzman. 'Or a more arrogant son of a bitch!'[26]

That both producers came from international backgrounds, with none of the hang-ups about British class, undoubtedly affected their final choice of actor; neither really wanted some cultivated thespian type or Brylcreemed-bonced Rank contract player. Alert to the world market, they needed their Bond to be less Ian Fleming's old Etonian and more of a brawling street fighter. Hence Broccoli's belief that Connery's virile, aggressive masculinity was crucial, arguing against the role being played by 'some mincing poof'.[27] It was a view shared by Bond screenwriter Richard Maibaum, that Connery was nothing like Fleming's concept of the character:

> But the very fact that Sean was a rough, tough Scottish soccer player made him unlike the kind of English actors that Americans don't like. Sean was not the Cambridge/Whitehall type – he was a down to earth guy. The fact that we attributed to him such a high-style epicure was part of the joke.[28]

Connery's friend and collaborator, the director John Boorman, has said much the same thing, that it was the disparity between the man and the role that made it so compelling.

Despite Connery's refusal to do a screen test, the producers sneakily asked the actor to come down to Pinewood to shoot some tests with potential leading ladies and it was this footage that was sent to United Artists for approval. Their response was blunt to say the least: 'See if you can do better.' To their credit Broccoli and Saltzman stood by their man, telling UA's top brass they intended going ahead with Sean or not at all. Instinct told Cubby this was the guy.[29]

Having cast Connery, the producers were a little hesitant about telling Fleming that they'd found his dashing hero in the guise of a former Scottish milkman. Once told, Fleming wrote to a friend: 'Saltzman thinks he has found an absolute corker, a 30-year-old Shakespearean actor, ex-navy boxing champion and even, he says, intelligent.'[30] A meeting between Connery and Fleming was arranged at the author's cramped business office near Pall Mall. They talked, and by the end Connery guessed Fleming regarded him as a compromise choice. This may have been true but Saltzman later admitted that Fleming was far from reassured. 'Fleming didn't like Connery because he spoke with a Scots accent. Fleming saw Bond as himself, high-born, very educated, very English, posh public-school accent.'[31]

On 3 November 1961, it was announced in the movie trade papers, with surprisingly little fanfare, that Connery had secured the role of James Bond. In today's climate of multi-million dollar deals it's striking to note that Connery's fee for *Dr No* was a modest £6,000. Connery's contract required him to make one Bond picture per year, along with a stipulation that his non-Bond films be produced under the aegis of Broccoli and Saltzman. For Connery this smacked of ownership, virtually making him a slave to Eon, and that particular clause was ultimately dropped.

Plenty of people in the film business found it terribly amusing that Connery had landed the role of 007. One day Saltzman met his old producing partner at Woodfall, John Osborne, and told him of his plans to make a Bond film. 'And who do you think I've got as James Bond?' he asked.

Osborne scarcely knew the books but gamely played along. 'I don't know Harry. James Mason.'

Saltzman stared back, dumbstruck. 'Hell, no.'

Osborne had another try. 'David Niven.'

'For Christ sake,' screamed Saltzman, before pausing for effect. 'Sean Connery!'

Osborne looked incredulous. 'Harry, he's a bloody Scotsman! He can hardly read.'[32]

While the producers had their Bond, they didn't have a script and were having enormous problems with several drafts floating around the place. 'Cubby nearly killed Harry, I mean physically,' said Young:

> He got in a rage, and Cubby's a very quiet, tranquil man, but by God he was inflamed. 'Look, we've paid all this fucking money for this James Bond book and we're not using a word of it.' He blamed Harry, because Harry was in charge of the script. Cubby was doing other things.[33]

After the monkey fiasco, Saltzman gave the script back to Johanna Harwood, then Terence Young did a rewrite; 'That didn't please anyone either,' said Johanna, 'so it came back to me. Then someone said, this isn't masculine enough, which irritated me intensely because all the situations and most of the dialogue was Fleming's own.'[34] This was probably the reason why Berkely Mather, an ex-soldier who'd fought in the war and was now a bestselling author of adventure and thriller books, was brought in. But that wasn't a success, either, according to Johanna. 'Harry gave the Mather script back to me and said, "Cut anything you don't like," which I did. I didn't like Mather's work at all, and we shot it like that.'[35] After which it was altered a lot on the floor by Terence Young, but that was par for the course in movies, said Johanna: 'It's like confetti, a script, by the time you get it in front of a camera.'[36]

While Saltzman had been attending to script matters, Cubby was busy putting a crew together, most of whom were people he'd worked with on Warwick productions, people that he knew were dependable and could deliver the goods. Sopel, installed as associate producer, recalled that the technicians were chosen with the same care and diligence as the actors. That's certainly Peter Hunt's testimony, too. 'Their job was to put together a group of people, who can work superbly, and come up with a desired result. Broccoli and Saltzman were absolutely ideal for that. They brought together a very good group of people and encouraged them; that was their real talent.'[37]

Key among them was Ted Moore, virtually Warwick's in-house cinematographer he shot so many of them, and production designer Ken Adam. Cubby wanted Adam on the strength of his outstanding work on *Oscar Wilde* but after reading an early draft of the script he had a mind to turn the thing down; this was potboiler stuff. Adam's wife Letitzia said he would be prostituting his art if he agreed to do it. But he liked Cubby, had met and spent a bit of time with Harry in Italy when he wanted the designer to work on a TV series, and also knew Young, so it was a belief in the talent of those involved, rather than the material itself, that changed his mind.

Other Warwick veterans included stuntman Bob Simmons, who'd built a reputation not only for performing stunts but co-ordinating fight and action sequences, and art director Syd Cain, a former RAF pilot. When *Dr No* was released an error resulted in Cain's name being omitted from the credits. As compensation he was presented with a solid-gold pen by Broccoli.[38]

It was Saltzman who brought in editor Peter Hunt, having tried to hire him for *Look Back in Anger*. Hunt had previously worked as an assistant cutter for Alexander Korda and eagerly accepted the assignment, being a fan of the books and an old friend of Terence Young.[39]

With the behind-the-camera talent installed, focus turned to casting. For their villain, Saltzman came up with the name of Joseph Wiseman, an actor he had known in New York best known then for his method-school creepiness in a 1951 film called *Detective Story*.[40] The producers also wisely ditched Fleming's clumsy concept of the villain having two hooks for hands, replacing them with metallic ones more in keeping with the atomic age.

As for Bond's allies in the story, film and television actor Jack Lord was chosen to play CIA operative Felix Leiter, but the role of Islander Quarrel proved problematic. Fleming wrote to Saltzman in August 1961, suggesting 'an extremely intelligent and attractive coloured man' called Paul Danquah, 'who is studying law here but has been very much taken up by the bohemian set, and I have met him on and off for several years.'[41] Ironically, Danquah had just made his film debut in *A Taste of Honey*, the film Saltzman tried to set up at Woodfall. The producers had their own ideas. Broccoli wanted Earl Cameron, a Bahamian-born actor who'd worked on three Warwick pictures, while Saltzman was after American actor John Kitzmiller. Cameron was invited to meet both men at their office, only to leave afterwards not feeling very confident. Outside in the lobby he bumped into Connery:

> I knew Sean quite well because I'd worked with his wife Diane Cilento and he said, 'Are you going to be in the film?' I said, 'It doesn't look like it, this guy Saltzman is very tricky.' And Sean said, 'Yeah, tell me about it.' I asked, 'How about yourself?' He said, 'I'm not sure.' So even Sean hadn't been signed yet. He was still waiting. This was early days.[42]

Ultimately, Broccoli was overruled and Saltzman bagged Kitzmiller.

The task of casting Bond's leading lady was certainly made more challenging by Fleming's comparison of Honeychile Rider to Botticelli's Venus; just how many of those are walking around, even in Hollywood? Cubby and Dana had spotted a young, unknown actress in a television play and invited her to meet with Harry and Terence Young. She arrived in jeans and 'terribly dishevelled', according to Broccoli, who couldn't hide his disappointment. 'I couldn't believe it was the same girl.'[43] Her name was Julie Christie.

Far from showing disrespect, this was Julie's style, as television producer Robert Baker, who the year before had cast her in a *The Saint* episode, recalled: 'She used to travel round with a bag and would sleep anywhere; she was a real hippie.'[44] Young saw beyond all that and recognised something special. He also felt sorry for the shy young actress entering what was a very masculine atmosphere. 'There were a lot of people hanging around Audley Street in those days, mentally undressing every girl who walked in.'[45]

Broccoli did tell a different story about that meeting, saying how by the time he got to the office, Harry and Young had already decided not to use her, for being 'Too flat chested.'[46]

With just two weeks before filming was due to begin, the producers took to shifting through hundreds of photographs that had been sent to the office.

One quite obviously stood out from all the others, it quite took Cubby's breath away. It was of a girl wearing a wet shirt that left very little to the imagination. Waving it at Harry across the desk he asked if he knew her. 'Oh, just a dame that Goulash (Harry's nickname for John Shepridge) introduced me to.'[47]

'Well, this is the girl, Harry.' Not waiting for any response, Cubby picked up the phone and called a friend of his, Max Arnow, a casting agent over at Columbia. 'Max, it's Cubby, do you know a girl called Ursula Andress.' He did, confirming that the young actress was married to 1950s matinee idol John Derek, was even more beautiful in real life, but unfortunately had 'A voice like a Dutch comic.' No problem, thought Cubby, that could be easily fixed in the dubbing theatre.[48] Ursula was hired sight unseen. The first time the producers and director Terence Young met her was on location in Jamaica.[49]

As plans were drawn up to fly the cast and crew to Jamaica, Cubby already had in mind a candidate to write the all-important music score. Some months earlier Wolf Mankowitz had been involved in a stage musical written by Monty Norman, a former big band singer and now a successful lyricist and composer. To raise funds to put it on in the West End, Mankowitz held a special preview and invited friends, financiers and producers, including Cubby. The entire budget was raised that very afternoon, with Cubby one of the main backers.[50]

The musical was called *Belle*, set in the Victorian world of music hall, and one of the main characters was Dr Crippen. 'At that time nobody had ever done a black comedy musical about a murderer,' recalled Norman:

> It was 20 years before its time. The critics were horrified. But I got to know Cubby quite well and liked him very much. When *Belle* absolutely died after about seven weeks, he said to me, 'I loved the show, I think the critics have been terrible, but one of these days we must work together again,' which was nice to hear but I didn't expect anything to come of it.[51]

It was a pleasant surprise, then, when Norman heard from Cubby again, who wanted him to come over to his office and meet his new partner. Told about all these elaborate plans they had for James Bond, Norman was asked if he would be interested in handling the score.

> Funnily enough at that time I was doing so many other things I was just about to say, it sounds like a good idea but give me time to think about it, when Harry chipped in, 'We're doing all the location stuff in Jamaica, why

> don't you come out with your wife, all expenses paid, and get a feel of the Caribbean.' And that was it; you could say I did *Dr No* for a free holiday.[52]

Having agreed to do the job, Norman vividly remembered being escorted out of the office by an assistant and being told, 'See if you can come up with a good theme because I reckon we've got two films and a television series out of this.'[53]

By mid-January, Norman found himself flying out to Jamaica with the bulk of the Bond team on what was going to be, if nothing else, an exciting adventure.

> Eon hired what must have been about the last turbo prop to cross the Atlantic with people in it. Everybody was on that flight; Cubby and his wife and Harry and his wife, the cameraman Ted Moore and his wife, Ken Adam and his wife, me and my wife, a lot of the actors, the stuntman Bob Simmons, and of course Sean Connery. And it became almost like a cocktail party, drinks were flowing and food. By the time we got to Jamaica we were all pissed. It was about a 20-hour flight, it stopped in New York or somewhere. It was absolutely a historic flight.[54]

While Fleming's book necessitated the bulk of the story take place in Jamaica, the producers certainly didn't want to cheat their audience by not shooting on real locations. 'There is simply no substitute for the exotic values you can get from shooting on location,' said Broccoli, a lesson learnt from his Warwick days, many of whose films were shot abroad. 'If entertainment is part escapism, taking the audience into this kind of paradise is the way to achieve it.'[55]

The Bond team shot up and down the island, in Kingston, Montego Bay, Ocho Rios, even the main airport. Expecting blue skies all the way, the production met with some poor weather conditions that set the schedule back. The classic scene where Ursula Andress steps out of the surf in a white bikini was filmed at Laughing Water, not far from Fleming's winter residence Golden Eye.

According to Monty Norman, Fleming didn't visit the set very much, content to let them get on with it as they saw fit. 'Although he would say his piece if he was asked. A group of us went to his house once for lunch. Cubby and Harry used to go there more often, along with Sean. I think Fleming liked Sean very much.'[56]

Norman stayed with the crew in Jamaica close on three weeks, during which time he began work on a lot of the calypso melodies for the film. 'The producers were very encouraging. It was Cubby's idea that Ursula should sing something as she came out of the water, so I wrote "Underneath the Mango Tree". Harry fell in love with that song, he absolutely loved it.'[57] Indeed, for one brief moment Saltzman wanted to put it at the top of the film, only for everyone else to say it was a crazy idea, especially if Bond was going to be a series. The last thing you wanted was a calypso number as the main theme going forward.[58]

When it was time for Norman to leave Jamaica and fly to New York on business, Harry grabbed him to ask if he could go and see the suits at United Artists and tell them how marvellous the film was, 'because they weren't convinced, they thought it was just a limey spy film'.[59]

By the close of February, the unit were all back at Pinewood Studios to be greeted by Ken Adam's startling interior sets. Having been given virtual carte blanche by the producers, Adam had allowed his imagination free rein, or as much as he could on what was a paltry budget of around £14,000. When Adam complained he couldn't do it for that sum, the producers gave him another £7,000 out of a contingency fund.[60] Still, Adam remained nervous that the finance people might come into his office demanding to know why he'd overspent by thousands of pounds. 'I said to Harry and Cubby, "What am I going to say to them?" And they said, "Hide!"'[61] Of course, as the Bonds went on to have huge success the situation changed completely for Adam. 'When I used to say something cost too much money, Harry would say, "What are you worrying about? It's only money."'[62]

He was, however, stumped when it came to designing Dr No's nuclear reactor, something which he knew absolutely nothing about. Luckily, Saltzman had a contact at Harwell, the Atomic Energy Research Establishment near Oxford, and arranged for two young scientists to spend a couple of hours with Adam at Pinewood explaining the principles of a nuclear water reactor.[63]

Principal photography on *Dr No* concluded on 30 March, after fifty-eight days.[64] Now in the hands of editor Peter Hunt, the film began to take shape and come alive. The most important thing for Hunt was to keep the film moving, to incorporate what Saltzman called a north American tempo. In other words, the film equivalent of a pulp paperback, the pace of which was so fast you didn't have time to question its logic.

Monty Norman had also been completing the score, as well as coming up with a signature tune for Bond, something the producers had discussed from the very beginning. Playing around with an old piece of music from an abandoned musical, Norman came up with something that worked perfectly. 'It had the mood, the ambience and especially, what I was looking for, the character of James Bond.'[65]

The Norman version of the Bond theme wasn't quite working and they wanted to bring someone else in to do a more lively and contemporary arrangement. John Barry's name came up, then the leader of his own jazz combo, the John Barry Seven, who had scored a string of pop hits over the last couple of years and was clearly a man going places.

The producers got Barry on the phone and a deal was made, a flat fee of £250 plus a promise of future work. Peter Hunt recalled that Barry felt quite nervous at first working for Broccoli and Saltzman due to their reputation in the film business:

> and they were pretty overbearing. Harry was a big bully and Broccoli was always trying to be nice, but never quite succeeding. They were tough guys – and it was a tough business. They were never really kind or sympathetic unless it suited them, so they would have been daunting for John.[66]

With the music taken care of, the last piece of the jigsaw was the credit sequence. What Cubby and Harry wanted was something innovative and imaginative. They recalled going to see Stanley Donen's 1960 comedy *The Grass is Greener* and witnessing the impact on audiences of the title sequence where the main cast members were represented by babies. The man behind it was a graphic designer by the name of Maurice Binder, and although he had another project on the go he was intrigued enough by the offer to work on *Dr No*, despite not knowing anything about the story. 'Well, come on over to my house,' said Harry, 'have some bagels and lox and we'll discuss it.'[67]

What is regarded as one of the best-known title sequences in film history came about as Binder experimented with white price tag stickers on a storyboard in his studio minutes prior to making his presentation to the producers. The notion of using these graphic dots as gun shots across the screen before Bond enters the frame was inspired, and when the producers loved what he was doing it was expanded into a full title sequence.

Binder forged a close relationship with Saltzman and Broccoli and went on to produce a total of fourteen title sequences for the franchise, many of them sexually risqué, falling foul of some country's censors. 'Maurice was always getting into trouble for showing a bit of nipple,' recalled Sir Roger Moore. 'I'd go and watch him shooting them, there'd be wind machines and all these naked girls. And suddenly he'd rush forward with a pot of Vaseline and smear it on these girl's pubic hairs because they were blowing in the wind.'[68]

On just such an occasion on *The Man with the Golden Gun*, Moore turned up with Cubby and there was Maurice smearing down some girl with his regulation pot of Vaseline. Cubby took one look and said, 'I'm the producer of this picture. Are you sure we're *paying* you for this?!'[69]

As soon as an answer print became available, the producers set up a screening for several of the executives at United Artists, including Arthur Krim. The film started promptly at 10 a.m., and when the lights came up around noon there was complete silence in the room. 'Nobody said anything,' Saltzman recalled, 'except a man who was head of the European operation for United Artists. He said, "The only thing good about the picture is that we can only lose $840,000." Then they all stood up, and Cubby and I were just shattered.'[70]

The film's sound editor Norman Wanstall was at another sneak preview and has never forgotten it. 'As the audience filed out of the theatre there was a look of sheer terror on Harry's face. No-one ever had any idea whether or not that first Bond would be a success.'[71] Jeremy Vaughan, who knew both Fleming and Kevin McClory, was invited to a morning press show in London. 'Everybody in the cinema pissed themselves with laughter. And Terence Young was pulling his hair out because it wasn't meant to be a comedy. All of us slightly cynical lot thought it was hilarious. But little did anyone know that history was made.'[72]

There's been much debate over how much the humour in *Dr No* was deliberate, whether it was encouraged on the set or grew naturally from the way Connery played the role and how Terence Young directed the material. Certainly, as the series evolved, humour and comedy played a much bigger role, though that was never the intention at the outset, recalled Johanna Harwood:

> When we were working on *Dr No*, everybody was treating it as serious. We used to sit round having script conferences and talking about Bond's psychological approach and that kind of thing. And there was nothing comic in the books. It wasn't until the sneak preview that we had any idea we had a comedy on our hands, so to speak, because the audience laughed.[73]

Len Deighton recalled his first ever meeting with Saltzman took place not long after *Dr No* opened in cinemas. During lunch, one of Saltzman's assistants arrived at their table with news on how it was playing with audiences. 'They're laughing,' the man said.

Saltzman frowned. 'Are they laughing at Bond or laughing with him?'

'I think they're laughing with us.'

The frown turned to a smile. 'It'll be all right,' said Saltzman and waved his assistant away.[74]

Much to United Artists' surprise, *Dr No* was a runaway hit in Britain. 'To them it was a B picture. They hated it,' Saltzman later stated. 'They said, "Hammer makes the same kind of pictures for one-third the price."'[75]

Terence Young put its success down to opening at exactly the right moment, when a particular mood was beginning to envelop Britain. On the same day *Dr No* premiered at the London Pavilion, in the heart of London's West End, 5 October, the Beatles released their first single 'Love Me Do'. Just twenty-four hours earlier, Roger Moore made his debut as *The Saint* on the ITV network. Things were starting to swing, the sixties were about to get into top gear. 'I think people were getting tired of the realistic school,' said Young. 'The kitchen sinks and all those abortions.'[76] Here was an absolute breath of fantasy and glamour, and the public lapped it up.

Critical reaction, though, was mixed. The Vatican condemned it as 'a dangerous mixture of violence, vulgarity, sadism and sex', thus virtually assuring its success. Highbrow critics were pompously dismissive. *Films and Filming* called it a 'monstrously overblown sex fantasy of nightmarish proportions', and 'the headiest box office concoction of sex and sadism ever brewed in a British studio'. The critic of the *Daily Express* reprimanded Bond for not behaving like a proper hero, accusing his methods of being indistinguishable from those of the villains.

Breaking box office records in Britain, things were different over in America, as Cubby recalled. 'Several of the UA bookers who saw the picture privately in our projection room expressed some doubt that they could sell a picture in the major US cities with, "a Limey truck driver playing the lead."'[77] So, instead of opening in key cities like New York, Chicago or Los Angeles, James Bond made his stateside debut at drive-in venues in places like Oklahoma and Texas. Thanks to some positive reviews and favourable word of mouth, *Dr No* went on to make a solid return at the US box office early in 1963, although both producers remained convinced had United Artists shown more trust and bravado they could have taken twice as much.

Either way, James Bond had arrived.

5

Calling Mr Hope

Given the impact of *Dr No*, it's curious that the producers didn't race ahead with a sequel. Instead, they decided to make another picture, the only non-Bond film they ever made together. *Call Me Bwana*, a tepid Cold War comedy, was largely Saltzman's baby, and it does appear that from the very get-go Saltzman was looking to diversify into other areas and other films; as Cubby said, 'He had a low boredom threshold, I guess.'[1]

He had already, for example, tried unsuccessfully to put a play on in the West End. Johanna Harwood had been asked to adapt an American play Saltzman owned the rights to called *The Marriage Game*, a farce about a group of girls looking for suitable husbands. The idea was to do a brief tour of places like Liverpool, Eastbourne and Brighton before landing in London, but the show just didn't work out. Returning home after the first performance, Johanna remembered the director and Saltzman discussing how things went. Saltzman was convinced that one scene in particular needed a drastic rewrite. The director looked at him somewhat bemused. 'But Harry, that's the best scene in the play.' For Johanna, that sort of summed up Saltzman for her, this need to keep meddling and not really knowing what he wanted, along with an inability to distinguish between what worked and what didn't work.[2]

Ken Hughes faced much the same problem when Saltzman asked him to work on an early draft of *The Ipcress File* screenplay. 'Harry has such an energetic mind he gets ideas in the middle of the night which are in complete contradiction to what we discussed the day before. As fast as I'd write up his old ideas, he'd change to a new one.'[3]

Eager to make *Call Me Bwana* on location in Kenya, Harry contacted Mort Lachman in Los Angeles, Bob Hope's head writer, to see if the comedian was available. Hope would play an African explorer who teams up with a female

CIA operative to find a space capsule that has crash landed in the jungle. His enquiries were welcomed, provided he knew the answer to one question: how far was it from the Mount Kenya Safari Club to the nearest golf course? Hope was, of course, obsessed with the sport.

'How should I know?' answered Saltzman.

'Find out and call me back.'

A short time later, Saltzman returned with the answer: it took just twenty minutes by helicopter. 'Then you might make a deal,' said Mort.[4]

Saltzman flew to California with a script and showed it to Mort. 'It's terrible,' said the writer. 'You can't show that to Bob.'

'What can I do?' asked Harry. 'I've got to make the picture.'

'Tell Bob how close it will be to the golf course and tell him you'll have the script ready in time.'[5]

As the script underwent a rewrite, Cubby thought he had a better alternative. A friend, Donald Zec, one of the country's leading showbiz reporters, had written an article about a new pop group going great guns up in Liverpool, and suggested maybe they would make ideal subjects for a movie. Whatever words of persuasion Cubby or Mr Zec could think of didn't pass muster with Saltzman.

'Listen, let me ask you something, Cubby,' said Harry at one meeting. 'Would you rather make a picture with four long-haired *shnooks* from Liverpool – what's their name?'

'The Beatles,' answered Cubby.

'The Beatles, who nobody's ever heard of, when we've got Bob Hope – BOB HOPE! – all ready to go.'[6]

There was no denying Saltzman's logic; Hope was box office, while the Liverpool lads were a gamble. So, production went ahead on Harry's *Call Me Bwana*. It was a film Broccoli never much cared for, since there were problems with it from the very start when filming in Kenya had to be cancelled due to political tensions. The jungle background was duplicated on the backlot at a wintry Pinewood.

Johanna Harwood, who co-wrote the script, remembered Broccoli around a lot on the film, though it was evident Saltzman was the one driving everything along, which is how she viewed their partnership at the time:

> Harry was the steamroller, he was the one who moved things and called meetings. Cubby would be there and was always very amenable, but he never fought a battle. He was the nice fellow. It seemed to me, until he got his hands on the Bonds, that Cubby made his career being the nice fellow

> because Irving Allen was rather like Harry Saltzman, brash, inconsiderate and tactless. And Irving worked very well with Broccoli because he came along after Irving rubbed people up the wrong way and calmed them down. And Cubby did exactly the same thing with Harry. He was there to be nice, and that's why at the beginning they worked very well together.[7]

Hope enjoyed making the movie and working again with Saltzman. The comedy legend certainly admired his chutzpah, never forgetting one ill-fated attempt to persuade the current pope to guest star in one of Hope's TV specials.[8]

Johanna recalled meeting Hope just the once, but found writing for him a breeze, since once again he had brought over his team of gag writers.

> The orders were, don't bother to give any lines to Bob Hope, his script writers supplied them. So, you just left a blank. There were three or four of these writers who worked in a caravan parked on the set and if Bob Hope didn't like a line, they had to write another one on the spot.[9]

One day at a script conference, Johanna watched as the director discussed a scene with Hope, in which the very last line went to another actor. Saltzman, 'buttering up Bob Hope obviously', took the star to one side and said, 'Oh, we'll change that Bob, we'll give you the last line.' And Hope replied, 'I don't mind not having the last line. What I want is the last look.'[10]

Hope's co-star in *Call Me Bwana* was the fiery Anita Ekberg. Len Deighton recalled arriving at Eon's office one morning for a meeting with Saltzman. He was asked to sit down and help himself to a drink as Saltzman needed to make an urgent phone call to Miss Ekberg. It went something like this:

> Hello Anita, you weren't on the set today. It's costing a lot of money and we've got to get everything done by next week. (Slight pause.) You're not feeling very well. Did you have the doctor in? (Another pause.) You didn't have the doctor in. Well, listen Anita, I'll be sending a doctor round tomorrow morning if you're not on the set. And I just want to give you a bit of advice. I've been in this business a long time, and once the insurance companies get the idea that an actor is unreliable from a medical point of view, whether it's authentic or whether it's not authentic, then it's bad news and you become anathema to the whole industry. Now if you take my advice, you'll be on the set bright and early tomorrow morning.'

Of course, she was. As Deighton recalled, 'It was a wonderful bit of iron bar inside a glove.[11]

After their successful collaboration on *Dr No*, Monty Norman was once again brought in to compose the score. 'They rang and said, do you want to do a film with Bob Hope and I said, wow, yeah. Absolutely. He was my childhood hero.'[12] Norman recalled that it was Saltzman who was the functioning producer on *Bwana*; Broccoli had very little to do with it, yet Norman found Broccoli the more approachable of the two men, especially in a social environment. 'He was somebody you enjoyed being with. Harry, although he was a consummate film man and knew how to get things done, he was a bit crazy. He was really a throwback to those old tough Hollywood producers.'[13]

Norman found it strange that the two men had gone into partnership together at all, since in his opinion they were chalk and cheese. 'Cubby was this large, warm, Italian New Yorker, and Harry always reminded me of this Napoleon-like figure, a tough pugnacious Canadian Jew. They did create sparks though in those early days. They were good for each other at the beginning.'[14]

Even so, Norman always used to feel that there was a kind of tension between both men. When he went to see them at their office, the atmosphere was always the same, 'as if a husband and wife have had a row and then you suddenly arrive unannounced, it was like that'.[15]

All through the time he was working on the music for *Call Me Bwana*, Norman was never able to get a contract out of Harry, and whenever he raised the subject or spoke to him about it the reply was always the same: 'Yeah, yeah, it's ok, don't worry.'

When the score was finished Norman rang Saltzman. 'I've done everything Harry, and the director is delighted with it.'

'Yeah, everybody's delighted, it's great, thank you very much, you've done everything we asked.'

'By the way Harry, I still haven't got a contract, isn't it time we talked money?'

Harry came back with a line that Norman thought was as good as anything Goldwyn ever said. 'Monty, if you wanna talk money, we can't do business.'[16]

It seemed to Norman that Saltzman was almost taken aback by the request. 'And we never recovered from it. My solicitor did eventually sort it out for me but that was the end. And with Cubby being loyal to his partner, I never worked for them again.'[17]

Neither did Norman believe this was an isolated case, having heard from a friend of his who wrote a screenplay for Saltzman. Wanting to know when he was getting paid, Harry responded with, 'I can't do that, I've just bought a Cadillac!'[18]

At this early stage in their partnership, the producers were actively looking for other projects to make together outside their Bond stable. They had already optioned Berkely Mather to adapt his recently published novel *The Pass Beyond Kashmir*, which Saltzman thought an interesting adventure story, with the intention of starring Connery in it.[19] They had also come into contact with a vibrant American novelist and journalist by the name of Terry Southern. In the winter of 1962, partly on the recommendation of Peter Sellers, Stanley Kubrick brought Southern over to London to help revise the screenplay of *Dr Strangelove*. Remaining in the capital, Southern began to look for more film work and came within the sphere of Broccoli and Saltzman. They set him up with a young new director called Peter Yates to work on a film treatment of *The Marriage Game*, the play Saltzman had earlier tried to bring to the West End.

Southern's wife, Carol Kauffman, was staying with him in London and recalled meetings and dinners at the producers' homes: 'They were in sweatshirts with their wives. They were very manic and funny, as they talked ideas. They were very dynamic.'[20]

Nothing came of *The Marriage Game*, though Southern went on to become a prominent figure in swinging sixties London, even contributing to the script of the infamous *Casino Royale* spoof. He later worked with Peter Fonda and Denis Hopper on the screenplay for *Easy Rider* (1969).

Saltzman also came to the aid of fellow producer Lord Birkett, who had fallen into financial chaos with his latest picture, an adaptation of Harold Pinter's celebrated 1960 play *The Caretaker*. Just days before filming was due to start, with Alan Bates and Donald Pleasance reprising their stage roles, with the addition of Robert Shaw, the American backers started making demands on Birkett. 'They said, we want a script supervisor and I said, not with Harold Pinter you don't.'[21] The result was the Americans pulled their £40,000 investment. 'We'll have to find the money privately,' Birkett announced the next day to the stunned cast. 'Let's go simply to friends who might back it. And I'm sorry, but we can't take money from friends and pay ourselves with it so you don't get paid.' Within days the money was raised and the roll call of new investors was so distinguished – along with Saltzman there was Richard Burton, Elizabeth Taylor, Noel Coward and Peter Sellers – that Birkett named them all on the opening credits of the film, before the cast, as a special thank you.[22]

6

Turkish Delight

Before the release of *Dr No*, Saltzman asked Johanna Harwood to start work on a script for a Bond follow-up. From all Fleming's available titles, the producers chose *From Russia With Love* for a number of reasons, key amongst them being the title's familiarity, especially to American audiences, thanks to President Kennedy's endorsement. Broccoli also considered it to be amongst Fleming's best stories, full of intrigue and interesting characters, although it was decided to steer clear of its Cold War politics, which the producers wisely concluded would date the film. There were commercial considerations too, according to Johanna, 'It was really the East European market they hoped not to lose!'[1] The Iron Curtain baddies thus became a non-political international terror group, SPECTRE.

As Johanna completed her first draft, matters changed dramatically when *Dr No* proved to be such a hit. Naturally, everyone hoped the film would be a success, but nobody envisaged it having the impact that it did. 'There was absolute panic in the production,' said Johanna, 'because suddenly they had a huge success on their hands and they didn't know why. And the great panic was, could they do it twice, since they didn't know why they'd done it the first time.'[2]

Frantic discussions took place about what they thought worked in the film and what didn't, the elements audiences liked and wanted to see more of, with the result that Johanna's script was more or less 'torn to pieces'.[3] It was Harry who told Johanna that he wanted her to team up with Terence Young to rewrite the entire script:

> We had just one afternoon working together and it was absolutely impossible because he didn't listen to anything I said. He'd re-write the scene

himself and say, 'That's better, isn't it?' We were supposed to meet again the next morning and I went to Harry straightaway and said, 'You're paying two people to do the job of one. There's nothing I can do to change Terence's mind on anything. So, if it's all right with you, I'm leaving.' And I left.[4]

It's common practice for sequels or follow-ups to cut corners financially, to offer up the public the same old thing only slightly frayed round the edges. As far as Harry and Cubby were concerned, that was a cheat. Right from the start they worked on the principle that each film had to be bigger than the last in every respect. United Artists also showed their faith in the producers by almost doubling the budget, while continuing to keep a check on where the money was spent, according to Stanley Sopel. 'We would have terrible fights if we went over budget in those days.'[5] It became almost a source of pride to make sure that every penny was seen on the screen.

Showing both loyalty and faith, Broccoli and Saltzman brought back the same key creative talent from *Dr No*. Terence Young resumed the director's chair, Richard Maibaum delivered yet another taut script, one of the best in the series, and Peter Hunt supervised the editing. The only main absentee was Ken Adam, who had been asked by Stanley Kubrick to take charge of the production design on *Dr Strangelove* after the director was impressed by his Bond work. Adam's assistant Syd Cain took over.

After the success of *Dr No*, confidence was riding high, with everyone on the crew feeling a greater freedom and a more relaxed creative environment. 'If we needed another day or some extra shots, we got them,' recalled Peter Hunt. 'So, it was a far better laid out production. We were also much more respected by the studio then. They no longer thought of us doing a little crappy picture; suddenly we were the big boys, and demanded all sorts of things.'[6]

Returning as Bond, Connery now regretted signing a multi-picture deal. His wife Diane Cilento recalled that the producers refused to listen to any talk about the contract being altered. 'There was a long legal wrangle, which entailed lawyers, agents, flaring tempers, shouting and lots of aggravation.'[7] In the end Connery's agent Richard Hatton managed to raise his basic fee considerably and exert a nice bonus on top. He also found the time to suggest that another of his clients, Robert Shaw, might be perfect for the role of Red Grant, the psychopathic assassin out to kill Bond. Shaw was of a mind to turn it down, calling the script 'rubbish', only for his wife Mary Ure, the ex-Mrs John Osborne, to urge him to swallow his pride and take it.[8]

The producers knew they had a tough job on their hands finding an actress who was going to have a similar impact on audiences as Ursula Andress. Visiting Rome, Paris, Sweden and Denmark, Young estimated they must have interviewed some 200 girls for the role of Tatiana Romanova, who finds herself an innocent pawn in SPECTRE's dastardly revenge plot against 007.[9] A former runner-up in the 1960 Miss Universe contest, 20-year-old Daniela Bianchi was eventually chosen.

Fleming had created a remarkable gallery of villains for his story and it was Saltzman who came up with the inspired notion of casting Lotte Lenya as SPECTRE henchwoman Rosa Klebb. The widow of composer Kurt Weill, and an acclaimed stage performer in her own right, Lotte was then appearing at the Royal Court in a revue of the life and works of Bertolt Brecht when Saltzman got in touch. 'Miss Lenya, we have a part for you. It's an Ian Fleming story.' There was a slight pause on the other end of the line, and then a quiet voice answered, 'I'm very sorry about my ignorance, but I don't know who Ian Fleming is.' No matter, assured Saltzman, he'd send a copy of the book over to the theatre for her to read.[10] She agreed to play the part, and made such an impact on audiences that for years after she was stopped in the street by people calling out, 'Look! There's the lady with the knife in her shoe!'[11]

The casting of Vladek Sheybal as chess master Kronsteen was also down to Saltzman, after seeing him in a play on the BBC. Born in Poland, and imprisoned in a concentration camp during the war, where he was forced to face mock executions by prison guards,[12] Sheybal was certainly not prepared to be intimidated by anyone. When Saltzman showed up on the set one day and began interfering in the way a scene was being acted, Sheybal simply stopped and informed him, 'This is the director Terence Young and he doesn't want me to play the part in any different way. Why should I do what you say?'

'Because I am the producer,' Saltzman answered.

'You mean that you represent money?'

Sheybal stood his ground, determined to play it his way, and found support in Lotte Lenya:

> And then Harry Saltzman became completely unbearable so I just said, 'I've had enough of it!' I just walked off and went home! And in the evening, Terence Young rings me up and he says, 'Vladek, I promise that Harry Saltzman won't be in the studio tomorrow. Will you come and finish the part?' So, I came in and finished it.[13]

One of the most memorable characters in the entire Bond series was Kerim Bey, Bond's main ally in the film and head of the Turkish secret service. Broccoli cast the fine Mexican actor Pedro Armendariz, only to discover during location shooting in Istanbul that he was a dying man, his body riddled with cancer. The producers debated whether to recast the role, not wanting to put Armendariz through any pain or discomfort, but the actor was determined to finish the picture so he could leave money to his widow and children. A solution was found: all Kerim Bey's scenes back at Pinewood were hurriedly lumped together and shot over a two-week period, after which Armendariz went back to America and entered hospital. The entire crew were devastated when news reached them a month later that Armendariz had taken his own life.[14]

Prior to shooting, Saltzman, along with Young, cameraman Ted Moore and Syd Cain, flew to Istanbul for a location recce. Everyone stayed at the Hilton and one afternoon Cain was looking in the hotel jewellery shop for a suitable gift for his wife. Saltzman saw him and made a suggestion, pointing to a gold ring with rubies that rested amongst the shop's most expensive items. Cain said he didn't have the money to buy it, made his excuses and left. At the end of the day, Cain returned to his hotel room only to find that very ring lying on his bedside table. 'It's very, very kind of you,' Cain told Harry later, 'but my wife would know immediately I couldn't afford that.'

'This is what you do,' said Saltzman. 'Tell your wife it's a present from me, for all the hard work you have done.' And that wasn't all, Saltzman insisted she came out to the location for a holiday – all expenses paid. 'And that was Harry,' said Cain. 'He was very generous.'[15]

From Russia With Love is often cited as the best film in the series. Cubby always singled it out as the film in which the Bond style was perfected and the success of the franchise was assured. 'By the time we'd made the second Bond, we knew we had a winning formula.'[16] It certainly introduced one of the mainstays of the series, the pre-credit sequence. It was Harry who came up with the idea of opening the new picture with something that would really startle the audience, Bond being stalked and then killed; only it's a double, of course.[17] The scene takes place at a SPECTRE training school, which was another notion of Harry's. Recalling the gladiator school in the film *Spartacus*, he thought it would be fun for the baddies to have something similar.

Harry really was the 'ideas man'. Often it was a case of sieving through the bad ones to get to the good ones. 'Harry would come up with 100 ideas a minute,' recalled Stanley Sopel. 'We'd have to throw 93 right out as being marvellously impractical because they would cost too much or be impossible to shoot.'[18] When one of his ideas fitted it was often a gem, and if the ideas weren't his but were good, according to one of his working associates, Andre de Toth, he would convince himself they were his anyway.[19]

Where Harry was infamous for churning out ideas with machine-gun rapidity, along with a love for gadgets and hi-tech gizmos for Bond, Broccoli's talents lay elsewhere, as Guy Hamilton observed:

> Cubby was very much concerned with the casting, making sure that the girls were pretty, worrying about the script, that it didn't get bogged down with too much dialogue, that it got on with the action, that the storyline was straightforward enough so people from ten to 100 could follow it.[20]

Cubby was also a people person and from the very start was keen to promote a sense of family amongst the crew. It was one of the reasons why the 007 pictures were crewed by many of the same people. Technicians would not take another job but wait for the next Bond movie so they would be sure to get on it. And not necessarily because they paid the best wages, simply because they wanted to work on them. This also included looking after the crew, especially on location, things like putting them up in good hotels, and as a result Cubby and Harry rarely had any of the run-ins with film unions that plagued other productions.

The producers were also keen to emphasise a friendly working environment. They expected everyone to do their job but were keen that the pictures should be fun, and not just hard work. 'I got on really well with Cubby and Harry,' said effects man John Stears.

> They were always on the set, and any problems that were about to arise, they had a handle on instantly. It was a wonderful combination, because the whole crew were totally integrated. We were all working for one cause, which was the love of the movie, and we were like one big family.[21]

This feeling of 'family' is something Tom Mankiewicz picked up on when he began working on the Bonds as a writer in the early seventies:

> Cubby would walk on the set and he knew the names of everybody on the crew. He knew a lot of their children's names. If he heard that the camera loader's wife was ill, he would go up to him and say, is there something we can be doing for you? As far as Cubby was concerned, Bond was a club and he loved that. Harry was a different kind of producer, and this wasn't

> because he was a terrible person, but he couldn't give a flying fuck what the camera loader's name was.[22]

It was all about teamwork, really, that was the secret of the Bond films; everyone worked as one complete unit, with no room for egos or individualists. 'If ever there was a team, it was Eon Productions,' confirmed Stanley Sopel. 'Those pictures were made by teams, headed by Broccoli and Saltzman, and everybody did everything.'[23] That meant chipping in, too, no matter one's position in the company hierarchy. On *Dr No*, Connery recalled Cubby and Harry both taking spades and preparing the beach for the sequence where Honey Ryder emerges from the sea.[24] And on *You Only Live Twice*, when poor weather restricted the use of a helicopter to transport people down the volcano, everyone had to lug the equipment down 2 miles, including Broccoli, happy to carry one of the cameras.

One thing Cubby was noted for was welcoming any newcomers to the team. Desmond Llewelyn had been cast as Q, taking over from the actor who had played him in *Dr No* and was now unavailable. His one and only day on the set of his first Bond film was made even more memorable when Broccoli made the time to personally introduce himself and welcome him to everyone. In Llewelyn's experience it was usual to meet the director, but producers rarely bothered with small-part actors. Cubby was different. Everyone was important. Everyone had a contribution to make. 'Cubby was one of the nicest, most thoughtful men I have ever met; one warmed to him immediately and instinctively. I knew if I had any problems he'd always help.'[25]

From Russia With Love is well served by its atmospheric location work in and around the city of Istanbul. On one occasion the crew even employed the unwitting assistance of the city's emergency services. For Bond's raid on the Russian consulate, the effects team, headed by John Stears, had to create the illusion of the building being on fire. Saltzman assured him that all necessary permits had been signed and that he could carry out his task of placing smoke pots both in and outside the building. When the cameras rolled and the black smoke started billowing, it wasn't long before fire engines and the police descended on the location. 'It was absolute pandemonium,' recalled Stears. 'Harry was going absolutely wild. He said, "Fantastic, fantastic, keep turning the cameras." It was the real fire engines, the real ambulances, the real police.'[26]

Whilst in the city, Harry led a party that regularly tracked down the best local restaurants. Harry considered himself to be a food and wine connoisseur. When Fleming arrived for a short location visit, he joined the group on his last evening and quickly wished he hadn't. There was Harry, as usual taking control by insisting on doing all the ordering. Plate after plate arrived, none meeting with the writer's approval. Exasperated, Fleming beckoned the waiter over and ordered a Spanish omelette.

One suspects Saltzman never forgot that rebuke. One of the many pleasures of reading Fleming's prose is the fine detail he brings into Bond's lifestyle, notably what he eats and drinks. Saltzman was eager to burst that particular balloon when he spoke to journalist David Lewin. 'I took Fleming to lunch at Les Ambassadeurs, which has Prince Philip among its members. Fleming ordered two dry martinis and scrambled eggs. He knew nothing about wine or food.'[27]

Whereas the shooting of *Dr No* had proceeded largely without incident, *From Russia With Love* was a plagued production. There was, of course, the sad death of Armendariz, then a boat chase had to be abandoned due to adverse weather conditions along with technical issues with the supplied boats. Rescheduled to be shot in Scotland, a helicopter carrying Terence Young on a location recce hit a crosswind and ditched into the sea. Suffering nothing more serious than a cut hand, Young was back directing that very afternoon, his arm in a sling.[28] And poor Daniela Bianchi. Being driven to the set early one morning, her driver fell asleep and the car almost landed in a river after turning over several times. Daniela received bruising to her face and couldn't work for two weeks.[29] All this was a real headache for the producers and the film inevitably went behind schedule and over budget.

One of the very last scenes shot was Bond's underground escape from the Russian consulate, hotly pursued by an army of rats. When this couldn't be filmed as planned in Istanbul, Cubby took a small unit to Madrid where a local rat-catcher procured 200 brown rats. Syd Cain built the set in a warehouse, a large sheet of glass protecting the crew. Alas, the rats escaped and Cain found himself outmanoeuvred to the nearest place of safety by his boss. 'Cubby was a man of some considerable girth but he moved like an Olympic runner to outrace me to a stepladder.'[30]

Having promised John Barry the chance to score the next film, after his sterling work on the Bond theme, Saltzman was now having second thoughts due to the young musician's relative inexperience and there was talk of Lionel Bart, who'd had huge success with his stage musical *Oliver!*, writing all the music. That was Terence Young's recollection, who very much championed Barry. 'Cubby was on my side, and in the end, it was two to one. I think Cubby was the decider that we should go with John. In the meantime, I think Harry had committed to Lionel Bart, and that's why Lionel wrote the title song.'[31]

Saltzman remained interested in Bart's work, and just a year later expressed an interest in bringing to the screen his musical comedy about Cockney low-life characters in the 1950s, *Fings Ain't Wot They Used T'be*. When he heard about his partner's interest in the property, Broccoli asked, 'Where are you going to get the money?' To which Harry replied, 'Details Cubby. Details.'[32]

Accompanying Bart's memorable song were some truly eye-catching titles by New York graphic designer Robert Brownjohn, brought in after Maurice Binder proved unavailable. Not long in London, Saltzman first met Brownjohn at a Chelsea dinner party and invited him to offer some ideas for the film. Brownjohn's memorable pitch took place in a darkened Soho theatre where the producers sat and watched as he turned on a projector and danced in front of the beam of light as projected images glanced off his body. 'It'll be just like this,' he explained, 'except we'll use a pretty girl!'[33]

Brownjohn next worked on *Goldfinger*, where if anything he outdid himself, coming up with a main title sequence that in pure style and innovation has hardly been bettered. Brownjohn enjoyed his time working on the Bonds: 'I'm lucky with Harry and Cubby because they let me get on with it, leave me alone and don't ask questions.'[34] But when the producers offered to set up Brownjohn in his own independent production company to make all their future titles, he turned them down and they went back to Binder.[35]

Anticipating that the film would do just as good business as its predecessor, the producers instructed their joint attorneys, Irving Moskovitz and Norman Tyre, to suggest to David Picker that the deal their clients had originally signed with United Artists be renegotiated. 'That in itself was not unusual,' said Picker. 'Although any changes would usually be tied to a new deal with new pictures. Here, after only two films the producers were already pushing for a change.'[36] The newly worked out deal meant a higher fee, overhead allowance and personal expenses. As an extra inducement, United Artists agreed that if both *Dr No* and *From Russia With Love* recouped all of their costs back, Danjaq's share of the profits for subsequent Bond pictures would rise from 50 per cent to 60 per cent.[37]

As it was, *From Russia With Love* exceeded everyone's expectation when it opened in October 1963. In London it was the first film ever to be shown in four West End cinemas simultaneously. The producers cannily announced over the end credits the title of the next film in the series, standard procedure for the Bonds that were to follow. It was reported that one woman, after a showing in London, attempted to book advance tickets for *Goldfinger*, which had yet to even enter into production. Bond fever was beginning and

From Russia With Love ended up the most popular film of the year at the UK box office.

Less positive was the criticism the film received in some quarters over its sadistic violence. 'If Odeon cinemas really think the new Bond is nice clean fun for all the family, then Britain has some pretty kinky families, or soon will have,' bemoaned *Films and Filming*. The *Sunday Express* compared the film to 'an expensive penny dreadful, enjoyably absurd, calculatingly sadistic'. The Fleming books had always been steeped in sadism, together with violence and misogyny, it was one of the reasons why they were viewed as unpalatable by so many producers and studios who turned them down. Cubby and Harry were only too aware of this and made a conscious decision not to replicate those elements too much on the screen. 'But we try to keep the character of Bond as a hard, sometimes cruel man in the films,' said Broccoli. 'You might even call it "sadism for the family".'[38]

7

All That Glitters

With *From Russia With Love* a massive hit in European territories and outpacing the performance of *Dr No* in America, the producers were on a crest of a wave, but a charismatic and highly ambitious Irishman by the name of Kevin McClory threatened to gatecrash the party.

Back in the spring of 1959, McClory had managed to persuade Fleming to give him the rights to make a Bond picture. Spurning the books, which McClory didn't think were filmable, the idea was to concoct a brand-new Bond scenario. Experienced screenwriter Jack Whittingham was hired, and melding ideas from both Fleming and McClory produced the first ever James Bond script, entitled *Thunderball*. As preparations were set in motion to begin shooting early in 1960, Fleming got cold feet due to McClory's inexperience as a filmmaker, having produced only one picture previously which flopped at the box office. With the project dead, Fleming used Whittingham's screenplay as the basis of his next 007 novel. He didn't even bother to change the title, nor did he acknowledge the work of McClory or Whittingham. McClory sued Fleming for plagiarism and the resulting trial in November 1963 was followed eagerly by the press.

Broccoli and Saltzman had been following the case closely and knew that victory for McClory would throw a huge spanner into the works. With Bond's debut adventure already beyond their clutches, they now looked like losing another Bond title. When news leaked of Fleming's intention to settle after just nine days into the trial, the producers offered to underwrite the costs of continuing the case for a further fortnight.[1] But it wasn't the money, Fleming's health was deteriorating and friends feared if proceedings dragged on any longer, he might not survive it, having already succumbed to one heart attack. Besides, the evidence against him was damning and he was staring defeat in the face anyway.

McClory emerged out of the High Court victorious, considerably richer and the proud owner of the film rights to *Thunderball*. And with the runaway success of the first two Eon-produced films he lost little time planning his own renegade Bond, with Richard Burton reportedly 'very amused' with the idea of playing the super spy and more than curious about the very large pay packet.

Shunting the problem of McClory to one side, Saltzman and Broccoli ploughed on with *Goldfinger* only to find themselves facing another problem, that of finding a new director. Terence Young had decided to move on, he simply couldn't see himself directing a fresh Bond adventure every year for the foreseeable future.[2] While this may have been true to a point, Young was also frustrated with the producers' refusal to give him a profit-share deal after the enormous success of the first two movies.[3]

As his replacement, the producers looked to the man who had turned them down originally and was now eager for the job: Guy Hamilton. Broccoli particularly liked his work, 'He shoots with a lot of pace and style, and also has a flair for comedy: all the elements intrinsic to Bond.'[4]

Like Young, Hamilton served in the war, with the Royal Navy, first on Destroyers and then as part of the 15th Motor Gunboat Flotilla, a covert unit which specialised in ferrying secret agents, escaping Allied service personnel and intelligence material to and from German-occupied Brittany and Norway. After the war, Hamilton assisted the likes of John Huston and Carol Reed before making his own solidly-British efforts, notably *An Inspector Calls* (1954) and *The Colditz Story* (1955).

Coming into *Goldfinger*, Hamilton already knew that Bond was different to any other kind of movie. 'It's a wonderful licence. It's the only sort of picture where the audience already knows the ground rules, you don't need to explain anything, you just give them a wonderful ride.'[5] He also quickly surmised that the Bond crew had got a little bit self-satisfied and, in his words, 'needed goosing up'.[6] However, the first thing Hamilton learnt, indeed the first thing anyone working for Cubby and Harry would have to discover, was their meaning of the word – Bondian. 'Core writers would arrive in industrial quantity and leave very quickly because they didn't understand Bondian.'[7]

For Harry and Cubby, Bondian was a combination of many things: that Bond behaves in a certain way, has certain props, he's got to be elegant and exciting. If you're going to give Bond a car it couldn't be something anyone could buy from a dealership, it had to be a car just off the factory floor or a car that only 1 per cent of the population could afford. Bond couldn't have a normal watch, it had to be the latest and the best. When Rolex declined to cooperate on *Dr No* there were no funds left to go out and buy a new one, so Broccoli simply took the Rolex off his wrist and gave it to Connery to wear.[8] When Bond stays in a hotel, he doesn't get a single room, he gets the penthouse. For example, in *Diamonds Are Forever*, it's the biggest and gaudiest suite in Las Vegas, complete with a waterbed and live fish, a nice touch that was Cubby's idea. Everything had to have an over-the-top style. It was Harry's circus philosophy again, make it bigger! 'Anything you had seen in another picture, we didn't want it here because it isn't Bondian,' said Hamilton. 'We've got to create our own world.'[9]

Locations could also be used in a Bondian way; it was a question of where do you take Bond. 'You couldn't take him to Marseilles,' claimed Hamilton:

> because all you've got there is tarts and Bond doesn't deal with tarts, it's got to be glamorous. So, he'd go to Monte Carlo or go on a yacht. That was the thinking, and very bright it was too because at that time there were no package tours, travel was still rare and the idea of Bond was that we would take you to the most glamorous places in the world where never in your lifetime will you go.[10]

Even the way villains perished had to fit in with the producers' notion of Bondian. Saltzman's son Steven recalled that his father would constantly doodle, and one day he asked him what he was doing. 'Thinking of another way to die,' was the unusual answer. 'Death is really quick,' said Saltzman, expanding on his theme. 'A bullet to the brain, you're dead. But what I've got to do is think of something glamorous, you've got to die Hollywood-style, like piranhas or electrocution. And it's got to give the audience a sense of revenge.'[11]

Once again, Richard Maibaum was hired to carry out a first draft on *Goldfinger*. Then, on Saltzman's suggestion, writer and film critic Paul Dehn was brought in to do some revisions, only for Connery to raise several objections and Maibaum was called back to do a final polish.[12]

Getting the right balance of writing talent was always uppermost in the minds of the producers. However, the Bonds were almost unique in that they were probably the only films written by committee. At the start of each new production Saltzman and Broccoli would sit down with their core creative team for a series of conferences to thrash out what was going to be put into the script.

Maibaum once brilliantly illustrated what those meetings used to be like:

> The most important ground rule is that everyone is expected to say exactly what he thinks. The wildest notion is encouraged. The floor belongs to whoever at any given juncture can command attention either by his fervent cogency or by the simpler expedient of shouting loudest. And all this is accompanied by an obbligato of insistently ringing telephones which Mr Saltzman seems incapable of not answering.[13]

For Maibaum, the toughest thing was always trying to keep the story moving along and coherent while having to include all the bits and pieces the fans were now coming to expect. As a result, these meetings could descend into what he described as a 'melee', in which 'tempers are lost, good manners waived and lacerated sensitivities are ignored and forgotten immediately after the melee ends'. It was always understood, though, that the producers had the final say.[14]

Of course, the producers had the added advantage of the creator of Bond available to them and Fleming did sometimes attend these production meetings, although he chose never to interfere or throw his weight around. As Broccoli recalled, 'He'd sit there in his detached manner, occasionally, but always diffidently, suggesting an idea or two.'[15] Part of his deal meant that Fleming had no approval over any script, although the producers allowed him to see them just the same, more out of courtesy than anything else, and the fact they valued his expertise.

Behind the scenes Dana was important, too. 'I think all the major decisions that he made he discussed with her,' claimed Barbara Broccoli. 'It was a real partnership.'[16] Being a writer herself, she was able to make practical and informed suggestions that were always helpful. 'Dana was a lovely lady,' said Monty Norman. 'A real tough business woman. She was certainly the queen behind the throne, so to speak.'[17]

The routine once the production was underway was that the producers left the director pretty much alone to get on with things. 'And that was marvellous,' said Hamilton:

> There was no interference whatsoever. One or other of them, or sometimes both, might come down for lunch on the set, to show their faces, but they tended to spend more time with the production supervisor or the associate producer to see how things were going, but leaving you in perfect peace and quiet. You felt confident that they were trusting you and you

> appreciated that enormously. Basically, all creative decisions had been made prior to shooting. Along the way we'd change things on the floor, of course, put in gags and change lines and if they laughed, they'd be happy and on we went.[18]

Expected to top the thrills of the first two 007 pictures, the casting of Bond's latest nemesis Auric Goldfinger, whose dastardly scheme is to detonate a nuclear device inside Fort Knox, would be crucial. 'I was worried that Bond was becoming superman,' said Hamilton. 'And that's never very interesting because you know he's going to win all the time. Bond is only as good as his villain; you've got to work hard on the villains.'[19]

Saltzman was keen to use the respected American actor Theodore Bikel and he was flown to London to undergo what turned out to be an underwhelming screen test. Meanwhile, Broccoli was convinced he'd found the perfect candidate in a German actor called Gert Frobe and asked Hamilton to come to the projection theatre to see some footage of him. It was in a film in which he played a child molester. He was sitting on a bench producing sweets from his pocket. Wonderfully evil, thought Hamilton. 'He looks marvellous Cubby, but can he speak English?'

'Yeah, I've spoken to his agent, he speaks English,' confirmed Cubby.

Gert Frobe duly arrived on set and introduced himself. 'How do you do. I'm very happy to meet you.' Well, that was about all he could say in English. 'We drafted in a dialogue coach and he worked like mad to get it right,' recalled Hamilton. 'Cubby and Harry when they saw the first rushes went ape, I had to calm them down. "Trust me," I said, "we'll dub him. It'll be all right."'[20]

It was a bit disconcerting for the rest of the cast, especially if you happened to be acting opposite him as Honor Blackman explained:

> I met Gert for the first time, we shook hands and Guy shouted, 'Action!' And all this gobbledegook came out and I thought, Dear God, what did he say? Why have they cast this man because I can't understand a single word he's saying. Guy explained that they were going to dub his voice later, so I had to just wait until his mouth stopped moving before saying my lines.[21]

In the end it didn't matter that Frobe couldn't speak a word of English (he was brilliantly dubbed by English actor Michael Collins); he inhabited that character so totally that it's now impossible to see any other actor in the role.

Equally memorable was Goldfinger's Korean sidekick, Oddjob. With Fleming describing him in the book as a man with 'arms like thighs', where the hell were the filmmakers going to find an actor like that? Hamilton was watching wrestling on television one Saturday afternoon when Harold Sakata came on and the crowd all booed – 'and there was Oddjob'.[22] A champion weightlifter and professional wrestler of Japanese descent, Sakata had no acting experience whatsoever, which didn't deter Broccoli at all: 'That square head and the sheer tonnage of the man made him the perfect henchman.'[23]

The girl quotient was also increased. Honor Blackman, cast due to her popularity as judo expert Cathy Gale in TV's *The Avengers*, was hired to play Goldfinger's tough, no-nonsense personal pilot, the wonderfully named Pussy Galore. Even today the name is risqué and one is baffled quite how the producers got away with it. Indeed, they almost didn't in America where the chief censor threatened not to release the picture. Cubby personally flew to the US to remonstrate with him, but what made the difference was a newspaper cutting of Honor Blackman meeting Prince Philip at a society event. The headline was: *Pussy Meets the Prince*. 'What's so wrong with that?' asked Cubby. The censor withdrew his objection.[24]

Shirley Eaton had made a name for herself in British comedy movies of the *Carry On* and *Doctor* variety and didn't need to test for the film; instead she was asked to go and see Saltzman. Having just returned from holiday in the South of France, Shirley was suitably tanned. 'I remember I had a nice little white chiffon dress on which showed off my long brown legs. I felt gorgeous.'[25]

All Saltzman really wanted to know was, did Shirley mind being painted nude in gold paint? 'I said, "No, not if it's done tastefully."'[26] Interview over, Shirley made her way back home. No sooner had she opened the door than her agent was on the phone saying she'd got the part. It was to change her life dramatically. That picture of Shirley painted gold became one of the 1960s' most iconic images. 'Getting it off was a real devil though, they scrubbed me down until I was pink raw. And a week later I sweated it out at a Turkish bath.'[27]

Shirley enjoyed working on the film, though remembered the producers as having very different personalities. 'Cubby was a very good businessman and he was friendly and warm, there was no side to him. Harry unfortunately had a much more brittle and divisive personality. He couldn't help the way he was.'[28] Honor Blackman also picked up on the vivid contrast between the two producers: 'Cubby was the cuddly one and Harry was the tough one. But Harry was lovely and had a very dry sense of humour. I liked him.'[29]

Girl number three was Tania Mallet, then one of the top models in Britain when she was talent-scouted by the Bond producers:

> I was on a photo shoot for *Vogue* in Spain and someone showed the pictures to either Harry or Cubby and asked, 'What do you think of her as a Bond girl?' and they said, 'Terrific.' I originally tested for the main female role in *From Russia With Love*, but in the end they thought I was too English-sounding, which was ironic because the actress they eventually used had to be dubbed anyway.[30]

With the date of *Goldfinger*'s premiere already established for 17 September 1964, Hamilton realised he was in a race to finish the film before he'd even started shooting in mid-January. He was further hampered by the fact that his leading man was in Hollywood making a film for Alfred Hitchcock called *Marnie* and he would have to start without him:

> Rather difficult because Sean was in practically every scene. So, I did a lot of car chases around the lot at Pinewood while waiting for Sean to be released from his picture. And that was making everything very, very tight, we had to keep up to schedule and we had a ridiculously short time for the editing. It was a bit of a nerve-wracking experience.[31]

When Connery did arrive at Pinewood early in March, he was not a happy bunny. As an actor he no longer existed. In the eyes of millions around the world he was James Bond. The strain was beginning to take its toll, what with the attendant fan worship and the growing media intrusion into his life, torture for a man who took his private affairs seriously. He had already begun to grumble about the Bond role restricting him from other acting challenges, something that started towards the end of production on *From Russia With Love*. Asked by Cubby who he wanted to make a picture with, Connery had replied Alfred Hitchcock. To placate his star, Cubby spoke with Hollywood agent Lew Wasserman, who was close to Hitchcock, and then to the director himself, with the result that Connery got the *Marnie* gig.[32]

To smooth things even more there was a new pay deal, £50,000 plus a percentage of the profits: 'By *Goldfinger* Sean knew he was indispensable to us,' said Broccoli. Or as Saltzman put it, 'When we had an ultimatum from Sean, it was either pay up or he went.'[33]

Cubby could sense the growing disenchantment with his star, and it was on *Goldfinger* that he saw for the first time the danger signals for the future of Connery playing the role, as he later admitted: 'It was after those first two films that our relationship deteriorated. He got mad at us about expenses early on and he became sick and tired of us later.'[34]

Yet Connery never allowed any personal problems to corrupt the atmosphere on the set. One of the actors on the film, Burt Kwouk, recalled that Connery was never less than totally professional. 'On the factory floor he had a job to do which he simply got on and did.'[35] He'd also greatly matured as an actor after working with Hitchcock, and gearing up for Bond number three he was in supremely confident mood. 'Sean was much more accomplished than in *Dr No*,' claimed Hamilton. 'There's a big difference in the performances. He was becoming more assured in front of the camera. His personality was breaking through.'[36] Connery's performance in *Goldfinger* is a wonderful show of cosmopolitan cool and casual send-up, befitting the new approach by Hamilton, who veered the series away from the hard-edged realism of the first two 007 pictures into the realms of comic strip fantasy.

On that first day of shooting at Pinewood, Harry arrived on the set with a bottle of champagne to wish everyone the best of luck. He then proceeded to smash it over the camera as if he was launching an ocean liner, not a motion picture. Instead of applause, there was stunned silence from the crew. He'd broken the lens and there was broken glass everywhere.[37]

Saltzman also had a habit of bringing friends and their children onto the set, as Guy Hamilton recalled. 'I realised for Harry it was a show. It's front row seats at the circus.'[38] When his daughter was 11, he brought her entire school class to Pinewood Studios to observe the voodoo sequence from *Live and Let Die* being filmed. He really did treat the Bond set like his own personal fiefdom. 'Chairs would be lined up for his visitors,' said Roger Moore.

> And he'd be showing off rather expansively and would go on talking and I can remember Derek Cracknell (assistant director) shouting for quiet and Harry is going on talking; everyone else is dead quiet and Cracknell said, "Quiet everybody! And that includes *you* Harry." For once I saw Harry slightly non-plussed.[39]

One of the many innovations on *Goldfinger* was establishing the pre-credit sequence as a mini adventure all of its own. 'We do these openings to make it very evident that it is tongue in cheek, that it is larger than life and we're not pushing any political ideology,' said Saltzman. 'We are making an entertainment.'[40]

It was during the night shoots on the pre-credit sequence at Pinewood that Richard Jenkins, the second assistant director, described an illuminating episode concerning Saltzman. Jenkins had only recently married and his young wife was nervous of being left alone all night at home, so would come along to watch. When filming broke for dinner the production manager refused to allow her to eat any of the food being served, because she was not an accredited crew member. Jenkins complained to the producers, and it was Saltzman who insisted she sit at the main table with all the other wives. 'Family was important to Harry. He was a great family man.'[41]

After his absence on *From Russia With Love*, Ken Adam returned as production designer on *Goldfinger* and his visual imprint on the film is undeniable, creating a style the rest of the Bond films would follow, his Fort Knox set being a perfect example of what he was trying to achieve.

Thanks to an old friend of Cubby's, a retired Air Force colonel by the name of Charles Russhon, the Bond makers were allowed access to the Fort Knox complex. Broccoli, along with Hamilton and Ken Adam, went up to Louisville to scout the famous gold depository. 'We were given special permission to fly over the outside, which was quite frightening because they had machine guns on the roof and there were loud speakers all over the place saying, "You are now trespassing, do not approach."'[42]

As for looking inside, they were politely told not even the President of the United States was allowed to do that. Adam had visited vaults at the Bank of England and knew more or less how gold was stored and it lacked any kind of visual punch. Letting his imagination run riot, he came up with a cathedral of gold concept.

> I reproduced the exterior of Fort Knox in every detail on the backlot at Pinewood, but the interior was a complete stylization – not for the sake of stylization. It was, I felt, the biggest gold depository and the public wants to see gold. This is what Fork Knox *should* look like.[43]

First, Adam made a sketch of his proposed design, since he had to sell the idea to Cubby and Harry. 'I came up with this idea of a gigantic 40ft grille with gold stacked to the top and that we the audience are kept outside the grill. That's the way I justified it to Harry Saltzman who said, "It looks like a fucking prison to me."'[44] Hamilton, who Adam recalled always backed him up in discussions with Harry and Cubby, was more taken by the concept, and in the end the producers gave their go ahead.

Ironically, after the film came out the producers received something like 200 letters of complaint about why a British film company had been allowed to make a movie inside one of America's most secret installations.

Working on the plans of the Fort Knox set was a newcomer to the Bond team, a young draughtsman by the name of Peter Lamont, who was to forge a close working relationship with Ken Adam and go on to take his place as production designer on nine 007 movies. Lamont fell easily into the workings of the Bond crew, noticing the special role Stanley Sopel played in being the buffer between the studio floor and the producers. Only a select few were allowed to go and see the producers, everyone else dealt with Sopel.

He also never forgot one of his first meetings with Saltzman. 'I was summoned to his office and he had three telephones going all at once and seemed to be speaking three different languages, and there was someone measuring him up for a suit.'[45] Lamont found Saltzman a colourful character, something of a wheeler-dealer. 'I don't know how true it is but I heard at one time Harry used to do money lending at high interest over the weekends when the banks were closed.'[46] He also knew all manner of extraordinary people. Lamont next worked on *The Ipcress File*, and one evening was invited to Saltzman's London home to meet a woman who had been incarcerated in a cell just like Harry Palmer in the story. 'It was fascinating. I don't know where Harry found this woman, but he did know all these weird and wonderful people.'[47]

Along with Fort Knox, Ken Adam was also instrumental in the design of Bond's gadget-laden Aston Martin DB5, which was to become one of the most iconic vehicles in cinema history, its sleek silver body encapsulating the new technological and consumer age of the 1960s. Originally Broccoli wanted to go back to Bond's car in the books, the Bentley, but Hamilton and Adam wanted to use a modern sports car and the Aston seemed perfect.[48]

Even in those early days, the producers employed a marketing strategy to tie up as many deals as they could with companies for the loan of their products in order to keep production costs down. Saltzman had already made a deal with the Ford Motor Company to feature two of their cars in key points of *Goldfinger* and they had been extremely cooperative. It was to be a different story with Aston Martin.

At first, when Saltzman called Aston Martin's general manger, Steve Heggie, there was little appetite to cooperate with the film. Frankly, it wasn't worth the company's time to indulge filmmakers, but he would be delighted to sell him a car at the going rate. Saltzman almost exploded. 'Haven't you seen *Dr No* or *From Russia With Love*?' he admonished. Heggie confessed that he hadn't. 'He thought I had just come down from the trees.'[49]

Saltzman tried another tack. He informed Heggie about an earlier conversation he'd had with his boss, David Brown, the company chairman, and that he had been promised cooperation. Heggie found this more than a little bit suspicious; surely Brown would have notified him about this. And so it proved when Heggie cabled his chairman, then on business in America, and learnt no such assurances had been given. Heggie called Saltzman and told him he was still happy to sell him a new Aston, at £4,500.[50]

Saltzman's persistence finally provoked a change of heart after he set up a series of meetings between the Aston Martin people and Ken Adam and John Stears, who finally were able to convince Heggie of the merits of featuring the DB5 in a film with the potential to reach millions of people. The company lent the production two models, one for the normal driving scenes and another to be converted with various gadgets and gimmicks by John Stears at a cost of £25,000. Filming in Switzerland, the 'road' car as it was known developed a faulty gearbox, and as they were always fighting against the clock the unit had no choice but to fly in the 'effects' car from Pinewood and cross their fingers nothing went wrong, as Joe Fit, Stears's right-hand man, recalled:

> Harry was a pretty highly-strung sort of guy at the best of times and with the necessity for using the 'effects' car on the chase sequence this only added to his volatile temperament. I'll never forget his face when he came out of the trailer and saw that it was missing. Here was a £25,000 car, one of a kind, and a crew member had borrowed it to collect his lunch from the canteen! Boy did he bawl out that young kid on his return.[51]

Shooting the scene where Bond is first introduced to the Aston Martin, Cubby was watching proceedings from behind the camera. There was Desmond Llewelyn as Q explaining all the gadgets to a disinterested Bond, everything was going smoothly, then Hamilton called, 'Fine, cut.' Broccoli walked over, a little mystified that Hamilton had allowed Llewelyn to miss out the car's *pièce de résistance*, the ejector seat.

'No, Cubby. I want the ejector seat to be a surprise. There is Bond with the villain next to him. He presses the red button and, whoosh, off he goes. I think that will get a big laugh.'

Cubby didn't agree. He knew the scene would get a big laugh anyway, the audience's enjoyment of it came from the anticipation of when Bond was going to use the gadget. 'You never argue with Cubby,' said Hamilton. 'You're wasting your time. So, we shot all the rest of the dialogue and Cubby was absolutely right, tell 'em what you're going to do and then do it.'[52]

The introduction of Bond's gadget-laden Aston Martin was a watermark in the series, henceforth 007 tended to rely on Q Branch more than his wits to get out of tricky situations. And it was Harry, rather than Cubby, who was the gadget master according to Guy Hamilton. 'Harry was particularly keen on gadgets and gimmicks, and quite a lot of people in the Pentagon and places like that were letting him know about the latest toys in the army. That was important because Bond had to be ahead of his time.'[53]

As we know from his behaviour on the set of *The Entertainer* and those bottles of Bass beer, Saltzman wasn't shy in utilising an early form of product placement in his films, and the Bonds were no different. In the scene aboard Goldfinger's private jet, Bond goes into the bathroom to shave. Arriving at the studio early, Hamilton walked onto the set only to see it looking like a Gillette ad, with strategically placed bottles of the company's foam and after-shave. 'Harry, what are you doing at 8 o'clock in the morning, when the crew haven't even arrived, dressing the set?' Hamilton was not amused. 'He'd done a deal with Gillette and he was being very naughty. It was too obvious so I threw all the props out.'[54]

The bulk of location work on *Goldfinger* took place in Switzerland and here Hamilton was accosted by Saltzman's wife Jacqueline, who wanted to know when he was going to film her cameo. 'It's a good luck thing that I put her in the background,' stressed Harry. She had appeared briefly looking out of a window on the Orient Express in *From Russia With Love*. Hamilton decided to cast Jacqueline in the role of a garage attendant who services Bond's Aston, but when he returned to Pinewood weeks later Cubby was steaming: 'No fucking way. Over my dead fucking body.' Jacqueline's brief appearance was cut.[55]

With the premiere date looming, there was just one more sequence to film: the plane gas attack on Fort Knox. Broccoli organised a skeleton crew to fly out to Kentucky and was driven to the airport by his stepson Michael, who had just graduated from university and was on summer vacation in London before going to law school. Cubby started thinking how he might need another pair of hands, but that it was too bad Michael didn't have his passport with him. As it happened, it was in his back pocket and Michael caught the plane out to New York with the crew and then down to Fort Knox. 'And that was my first taste of working in the film business.'[56]

Thanks once again to Charles Russhon, permission was granted for private planes to fly over the gold depository. Cubby was on the ground reassuring the man who ran the place that each plane was flying at the requested height of 5,000ft and not breaking restricted air space. As the aircraft headed closer, it was obvious that they were much lower. 'My goodness,' exclaimed the man. 'They're not 5,000 feet.' Quick as a flash, Cubby said, 'Oh no, it's an optical illusion. I'm sure they're 5,000 feet.' Far from it, and Broccoli needed all his persuasive skills to keep a lid on the situation. 'The poor man was screaming,' recalled Hamilton. 'He was very, very unhappy.'[57]

Next, Hamilton borrowed a platoon of men stationed at the adjacent army base. He told them that at the sound of a whistle they were all to look up into the sky, and when it blew a second time, they were to all drop to the floor and play dead. 'We gave them ten bucks and a bottle of beer each. They all thought this was the dumbest thing they'd ever been asked to do.'[58]

With time running out, the Fort Knox footage was raced back to England where *Goldfinger* was due to open in less than a month. Post-production was frenzied. John Barry was scoring scenes fresh from the cutting room and having battles with Saltzman over the title song. The producer hated it and only capitulated in the end saying, 'The only reason this song is staying in the movie is because we don't have any goddamn time to redo it.'[59] As sung by Shirley Bassey, 'Goldfinger' went on to receive a gold record for sales and is the series' most iconic anthem. One night not long after, Barry was sat in The Pickwick, a favourite actor's club/restaurant situated in the heart of the West End, with his pal Michael Caine when Saltzman approached him and said, 'Thanks, it works,' and that was it. 'But it was such an off-handed compliment that it didn't really make up for anything at all.'[60]

★

Just prior to the premiere of *Goldfinger*, Ian Fleming died after suffering a fatal heart attack. Cubby and Dana were particularly saddened by the news, both of them had liked him immensely. Broccoli was particularly sad the author missed the opening of *Goldfinger* and the Bond mania it spawned, although he'd been shown some of the early rushes and was pleased with what he saw. 'All in all,' said Cubby. 'I believed we served him well.'[61]

A 5,000-strong crowd gathered outside the Odeon Leicester Square for the premiere of *Goldfinger*. After attending the first two Bond openings, Connery was conspicuous by his absence. Even without him, emotions ran high that evening. Tania Mallet witnessed the madness firsthand. 'I heard this huge explosion to my right. The crowd just surged forward, the police had completely lost control and the glass doors of the cinema foyer caved in. I quickly ran inside the auditorium. It was terrifying.'[62] Bond mania had begun.

Broccoli and Saltzman really hit the jackpot with *Goldfinger*. *Dr No* and *From Russia With Love* broke records, but this time around they were obliterated. The film's $3 million budget was recouped in just two weeks, earning it a place in the *Guinness Book of World Records* as the fastest-grossing film up till then.[63] Some cinemas in America ran *Goldfinger* twenty-four-hours non-stop, such was the demand. Its success triggered United Artists into reissuing the first two Bond movies in America as a double feature during the Easter holidays of 1965, bringing in another $8 million.[64] Not for nothing did *Playboy* hail Bond as the hero of the age. Even the Beatles used to come to private showings of the films at the producers' own viewing theatre at South Audley Street.[65] In the words of Saltzman, they had created a modern mythology. 'James Bond is the Tarzan of the 1960s. He is the Superman. We live today in an age of violence and James Bond exemplifies the hero in an age of violence.'[66]

Perhaps Penelope Gilliatt, the *Observer* film critic, summed it up best: 'The Bond pictures are pure producer's pictures, the circuses of the age, made with extraordinary flair and commercial instinct and a skin-crawling sense of the times.'

According to Broccoli and Saltzman there were two kinds of producers: the business and administrative producer, and the creative producer. Both men identified themselves as creative producers, involved in all aspects of the filmmaking process, offering ideas and guidance and ultimately putting their individual stamp on the pictures. On *Goldfinger*, for example, it was Cubby who picked up the notion of the tranquiliser gun from a science magazine he read, and a news photograph of a crushing machine for used cars seemed a very Bondian way to kill a baddie.[67] For Cubby especially, the fun of making a picture was to be where the action was. Ken Adam recalled that he 'covered half the globe looking for exotic locations' with the producers.[68] 'I remember once I wanted to look at a really dangerous location in the jungles of Guatemala in a tiny plane and I said, "Cubby, I'm going by myself." He said, "No, I'm coming with you." He would never let me go by myself.'[69]

In post-production, too, they were a presence in the cutting room and at rushes, which were normally screened in a little theatre in South Audley Street. Even when the film was in release their job wasn't finished; they'd scrutinise ad campaigns, carefully go through every detail with the distributors, attend opening nights round the world and read reviews to gauge what the critics were saying. This was especially important to Broccoli, according to Dana. 'When we were in a strange city anywhere in the world, and if there was a Bond film playing, Cubby would go in and sit and listen to the reaction of the audience to find out what they liked, and what they didn't like. He had a great respect for the public.'[70]

He would also make an effort to talk to cinema managers to find out if there had been any complaints about a particular scene. While Cubby had playfully tagged Bond as sadism for the family, he was keen never to overstep the mark in terms of taste and decency. As Tom Mankiewicz later observed, 'Cubby would talk about the soul of Bond or Bond would never do that. And Harry would sometimes get short with him and say, "James Bond will do whatever we want him to do."'[71] Cubby would never, for example, succumb to studio pressure to take the Bond franchise in directions that he felt were unsuitable.

Both Cubby and Harry felt enormously proud of what they had achieved, and they had done it working as independent producers and in defiance of so-called experts who said Bond would never work. In the words of Broccoli, what they had accomplished 'was unique, even by Hollywood standards'.[72]

And of course, the renumeration was considerable. Roger Moore recalled Guy Hamilton telling him a story of when he was in the office and the money was coming in faster than either of the producers really knew what to do with. It was Harry who figured they ought to buy gold bars. Hamilton envisaged the next time coming into the office the carpet being piled high with hundreds and hundreds of them.[73]

But how long was it all going to last? Even the producers didn't know. All they promised was to keep on making them as long as there was an audience. 'Perhaps five or six more,' predicted Cubby, hopefully.[74]

8

Kitchen Sink Bond

It's no surprise that after Len Deighton's first novel – *The Ipcress File*, an ironic and downbeat take on the spy game – was published late in 1962 to critical acclaim, the author came into the orbit of Harry Saltzman. Invited to lunch at Pinewood Studios, Deighton's first impression of Saltzman was that he epitomised a certain type of film producer, 'the chubby, cigar-smoking figure that Central Casting chose as a "Hollywood film producer" in the old black and white movies with which I'd grown up.'[1] So quickly did Saltzman want to tap into what Deighton could offer that he was asked to begin a film treatment of *From Russia With Love* and the pair of them went out together to Istanbul.[2]

Having secured the film rights to *The Ipcress File* for £12,500,[3] Saltzman looked for the right person to adapt it. Picking up the phone he called the agent Richard Hatton to ask if his client, Lukas Heller, was available. The German-born Heller had recently won plaudits for writing the screen adaption to *What Ever Happened to Baby Jane?* Heller was busy elsewhere but Hatton made an interesting suggestion: why not try another of his clients, Robert Shaw, who had branched out into writing with two successfully published novels. Having read Deighton's work, Shaw was enthusiastic and his passion moved Saltzman into hiring him to write a first draft screenplay.[4] That draft did not find favour with Saltzman, who removed Shaw from the project, something of a blow for the actor who had rather fancied himself in the title role.[5]

Someone else who had a go, along with being considered as a potential director, was Ken Hughes, but according to his wife Cherry Hughes he struggled with the script. 'He said, "I can't make head nor tail of this bloody thing," and turned it down.'[6] In the end Saltzman went through six writers before he was satisfied; only Bill Canaway and James Doran earned a credit.

Finding the right actor to play Deighton's spy hero proved even more difficult. Saltzman's first choice was fellow Canadian Christopher Plummer and he put the actor under contract. Not long after, Plummer asked to be released to go and make *The Sound of Music* (1965). 'And Harry said ok,' recalled Deighton. 'There was no punitive action taken against him, and that was very unusual amongst film producers to just give actors their freedom like that. Harry was wonderful at tearing up contracts.'[7]

At Pinewood one afternoon Saltzman bumped into Lindsay Anderson, who had just finished shooting *This Sporting Life* with Richard Harris. Saltzman made the suggestion that *Ipcress* would be an ideal role for the up-and-coming actor and he'd send over the script. 'And send it he did,' Anderson wrote in his diary. 'It was there, with the sequel, *Horse Under Water*, delivered by hand through my letterbox when I got home that night.'[8] In the end Harris turned the job down.

Meanwhile, Deighton was a fan of the BBC sitcom *Steptoe & Son*, and believed that Harry H. Corbett could play the role. Saltzman didn't agree that someone associated with a comedy show would make a believable spy for audiences. But earlier in his career Corbett was regarded as an actor of note, performing Shakespeare and working under Joan Littlewood. Deighton's persistence eventually paid off:

> Harry totally bought the idea of using Corbett and was on the verge of signing him when Corbett got the chance to make a movie called *The Bargee* and the makers of that film really wanted to utilise his image as Steptoe. That's when Harry said, 'No, no, we can't use him after that comedy film because he'll just get laughs and it won't work.'[9]

One evening, Michael Caine and his close friend Terence Stamp were having dinner at the Pickwick. Over at another table were Saltzman and Jacqueline. When they spotted Caine, both of them urged the young actor to join them. 'We've just come from seeing *Zulu*,' said Jacqueline, as Caine took a seat. Both of them had enjoyed it immensely, especially Caine's performance. 'We both agree that you could be a big star,' said Saltzman. 'You really come over well on the screen.' Caine couldn't believe it, that was the first time anybody had said that to him – 'and it was from somebody who knew what he was talking about'.[10]

The next two minutes were to change Michael Caine's life. Saltzman was not only offering him the lead in *The Ipcress File*, his first starring role in a movie, but a seven-year contract. 'I sat there dumbfounded,' said Caine. 'I had only just met the man!'[11]

Caine was asked to meet Saltzman for lunch at Les Ambassadeurs the following afternoon. When he arrived, 'very quickly realising that I was the only person there I had never heard of', Saltzman had already ordered caviar and vodka. 'First class all the way for you Michael, from now on,' he said. And he was right.[12] The strange thing was Deighton had already met Caine when the journalist Peter Evans introduced the two of them, and is still mystified why he didn't bring up his name to Saltzman, 'because when I look back on it, I can't think of any other actor who could have come anywhere near Michael.'[13] Caine was to receive the sum of £6,000 for the film, exactly the same figure Connery got for *Dr No*.[14]

In the novel Deighton deliberately kept his spy hero nameless, so Saltzman called a meeting to thrash out a suitable name for the character. 'We need a name that means absolutely nothing, a common or garden name that means nothing at all.'

Caine knew a kid at school called Palmer who was the dullest he'd ever met. 'Good,' said Saltzman, 'Now, what's a really duff first name.'

Without thinking, Caine said, 'What about Harry?'

'Thanks very much,' said Saltzman. 'Just for that we'll call him Harry.'[15]

Then there was the problem of Deighton's hero wearing glasses, something Saltzman was dead against. No matter how many times Deighton and Caine brought up the subject, Saltzman waved it away. One evening both of them were invited for dinner at Harry's Mayfair home. Once again, the thorny question of the glasses was brought up. Harry sighed. 'No, no, no. What film star have you ever seen wearing glasses?' Just then, Jacqueline made an interjection that swayed the whole thing. 'Harry, darling. Cary Grant looks lovely in glasses.' This was one of the very few times Deighton ever recalled Harry at a loss for words. 'Very well,' he said eventually. The glasses were in.[16]

Over the years Deighton got to know and like Jacqueline very much and was in no doubt that theirs was a happy marriage. One insight into the Saltzmans' domestic life occurred when he arrived at their home early one evening for a meeting, only Harry was late coming back from a trip to Switzerland. Deighton sat down and was talking to Jacqueline when Harry came in, complaining about the fact his flight was delayed. She got up to fetch him a drink and then said, 'Did you bring me a present?'

'No honey, I didn't bring you a present. It's been a terrible day.'

'Didn't you bring me anything?'

'No honey,' stressed Saltzman. 'I just didn't have time to go to the shops.'

'Didn't you even bring me one of those little gold bars that they sell at the airport?'[17]

In a way, *Ipcress* represented a return to Harry's Woodfall days. Palmer was the kitchen sink Bond, something that unnerved Broccoli. 'We had a lot of problems with Cubby,' said Ken Adam, hired by Saltzman as the film's production designer, 'because he thought Harry was going to make a poor man's Bond.'[18] This, however, was the genius of Saltzman's plan. With the recent surge of Bond imitators in movies and on television, Saltzman had decided to go to the other extreme and make the absolute antithesis of Bond. Perhaps Saltzman recognised in Deighton's Palmer the same anti-authority credentials that made Sillitoe's Arthur Seaton resonate so much with the British public. Indeed, one of the first things Saltzman ever said to Deighton was, 'I'm the only man in the world who you can be sure won't make your story into a James Bond story.'[19]

It was that feeling which led Saltzman to hire Sidney J. Furie as his director, a Canadian who had relocated to England and just come off a working-class biker picture called *The Leather Boys*. 'Harry had a feel for that kitchen sink stuff, so when he saw *Leather Boys* he knew I'd be cheap and available.'[20]

When filming began on location around London in September 1964, turmoil reigned, 'but good turmoil, healthy turmoil', insisted Furie.[21] Worried about the inadequacies in the script, that the writers had, in his words, 'tried to make an American B movie' out of the novel, Furie began to employ bravura camera shots and other techniques. As he told Caine one day on the set, 'Look, the only way we're going to get through this shit is to give it ambience.'[22]

Another thing he did was employ new writers who were working as he was shooting:

> Literally, we'd get there in the morning and sometimes there were no pages. So, I'd say to our cameraman Otto Heller, take two hours to light that staircase, by which time pages arrived, we made carbon copies of them and the actors would quickly learn the lines and away we went. And that happened a lot.[23]

Saltzman just couldn't get to grips with what Furie was doing. After a week of shooting tension reached a head as the crew were filming in Shepherds Bush. Following yet another heated discussion between director and producer, Furie came sweeping past Caine in floods of tears, quite inconsolable. 'Fuck it, I'm off this picture.' And with that he hopped onto the number 12 bus heading towards Oxford Street. Saltzman wasn't far behind. 'Where the hell is he?' Caine pointed to the red London bus on its way down the Bayswater Road.

'Nobody leaves my set on a fucking bus.' Saltzman grabbed Caine and they both piled into his Rolls-Royce Phantom and gave chase.[24]

Urging his chauffeur tactfully to get a fucking move on, as the Roller edged alongside the bus Saltzman wound his window down to scream at the conductor on the back, 'Stop the fucking bus! You've got our director on board.'[25]

Furie decided to return to the film, but relations stayed frosty. 'Harry despised me so much, he really did. But I stood my ground.'[26]

After another week of disagreements, and still baffled by Furie's shooting style, Saltzman had reached a shattering conclusion:

> Saltzman came by one day and saw the footage and thought it was the worst shit he'd ever seen and told me that when the editor Peter Hunt returned from his holiday, if he didn't like it, he was firing me. 'Well fuck you,' I said, and I tore up the pages of what we were shooting, 'Here, you can have it all back.' And then Michael said, 'no, no, just stay.' Because I was walking. No producer's going to tell me the editor will decide my fate. But then a few days later Peter Hunt came back and he said, 'Harry, I've just seen the rushes and you shouldn't be mad at Furie, you should kiss him.' After that day Harry never really talked to me again.[27]

It wasn't long before Hunt began to see what was going on and had a great deal of sympathy for Furie. 'Saltzman was a terrible bully towards Sid, and could be towards others. I don't know why he carried this on with him. Everything was this intense battle of wills between the two of them.'[28]

Other problems emerged. Caine's co-star Sue Lloyd had become romantically entangled with Furie, a situation that reached a very public boiling point, as the actress recalled:

> Sidney arrived with his suitcases on my doorstep, which was not cool at all because his wife was in the pudding club. Harry Saltzman's wife, which I didn't blame her for at all because she happened to be a great friend of Sid Furie's wife, together they decided that I should never work again. My agent told me that Saltzman had said he will see to it that you will never work again.[29]

Whether Saltzman carried out this threat one cannot really gauge, save that Sue Lloyd claimed she did not receive many offers of work for the next few years and had to eventually take a television series, *The Baron*, against the wishes of her agent. 'And to think I had the same contract as Michael Caine on *The Ipcress File*. And I blew it.'[30]

While the film was very much anti-Bond, Saltzman was still in many ways tied to the logic of the 007 universe. Ken Adam had found a building in Grosvenor Place he thought ideal for the MI5 office; it had these very large empty rooms, with tall windows. Harry came by promising to fill the place with all manner of computers and hi-tech gizmos. Whatever he wanted, Harry would get him. This placed Adam in rather a difficult position, since he already had a completely different kind of vision for what he wanted to do. After a sleepless night Adam approached Furie on the set the next morning.

> I have an idea, Sid, what do you think, if instead of the head of MI5 having all sorts of gadgets and gimmicks, he sits behind a trestle table, he has a camp bed on one side, he doesn't even have a chair for the person who comes in, and maybe he's got a bust of the Duke of Wellington, and that's it.

'Let me think about it and I'll let you know,' Furie answered.

After five minutes the director came back to talk to Adam. 'It's a brilliant idea, we'll shoot it that way, and get rid of all the other stuff.'

About an hour later Saltzman arrived. 'He sees this bare set, and he went ape,' recalled Adam.

> He started screaming at me, he said, "You're trying to get between me and the director." I said, "I discussed it with the director." And, of course, for the unit it was great fun because they always enjoyed a big fight going on.

The result was that Saltzman left the building in a foul temper. When he came back two hours later it was as though nothing had happened and he gave the set a thumbs up.[31]

This was the infamous Saltzman temper in action. The producer had a notoriously short fuse, although as his son Steven confirmed, 'By the time everyone was really upset, he'd actually forgotten what he was upset about.'[32] When his temper got out of hand, though, he was quick to fire people, if only to later sometimes reinstate them.[33]

Saltzman himself didn't think he was ruthless at all and that his tantrums were justified, in that he had little patience when it came to artists or technicians behaving in an unprofessional manner or people with no talent. 'I heartily dislike dilettantes and amateurs, and I won't be bothered by them.'[34] Quite simply, he didn't suffer fools of any sort. 'I saw him fire people on the spot a couple of times,' claimed Paul Tucker, location accountant on *Live and Let Die*. 'I saw him fire a set decorator who started a backchat conversation with him as if he knew better and that was it, a new set decorator arrived the next day.'[35]

He was also known to argue with airline officials to change the scheduled picture if he'd already seen it.[36] It was reported at a film festival that Saltzman turned on a publicity person who failed to recognise him. 'If you don't know who I am, you have no place in showbusiness,' he raged.[37] Richard Jenkins recalled one incident that took place at Pinewood Studios. 'In those days parking at Pinewood wasn't an exact science with cars parked everywhere, and one morning Harry couldn't find a place and he stormed onto the studio stages shouting and screaming.'[38]

Of course, as Saltzman said, you had to be tough in this business. If you weren't, you'd get eaten alive. 'But I only pick on people my own size. I hate people who yell at secretaries.'[39] Although journalist Leonard Mosley, who spent a long time with Saltzman during the making of *Battle of Britain*, observed: 'He let his underlings argue with him and shout at him, and bore it patiently, even when they were manifestly wrong or merely trying to demonstrate to outsiders that he didn't overawe them.'[40]

When it came to Harry's temper, Cubby dealt with it in much the same manner as he'd done with Irving Allen, collecting the 'wreckage' and then having to apologise to whomever had been offended: 'Don't worry. You know he doesn't mean it.' As John Stears was to say, 'Cubby was the soothing factor and Harry was the fireball.'[41]

And yet Cubby, too, could be volatile at times and his rages, according to Richard Maibaum, were somewhere on the volcanic register. 'His eruptions, preceded by ominous rumblings of discontent, are infrequent but devastating.'[42] Everyone used to say 'cuddly' Cubby, and he was overtly, but beneath that usually calm persona was a man of fierce determination and toughness, as his friend the actor Topol commented. 'It would be wrong to take his gentle manner for vagueness, indecision or softness, for he is a man who knows what he wants and how to get it.'[43] William P. Cartlidge worked on a number of Bond pictures and recalled during pre-production on *Moonraker* Cubby was in talks with Industrial Light and Magic, who worked on *Star Wars*, to provide the complicated special effects. 'The negotiations were all going very nicely until they asked for 2 per cent of the profits, at which point Cubby told them to fuck off.'[44]

Perhaps the strangest thing about Cubby, and this is true sometimes in marriages, was that he did seem to be attracted to the Harry Saltzman type of personality. 'Whether it was by accident, he did seem to attract partners that were rather aggressive,' said Cartlidge. 'I'm not a psychiatrist but it makes you wonder.'[45]

Originally, Saltzman made a deal with Rank and Columbia to finance *The Ipcress File*, but when the American studio pulled out late in the day, he was forced to quickly cut costs and invest his own money during the time it took to bring in another US studio, Universal, to cover the modest £309,000 budget. As a consequence, several scenes intended to be filmed in Beirut and at Cape Canaveral were dropped from the schedule.[46] Another investor was an American by the name of Charlie Kasher, who had made a small fortune selling hair products on US television and wanted to get into movies.[47] Saltzman took a £35,000 producer's fee.[48]

The majority of the film was shot on real locations, the exception being the 'programming box' climax where Palmer is strapped into a large metallic container and subjected to hyper-kinetic images and disorientating sounds. According to Deighton this was Saltzman's idea:

> Harry had got hold of a copy of *Life* magazine and read this article about people being brainwashed in Korea or something and it captured his imagination. He took it I think first to Cubby and some of the other Bond people and said, 'We've got to have this brain washing sequence,' and they said, 'No Harry, it's not a good idea.' So, having been repelled by the Bond people, Harry put it in *Ipcress*. In the end they shot it at Pinewood.[49]

After the end of principal photography, Saltzman did what he'd threatened to do almost from the start of shooting: he got rid of Furie. What's more, Saltzman banned anyone connected with the film to have any dealings with Furie or even talk to him. 'That's how small-minded he was,' said the director.[50]

That included John Barry, hired by Saltzman to write the score. Furie remembered that the two of them wound up meeting in secret at the Pickwick club.

> John called me and said, 'Come over for dinner, I want to review the score with you.' And he had all the music sheets and told me what he had done, and did I have any thoughts. I had a few and he said, 'Ok, I'll change it.' And Harry never knew John did that.[51]

It didn't end there. Banned from the cutting room, Furie met with Barry perhaps two or three times a week to keep updated on how things were going, asking questions like, 'Did they keep that shot in?' It was a crazy situation.[52] 'Harry was a tyrant,' said Furie. 'But a lovable tyrant.'[53]

While Barry was helping Furie out, he was facing problems of his own. After the troubles with Saltzman over the theme song to *Goldfinger*, this time his entire score came under scrutiny. Barry had employed a Hungarian zither to lend much of the music a Middle European flavour. This was something that did not sit well with the producer according to Caine. 'There were huge rows about the music. I think Harry literally wanted ersatz Bond, and when he heard all this foreign stuff he thought: "Christ! What's this?" But you could talk Harry round anything; his bark was very much worse than his bite and he loved John really.'[54]

When it opened in March 1965, *The Ipcress File* was an instant hit with the public and critics alike. It also made an impact in America, where *Time* magazine called Palmer 'A new breed of spy hero', and the *New York Times* labelled the film 'as classy a spy film as you could ask to see'.

The biggest beneficiary was undoubtedly Michael Caine. Prior to its release, Saltzman told Caine that he was going to put his name above the title in both the credits and the poster. 'Gee, Harry, that's great. You mean, you thought I was good in it?'

'No, it's just that, if I don't think you're a star, who the hell else is going to?'[55]

Ipcress was a personal triumph for Saltzman. Chosen as the official British entry for the Cannes Film Festival (Furie was banned from the screening party), it was also nominated for five BAFTA awards, ending up winning three, including Best Film and Production Design for Ken Adam, who was nominated for *Goldfinger* on the same night. Broccoli had booked a large table for his Bond team and was not best pleased when Adam won the award for *Ipcress*. 'Cubby practically didn't talk to me for the rest of the evening.'[56]

On the back of the success of *The Ipcress File* there were plans for further adaptations of Deighton novels. While Broccoli intended to remain focused on Bond, Saltzman had already begun to build a producer's portfolio of projects. This aspect of his partnership with Saltzman was something Broccoli never came to terms with, this need to do other things. To him, sustaining Bond as a top international box-office attraction meant staying with it, living with it, without hankering for other things. In other words, a full-time occupation. But Harry never saw it that way, as Dana Broccoli recalled: 'Harry had a lot of energy and he liked to do six things at the same time or he became very restless. And Cubby was quite different because he loved the project of Bond and he put all his energy into that.'[57]

Indeed, as preparations got underway for Bond number four, Saltzman had two other productions on the go. One was a dramatized study of the life of Pope John XXIII, based on his youthful journals. It was partly financed by an

American Saltzman had met by the name of Leonard Rosen, who had made a fortune through real estate in Florida.[58] Despite starring Rod Steiger and being directed by the respected Italian Ermanno Olmi, *A Man Named John*, as the film was called, only had a limited release in late 1965 and was not favourably received.

And there was a new film from Vittorio De Sica, a leading figure in the neorealist movement of Italian cinema and the legendary director of *The Bicycle Thieves*. Saltzman had great admiration for De Sica and approached him with an offer that he could have complete freedom to write and direct a film of his own choice. The result was *Un Monde Nouveau*, a little-seen drama that landed both Saltzman and De Sica in censorship troubles since the plot revolved around an abortion, at that time a taboo subject in Italy. Banned from making the picture in his homeland, Saltzman arranged for De Sica to shoot in France.

What's certain is that it must have been an experience, if a tiring one, working for Saltzman during these heady times. There's a story that he asked an assistant to fly to Rio in his place for a film premiere. This chap had always wanted to go there and Saltzman presented him with a free ticket and the words: 'When can you be back, baby? I want you in Nice next Wednesday!'[59]

Saltzman was also approached by Spanish filmmaker Jesus Franco, who was scouring Europe for someone to bail out Orson Welles's latest project. There weren't any takers. Welles was revered all right but no one trusted him with any money.

Chimes at Midnight was an adaptation by Welles condensing all of Shakespeare's plays featuring the character of Falstaff into a single focused narrative. It was to be gritty and poetic, a lament, said Welles, for the death of Merrie England. Bringing together an impressive international cast that included Jeanne Moreau, Fernando Rey, Margaret Rutherford and John Gielgud, Welles, who played Falstaff, had begun shooting in the summer of 1964 on various Spanish locations with the financial backing of producer Emiliano Piedro. By the new year funds had dried up. Jesus Franco, brought on to the film as assistant director, was unclear whether Piedro had flat run out of money or whether Welles had simply underestimated what it was going to cost to make the film. Whatever the case, Franco was sent out into the world to find cash.

Saltzman was interested in helping. Having his name on a Welles picture would certainly lend him a measure of artistic kudos within the film community. But it was Jacqueline who tipped the balance, according to Keith Baxter, who played the pivotal role of Prince Hal. 'I heard Saltzman's wife was very enthusiastic about the film and it was her encouragement that prevailed. Thank God.'[60]

A delighted Franco returned with the good news, only to face a less-than-convinced Welles. 'Orson did not want to hear about him (Saltzman), claiming he was an idiot who did not understand anything about cinema! I fought hard to change his mind.'[61] Welles's reluctance to deal with Saltzman perhaps dated back to a TV series the two men were preparing in 1955 for CBS. Welles was due to direct and star in a series of prestigious colour programmes based on contemporary and classical plays and novels. *Anthony and Cleopatra* was mooted, as was *Trilby*, George du Maurier's popular novel in which Welles would play Svengali. Saltzman was due to produce. The series never materialised.[62]

With Saltzman the only game in town, Franco was dispatched once again, this time to make a deal. What happened next would have repercussions for the next forty years. Saltzman was prepared to bail out the film to the tune of $750,000; in return, he wanted his name to be prominent and before the title on the credits. In the end, his credit ran: 'Harry Saltzman presents.' The copyright of the film would be shared 50/50 between him and Piedro, but Saltzman would get distribution rights throughout the world, except for Spain, Portugal and all the Spanish speaking territories, and those distribution rights would be in perpetuity.[63]

Welles was incandescent with rage when he heard what had been agreed and there is a story that he physically attacked Franco.[64] Certainly it created problems later on as to who exactly owned the film, and for many years the rights were in dispute and the picture withheld from distribution.

Whatever the legal implications, what is indisputable is that Saltzman's money saved the film. 'Without Harry's intervention the film wouldn't have been finished,' revealed Saltzman's widow Adriana:

> Francois Truffaut said that by the time of *Chimes at Midnight*, Welles used to spend many evenings with powerful producers, who offered him cigars but wouldn't have given him 100 metres of film. Harry was the only one who did it. Without him it would have been one more film by Welles that was never completed.[65]

Keith Baxter recalled that the bulk of the work had already been done by the time Saltzman's money arrived, with most of the crew and the principal actors having left. Baxter remained behind since Welles had yet to shoot his very last scene:

> Orson wouldn't let me return to England. I think he thought I might not come back! He wasn't idle, though the film had been closed down. With just a few people he shot little bits and pieces. Often in the kitchen of his flat. He needed a hand to pick up the crown and hand it back to Gielgud after he had knocked it onto the floor. Rough tiles were laid down over the kitchen in his apartment and that is my hand that picks it up.[66]

For the final battle scene, Welles wanted a close-up shot of some feet writhing in mud. Again, they put earth down on the kitchen floor and made it muddy. 'Those are my feet in chain mail writhing in the mud,' said Baxter.[67] Orson then told Baxter to go to Morocco. He had to promise to go to American Express every Monday morning and every Friday evening to see if there was a message for him. 'For three weeks there was never a message. Then one Friday I went and there was a message: "Money arrive. Come back." So, I returned and shot my final scene and my work was over. Maybe that was Saltzman's money.'[68]

Chimes at Midnight was well received by the critics but suffered a scattergun release schedule, opening first in Spain at the close of 1965 but not reaching the US or Britain until March 1967, and so never found its audience. Today it's considered not only one of Welles's finest works, but amongst the best screen adaptations of Shakespeare put on screen. Welles always considered it a personal favourite. Falstaff had always been a literary figure that fascinated him, a comic rapscallion that in the hands and performance of Welles becomes a robustly funny and ultimately tragic screen antihero.

9

Bond in the Bahamas

Throughout the making of *Goldfinger*, the shadow of Kevin McClory loomed large over the Bond producers. However, despite the interest of Richard Burton, McClory must have felt that his 007 project was caught between a rock and a hard place. By the time he won the film rights to the *Thunderball* novel, the opportunity to put out a successful picture first and independent of Broccoli and Saltzman had been lost. Their series had already been fixed in the public's mind: the opening gun barrel, the Bond theme music and, most importantly, Connery, all would be missing from McClory's production. The only real chance left for the Irishman was to join ranks with the producers he threatened to rival.

Broccoli and Saltzman, too, naturally felt that a rival Bond at this early stage would harm their product. With three films already in the bag, the producers naturally felt they knew more about making a Bond picture than anyone else. So, it was almost by mutual consent that the two forces joined together. In the summer of 1964 Broccoli flew to Dublin, where he and McClory met at the airport and a deal was struck.[1] Roughly, McClory would get $250,000 plus 20 per cent of the profits, all this on the understanding that he would not exercise his rights to the *Thunderball* material for ten years. He would also receive full producing credit,[2] though essentially all three men acted as producers.

By the time *Thunderball* was ready to go before the cameras, the Bond formula was well and truly established, as described by Richard Maibaum:

> Hitchcock said to me, 'If I have thirteen bumps, I know I have a picture.' By 'bumps' he meant shocks, highpoints, thrills. Broccoli and Saltzman and myself have not been content with thirteen 'bumps.' We aim for 39. Our

> objective has been to make every foot of film pay off in terms of exciting entertainment.[3]

After the unprecedented success of *Goldfinger* Guy Hamilton was the obvious choice to direct, only he wasn't interested:

> I was spending a weekend in Las Vegas and Cubby and Kevin McClory came out to see me. McClory was an old mate of mine because we'd worked on *The African Queen* together, and he pushed the script into my hands and I said, 'Honestly fellas, I've run out of ideas,' because Bond takes a lot out of you, 'And I have nothing fresh to add. So, I'll have to pass.'[4]

With Hamilton passing, Terence Young reconciled his financial difficulties with the producers and reclaimed the director's chair, a decision that was welcomed by the Bond crew according to assistant director Richard Jenkins. 'Terence had a very good relationship with Sean, and really Harry and Cubby were so lucky that he directed the first Bond film. I liked Terence very much. He was a very sophisticated man and had great style.'[5] At Young's disposal was a budget of $5.6 million, over five times the amount spent on *Dr No* just three years before, which gives some indication of how big Bond had grown in such a short space of time.

It's widely acknowledged that one of the areas that Cubby excelled in was casting the Bond girls. One of the theories he espoused was that Bond's ladies, 'must stay in the background and must give the impression of being experienced with men. They must be strong but elegant. And something has to happen when you look at them.'[6]

They also needed to be well developed in a certain department, or as Guy Hamilton put it, 'Cubby had fixed ideas about the type of girl he wanted in Bond's bed. And one thing he wanted was good tits.'[7] Such views were more easily voiced and accepted in the sixties and seventies, as Cubby explained to film journalist Tony Crawley:

> I don't say the girls have to be necessarily endowed that way to do the film. We like to think that the male audience – and I don't wanna sound chauvinistic at this point – like to see a beautiful bosomed lady. And I do, too. So, there we are. If I had the choice, I'd go for the bosomed girl – with an obvious amount of acting talent, as well.[8]

A definite 'boob' man, Cubby was not averse to the alluring mystic of a woman's rear end, either. Roger Moore once heard him say as one of the girls walked past that she had 'a particularly lovely derriere'. Hearing this, the girl turned on her heels to confront Broccoli and called him 'A sexist, misogynist swine' to his face, and how dare he treat her like a bimbo.[9]

According to one report, the producers spent $75,000 finding the *Thunderball* girls. 'There's a great shortage of beautiful women who can act,' claimed Saltzman. 'Lots freeze before a camera and lose their beauty.'[10]

For the main role of Domino, the fragile and vulnerable mistress of the film's villain, one serious contender was Raquel Welch, after the producers saw the young American actress on the cover of *Life* magazine. Convinced her earthy sensuality was perfect for the role, they flew to Hollywood and signed her up. Back in London, Cubby took a call from a frantic Richard Zanuck, production chief at 20th Century Fox. He'd been hoping to use Raquel in their big sci-fi film for that year, *Fantastic Voyage*. Would they consent to release her? Cubby and Harry still wanted to use Raquel, but as a favour to Zanuck agreed to his request.[11]

Next, their attention turned to another up-and-coming actress, Faye Dunaway. 'We sent her tickets to fly over but she never turned up,' said Cubby.[12] The final choice was a former Miss France, Claudine Auger.

Another actress in the running for Domino was Luciana Paluzzi, who recalled arriving at Pinewood for her test and seeing something like 300 girls there. While she lost out to Claudine, 'they wanted to launch a newcomer with each new film and I was already well known in the industry,'[13] Luciana was asked to play the film's femme fatale, Fiona Volpe. Unhappy with the fee her agent had negotiated, Luciana went to see the producers at South Audley Street. 'They're both on the phone at the moment,' said a secretary. 'But go in, they'll be off in a minute.' Luciana walked in and calmly sat down:

> And the two of them are talking business, but Harry was screaming at the top of his voice. 'And you tell your client that if he doesn't want to do this role there are a hundred people outside my door lining up to do it.' And he slammed the phone down. Then they both turned to me, 'What can we do for you Luciana?' And I thought I was going to die because the timing of my request was so bad. I had to muster all my courage to ask for a rise, and I thought they were going to explode. And Cubby said to me, 'You're not happy, what do you want?' I asked for double. And they looked at me and then they looked at each other and said, 'Ok.' And I couldn't believe it.[14]

Making up *Thunderball*'s four-girl roster were Mollie Peters and Martine Beswick. Having appeared in *From Russia With Love* as one of the fighting gypsy girls, Saltzman was against Martine being in the new film. 'We don't have the same one twice,' he said. 'They're all Kleenex, throw 'em out.'[15] Young fought for Martine's inclusion as Bond's contact in the Bahamas and she was cast. Mollie Peters was another choice of Young's, having spotted the former model as an extra. Making her first real acting debut, Mollie was understandably nervous but found the Bond team warm and encouraging, especially Cubby, Young and Connery. 'Cubby was friendly, cuddly. I liked him. Sort of dad-like, as far as I was concerned. Harry, I never really ever got to know.'[16]

Mollie isn't alone in categorising the two men in this fashion. 'Cubby did come over as a father figure, loved by all,' said sound editor Norman Wanstall. 'Harry was in his own world and I don't know if anyone got close to him.'[17] Wanstall worked on five Bond films in total and can't recall Saltzman speaking to him even once, not even after he won an Oscar for *Goldfinger*! Special effects technician Albert J. Luxford also saw a clear difference between the two producers: 'Cubby was always warm and affectionate whereas Harry was a bit more the stereotypical film producer. Harry was always Mr Saltzman and Broccoli was always Cubby – that's how it was. If you called Cubby "Mr Broccoli" he didn't really like it.'[18]

Filling out the rest of the cast was Adolfo Celi as Largo, chief operative for SPECTRE whose latest plan was the theft of two atomic bombs to hold the world to ransom, and Rik Van Nutter as Felix Leiter. Nutter was married at the time to Anita Ekberg and it was through the couple's friendship with the Broccolis that the actor was cast.

Filming began on *Thunderball* with the exciting pre-credit sequence at the sumptuous Chateau D'Anet, outside Paris, on 16 February 1965. Here audiences were treated to one of Bond's most iconic gadgets, the one-man jet pack. Again, this piece of military hardware was sourced by Cubby's friend Colonel Charles Russhon, 'Mr Fixit' in the words of Peter Lamont. It was on *Thunderball* that Russhon really came into his own, not only supplying the jet pack but the Fulton Skyhook that featured at the end of the picture, the high explosives used to blow up the Disco Volante yacht, and facilitating the use of the US Coast Guard and the Air Force Aqua-para rescue team for the film's stunning underwater battle climax.

Russhon continued to work on the Bond films into the early 1970s, his clout rarely questioned. Peter Lamont recalls on *You Only Live Twice*, Russhon arriving at Heathrow airport with a huge trunk full of weapons and getting it through customs. 'He just changed into his Colonel uniform and said he was on official business.'[19] Russhon was also a close friend of Connery. According to Russhon's widow, Claire, when the actor was at odds with the producers it was often Russhon who acted as a go-between.

Russhon's involvement and influence on the series is huge but he wasn't the only one passing on 'insider' information, according to Paul Tucker, a production accountant who worked on the early Roger Moore Bonds. 'Both producers had amazing contacts in America with the military. They were always able to get the latest equipment or advanced warning of what was coming up so Bond was always one step ahead of every other film.'[20]

In Paris, staying as he always did at the George V, a luxurious landmark hotel off the Champs-Élysées, Saltzman was as busy as ever. According to Guy Hamilton, the producer went over to Paris once a week. He loved London, was a real Anglophile, like Cubby, but there was something about Paris that was in his heart and never left him, and there were friendships there that Hamilton knew meant a great deal:

> Just after the war, Harry had been very broke in Paris and saw the rough side of life. He had to haggle to survive. And one or two friends had helped him out and so now with the money he'd earnt from Bond he loved to go over and see all his old friends who'd helped him when he was down on his luck and return some of that hospitality.[21]

In Paris, Saltzman visited the street locations where De Sica was shooting *Un Monde Nouveau*, telling reporters that this film marked a return to the famous director's neo-realism roots. He caught a rough-cut screening of his Pope film, boasting that he had won permission to hold the French premiere in Notre Dame. There were also rumours of him visiting the Vatican in order to persuade the current Pope, Pope John, to fly to New York to attend the US opening. There were also a couple of dinners with Rex Harrison, who was keen to move behind the camera and direct his first film, with Saltzman producing.[22]

While he may have had all these films brewing at the same time, Saltzman was a marvellous delegator. His method was to have one or two producers handle a particular group of films, then he would form another group of films and select producers for those. Once a script had been agreed, along with a cast and a director, the producers then handled the actual production, with Harry keeping in close contact by phone and the odd set visit. But when he was there, in person, he gave a film his undivided attention, involved 100 per cent in everything connected with the production, as his daughter Hilary explained. 'He wanted to know what the designer was doing, what the

Director of Photography was doing, how the sets looked. He always had a say in everything and an interest in everything.'[23]

After their stay in Paris, Saltzman and Jacqueline caught a flight to Madrid, where Orson Welles had organised a screening of the uncut version of *Chimes at Midnight*. The couple arrived at a film studio where a large screen had been erected on one of the sound stages. During scenes where some of the dialogue hadn't been recorded, Welles boomed out the lines in the darkness. During the battle scene he barked, 'This is going to be terrifying. They're all yelling and you hear the armour clanking; it isn't just music playing.'[24]

Someone else at the screening was Broccoli's cousin, Pat De Cicco. 'It's a masterpiece,' he told Saltzman afterwards. Whether it was going to make any profits, and how long the producer would have to wait to see them, was another matter. 'That's ok,' said Harry. 'It's not all right,' countered De Cicco. 'Listen, Harry, are you in this for art or for the money?'[25]

It was an interesting question. Both Cubby and Harry were quite open about the fact they were in the entertainment business and not out to preach to their audience. But as Saltzman was to claim, Shakespeare was entertainment too, and he was hopeful that *Chimes at Midnight* was going to make money; he was pretty damn sure it wouldn't lose any. After all, Shakespeare wasn't meant to be for the masses, but he felt sure there was a sufficient audience to make it pay off. 'I don't believe in trying to mix education and entertainment. Trying to put a message in a film that purports to be entertainment is a kind of moral dishonesty and, besides, it never works. The pictures always fail.'[26]

Meanwhile, Broccoli had arrived in Nassau with the rest of the Bond team to start location shooting on *Thunderball* and faced an immediate problem when customs impounded all of the movie equipment. This kind of thing happened back then in certain countries where authorities tried to make a fast buck out of film companies. According to actor Earl Cameron, who played Pinder, Bond's ally in the film, Broccoli wasn't having any of it. 'He said, "Look, make up your mind because if you don't want us to make the film here, we'll go somewhere else to make it." So, he just frightened them and they let it go, of course.'[27]

Saltzman arrived at the location a few days later and Earl Cameron quickly noticed how elements of the Bond crew reacted towards him as opposed to Broccoli:

> If they said, Cubby's coming tomorrow, it was – oh great. If they said, Harry's coming tomorrow, it was – oh shit. That was the attitude of the crew. They

> didn't like him at all. He wasn't a nice man. Cubby was well loved. He was a really nice man. A charming man. I liked working with Cubby.[28]

Broccoli was really the practical one out of the two producers. He sorted out problems during the shoot or if anyone on the crew had any personal issues. 'You always felt you could go to Cubby about any problem and he would understand,' said Honor Blackman.[29] Broccoli would also listen to ideas and suggestions from any member of the crew; he might not necessarily agree, but he listened – and that was a quality that endeared him to everyone.

In Nassau, McClory came into his own as producer. Living as he did on the island, he had many contacts amongst the local jet set and was able to smooth the way for the production and provide access to many desirable locations. On the whole, though, McClory's producing marriage with Broccoli and Saltzman didn't work. There was a feeling that he was merely being tolerated for the duration of this one film. 'Kevin did not fit in well with the Bond team,' recalled Ken Adam. 'He had occasionally some good ideas, but he must have felt too that he wasn't one of the boys.'[30]

One of the locations McClory managed to procure was Palmyra, Largo's mansion, in reality the holiday home of Nicholas Sullivan, a millionaire from Philadelphia. He and his wife were staying there at the time, indeed would invite friends round to watch the filming, all sat in evening dress sipping cocktails. 'I was worried,' said Ken Adam, 'because Mrs Sullivan was an alcoholic and I thought at night time she might fall into the pool holding the sharks. I asked Cubby to station some guards there just in case.'[31]

As one of the mainstays of the series, it was crucial that someone like Adam had a good relationship with the producers. As it happened, Adam liked both men enormously and they worked extremely well together. He knew that Saltzman could be volatile, but appreciated his talents, referring to him as a showman brought up in showbusiness and that had never left him. 'Cubby was more "one of the boys,"' he said. 'But I got so used to working with them and their idiosyncrasies that it didn't really worry me too much.'[32]

Adam recalled one amusing incident on location in the Bahamas. While never completely comfortable around the sharks used in the film, Adam was never unduly worried; it was the barracudas he never acclimatised to:

> I'll never forget Cubby making fun of me. I used to swim every morning and one day Dick Maibaum joined me. And on that morning, there was a barracuda lying dead still on the seabed. And I said, 'I'm not going in.'

> And Dick said, 'Are you scared of that little fish?' I said, 'Yes, I'm scared of that little fish.' Because the moment you tried to get in the water his jaws opened. And Cubby was standing on his hotel balcony watching and said, 'My God, what a bunch of heroes.'[33]

Despite the sharks and the barracudas, shooting out in the Bahamas was a career highlight for the designer.

> We had a lot of fun on that picture because Terence was the sort of director who was full of fun and very sociable. Cubby was very sociable too and knew all the wealthy Americans in Nassau. So the atmosphere was wonderful. I must say in terms of ambience the Bahamas was one of the most pleasant experiences for all of us.[34]

Whilst on the island the producers recreated the famous Junkanoo festival, a sort of Mardi Gras that took place every year on Boxing Day, believing it would make a lively backdrop for a chase sequence. To ensure the locals turned out in force, they offered £1,000 prize money for the best costume and carnival float. Terence Young instructed his camera crew to weave in and out of the crowd, almost cinema verité style. One unusual image caught on camera was a dog lifting its leg to take a leak in the middle of the street. When he saw it, editor Peter Hunt thought the shot in poor taste and removed it. Running the sequence for the producers a few weeks later, both men yelled, 'Where's the dog, Pete?' Hunt said, 'You don't want that shot of the dog?' 'Yes, we do.' Hunt put it back in.[35]

One shot that did prove to be beyond the pale occurred during an underwater love scene between Bond and Domino. The pair disappear behind a convenient rock and the camera tracks an explosion of air bubbles released towards the surface. A shot of Domino's bikini was to have been included, but Broccoli felt it was too suggestive and ordered it to be cut.[36] The producers were always aware of having to tread a fine line when it came to sex and violence. Bond was a man who lived by his senses, with a voracious sexual appetite, he was also a ruthless killer, and yet the 007 films were broadly aimed at an audience of all ages, something Broccoli especially never lost sight of, according to Richard Maibaum: 'Cubby has tried very hard to keep the pictures from being vulgar. If someone suggests something that is really vulgar, he'll wince.'[37]

On the set of *Thunderball* it was obvious that Connery's relationship with the producers was getting worse, especially with Saltzman. Nor was his mood lightened much when the producers chartered two planes to bring something like 200 journalists to the island. 'Even on *Goldfinger*, as far as I can remember, Sean was very bitter against the producers,' said Richard Jenkins.

> They'd got him on a multi-film contract and they absolutely refused to negotiate. Even though he had been tremendously popular and they were making huge amounts of money they wouldn't share it. I think Terence told me that. And on *Thunderball* it was really Terence and Sean against Harry and Cubby, with Kevin McClory as the good guy as far as Sean was concerned.[38]

It got so bad that one evening Connery told Young, 'Don't engage too many extras tomorrow, I may not be here.'[39] But Connery was too much of a professional to let the team down and never carried out his threat, though he refused point blank to talk to any journalists. It even reached the point where Saltzman was prepared to drop Connery. 'I just didn't know who to replace him with.'[40]

It was all about money, of course. Connery was after a full partnership with the producers. 'He wanted it because he felt it was his due,' said Young. 'There they were, Cubby and Harry, sitting on millions and Sean outside the door calculating that maybe a third of it should be his.'[41] According to Ken Adam, Connery wasn't especially quiet about his grievances with the producers. 'He would talk about them all the time, complaining about how they were exploiting him.'[42] At one point during filming Connery tried to renegotiate his contract and reportedly settled eventually for a large cash settlement.[43]

Despite these problems, Luciana Paluzzi recalled that there was no tension on the set, largely because Saltzman and Broccoli knew *Thunderball* was going to be a success. 'Sometimes when you work on a movie the producers get upset when there is a waste of time because something doesn't go right. Nothing like that with Harry and Cubby. Truly it was the easiest and the most fun movie I've ever made.'[44]

Back from the Bahamas, the congenial atmosphere of filming in the tropics was certainly transplanted to London. After all, this was the swinging sixties and there were showbiz parties aplenty to enjoy, as Mollie Peters remembered. 'Somebody had a flat near the Dorchester Hotel and there used to be a number of supper parties. I'd go along and Sean would be there, Michael Caine, Claudine, Harry and Cubby, and Terence of course. It was great.'[45]

The producers were now the undisputed kings of Pinewood. Cubby, a regular at the studio's ornate dining room, sat at a large round table where once Emeric Pressburger held court; now it was Cubby's turn. 'Here he entertained bankers, sponsors, royalty and visiting journalists over sumptuous lunches,' recalled Roger Moore.[46]

On the eve of *Thunderball*'s opening, a disagreement flared up over how Kevin McClory wanted to be credited. The lawyer Peter Carter Ruck, who acted on McClory's behalf in his plagiarism case against Fleming, sent a stiff letter to the producers and the matter threatened to stall the first screening of the film, which was set to take place in the private cinema at South Audley Street. With things still unresolved, the preview took place nevertheless and Carter Ruck and his wife Ann took their seats along with a small invited audience. About halfway through, Ruck received a tap on his shoulder and was asked to go to a private office. There he saw McClory in a heated argument with the producers over the issue of his credit. 'It was a serious matter,' said Ruck. 'But I could not help being amused when Harry Saltzman started beating his desk, shouting, "We must not get emotional!"'[47]

In the end everything was sorted out and Ruck returned to his seat. 'It's a pity you missed the last half hour,' said Ann. 'It's been so exciting.' To which Ruck replied, 'It was nothing like the excitement which I have been experiencing in Harry Saltzman's office.'[48]

Thunderball marks the point in the series where the machines began to take over, and where Fleming's character moved further away from his literary roots into the realm of Superman. Even some of the core Bond talent knew it, like Ken Adam. 'We were getting less and less input from the Fleming books, and the producers relied more and more on spectacle.'[49] It's true to say there was now tremendous pressure on Cubby and Harry to make each Bond an 'event' movie, in other words bigger than the last, since the audience had come to expect nothing less. That was the aim, while also trying to maintain the quality they had begun the series with.

A lot of the critics agreed that Bond was getting swamped by gadgets. *The Observer* likened the new Bond to, 'A prodigious toyshop-cum-travel agency. The film is always jolly to watch but the toys have clearly taken over.' While Alexander Walker in the *Evening Standard* warned: 'Broccoli and Saltzman have given 007's adventures the extravagance and velocity of a comic strip and the only alarm may be whether they have overdone it.'

Yet if *Thunderball* proved anything, it was that the 007 franchise was critic-proof. As the *New York Times* critic was to observe in his review of 1969's *On Her Majesty's Secret Service*: 'Serious criticism of such an esteemed institution would be tantamount to throwing rocks at Buckingham Palace.' It was the same in Cubby's Warwick days; he didn't worry too much about what the reviews said. The kind of movies he made weren't meant to earn the admiration of critics or win plaudits and statuettes at film festivals; they were for the public. 'The only award I need is green with Washington's head on it.'[50] Saltzman felt the same, referring to both Cubby and himself as troubadours. 'We're minstrels, story-tellers in the market place.'[51]

And *Thunderball* was packing them in, selling 58 million cinema tickets in America alone.[52] Internationally, the film just about broke every record going. The Bonds had become the box office phenomenon of the age, and United Artists' biggest ever money-spinner. Just in time, too, since the company was haemorrhaging money due to the spiralling budget of their biblical epic *The Greatest Story Ever Told*, which ended up costing $21 million.[53] Expected to be a blockbuster when it opened in time for Easter 1965, the film fared badly, so the huge revenues for *Goldfinger* and then *Thunderball* certainly came in handy. According to Eric Pleskow, an executive at United Artists in foreign distribution and later head of the company, 'The Bonds kept us from going bankrupt.'[54]

It wasn't just box office receipts that interested the producers. In New York, Broccoli found time in his day to check the sale of popcorn at the Paramount Theatre on Times Square, where *Thunderball* was being screened twenty-four hours a day to cope with the crowds. Such was the pull of Bond now that the producers insisted on a cut from the confectionary concession.[55]

The producers also had a large share in Bond merchandising, everything from 007 vodka to deodorants, even the London Hilton had a 007 bar. They did, however, baulk at the request to manufacture a 007 condom.[56] In 1965 alone over 250 companies applied for a licence to make Bond-related products and rights were sold in some seventy countries.[57] All this was an unexpected bonus for the producers, but they were quick to exploit it, and formed a branch of companies, together with United Artists and the Fleming estate, to handle the demand for products. This boom carried on for the next few years, though by the close of the decade it had pretty much run its course. Even so, over those few years it was estimated that worldwide income from Bond merchandising reached $100 million retail.[58]

The money even started trickling back to the crew. '*Thunderball* was the one that we all eventually got a bonus on, nine months after it came out,' said Richard Jenkins. 'There was a huge furore because United Artists' staff got a bonus because *Thunderball* did such good business, and I think the technicians' union shamed Harry and Cubby into giving us, the crew, a bonus.'[59]

These years, 1965–66, were also the years of the Bond spy craze, with hundreds of rip-offs and spoofs being made around the world. Always careful to stay one step ahead of the competition, the producers screened some of these films at their private viewing theatre, just to see if they had anything to worry about. It was something Peter Hunt was especially cognisant of.

> One thing I said at the time of *Thunderball* and again later on, was that we had to be careful that we didn't become imitators of our imitators, because by then everybody had gotten on the bandwagon, so we had to be very careful of copying them, because that would have been a disaster.[60]

Cubby had his own theory why the bulk of these pastiches never worked. 'Audiences don't like to see their heroes lampooned. When Bond pays off a terrifying situation, or kills off an adversary with a quip, it works as a tension-breaker, the audience laughing with relief. But making Bond into a kind of spoof spy doesn't work.'[61]

10

In the Money

By 1966, Broccoli and Saltzman could quite comfortably claim to be the most financially successful independent producers in the business. A journalist visited their offices at this heady time and reported what he saw as a typical day. While Saltzman had his own office suite at South Audley, he was usually in Cubby's large old-fashioned office, both of them sat opposite each other at those two big desks pushed back to back. Papers were strewn over the floor. The phone rings and rings incessantly (the partners' phone bill was $12,000 a month), while people wander freely in and out, everyone talking at once. Harry and Cubby keep up a steady patter: 'Hey, Harry, think he'll take a hundred thousand?'

'What about her?'

'She's got a good face but Christ, the legs. Have you ever looked at her legs, Cubby?'

'I never got as far as the legs.' Cubby lit a cigarette using matches with 007 on the cover. 'What about the other one?'

'No breastworks,' Harry replied.[1]

Life was good since both men knew what it was like to face financial hardships; Cubby when he was forced to sell Christmas trees on frozen sidewalks and Harry when he used to stay in different friends' hotel rooms, sometimes even sleeping in the bathtub.[2] George Lazenby recalled Jacqueline once telling him that things got so bad during one period that Saltzman took to hiding in the toilet to avoid debt collectors.[3]

Now Broccoli had a five-storey town house in Green Street, off Park Lane which he decorated with Georgian silver, antique furniture and paintings that he and Dana picked up in auctions at Sotheby's and Christie's. During the filming of *Diamonds Are Forever*, Jill St John rented an apartment near the South Audley office and remembered that whenever Cubby won some money gambling, Dana would immediately go out and buy a painting, perhaps some jewellery or a good piece of furniture. 'It was usually something of lasting value.'[4]

One curious point about Cubby's address on Green Street: whether he knew this or not is unclear, but on that very road, number 27 to be exact, Ian Fleming was born.[5]

For Cubby, family was everything, an obvious by-product of his Italian background. When he joined the Bond team in 1970, Tom Mankiewicz grew very close to Cubby and Dana, 'and it was a real Italian family and Cubby was the godfather'.[6] There would be huge family gatherings and social occasions. The dining-room table seated ten and as one visiting reporter wrote, 'even an informal meal takes on the air of a banquet'.[7]

Broccoli loved to share his wealth, not in any vulgar way, but from sheer generosity of spirit. 'Cubby loved to show largesse,' said Mankiewicz:

> It was part of his personality, and part of the fact that he never dreamed in his life that he was going to be in this position. To give someone a gift was so important to him. Also, he didn't seem to have another agenda, he didn't want to take over General Electric or Barclays Bank, he really wanted to enjoy his life.[8]

Cubby relished the lifestyle. Early in his film-producing career he'd bought a stud farm in Newmarket, with the intention of going into the horse racing business. As it turned out, he was too busy with his movie activities and sold out to a partner. It wasn't until the 1980s that Cubby got back into the horse racing game.[9]

Another luxury was his Rolls-Royce, with the distinctive number plate of CUB 1, something he was enormously proud of. According to Tom Mankiewicz, though, he very nearly came to lose it. 'Britain had just recognized Fidel Castro and the Cuban ambassador was coming over to London and he wanted CUB 1, and Cubby called somebody in government circles, "Who is more fucking important to this island and this economy?" He got to keep his licence plate.'[10]

Harry also lived in Mayfair, in Mount Row. It was a mews house that had been substantially rebuilt so the rooms were quite large and light, especially the living room with its oak-panelled doors, marble-top tables and a huge multicoloured globe. According to Tony Bramwell, who later worked for Saltzman, Frank Sinatra often stayed there, so often in fact that many people thought the place was his. 'Frank loved it because it overlooked the American embassy. He felt safe because he could park his car behind the embassy, where the US marines kept an eye on it.'[11]

Like Cubby's, the property was filled with paintings and antiques. 'He was a compulsive spender,' said Len Deighton.

> At airports he would impulsively buy all manner of goods – from kitsch to works of art – and then hand the packages to whichever member of his entourage was nearest. 'Always keep at least one person between you and Harry,' an art director warned me too late when I was burdened with a prayer rug at Athens airport.[12]

Deighton was a frequent visitor to Mount Row. He'd get there maybe six or seven in the evening and when the whole place was full, Harry would announce, 'Ok, where are we going to eat?' Off they'd all go, sometimes twelve or fifteen people in a party. Around the table the waiters would try and give out menus, but Harry would snatch them all. Saltzman would never read a menu; he'd just sit down and tell the waiter what he wanted. 'We'll have Pasta e Fagioli to start,' which is a soup with a lot of pasta and beans. One particular evening Deighton never forgot:

> This pasta soup arrived and Harry took one sip of it, 'No, no, no, no, this is not the way we do it, take it away.' As commanded, the waiters started picking up these plates and there was Maurice Binder saying, 'No Harry, it's great, I like it like this.' And I can see it now, the waiter leaning across holding the plate and Maurice holding the other side still eating, it was like a battle of wills over this plate, which needless to say Harry won because he was paying the bill. That's what it was like to go out to a restaurant with Harry. Everybody had to eat what he wanted.[13]

A 1966 newspaper profile on Saltzman revealed that the producer worked at least twelve hours a day.[14] Len Deighton was to record that he would take meetings with Harry in the morning and leave him at Crockford's (an exclusive Mayfair casino) at 3 a.m., still as agile and fresh as he began. 'He seems to manage on almost no sleep.'[15] He read nine newspapers daily, in both French and English. He also owned a Lincoln Continental Convertible, which was replaced by a Rolls-Royce Phantom V;[16] number plate – EON 1.[17] When it came time, a few years later, to dispense with this car, he told the film director Michael Winner that his decision was based on the fact that a new model, the Phantom VI, had just come out. 'It looked exactly the same,' said Winner, 'but he wanted the latest car.'[18] It was Winner who bought the old Roller for a little over £8,000, and kept it for years. 'There was a problem, though. On each of the four doors Harry had his initials HS embossed in gold. I either had to change my name or have the car re-sprayed.' The latter was certainly the cheaper option.[19]

Harry also had a country home, less than a ten-minute drive from Pinewood Studios near Denham. There was a paddock for horses, a home farm which supplied milk, cream and butter, and a large park full of massive oaks and an ornamental lake. The house itself was large, with ten bedrooms, four reception halls, a billiard room and a wine cellar. Outside there was an open terrace and a modest swimming pool.[20] In the summer, visitors could often see Harry reading scripts as he floated in a chair in the middle of the pool. Alongside was a sign that read – 'Do Not Urinate in This Pool.'[21]

Director Ken Hughes and his wife Cherry were often dinner guests at the house in the late 1960s and early '70s. 'It was very elegant and Jacqueline was a very stylish hostess. You were never intimidated going to their place. It was a family home more than anything. I'd say it was comfortable luxury rather than ostentatious.'[22] It was also the scene of many poker games that stretched long into the night. Sometimes the children would be getting ready for school in the morning and a game was still going on.

Work was never very far away, even here, since there was a switchboard in the hall with six lines and thirty-five extensions. It was calculated that during the height of Bondmania in the mid to late 1960s, Saltzman's personal telephone bill was rarely below £1,000 a month.[23]

It was a great environment to bring up his family, and Hilary and Steven have fond memories of the place. Walking into her father's study or the living room, Hilary would never know who she was going to meet next; the likes of Peter Sellers, Connery, Caine and Roger Moore were frequent visitors. Coming back from school one day, Hilary brought a friend who, on seeing a group of celebrities of mega-wattage, fainted dead away.[24]

When she was young Hilary thought James Bond was a real person, since her father used to talk about him so much, and was left to wonder when she was ever going to meet him. Many of the key Bond team felt like family. Maurice Binder would dress up as Father Christmas around the holidays and when Hilary was old enough taught her how to drive.[25]

Harry also took his role in the community seriously and was proud of being the squire of nearby Iver village, attending fetes and charity events throughout the year.[26]

★

With Bondmania at its height, the producers faced a huge new obstacle: their star was looking for a way out. Bond had established Connery as an international name and a wealthy man, though not as wealthy as he would have liked. The drawbacks, however, now far outweighed any of the benefits: the erosion of his valued privacy, typecasting, and the long, punishing schedules which left him little time for other more challenging work as an actor.

Connery had two more films to do on his contract, with *On Her Majesty's Secret Service* planned first, to be followed by *You Only Live Twice*. The producers were keen to start shooting in January 1966 when the snow was at its best in Switzerland, but Connery said he wasn't going to be free. 'I don't want to rush it. I'm not going to rush anything anymore.'[27]

To placate their star, the producers thought it was worth the gamble releasing Connery from his contract and then re-signing him on a one-picture basis, obviously in the hope they could persuade him to carry on.[28] And as one of his main grumbles was how long each production took to make, a decision was reached to change the release pattern of the films, bringing out a new Bond now every two years rather than every twelve months. The fact that the movies had incrementally grown in size and logistics was also taken into account.

Interestingly, it was around this time that Broccoli began testing the waters for his own solo production away from Bond. He had given David Lean a copy of Stuart Cloete's 1963 historical novel *Rags of Glory*, about the Boer War. Lean did consider the proposal for a while but in the end was put off by the story material, which he found to be distasteful, as he wrote to a friend: 'Very good in an awful sort of way. Horrible revelations, to me, of white slave traffic and how they used to batter wretched girls into tartdom. Very shocking and I see exactly how Cubby Broccoli will make an enormous money-spinner out of it – but not with me.'[29] The idea went no further.

As usual, Saltzman had a drawer full of projects on the go. By far the most interesting proposition was a screen biography of one of Canada's most colourful historical figures: Cuthbert Grant. Born of a Scottish father and a half-Cree Indian mother, Grant is considered the first leader of the Metis Nation, that is, people of Canada who can trace their descendants to the indigenous population and the first settlers. As warden of the plains, also a sheriff, a magistrate, a doctor, a teacher and a bit of a drinker, Grant brought peace to western Canada during the bloody fur-trade wars of the early 1800s. In a bid to boost the Canadian film industry, practically non-existent at the time, Saltzman planned to use a majority of Canadian technicians and actors, along with the hope that Sean Connery would play Grant, a man the producer called, 'a fabulous character'.[30] Probably the sheer scale of the production thwarted Saltzman's ambitions for it and he instead returned to safer ground and another Harry Palmer thriller.

Funeral in Berlin was based on the third novel in Deighton's series and sent Palmer to Germany to arrange the defection of a high-ranking Russian intelligence officer. After their fractious relationship on *Ipcress*, Sydney J. Furie was never considered for the director's chair, a decision Deighton ruefully regretted, so Saltzman turned to Guy Hamilton.

Having expertly contributed to the *Thunderball* script, Saltzman brought in John Hopkins to work on the screenplay. Like Cubby, Harry worked closely with his writers and Hopkins enjoyed his time with the producer, recalling particularly one long discussion with him about the dramatic use of irony. 'He'd say things like, "This point is too important for implication," while the telephone was going non-stop. His telephone has an inferiority complex, it rings all the time.'[31] In the end, Hopkins left the project to be replaced by Evan Jones. As Deighton observed at the time, 'Harry goes through writers like a meat chopper.'[32]

Following the success of *The Ipcress File*, Saltzman was able to double the budget on the new film, allowing for extensive shooting across West Berlin, from the Tempelhof Airport to the cabaret district at night. Things were tenser when they shot near the heavily patrolled Berlin Wall. East German border guards deliberately shone mirrors into the camera lenses until the crew had to move to another location.[33]

For one exciting sequence a mock-up of the wall was built by the art department on a nearby stretch of land, leading to an amusing incident that Peter Lamont recalled. 'Some old boy used to walk past every day and suddenly overnight the wall went up and this poor bloke almost had a heart attack. He said, "Ven did zis happen?" He couldn't believe it because it looked just like the real thing.'[34]

Saltzman still maintained a good relationship with his star, though Caine was the first to admit that there were two quite distinctive Harrys. 'One is the social Harry, who is extremely charming and witty. Then there's the other Harry, the one you hardly ever see until he descends on the set like a whirlwind.'[35] This was the side of Saltzman that earned him a lot of enemies in the business. In a 1966 newspaper profile of the producer it was revealed that Saltzman was known to walk onto a set and vilify an actor in front of the whole crew for laziness.[36] Honor Blackman claimed that those who hated him did so because he told the truth, 'And is usually so scathingly, brutally honest, he knocks you down.'[37] Caine himself had to acknowledge that Saltzman was a very insensitive man. 'Whereas someone else would coach their criticism in language that would let you off lightly, Harry would start with, "This is crap!" and it went downhill from there.'[38]

While *Funeral in Berlin* was in production, Saltzman took time off to travel down to Cannes for the film festival that May, 1966, where a great deal of shenanigans went on regarding the screening of *Chimes at Midnight*. That year director Richard Lester was on the jury, and one morning he received a phone call from Saltzman asking him to come to his suite at the Carlton hotel at four o'clock, it was very important. Lester duly obliged. 'I knocked on the door, the door opens, and inside is Orson Welles and a lot of people and champagne and tits and ass and Wow!'[39]

Saltzman sees who it is and walks barefoot over to the door and pushes Lester out into the corridor, then closes the door behind him. 'We're counting on you, you know.' This is said, Lester recalled, 'with a CIA-operative menacing tone'. Lester asks what he means by this. 'You've got to be more realistic. Anyway, I've got to get back.' With that Saltzman is gone and the door is firmly closed in Lester's face. Walking back to his room, Lester was at a loss as to what to make of it all. He assumed they must have guaranteed Saltzman the Palme D'Or if he got Welles to turn up. As it was, there was not much appetite within the jury to award *Chimes at Midnight* with anything. Instead they came up with a compromise and presented Welles with a special prize.[40]

11

Twice is the Only Way to Live

Before a frame was even taken on the new Bond film, Connery had already revealed his intention to throw in the towel. The producers must have known it was coming, indeed had probably reached the conclusion that the public came to see James Bond in action, not necessarily Connery, a prognosis proven correct when the remainder of the series continued to be a box office success regardless of who inhabited the role. As Broccoli confirmed to television journalist Alan Whicker during filming, this Bond would certainly not be the last. 'If Sean doesn't want to do it, after all we can't force him, then this won't stop us from making another Bond that audiences out there want to see.'[1]

Connery wasn't the only defection in the camp. Peter Hunt had always coveted ambitions to direct and felt his contribution to the series warranted promotion to the director's chair. When Harry and Cubby refused, loath to lose someone they regarded one of the best editors in the business, Hunt threatened to walk out. To calm matters, Cubby suggested he take a holiday, chose any location he liked and Eon would foot the bill. Hunt said he'd always rather fancied a trip around the world, to which Saltzman reportedly replied, 'Why can't you go to Brighton for the weekend like everyone else!'[2]

Fast forward a bit to when the producers arrive in Tokyo on a location recce, and who should they bump into at their hotel but Peter Hunt, just flown in from Australia; was this luck or strategically planned? Either way, Cubby asked Hunt if he would take on second unit duties with the promise of helming the next Bond. Hunt agreed.[3]

The producers' choice to direct *You Only Live Twice* was Lewis Gilbert, who had made something of a career helming patriotic British war films like *Reach for the Sky* (1956), *Carve Her Name with Pride* (1958) and *Sink the Bismarck!* (1960), then surprised everyone with the Michael Caine hit *Alfie* (1966).

Only Gilbert's first instinct was to turn the job down, saying, 'It was like being Elizabeth Taylor's fifth husband – I knew what I had to do – but I didn't know how to make it different!'[4] Broccoli called Gilbert the next day. 'You can't turn down this film, because you have one of the world's biggest audiences waiting to see what sort of a hash you'll make of it!' How could Gilbert refuse such an approach. This was one of Cubby's great skills: he knew how to handle people, 'he was persuasive in a quiet way.'[5]

As a newcomer, Gilbert found the heady world of Bond an overwhelming experience, especially the producers themselves:

> You'd go to see Harry and he'd be getting his hair cut and having a suit made while he was talking to you. And there'd always be at least five people hanging around outside to see him, bringing him updates on hare-brained schemes that never came to anything. Harry was a man of intuition and he was always buying into new systems and ideas. Cubby was always much more conservative.[6]

It did seem that Saltzman revelled in chaos. An agent recalled going to his office to conclude a deal on behalf of his client and having to conduct business leaning out of a window, since the room was so crowded. At the same time the phone was constantly ringing, and every so often Saltzman would shout over his shoulder to someone. Then, spotting some people he recognised down in the street, he started another conversation with them.[7]

With Gilbert on board, the first problem the producers identified was that the Fleming novel was not going to translate adequately enough to a traditional Bond screen adventure, certainly not the type that audiences had grown accustomed to. Fleming himself had identified this problem when he sold the film rights and told Broccoli, 'You're going to have to update my stories eventually, just try to have the scripts written the way I have done in my early books.' Certainly, Cubby was the first to suggest that as they went on with the series, the books became largely redundant. 'They have had to be updated, rewritten, made more spectacular.'[8] *You Only Live Twice* became the first Bond film that differed radically from the source material, with its fantastical plotline, clearly influenced by the then current space race, of SPECTRE hijacking orbiting Soviet and US capsules in an effort to inaugurate a third world war.

With Richard Maibaum unavailable, Saltzman brought in an American television writer called Harold Jack Bloom, but his screenplay ideas didn't work out, though enough elements did remain that entitled him to a screen credit.

Next, the producers made an unusual if imaginative choice in recruiting short story and children's author Roald Dahl. It was Cubby who called the writer at home. 'I remember this man saying his name was Broccoli. I thought he was joking. After all, a man with the last name of a vegetable? It was funny. I really hadn't heard of him.'[9]

Dahl was invited to meet the producers at South Audley Street and began things by confessing he wasn't really a Bond fan and had only seen *Goldfinger*. That could be easily rectified: prints of all the films and a projector, along with someone to work it, would be sent to his home. 'This was the first small hint I was to get of the swift, efficient, expansive way in which the Bond producers operated,' said the writer.[10]

Next, Dahl was told that they were using hardly any of the Fleming novel. The Japanese setting would remain intact, along with the names of the characters, but the scenario would have to be completely invented. He was then asked if he could deliver a first draft in six weeks, and a second one fourteen weeks after that. Dahl said he could manage that. Cubby reached across the desk and put a call through to Dahl's film agent in the States, the famous Swifty Lazar, and a deal was made on the spot.[11]

Before starting work, Dahl attended three story conferences with the producers: 'Harry would usually nod off to sleep in the middle.'[12] Afterwards he was under no illusions that he was writing to a strict formula, especially when it came to Bond's women, of which there had to be three. 'The first gets killed. The second gets killed. And the third gets a fond embrace during the closing sequence. And that's the formula. They found it's cast-iron. So, you've got to kill two of them off after he has screwed them a few times.'[13]

With Ted Moore unavailable, the producers brought in one of the most revered cameramen in world cinema: Freddie Young. It's no fluke *You Only Live Twice* is one of the best shot films in the Bond canon. In London, Cubby and Harry arranged a party with over 200 guests to celebrate Young's fifty years in the industry; it was a nice gesture. Later, Broccoli asked Young to fly out to Hollywood to personally review and pass all 600 prints of the film due for wide release. Young recalled that he and his family were given the VIP treatment by Cubby, a sumptuous suite at the Beverly Wilshire hotel, plus days out to Disneyland and baseball games.[14]

With much of the film taking place in Japan, the producers arranged a location recce to look for suitable locations in the spring of 1966. Cubby rented a helicopter and together with Ken Adam, Lewis Gilbert and Freddie Young covered something like two thirds of the country over the course of a couple of weeks. A nervous flyer at the best of times, Gilbert was not the calmest of passengers, especially when he met their pilot, an elderly chap. 'He laid the map on the table, and as he pointed out our route his hand didn't stop shaking. Cubby and Ken, enjoying my misery, were struggling not to laugh.'[15] It actually turned out that the pilot trained in the war as a kamikaze. Much more appealing was the way that, after each trip, Cubby would radio ahead to wherever they were flying and order a massage for everyone.[16]

In the novel, Fleming has Blofeld hiding out in a strange island fortress. By the final week of the recce nothing matching its description could be found and things were looking desperate. Flying over the island of Kyushu, the south-westernmost of Japan's main islands, the helicopter passed over an area of volcanoes. It was a great visual image. Broccoli suggested it might be fun to put the villain's headquarters inside one of them. 'Cubby always looked for a hook for the storyline,' related Dana. 'When he saw the top of this volcano, that was his hook and he thought everything is going to now start out of this.'[17] The idea immediately appealed to Adam. 'I thought it would be great fun to design and I did a quick scribble. Cubby liked it and asked, "How much is it going to cost?" I said, "Cubby I have no idea." And he said, "If I give you a million dollars can you do it?" And that's when my worries started.'[18]

A million dollars was a huge figure in 1966, and almost the entire budget of the first Bond film, but as Adam recalled Cubby didn't blink an eye as he told him to go ahead. That was the mark of Cubby: not only did he show supreme confidence in Adam's abilities, but the balls to take this huge gamble. Both he and Saltzman were playing with the biggest set of toys around, and in the movie industry no one could touch them. Harry, though, had quite a shock when he heard what Broccoli had agreed. 'But Cubby was the gambler, more of a gambler in that sense,' said Adam.[19]

At the end of the recce everyone had seats booked on BOAC Flight 911 from Tokyo's Haneda Airport to Hong Kong on 5 March. Just hours before take-off, Broccoli was invited to watch a ninja demonstration and cancelled the reservations. It was an incredible piece of luck. Just twenty-five minutes after taking off, Flight 911 suddenly encountered abnormally severe turbulence which caused the aircraft to break up and it crashed on the wooded slopes of Mount Fuji, killing all 124 people on board.

The producers managed to secure a healthy budget of $9.5 million for what was to be one of the most logistically challenging and technical films to make in the entire series. By this time the producers could pretty much name their price. When a franchise was delivering the kind of box office numbers the Bonds were, no one at United Artists was going to say no to them. This was also reflected in the personal payments Broccoli and Saltzman received

Cubby on the set of his first picture as producer *The Red Beret*, starring Alan Ladd.

ɪrry the dreamer, Harry the showman, a ɪirligig of ideas and mad schemes.

The producers had a good relationship with Ian Fleming and valued his expertise and ideas. (Courtesy of Rex Features)

Saltzman was at the forefront of the British new wave cinema that made a star out of Albert Finney. (Courtesy of Rex Features)

Cubby's salute to the Royal Marines won favour with both Earl Mountbatten and Prince Philip.

At the premiere of *From Russia With Love* with Sean Connery and his wife Diane Cilento.

Broccoli tried to maintain amicable relations with his star, but Connery was to fall out with both men.

Saltzman put Michael Caine on a 7-year contract to play Harry Palmer, the role that made him a star

The producers and their wives, Jacqueline and Dana (in white), the queens behind the throne. (Courtesy of Rex Features)

Considered a flop on release, the Broccoli-produced *Chitty Chitty Bang Bang* has endured to become a children's classic.

The producer's relationship was fraught almost from the start, with many amazed it lasted as long as it did. (Courtesy of Rex Features)

Saltzman hoped his all-star epic tribute to the RAF would bring him a knighthood.

With George Lazenby, the man given the daunting task of replacing Connery as Bond.

e producers present Bond No. 3, Roger Moore, to the press. (Courtesy of Rex Features)

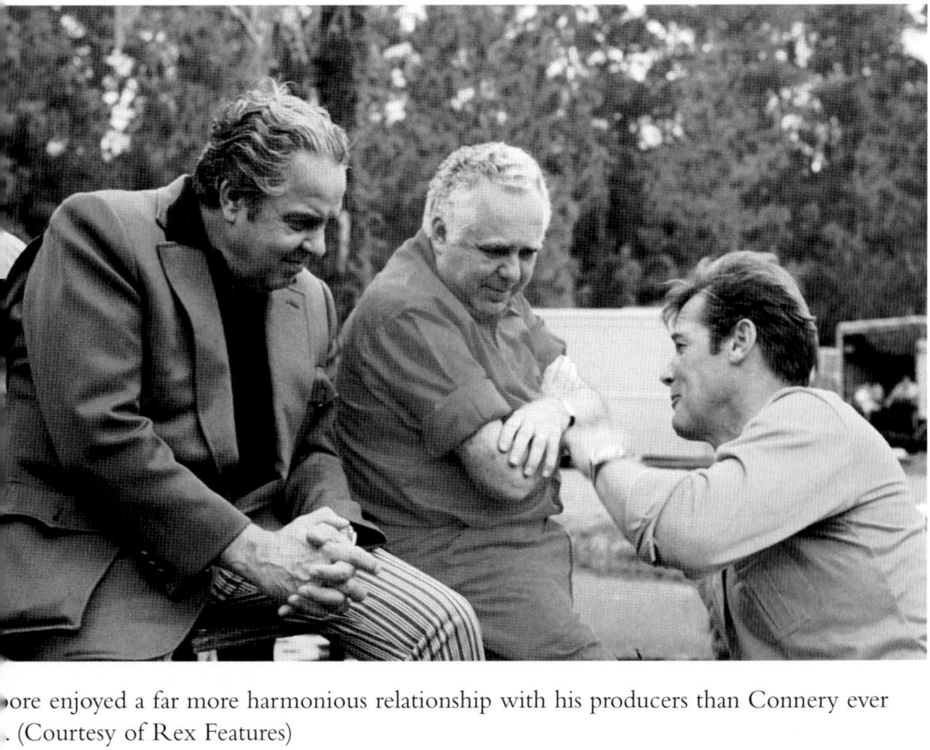

ore enjoyed a far more harmonious relationship with his producers than Connery ever . (Courtesy of Rex Features)

Broccoli first worked with Bernard Lee, who played Bond's boss M, in 1957 and the two men became life-long friends. (Courtesy of Rex Features)

On the set of *Live and Let Die*, within just two years the producers had gone their separate ways. (Courtesy of Rex Features)

as producers, which United Artists kept bumping up as the pictures grew in popularity, starting with $80,000 on *Dr No*, $120,000 on *From Russia with Love* and ever higher, until by 1967 the figure hit $420,000.[20]

Another reward saw an improvement in their profit participation, rising from an original figure of 50 per cent to 75 per cent.[21] It was a huge sweetener from United Artists, no doubt in part to discourage the producers from thinking about going to another studio, but also an acknowledgement of what they had achieved. United Artists could afford to be so generous; even though they were putting up all the money, the company incurred few financial risks since the Bonds were now such huge money-makers. Nor could anyone see an end in sight. An assessment that might have been better coming with a caveat had the true extent of the parlous nature behind the scenes been truly known.

Ironically, at the moment the Bond films reached their peak, in terms of popularity and financial muscle, not only did the producers face losing their star, but their own relationship with each other had reached something of a crisis point. There had always been tension between Cubby and Harry, heated arguments behind closed doors, but these disagreements had begun to seep out into the public domain. An article in showbiz bible *Variety* that April had already raised the possibility of the two partners splitting. But it was more than just a conflict of personalities according to Broccoli; 'It was two totally contrasting attitudes to Bond.'[22]

As we have seen, once Bond was up and running, Saltzman was off looking for new lands to conquer. While Broccoli retained his enthusiasm for Bond as the sole interest in his career, Saltzman saw the franchise as merely a platform to expand. 'Cubby just wanted to make films, make them well and sanely,' said one of Saltzman's associates, the film director Andre de Toth. 'Harry wanted to make them to have power and money for the fulfilment of his dreams.'[23]

Cubby always admired Harry's supreme ability, that wasn't in question; what did begin to grate with him was the feeling that his partner wasn't 100 per cent committed to Bond. 'He'd make an appearance on the set or location, do a lot of shouting, then he'd be off to France, Italy or someplace else, making a film, taking over a company, doing what he loves most of all, playing the celebrated entrepreneur.'[24] There is no better example of this than the summer of 1968 when Harry was overseeing the close of filming on the *Battle of Britain*. Despite his war epic being one of the most challenging films ever made, Saltzman was also involved in the latest Bond film, including the search for a new actor to play 007, a science fiction musical, a comedy about a modern Jesus to be shot in France by Luis Bunuel, a film about the daughter of Karl Marx, a Zola novel he wanted to make with Simone Signoret and

Jeanne Moreau, and the life of Nijinsky starring Rudolf Nureyev; no wonder Broccoli often lost patience with him. As Saltzman himself admitted, 'Cubby was only interested in the Bonds. He said I was crazy to want to produce other films.'[25]

For Broccoli, making Bond into the biggest thing in movies was enough of a challenge, and he never understood why Harry didn't feel the same and needed all this extracurricular stuff. Maybe it was part of his nature, as Saltzman's daughter Hilary observed: 'He had the attention span of a gnat. He couldn't be idle. He needed to be entertained and for him to be entertained it had to be a constant, there couldn't be a pause. He just always wanted to go one better, one higher, one longer, one stronger.'[26] This growing imbalance between the two men in their commitment to the Bond pictures, however, had reached a point where Cubby felt aggrieved that he was carrying the load of the franchise almost on his own.

These fissures also caused problems for those closest to the producers, key members of the Bond team like Ken Adam who found it increasingly problematic to maintain a close friendship with both of them. 'I began to feel like an unfaithful mistress because my wife and I used to play gin rummy at Harry's house in Denham and then Cubby wanted us to be with them at his house. It was very difficult to keep the balance.'[27]

The immediate result of all this was that Broccoli effectively became the working producer on *You Only Live Twice*, according to William P. Cartlidge, who had been brought onto the film by Lewis Gilbert as assistant director. 'Harry was around for pre-production,' said Cartlidge, 'and I did my best to avoid him. He was a bit of a bully and quite aggressive, the sort of guy you might have easily fallen out with. But once we started shooting Harry never came to Japan.'[28]

Neither was Saltzman much welcomed on the set by a certain actor. Connery could just about live with Broccoli, being the more accommodating of the pair, but it was a different story with Saltzman. 'Sean disliked Harry and the feeling was mutual,' confirmed Saltzman's assistant Sue St John. 'Harry considered that they'd created a monster.'[29] According to Cartlidge, the animosity between the two men was palpable. 'Sean told us that he would literally stop working if Harry came on the set. And Harry did suddenly turn up once on the stage at Pinewood and Sean stopped work right in mid-sentence.'[30]

This hatred of Saltzman by Connery was something Len Deighton for one could never really understand. Deighton knew Connery fairly well personally, and on more than one occasion asked him about it. He'd say, 'The way I see it Sean, is that neither you or I would be around here comparing Gucci shoes if it hadn't been for Harry.' But Connery wasn't having any of it. 'It was something deep-rooted in him,' said Deighton. 'And I just don't know what it was.'[31]

According to Ken Adam, who was close to the actor, Connery had begun 'An almost pathological dislike' of both Harry and Cubby.[32] This, combined with his frustrations and boredom of playing the role of Bond, resulted in his professionalism as an actor being tested to the limits on *You Only Live Twice*. 'He was fine with the crew Sean, but he was grumpy,' recalled William P. Cartlidge. 'He was, what you might call in any other business, working to rule. He was doing what he had to do, no more and no less. And that was all to do with him falling out with the producers.'[33]

In London, the obligatory trawl through hundreds of actresses to select the right combination of Bond women had been long-lasting and exhaustive. Two Japanese actresses were selected, Akiko Wakabayashi and Mie Hama, while the role of the latest femme fatale was judged to be better suited for a European to play. German actress Eva Renzi had recently appeared as an Israeli agent in *Funeral in Berlin* and Saltzman was keen for her to jump ship from Palmer to 007, but Eva had no intention of being a Bond girl. Her refusal enraged Saltzman, as she was to recall. 'He said, "Who do you think you are, you think you're Elizabeth Taylor, there are 50,000 girls standing in line, you bitch!" He hated me for having the guts to say no, I don't want to be this fucking Bond girl.'[34]

Instead, fellow German Karin Dor was flown to London and put up in the Dorchester while she made her test alongside numerous other competing candidates. After being chosen, Saltzman was sanctioned to carry out contract talks with her agent, Ruth Killer, who was aptly named given her tough, no-nonsense reputation. 'The negotiations took six hours,' Karin recalled. 'After which my agent came down and said, "Let's go, I cannot negotiate with that man." We were about to take off and Saltzman came running down, took her arm, pulled Ruth out of the car and said to me, "You have the worst agent I have ever worked with!"'[35] Saltzman had obviously met his match. Ruth Killer knew how poorly paid some of the previous Bond girls had been, and fought hard to get her client the kind of money her experience and profile in Europe merited. It was pay up or don't. Saltzman paid.

Filming on *You Only Live Twice* got underway as usual at Pinewood Studios. With the World Cup just days away from kicking off, the English football team made a well-publicised visit to the studio. Cartlidge can't be sure, but is fairly confident that it was Broccoli who organised it. 'He was good at that kind of stuff.'[36] The players met with Connery, were given a guided tour around and then everyone had lunch together in the studio restaurant.

By the time the final took place, the crew were in Japan shooting and obviously most keen to find out how the England team got on. Cartlidge led a delegation to the Japanese production office to ask, 'Who won the World Cup?' Only for the Japanese to reply, 'What World Cup?' At that time, football was not of particular interest to anyone in the country. Eventually news reached them of England's success and Broccoli managed to get a 16mm copy of the game and showed it to the crew.[37]

Had Connery not already decided to leave Bond, his experience in Japan may very well have proved the final straw. 'It was a nightmare,' recalled Cartlidge.[38] Filming on the streets of Tokyo was a trial due to excessive crowds and Connery was followed everywhere by the press, not giving him a moment's peace. As a result, Broccoli hired fourteen security men to look after him and keep photographers at bay. 'So, the first morning we lined up these security men as Sean's car arrived, six on each side,' Gilbert recalled. 'Sean got out of the car and suddenly twelve guards whipped out twelve cameras and all started clicking away. Well, that was the end of the security guards.'[39]

Roald Dahl was brought over to Japan to be on hand should any script revisions be needed, and saw first hand just how well-drilled the Bond unit was. 'You went everywhere by helicopter. If the location was 10 miles away and rather hard to get to, like a fishing village, you would go there by helicopter and find that they had already dug a helicopter landing pad out of a cliff.'[40]

The writer was also well placed during the whole shoot to observe the growing acrimony between the two producers. 'Cubby was marvellous with us. He took that one over. He was in charge. Harry put in an appearance, but he didn't get too close to Cubby.'[41]

Back in England, work began on Ken Adam's colossal volcano set, built on the Pinewood backlot. Such was the size of the construction it took practically every lamp in the studio to light, according to Freddie Young.[42] When filming ended, Cubby and Harry were of a mind to leave the set standing in order to adapt it for future productions or lease it out, since the damn thing had cost so much. Unfortunately, the construction hadn't been designed for that purpose and was demolished. Broccoli and Ken Adam were never to make that same mistake again, and working on *The Spy Who Loved Me* the super tanker set used for the climactic battle was designed and built at the same time as the construction of a solid stage around it to be used again and again – the now iconic 007 stage.

With the film's climax taking place within the volcano, audiences got to see for the first time Bond's nemesis Ernst Stavro Blofeld. Finding a suitable actor to play the role proved something of a problem, until Cubby and Gilbert received a telegram from Saltzman, who was in LA. He'd seen the perfect guy, a Czech actor called Jan Werich, and he was flying him to England to start work that very week. Neither Cubby nor Gilbert had heard of Mr Werich, didn't know what he looked like, if he could act, or even speak English. A quick fact-check established his credentials but really the two men were none the wiser. 'So, on Harry's word we took this guy,' said Gilbert. When Werich arrived at the studio he just didn't look menacing at all. Gilbert thought he resembled Father Christmas with his elderly looks and white beard. Cubby made the decision to shoot on the actor for a day to see if it worked out. It didn't.[43]

Phoning round trying to find a replacement, they heard Donald Pleasance was available and he was rushed in. Given how little time Pleasance had to prepare, it's even more impressive that he was to give what is now an iconic performance. Pleasance later admitted that the producers liked the little quirks he'd given the role but didn't find him 'physically imposing'.[44] It was agreed at the last minute to give the bald actor a jagged scar down his face, which critics later joked made him resemble a cracked boiled egg.

Returning to score his fourth Bond movie, John Barry's sound had become one of the unmistakable traits of the Bond formula, which made Saltzman's decision to hire a musical director, without the composer's knowledge, baffling to say the least. It was another nail in the coffin of their fraught relationship, following the problems over the *Goldfinger* song. Barry had come to find Saltzman a particularly difficult person to deal with, sometimes impossible to deal with. 'There were times when I would tell him to go to hell.'[45] And now he found his authority being undermined. Cubby stood by his composer, complaining, 'Why does he need help?' but Saltzman was insistent. It was a collaboration doomed to fail; Barry simply ignored most of the man's advice and he eventually left.[46]

Following the now established tradition of a popular recording artist performing the title song, numerous names were considered, including Aretha Franklin and The Walker Brothers. In the end, Cubby called his good friend Frank Sinatra and asked him to sing it. 'No, I don't want to do it,' the legendary crooner replied. 'But, you know, my daughter, she's really good. Have Nancy do it.'[47]

Opening in the summer of 1967, *You Only Live Twice* was another international hit, although its financial performance was certainly compromised by the release a few months earlier of the all-star comedy spoof *Casino Royale*. This was the one title not included in the deal the producers originally struck with Fleming, being the property of director Gregory Ratoff. On the occasion of his death, Broccoli contacted Ratoff's widow in the hope of striking a deal, but the rights were snapped up by Charlie Feldman, who represented the widow's business affairs. This was something of an irony given Feldman's past association with Cubby. Feldman originally intended to make a serious screen adaptation, and even approached Broccoli to see if he would loan out Connery for his picture. When that request was instantly quashed, Feldman suggested a partnership. This time Broccoli was interested, envisaging a similar arrangement to the one made with Kevin McClory. Only Feldman's terms proved unacceptable: 75 per cent of the profits for him, 25 per cent for Cubby and Harry and United Artists. 'Charlie,' said Cubby. 'You're going to have to make the picture on your own.'[48]

Critical reaction was polarised, some enjoying the grandiose spectacle, others complaining that the outlandish visuals came at the expense of logic and a decent plot. Alexander Walker in the *Evening Standard* had no illusions as to where he thought the series was going. 'The Bond formula has now been run into the ground and only requires a headstone. But the hallmarks of a Broccoli-Saltzman production may ensure another box office hit.' Nor did he think the producers ought to be worried about Connery's impending exit. 'I'm sure Ken Adam could now run up a robot Bond to replace him.'

Despite the problems and logistical challenges of *You Only Live Twice*, Lewis Gilbert enjoyed his time working on Bond and would return to direct two more the following decade. He acknowledged that of all the producers he'd worked with previously, Broccoli and Saltzman were the only two who had creatively contributed to the film. He placed as one of their greatest strengths a knowledge of what audiences wanted to see:

> Directing is really very national. You tend to think only in terms of what will go in Britain. You're not practised into thinking what will go in Cambodia and Hong Kong. Cubby and Harry know. They've seen it happen on the other films and they have become experts. They're the only producers who really know their audience.[49]

However, on a personal level, Gilbert didn't particularly like Saltzman. 'Harry was ill for most of the picture, but he was quick tempered and mercurial, and not very charming to people, whereas Cubby was the opposite. He was very lovable, cheerful, always behind you, always helping you.'[50]

Midway through the shoot of *You Only Live Twice*, Gilbert, whether instructed by the producers or under his own volition, talked to Connery about his decision to leave Bond and attempted to change his mind:

> I was against him leaving and I used to say to him, 'Sean, you are taking a risk, because in a sense you are typecast now. You're in an incredible situation here, because when you're Bond you can do what the greatest actors in the world can't do. If you say to United Artists, I'll do the next Bond film, but I want to play Oedipus Rex or I want to do Hamlet, they'd say, 'Ok Sean, here's the money.' But he wouldn't listen, his mind was made up.[51]

One way in which the producers might have persuaded Connery to stay would've been to cut him in on the millions the series was raking in, both at the box office and in merchandise, most of which bore the actor's image. The fact that Dean Martin made more money with the first Matt Helm spy movie than Connery did on *Thunderball*, which took almost four times as much at the box office in America, was probably not lost on the actor.[52]

On Connery's behalf, Terence Young implored the producers to take him on as a partner. 'Make it Cubby, Harry and Sean. He'll stay with you because he's a Scotsman. He likes the sound of gold coins clinking together. He likes that lovely soft rustle of paper. He'll stay with you if he's a partner, but not if you use him as a hired employee.'[53] Remember, this is an actor who bought his own bank.

As far as Broccoli was concerned, the Bond films made Connery both a star and a very rich man, and as the series progressed he began to 'attribute his success to himself, rather than to anyone else' and to make impossible demands.[54] Neither did Broccoli appreciate some of the actor's remarks about how badly he was treated, quotes like, 'What I'm really tired of is a lot of fat-slob producers living off the backs of lean actors.'[55]

While their relationship was sometimes strained, at times only speaking through intermediaries,[56] Broccoli always reassured himself that on both a professional and personal footing he had always strived to keep good relations with his star, unlike what had happened with Saltzman. And yet, as Connery stepped down from his Bond role, the two men had never been further apart, a state of affairs that would never fully reconcile itself.

12

Palmer's Last Stand

Just a few days after *You Only Live Twice* opened in both the UK and US markets, Saltzman sent the writer Wolf Mankowitz and the accomplished British film director John Schlesinger, along with a small camera crew, to make a documentary in Israel about the current frayed political climate. The Six Day War had recently taken place between Israel and the neighbouring states of Egypt, Libya and Jordan. In London, Saltzman and Broccoli attended an emergency meeting of entertainment leaders at the Café Royal to raise funds for Israeli welfare projects in the immediate aftermath of the conflict. The two producers each pledged £25,000.[1]

Saltzman was clear about what he hoped his film might accomplish, the title said it all: *Israel: A Right to Live*. 'It's not a commercial venture. We're making a television film, rather like *Panorama*.'[2] Once finished, Saltzman hoped to make it available to TV stations around the world. However, apart from a few showings the film was to disappear completely.

Saltzman also lent his name to the second film directed by a new young filmmaker called Costa-Gavras. *Shock Troops* was adapted from a Second World War novel and followed a group of resistance fighters who free a group of political prisoners from a Nazi jail. The film failed both commercially and critically, but was invited to the Moscow Film Festival.

On safer ground, Saltzman turned once again to Harry Palmer, looking to bring the latest literary instalment to the screen, *Billion Dollar Brain*, in which Deighton had his hero up against an eccentric Texan billionaire and his private army set on bringing down the USSR by creating civil war in one of the Baltic states.

The first Palmer films had served as more realistic and serious takes on the spy genre; however, this time Saltzman wanted a fresh approach and that meant a new director. Returning for a third time as Palmer, Michael Caine had seen the documentary work of Ken Russell for the BBC arts programme *Monitor* and put his name forward as director. Russell was summoned to Saltzman's office. 'I know you do art films,' said Harry. 'And you're a very clever filmmaker, everyone knows that, but you need to break into features.'

'I've already made a feature, *French Dressing*,' said Russell. This was a rather lacklustre comedy made in 1964.

'Was that in black and white?' asked Saltzman.

'Yes.'

'Black and white doesn't count.'[3]

Deep down, Russell knew that Saltzman had no option but to make a deal since Caine wanted him for the film, and after a short pause the producer made his pitch: do *Billion Dollar Brain* and he would bankroll an art feature. Russell agreed and signed up.

Otto Heller, who had photographed the previous two Palmers, was hired and immediately went out to the main location of Finland for a recce. By the time of his return the film's production manager, Eva Monley, had raised concerns that working in such a cold environment might prove a problem for the veteran, now 70 years old, and that he ought to have a medical. Saltzman agreed and raised the issue with Heller, who point blank refused to undergo one.[4] Saltzman had no choice but to let the cameraman go and replaced him with Robert Krasker, the Oscar-winning cinematographer of *The Third Man* (1949). That didn't last long either, when Russell complained that Krasker's working methods went against his vision for the film. Saltzman was furious. 'Best cameraman in the world not good enough for you, huh? What're we gonna do now? We're not making *Nanook of the North*, y'know.'[5]

Russell ended up choosing Billy Williams, with whom he'd collaborated on a number of television ads. Williams had shot only a couple of minor British films but had recently worked for Tony Richardson on a short film and took a couple of reels of his work to show Saltzman. The reaction was positive: 'Let's give the kid a break,' said Saltzman. Williams was 38 at the time.[6] He went on to become a highly respected cinematographer, working on Russell's *Women in Love* (1969), *The Wind and the Lion* (1975) and *Gandhi* (1982).

Sharing producing chores with Saltzman on the picture was Andre de Toth, a charismatic Hungarian-American film director who had made his name in the late 1940s and '50s with a series of film noirs and Westerns. In recent times de Toth had found assignments hard to come by and was recovering from a serious skiing accident when Saltzman put him on his payroll, installing him in an office at South Audley. De Toth noticed there were two telephones in his office, one of which he was told never to use; it was so Saltzman could reach him at any time. 'He didn't like to wait.'[7]

Working within the Eon offices, de Toth judged Harry and Cubby to be 'the oddest odd couple', and that it was the 'biggest miracle' that their partnership lasted as long as it did.[8] He came to understand the working methods of Saltzman, too, and his capricious nature:

> He loved the idea of making pictures and he had flashes of genius, but his brilliant ideas usually didn't fit the characters or the situation. But before you could object, he came up with at least five more new ingenious ideas that had equally no place in that particular story. Luckily, he got bored quickly and left the story, the picture and you alone.[9]

To kick things off, Saltzman hosted a start-of-picture party in Helsinki, though by the end of it he was shrieking at the waiters to go easy on the caviar, 'You're ladlin' it out like stewed spinach. And quit serving vodka by the pint.'[10]

Inevitably, the country was experiencing one of the warmest winters for something like two centuries. The unprecedented early thaw resulted in streets bereft of snow and an armada of trucks had to drive out of the city in the early hours, load up with snow, and return to the city where laborers shovelled the snow over the streets ready for filming that day. Not just an inconvenience, the conditions were dangerous too. Filming in Helsinki on the bay, the crew had driven out onto the ice, which was a little unnerving when the wheels of the vehicles sank up to the axle hubs. Saltzman flew out one day to see how they were getting on and drove out to the location. 'All this slush!' he said. 'Can't you shoot it someplace else?'

'But Harry,' protested Russell. 'The scene is set on the sea. We need this vast expanse.'

There was a slight pause. 'The sea!' Saltzman exclaimed. 'You mean we're on the sea?' According to Russell, Saltzman hadn't realised he was out on the ice with 3,000 fathoms of Baltic Ocean beneath his feet. 'Get out!' he ordered and drove back to Helsinki as fast as he could. Saltzman was right, it was getting perilous out there. 'We were walking about up to our ankles in slush,' said Russell. 'And at the end the ice did start to crack up. Michael Caine, to his credit, was jumping from ice floe to ice floe as the ice melted around us.'[11]

Billion Dollar Brain was released at the close of 1967 and met with a lukewarm critical and box office reception. In some quarters the film was criticised for being too pro-Russian. 'I didn't realise the writer was a rabid communist,' recalled Russell. 'Actually, it's one of the very few films made in Hollywood where the communists were the heroes. The Texans were the villains.'[12]

Caine, too, had grown weary of the series, and was eager to avoid the sort of typecasting trap that his friend Sean Connery had experienced with James Bond. Telling Saltzman that he no longer wanted to play Palmer, the producer toyed with the idea of replacing Caine with another actor in a proposed fourth instalment, but in the end dropped the series altogether.

Deighton was a little disappointed his hero wasn't going to star in any more big screen adventures, but had begun to diversify anyway. This included purchasing an option on the film rights to *Oh! What a Lovely War*, a stage musical developed by Joan Littlewood in 1963. One of the first people he sought advice from was Saltzman, and he popped over to see him one afternoon:

> We sat and drank coffee together and he talked to me about the dangers and pitfalls, the treachery and delusion of the film world as if I was his son. As I got to my feet to leave, he added a final warning: 'Make sure you don't buy yourself a packet of litigation, Len.' A little chuckle. 'There are cheaper ways of getting into court.'

Years later, Deighton was to dwell upon the irony of those words.[13]

Deighton always enjoyed these meetings with Saltzman, and never forgot one encounter in his office when his gaze was directed by Harry to a large cupboard piled high with screenplays, books and stage plays. 'There's maybe 200 screen rights in there,' Harry boasted. 'There are things I'll probably never make.' He grabbed one at random. 'Look at this, I only bought it for the title. And this, let me show you this.' Harry took a book off a shelf. 'Read that,' he said, opening it at the first page. Deighton read it. 'Isn't that a great beginning,' said Saltzman. Deighton agreed, it was a very gripping first paragraph. 'That's all I bought it for,' Harry admitted. 'For that beginning.' This was an incident that seemed to sum the man up for Deighton. 'Harry was like a magpie.'[14]

As for Ken Russell, he was to look back with mixed feelings on his Saltzman experience, left with the undeniable feeling that everyone on the film was working for the producer and against him. 'It wasn't from me they were getting their next meal ticket.'[15] This was especially true whenever Russell and his wife were taken to dinner by Saltzman. Here the restaurant staff acceded to his every whim and Harry would always order the appetizer without anyone's consent. 'You're at liberty to choose the next course,' recalled Russell:

> but he'll often say, 'That looks good' and reach across to take half your food. Or say, 'Try this' and ram a forkful of his own dinner down your throat. It's very funny for the first few months, then it begins to lose its flavour and you see you're paying for your dinner by being courtiers.[16]

Despite all this, Russell recalled that Saltzman had promised to finance an 'art' film and turned up at his office one day to remind him.

'Yeah, yeah,' said Saltzman hesitatingly.

'I'd like to do one on Tchaikovsky.'

Russell saw Saltzman's face fall. 'Come back in a week,' he finally said.

A week elapsed and Russell duly returned. 'Ok, what about the Tchaikovsky film?'

Saltzman's face was beaming this time. 'The Soviets are doing one already with Dimitri Tiomkin and he's already started writing the music!'

This was indeed true. 'And when I saw the film,' said Russell, 'he'd re-scored Tchaikovsky's *Serenade for Strings*. It didn't sound like Tchaikovsky at all.'[17]

As it was, Russell did finally get to make his Tchaikovsky picture when United Artists asked him to do another film for them after the success of *Women in Love*. 'I said, "Yes, a film on Tchaikovsky." Their faces fell again. They asked what the story was about and I said, "It's about a homosexual who falls in love with a nymphomaniac." They gave me the money instantly.'[18]

Saltzman, though, had made a promise to Russell, and having discarded Tchaikovsky asked if the director had another idea. Yes, as it happened: what about a biopic on the great ballet dancer of the early twentieth century Vaslav Nijinsky? This left even less of an impression on the producer. 'What film on a dancer ever made money?' he snapped back.[19]

Despite reservations, Saltzman took Russell to Paris to see Maurice Bejart's production of *The Rite of Spring* by Igor Stravinsky, for which Nijinsky provided the scandalous choreography on its 1913 premiere, only Saltzman nodded off halfway through.[20]

Still unconvinced, Saltzman nevertheless put some money into pre-production; Melvyn Bragg wrote a script and Russell wanted ex-Royal Ballet member Christopher Gable to play the lead, with Oliver Reed pencilled in as Nijinsky's lover, the ballet impresario Diaghilev. Ever mindful of the box office and publicity opportunities, Harry insisted on Rudolf Nureyev, who since his defection to the West in the early 1960s had been courted by numerous movie producers into making his screen acting debut. Saltzman arranged for Nureyev to meet with him and Russell at a London restaurant. It was an unmitigated disaster. 'He was two hours late,' Russell recalled. 'He arrived with a girl to whom he never introduced us, consumed vast quantities of vodka and caviar, and looked over our heads all the time.'[21] After dinner they took a cab to a Mayfair cinema, where Saltzman had laid on a private screening of Russell's 1966 BBC film on Isadora Duncan. Nureyev hated it, lamenting the fact that Russell had desecrated a dancing icon. He would do the Nijinsky film only if Russell was not involved.

By this time Russell was happy for his association with Saltzman to come to an end. It was his belief that here was a producer unable to carry through his initial enthusiasm for a project, found reasons for not doing them and firing the director or writer, and then, if the enthusiasm returned, thought he could buy them back. 'I wouldn't work for him again. But my experience is the richer for having been associated with him. Although I went through hell, even hell is an experience.'[22]

Saltzman, though, was keen to keep the Nijinsky project alive and suggested Herbert Ross as director; Nureyev much preferred Franco Zeffirelli or Ingmar Bergman. Progress was slow until Saltzman contacted Tony Richardson, his old Woodfall comrade. Richardson responded immediately to the material and brought in the celebrated American playwright Edward Albee to produce a new screenplay. Albee's approach to the subject won the approval of Nureyev; here was an opportunity for a mainstream picture to present a frank depiction of a homosexual relationship and its aftermath when Nijinsky descends into madness after his affair ends with Diaghilev, now to be played by Paul Scofield.

With filming due to start in the late summer of 1970, Richardson flew out to St Petersburg to scout locations when news filtered back to him that Saltzman had pulled the plug. A stock market crisis meant the producer was unable to raise the money despite having already spent $1 million on the project.[23] Saltzman next proceeded to talk his way out of paying for the work already carried out, by pointing out the fact that Albee had written a number of scenes in the script containing no dialogue whatsoever: 'Harry claimed that these were amateurish and unprofessional,' said Richardson, 'and reneged on the deal.'[24] The director was furious. It was a sour end to a relationship that had done so much at Woodfall.

13

It's Fantasmagorical

As early as 1965, Saltzman and Broccoli hoped to make *Chitty Chitty Bang Bang* as a joint production, the first of what both men hoped would be a number of family-orientated pictures. There were also reports that the pair of them were going to produce a movie together about the notorious Australian outlaw Ned Kelly,[1] along with a television documentary based on Ian Fleming's 1963 travelogue *Thrilling Cities*,[2] in which the author gave his views on several major cities including Hong Kong, Tokyo, Honolulu, Los Angeles, New York and Berlin.

What happened in the interim is anyone's guess. Did they fall out over how to approach the material, or was Saltzman just too preoccupied elsewhere? Whatever the reason, it was only *Chitty Chitty Bang Bang* that went ahead and as a solo Broccoli production.

Interestingly, right from the time of *Dr No*'s success Broccoli, like his partner, harboured a desire to produce other kinds of pictures on his own, but each 007 epic became so complicated to make, especially when they were coming out once a year, that they consumed too much of his time. He also felt a strong responsibility to audiences round the world who were waiting for each new Bond to come out. That desire to occasionally break away from Bond was always there, though, and one ambition was to make a big Western with someone like John Ford.[3] As it turned out, *Chitty Chitty Bang Bang* became Cubby's one and only non-Bond movie post-1962.

The origin of *Chitty Chitty Bang Bang* goes back to 1961 when Ian Fleming already knew he was a dying man. Having suffered two heart attacks, and ignoring doctors' advice to reduce his alcohol and nicotine intake, Fleming decided to leave something permanent for his beloved only child, Caspar, then 9 years old. He drew inspiration from the bedtime stories he used to read to Caspar about a magical car, and like his other alter-ego, James Bond, injected more than a little wish fulfilment into the story's protagonist, an eccentric professor called Commander Potts, whose motto for his children is: 'Never say "no" to adventures. Always say "yes," otherwise you'll lead a very dull life.'

By May, Fleming had sufficient material to send to his publisher and received only positive noises back. The hope was this could be the first of an entire series of stories. This was not to be after Fleming suffered that fatal heart attack, ironically on Caspar's twelfth birthday. *Chitty Chitty Bang Bang* was published posthumously two months later.

Cubby was first drawn to the book when he began to read it to his children and no doubt saw its potential as a film after the huge success of Disney's *Mary Poppins*, which had vied with *Goldfinger* to become box office champ of 1964. Cubby began pre-production work on *Chitty* early in 1966, and such was his desire to emulate *Mary Poppins* in both tone and style that he was determined to hire the same songwriting team, brothers Richard and Robert Sherman. The problem was they worked exclusively for Disney, and would he be able to prise them away? In the end, Walt was happy to give the brothers his blessing to work on the project.

Broccoli set up a meeting with the Sherman brothers at his suite in the Beverly Hills Hotel. Bud Ornstein of United Artists was there, anxiously looking at his watch. Cubby had hired Roald Dahl to write the script and the two men had just flown back from the Far East, researching material for *You Only Live Twice*. 'Dahl will be here very soon,' said Ornstein. 'He must have just fallen asleep or something. You know it's a fifteen-hour flight from the Orient.'[4]

Robert Sherman didn't think much of that excuse, Broccoli was there, jetlag or no jetlag, but he was content to wait a bit longer. Time passed, and there was still no sign of Dahl. Finally, he arrived, looking somewhat bedraggled, and Broccoli made the introductions. 'These are the fellas who wrote all those terrific songs for *Mary Poppins*.'

Suitably unimpressed, Dahl refused to acknowledge the Shermans with a handshake, and instead turned to Cubby. 'You got me all the way back from Bangkok today to meet two Jewish Hollywood songwriters?! Jesus Christ!'

Robert Sherman took one look at Broccoli, 'I'm sorry, Cubby,' and then facing Dahl square in the face said, 'Fuck you, mister.'[5]

The two brothers promptly marched out of the suite. Robert Sherman took one look behind him and caught a glimpse of Broccoli's expression. 'He was dumbfounded.' Bud Ornstein ran after them, imploring both to come back. 'Really guys. It means so very much to Cubby to have you both aboard. Believe me. Roald was just exhausted.'

By this time Robert Sherman had reached the bar, Richard had already left. 'What will I tell Cubby?' implored Ornstein.

'Tell him to get rid of the shit heel or forget about us.'[6]

Dahl later apologised for his insensitivity, and he and Robert Sherman became keen drinking buddies and worked well together on the film.

Broccoli was delighted about the writers' reconciliation, since the Shermans were pivotal in what he was trying to accomplish, building a film that was to be the best of two worlds – Disney and Bond. It made sense to recruit from the Bond team, people he trusted and felt comfortable with, such as Ken Adam, Peter Hunt, Peter Lamont and John Stears. But he also brought in a lot of the *Poppins* crew, not just the Shermans but the same musical supervisor, Irwin Kostal, and the same choreographers, Marc Breaux and Dee Dee Wood.

Most ambitious of all, Cubby wanted to reunite Julie Andrews with Dick Van Dyke, but he fell at the first hurdle when Andrews rebuffed his advances. Van Dyke didn't want anything to do with it either and turned the role down several times, citing a weak script. 'However, each time I said no, Cubby came back with more money.'[7] Eventually it came to a point where the money on offer was just too dumb to refuse. By then he'd also been given a sneak preview of some of the Sherman compositions and liked what he heard. There was one stipulation: no way was he going to repeat his mistake on *Mary Poppins* and even attempt another British accent, it would be his own American voice. Cubby agreed.[8]

Losing out on Julie Andrews, London-born actress/singer Sally Ann Howes was chosen to play Potts's love interest in the film, the deliciously sounding Truly Scrumptious, who drives a car with the registration plate CUB 1, presumably a homage to the producer. Mixing the requisite amount of sex appeal with Edwardian schoolmarm primness, Howes makes the part her own, and has perhaps stated the reason for the film's enduring appeal better than almost anyone else when she said: 'If you put *Mary Poppins* together with James Bond this would be their child.'[9]

For his director, Cubby turned to a man whose talent he greatly respected and whose excellent work on the *Oscar Wilde* film he had never forgotten, Ken Hughes. Only Hughes wasn't sure whether or not to accept the job and discussed the prospect at length with his wife Cherry. 'He didn't want to get stuck in the children's musical genre. Nor did he think it was right that Cubby was making *Mary Poppins* part two, which is what Cubby really wanted to do.'[10]

Finally accepting, Hughes voiced concerns over the script and there were some messy disagreements between himself and Dahl that left the writer fuming. 'I was very badly treated by Cubby on that one,' Dahl later claimed. 'Ken Hughes completely rewrote my script and Broccoli did nothing to interfere.'[11] Nor did the problems end there either, since Broccoli felt the need to draft in Richard Maibaum to carry out some uncredited script doctoring.

Shooting began in July 1967, and for Van Dyke it turned into the most exhausting picture he ever worked on. The dance numbers took weeks to rehearse and shoot. The final shot of the 'Me Ol' Bamboo' sequence required twenty-three takes in order for all the dancers to execute their moves in perfect synchronisation.[12]

Van Dyke had arrived in England with his entire family in tow, though as time went on his wife Margie began to complain of ill health and the opinion of a doctor was urgently sought. The prognosis was not good: there was a possibility she might have cervical cancer. As Margie rushed back to the States with her children to undertake medical tests, Van Dyke told Cubby the situation and that he needed some time off to fly home to be with his wife. Cubby said he understood totally, indeed would do the same in his position. 'Before I left, he even put his arm around me and said, "Don't worry, we'll shoot around you."'[13]

Thankfully it was good news, the tests came back negative and after a few days Van Dyke was ready to return. 'I flew back to Europe only to have my agent inform me that Cubby had docked me $80,000 for missing work. Furious, I didn't want to talk to him after that.'[14]

In spite of that, Van Dyke did reveal an extraordinary conversation with Broccoli just as the picture was winding down. With Connery having walked out on Bond, how did he fancy taking on the role of 007? Van Dyke wasn't sure if Cubby was kidding. 'Have you heard my British accent?' he said, referring to his much downtrodden attempt at playing a Cockney in *Mary Poppins*. 'Oh, that's right, forget it,' answered Broccoli.[15]

As for the Sherman brothers, they couldn't have found Cubby more accommodating. Both of them spent a lot of time in England preparing the film, but when shooting began Richard went back to Los Angeles because his wife was giving birth to their third child. Robert remained in England, and as the production dragged on he asked Broccoli if he could bring his wife Joyce and young family over. Broccoli thought it was a great idea and said not to worry about the cost. It was on him. That included booking a series of adjoining suites at the Dorchester Hotel, one for each of Robert's three kids and one for Joyce and himself:

> The suites took up half of the eighth floor and had a view of Hyde Park. On the other side of the hallway resided the Shah of Iran. His rooms weren't park side though. Ours were! This would become our headquarters for the next number of months. What luxury! And what a generous man Cubby was![16]

When Broccoli heard that Robert's 7-year old daughter, Tracy, and his own daughter Barbara had birthdays just one day apart, he and Dana threw a lavish party at their home in Green Street. 'In addition to this, Cubby purchased dozens of colour television sets and donated them to London children's homes in the girls' names.'[17]

Broccoli assembled an exceptional supporting cast to back up the talent of Dick Van Dyke, many of them comic actors familiar to British audiences such as Lionel Jeffries (playing Grandpa Potts despite being six months younger than Van Dyke), Benny Hill and James Robertson Justice. And there was a smattering of familiar Bond faces, too: Goldfinger himself Gert Frobe and Desmond Llewelyn. Making by far the biggest impact was ballet star Robert Helpmann as the Childcatcher, one of cinema's true grotesques.

In the vital roles of Potts's two young children, Broccoli and Ken Hughes interviewed and tested hundreds of kids before finding their perfect Jemima and Jeremy in Heather Ripley and Adrian Hall, both 9 years old at the time. Both had conflicting experiences working on the film: Heather did not enjoy the process, while Hall looks back with fonder memories, especially a Christmas present from Broccoli. 'Expecting a standard toy, I was amazed to discover a microscope with slides which would not have been out of place in a professional laboratory! I treasured it for many years and my sons also got many years of pleasure from it.'[18]

Another time Hall mentioned to Cubby his love of the Bond movies. 'Within a week we were taken to his private cinema for a personal showing of *You Only Live Twice*.'[19]

Inevitably, bad weather in England led to long delays that in the end necessitated the production moving backwards and forwards to the South of France to find the sun. Back in England, logistical nightmares cropped up, one involving a gigantic airship which had a mind of its own. Graham Hartstone was a member of the sound crew and saw the airship hit the ridge of a hill and lose all the sandbags acting as ballast:

> It then spiralled upwards apparently out of control. I chased it over the Chiltern Hills in my 1949 Jaguar with a radio aerial on a long pole protrud-

> ing from the sunroof, trying to keep in range with the pilot. It was finally pulled down by willing helpers who grabbed the 250ft rope it was trailing.[20]

Hartstone recalled Broccoli joining the unit on location in Germany a few days later, partly to avoid all the complaints he was receiving about the havoc wreaked by the airship back home over three counties. Hartstone enjoyed working for Cubby. 'He was the most generous and appreciative producer. A gentleman producer. Cubby was highly respected by all who worked for him. He threw the most lavish parties for the crew at the end of shooting.'[21] When Hartstone got married midway through the *Chitty* shoot, his wife was allowed to join him on location in Germany and the South of France. 'A working honeymoon courtesy of Cubby.'[22]

In Germany, the crew were based mainly in the scenic town of Rothenburg in Bavaria. Hughes's wife Cherry was working on the film, in continuity, and recalled Saltzman giving her a bit of advice before she went out there. 'Listen, Cubby is not a nice man, so don't be fooled by that uncle Cubby act. It's bullshit.'[23]

Cherry soon learnt what he meant when she joined her husband and a few others to watch rushes one morning. Looking at the screen, she nudged Ken and told him how she thought they'd used the wrong location and as a result the scene didn't work. One of Broccoli's people overheard this and rushed to tell the producer. The next day, Cherry arrived on set and there was Broccoli:

> And the minute he saw me he started shouting at me, 'Don't you fucking well criticize me. Who the bloody hell do you think you are?' And I said, 'Let me tell you something Mr Broccoli. I'll tell you exactly who I think I am, not you, and I'll criticize if I want to, and if you don't like it, you know what you can do, stick it.' And I walked off.[24]

As it happened, Cherry was due to fly back to London that day for a family occasion, but driving to Frankfurt airport she had no intention of coming back. 'Ken was devastated. He felt an outsider amongst this bunch and didn't want to go on directing the film unless I came back. And 24 hours later an enormous bouquet of flowers arrived with a note of apology from Cubby Broccoli. And he was never rude to me again.'[25]

Chitty Chitty Bang Bang opened in time for Christmas 1968 and met with decidedly mixed reviews. *Time* commented that *Chitty* was, 'A picture for the ages – the ages between five and 12. After that, interest is bound to slacken into hostility or slumber.' Roger Ebert, writing in the Chicago *Sun-Times*, was more forgiving, calling it, 'About the best two-hour children's movie you could hope for. But the trouble is, these two hours of fun are surrounded by about another 45 minutes of soppy love songs, corny ballads and a lot of mushy stuff.'

Even Ken Hughes spoke out against the film not long after it opened, admitting that he considered it a disappointment. 'We took too long to make it. I sweated over it for about a year and really it was only a children's film. I think such a thing should be made quickly and with enthusiasm. My enthusiasm ran out long before the end.'[26]

While the picture performed well at the box office it wasn't the resounding success Cubby had hoped for. Since then, of course, with repeated viewings on television the film has become an enduring classic, and in 2002 was turned into a hugely popular stage musical.

For the Sherman brothers, working on *Chitty* was one of the most personally rewarding experiences of their careers. For Robert Sherman, much of that was down to the generosity of Broccoli. It wasn't just that he could visualise the end product, he was also emotionally connected to the material. Sherman recalled visiting Broccoli at his hotel suite to play him one of the songs, 'Lovely Lonely Man', and saw that by the end he was in tears it had affected him so much. As his son Robert J. Sherman explained, 'In his later career, my father lamented the fact that there weren't the gentleman producers like Cubby Broccoli and Walt Disney around. They respected the creative process and did what they needed to do to facilitate the creative talent.'[27]

14

Wargames

Besides film projects, screenplays, books and other sundry miscellanea, Saltzman also collected people, and was always on the lookout for emerging talent that he could use. Philip Saville was one of those, a talented television director Saltzman had kept tabs on for some time before calling a meeting with a view to offering him a two-year contract. 'Meeting the enthusiastic and persuasive Mr Saltzman at his Mayfair offices was quite an eye opener,' revealed Saville. 'He had a flamboyant charm with a pushy presence. Immensely confident, like a chromium-plated tank, whose force you didn't cross because of its fire power.' Saville was one of three directors Saltzman had accumulated, along with Ken Russell and Anthony Simmons. 'I think he regarded us as race horses, trained to come first at film festivals.'[1]

Excited at the prospect of some financial security, Saville was led to understand that he would be in a position to option books he wanted to make into films, along with developing original screenplays. All these issues were set out in an exclusive contract devised by Saville's agent, Dennis Selinger. 'Harry agreed and I went out immediately and bought a new suit.'[2]

The next six months were to prove a frustrating time. For someone used to the urgency of working in television, the film industry seemed positively moribund by comparison. Saville had a personal project he was keen to pursue, about three handicapped children trapped underground as a result of a gas explosion, only he ended up being wined and dined in fashionable restaurants, especially Les Ambassadeurs club, which Saltzman tended to use 'as an alternative office' to cushion the rejection.[3]

In Saltzman's office, Saville was handed any number of books and scripts that had been collecting dust over the years, with the promise of total cooperation if he wanted to direct one. Most of them Saville found to be scarcely on the pulse of contemporary cinema, a little too old-fashioned. Yet there was one that did have merit and Saltzman hired novelist and film critic Penelope Gilliatt to adapt it. Saville undertook weekly meetings at Penelope's house in Bloomsbury, but Saltzman eventually dismissed her draft screenplay and like so many other projects it ended up like dust in the wind. That was the final straw for Saville and he asked Selinger if he could arrange for him to be released from his contract. 'Saltzman was sympathetic and agreed, and ended by mentioning he might have some good news by the end of the week.' That good news turned out to be a meeting with renowned producer Carlo Ponti, which led to Saville directing his first mainstream picture, *The Best House in London*.[4]

One film Saltzman was eager to push ahead with was *Play Dirty*, a nihilistic war movie in *The Dirty Dozen* mould, about British officers leading a bunch of criminals in a mission to destroy a German fuel depot behind enemy lines in North Africa. No sooner had Saltzman hired acclaimed French director Rene Clement to helm the movie than they began to clash over conflicting visions, as Andre de Toth recalled. 'Genteel Rene wanted to make a "poetry of war." Harry wanted blazing guns and roaring tanks.'[5]

Nor did they see eye to eye on where to shoot the picture; Saltzman wanted to make it out in Israel, while Clement saw the sense in using actual North African locations. When Saltzman rejected the idea of going on a recce to North Africa and Clement refused to go to Israel, it was an impasse. The compromise choice ended up being Almeria in southern Spain.

Michael Caine was going to play one of the British officers, keen to work with such a respected artist as Rene Clement. That ambition barely lasted a few days when Clement left the picture. It was location manager Andrew Birkin who collected Saltzman from the airport after he'd flown in with the express intention of dismissing Clement. Their earlier disagreements about how to approach the subject had evidently not been rectified. 'Clement was an auteur,' said Birkin. 'And he was making what Saltzman feared was going to be some kind of an art movie.'[6]

After a three-day hiatus where nothing got shot, Saltzman asked de Toth to take over. Birkin thought de Toth was the perfect replacement, having exactly the right temperament: 'He was more of a sergeant major and he made the picture that way, which was probably the right way to do it. I remember Saltzman gave a speech on the set about how we all had to rally behind the new Reich Fuhrer, as it were.'[7]

That wasn't the end of the problems. Richard Harris had agreed to play opposite Caine. After discovering rewrites were in progress, he insisted a clause be put in his contract stating that the substance and nature of his role would not 'change to any appreciable degree'. This was agreed and both parties signed. 'But then, when I arrived in Spain, I was given 30 new pages, with four of my main scenes cut to ribbons. I told Saltzman, "You are a contemptible low-life fucker," and I walked off. I wasn't going to play second fiddle to Caine.'[8]

Apart from all the troubles, Birkin recalled it was quite a fun shoot. Pretty new to the industry, having started as an assistant on the Beatles TV film *Magical Mystery Tour* and then *2001: A Space Odyssey*, Birkin had been recommended to Saltzman. Walking into South Audley Street, Birkin tagged Saltzman as 'the archetypal film producer, sat behind a big desk with a cigar'.[9] Despite being just 21, Saltzman took him on, seemingly unaware of his Bond connection; Birkin's sister Jane was currently married to John Barry.

Not far from the *Play Dirty* location, almost literally over the next sand dune, Sean Connery was making a Western that he hoped would obliterate his 007 image: *Shalako*, with Brigitte Bardot. This presented its own special set of problems as the local authorities carefully regimented the area, especially the sand dunes which David Lean had made famous in *Lawrence of Arabia*. 'You got them for two weeks because another picture was coming in,' said Birkin.[10] There was always a communication breakdown of sorts, though, as Caine recalled: 'One day we had a shot where the tanks of Rommel's Afrika Korps were advancing, only to be greeted as they rounded a hill by a stagecoach being chased by American Indians coming in the other direction.'[11]

During shooting Caine celebrated his 35th birthday. Since signing his seven-year contract with Saltzman, Caine had become a substantial box office draw and was now clearly unhappy with this binding arrangement. In the face of the lucrative offers coming his way, Saltzman was still only obliged to pay Caine the small sums agreed in that now outdated contract. Instead, every year on Caine's birthday, Saltzman redrafted a new contract at a much higher and more competitive rate. 'This year, however, when I opened the envelope it contained the contract itself, torn into small pieces, and with a note that just said: You're on your own now. Happy birthday – and it was signed Harry.'[12]

Following production on *Play Dirty*, Andre de Toth returned to his office at South Audley Street where Saltzman put him in charge of a string of new projects, most of which the veteran filmmaker categorised as pie-in-the-sky stuff. 'Harry's dreams were commendable and absurdly impractical.'[13] One potential film idea was *The Pass Beyond Kashmir*, which had been slated as an Eon production back in 1963 and which de Toth considered terribly old-fashioned and was going to cost a fortune to make. He voiced his reservations but Saltzman wouldn't listen; instead, he bought first-class air tickets for de Toth and a small crew to go and scout locations. It was nothing short of madness, thought de Toth, and he announced his intention to quit. 'Why?' asked a bewildered Saltzman. 'You're earning a good salary.'

'No, it's not enough, I want $100,000 a week. You're spending your money so foolishly, why not give me a raise?'

De Toth's words trailed away into silence, leaving the two men looking blankly at each other. Then Saltzman turned and left the office. It was the last time the two men ever saw each other.[14] 'One had to feel compassion for Harry,' de Toth lamented. 'Hidden, well hidden inside him was a generous, beautiful, tortured man.'[15]

It was a sad end to the relationship. De Toth was always beholden to Saltzman for helping put his career back on track, but he had come to see his employer as something of a drowning man who didn't want to be saved. 'The man had absolutely no idea where he was going, or why, or what he wanted to do. Staying on his gold-dust-sprinkled merry go round ultimately would have hurt him and, above all, my integrity.'[16]

*

It was a lone Spitfire traversing the sky above Hyde Park rehearsing a fly-past over Buckingham Palace that provided the inspiration for producer Benjamin Fisz, who saw combat during the Second World War with the Polish Air Force, to bring to the screen the full story of the summer of 1940 when the RAF, fighting against odds of four-to-one, stood against the German Luftwaffe who craved mastery of the air as a prelude to invasion.

This was the summer of 1965, and by late autumn Fisz had interested Rank to put up the money, with Lewis Gilbert voicing an interest in directing. Then nothing. Fisz had hoped to begin shooting in the spring of 1966 for a summer 1967 release, but Rank was stalling. Then Fisz took a call in his office that changed the whole dynamics of the project. It was Saltzman. The two men met over dinner at a restaurant in Soho. Saltzman was keen to come in as Fisz's partner on the film and asked how much Rank were prepared to commit. The answer was £1.2 million.

'How much do you visualise your budget?' asked Saltzman.

'Three and a half million pounds.'

Without a pause, Saltzman said, 'I can get the rest.'[17]

Obviously, Saltzman saw a lot of box office potential in the project; war movies were still a popular attraction at cinemas. He also believed that it was an episode of history that had been more or less forgotten, especially by a youth who he viewed as having next to no knowledge of the enormous sacrifice that took place. But there were other more personal issues at play according to Tom Mankiewicz, who was soon to join the Eon family. 'What everybody at his office told me was that Harry wanted to make the ultimate tribute to the RAF and Britain in World War Two because he really, really believed that there was a knighthood in it for him.'[18]

With his military background, Saltzman thought Guy Hamilton was the perfect candidate for the director's chair. During the shooting of *Funeral in Berlin*, the producer approached him one day on the set. 'I've got a present for you.'

'That's very nice,' said Hamilton. 'Put it in the car.'

'No, it's *Battle of Britain*. How would you like to direct it?'[19]

Saltzman put Hamilton in touch with Fisz, who gave him bundles of research material. It was the Polish producer's enthusiasm for the project that sold Hamilton and he quickly signed on.

Rank's participation in the film was in return for 20 per cent of the world profits and the right to distribute the film in the eastern hemisphere, but when they began to demand a better deal, Saltzman refused to budge, telling them, 'Nothing doing. You should stick to the terms you agreed to.' Fisz was of a mind to give in; Saltzman, however, remained adamant and as a result Rank pulled out.[20]

Far from worried, Saltzman was confident in making a deal over at Paramount, due to his friendship with its chief, Howard W. Koch, and the fact that the company had released *Funeral in Berlin*. For once Saltzman's timing was lousy. Koch had left Paramount to form his own production company and been replaced by Charles Bluhdorn. Following a number of meetings, it was clear that Saltzman and Bluhdorn were so different in temperament that they would never be able to work together. Reports also emerged that Paramount were unsure about financing a movie with zero American involvement. Saltzman had always maintained that this was a wholly British story and attempts to introduce American characters would dilute it. So, Paramount was out. Saltzman told Fisz they had no alternative but to postpone the film.[21]

As news filtered out that the production was on hold, both Saltzman and Fisz started to receive thousands of letters and donations from members of the public. War widows sent in their scrapbooks and ex-RAF mechanics volunteered their services. However gloomy things might have seemed as the delay stretched into 1967, Saltzman was busy behind the scenes, his enthusiasm for the project undimmed. It was Saltzman's money too that paid for a large staff to carry out pre-production duties, although everyone working in that office knew the money wouldn't last forever and that a decision to keep them on would have to be made sooner rather than later.

That day arrived when Saltzman turned up unannounced and called a special meeting for the entire production staff. The tension in the room was palpable as Saltzman began to speak. 'Well, gentlemen,' he began. Out of the corner of his eye he spotted Ron Allday, the film's chief accountant, and asked how his wife was, aware that she was expecting a baby. 'I love babies,' offered Saltzman. This kicked off a large debate amongst everyone about children; photographs were brought out, discussions about teething problems and what age they start to walk and talk. After thirty minutes of this, Saltzman called for quiet. 'Gentlemen, I think it's about time we wrapped up this meeting. We start making the film next year.' Before anyone could say a word, Saltzman had left the room. Unbeknownst to anyone, he had flown to New York and negotiated a deal with David Picker at United Artists.[22]

The first hurdle to cross was assembling something like 140 aircraft required for the aerial combat scenes which comprised something like forty minutes of the film. The task was assigned to Group Captain Hamish Mahaddie, one of the film's technical advisors. Tipped off that the Spanish Air Force largely consisted of Luftwaffe rejects, Mahaddie flew to an airbase in Seville and discovered several Messerschmitts in good flying order. On a nearby scrapheap he also discovered enough material and spare parts to build thirty fighters.[23]

The Spanish Air Force also used Heinkels as part of their bomber force and lunch with one of their top brass resulted in Mahaddie making a deal to use fifty of them for the film. The problem was they were all decorated in Spanish national colours, so they had to be dressed up with Nazi emblems. This resulted in an amusing incident when the Spanish planes were required for a NATO exercise in the Bay of Biscay. The only thing was, there wasn't time to remove all the Nazi insignia, as Guy Hamilton recalled:

> I was in the navy during the war and I love the idea of these NATO top brass on a battleship and someone says, 'Aircraft approaching on the starboard bow' and they all look through binoculars and here are these Heinkels and Messerschmitts in Nazi colours coming flying past – they must have been absolutely stunned.[24]

Locating the British planes, like Spitfires and Hurricanes, proved more troublesome, especially since only six Hurricanes were known to exist. A worldwide hunt was conducted with aircraft turning up as far afield as Canada and Malaysia. By the close of 1967 the production had acquired fifty Heinkel bombers, twenty-eight Messerschmitts, two squadrons of flying Spitfires and four Hurricanes, at a combined cost of £100,000. The number of planes was boosted by fibreglass replicas constructed at Pinewood Studios. Nicknamed Saltzman's 'Private Airforce', the production could genuinely claim to be the thirty-fifth biggest air power in the world.[25]

Using their contacts in the business and powers of persuasion, Saltzman and Fisz gathered together top British acting talent including Michael Caine, Trevor Howard, Laurence Olivier, Ralph Richardson and Robert Shaw. Saltzman reportedly rejected the idea of casting Christopher Lee on the grounds that audiences would not accept Count Dracula as part of the RAF.[26]

To avoid any problems when it came to paying star wages, Saltzman and Fisz proposed that there should be a flat rate for all the main players, 'plus a contribution to the Actor's benevolent fund', said Hamilton.[27] Saltzman revealed that the film would have cost 50 per cent more if every star had demanded their normal fees. 'But they felt this was an important story that should be told.'[28]

Cameraman Freddie Young recalled a string of prominent Battle of Britain veterans who worked on the film or visited the set, people like Squadron Leader Ginger Lacey, who had more 'kills' to his credit than any other pilot, and Douglas Bader, already immortalised on screen in *Reach for the Sky*. But it was a very special occasion when Lord Dowding, who had been Air Chief Marshall during the campaign, visited the location. 'When he came down, those old war heroes quarrelled for the honour of pushing his wheelchair, they venerated him so much.'[29]

From the outset the ambition of the producers was to tell the story of the conflict from both sides, and with this at the forefront of their minds Germany's top air ace of the war, Adolf Galland, was brought over to act as a technical advisor. Galland was quite a difficult character, especially when anybody brought up the fact that the Luftwaffe lost the Battle of Britain, something Saltzman was only too happy to do whenever Galland was within earshot. On one occasion Caine witnessed the sight of Saltzman, this Jewish movie producer, and the ex-leader of the Luftwaffe almost coming to blows over who really won.[30]

Principal photography began in mid-March 1968 on location in Spain, where much of the aerial footage was staged. These stunning sequences were filmed from a converted B25 American Mitchell bomber with five camera shooting points; Hamilton directed the action sitting in the mid-upper gun turret. 'The pilots hired to fly the planes were some of the best in the world,' said Nick Alder, who worked on the aerial unit.[31]

The production was almost a paramilitary operation in itself. Saltzman said it was like making five pictures at the same time. Something like 500 cast, crew and technicians were on the payroll. Every week Ron Allday, the film's accountant, spent hours signing pay cheques for everyone, so many cheques in fact that it took two suitcases to contain all of them.

United Artists had given the film a budget of $8.5 million but no one thought that was really going to be enough, and by the end of June there was just about enough money left to carry on shooting for a few days. Saltzman announced he was flying to New York to raise more finance. Three days later he returned with $2 million. The film was able to carry on, but from that moment on the United Artist top brass were exerting huge pressure on Saltzman about the rising cost. In the end, the film wound up costing $13 million.[32]

As production neared its end, thoughts turned to who would write the music score. Saltzman asked his office staff a simple question, 'Who is England's greatest living composer?' There was a gentle murmuring and then one of them said, 'Well, I suppose without a doubt Harry it would be Sir Benjamin Britten.' Saltzman nodded, 'Ok, he's going to do the score.' Saltzman was now determined to get his man. Tom Mankiewicz was told what happened next:

> They kept trying to get in touch with Benjamin Britten and Benjamin Britten would never call back. Harry sent down messengers with letters to him, patriotic notes, never was so much owed by so many to so few, that kind of stuff, still he never called him back. Finally, one day the phone rings in Harry's office and it's Benjamin Britten. Harry says, 'Sir Benjamin, this is Harry Saltzman…' and he goes off again with never was so much, and Benjamin Britten says, 'I think you should know Mr Saltzman that for the entire duration of the war I was a pacifist and a conscientious objector,' and Harry hung up on him. Then he turned to his staff and said, 'Ok, who's the second greatest living composer in England.'[33]

That composer was Sir William Walton, by then in his mid-60s. Saltzman arranged for Walton to see a rough cut of the film, after which the composer was determined to write something rousingly British. Only his score was rejected by United Artists on the grounds it was not long enough to issue as a soundtrack album. According to his wife Susana, Walton couldn't sleep for weeks after hearing the news. 'The anguish that discarding his score caused him was devastating.'[34]

As for a replacement, once John Barry ruled himself out, it was Ron Goodwin, famous for his war picture scores of *633 Squadron* (1964) and *Where Eagles Dare* (1968), who stepped into the breach. 'I only had three weeks to write it,' recalled the composer, who normally required twice that length of time, 'because they were madly behind schedule. So, I just had to get on with it. You didn't have time to sit around waiting for flashes of inspiration. It was very much a musical journalist job rather than a musical author's job.'[35]

Saltzman soon found himself having to face down another problem. Walton had made his reputation as a film composer with Laurence Olivier's trilogy of Shakespeare films: *Henry V* (1944), *Hamlet* (1948) and *Richard III* (1955). When Olivier heard what had happened, he informed Saltzman and United Artists that he would be removing his name from the credits unless at least some part of Walton's score was reinstated.

Saltzman contacted Goodwin about the Olivier situation, saying, 'We can't afford to upset him,' and that it was going to be a clear choice between his music for the climactic air battle and Walton's. It wasn't until the press show that Goodwin discovered Walton's music had been chosen, as he expected all along. 'Nobody at the film company had bothered to call either Sir William or myself to tell us their decision. The whole thing was a very regrettable situation.'[36]

Battle of Britain premiered in London on 15 September 1969, where the stars mingled with war heroes. Lord Dowding was almost overcome by the evening. 'It is an emotional experience seeing it all again on the screen,' he told reporters. 'I am seeing my boys die again.'[37]

Critics were lukewarm about the film, and despite a strong showing in British cinemas the movie was a commercial disaster in America and other international territories, leaving United Artists heavily out of pocket. David Picker later regretted having greenlit the project.[38] According to Tom Mankiewicz, when Broccoli made *Chitty Chitty Bang Bang* for United Artists, or Saltzman with *Battle of Britain*, they were cross-collateralised at the studio. 'So, if the film lost money it was taken out of your Bond profits.'[39]

Licking their wounds, the two producers turned their attention once again to the commercially sound Mr Bond, determined that Connery's departure would not mean the end of the franchise, as some commentators were predicting.

15

The One Hit Wonder

Sean Connery's resignation from the Bond films came at a momentous time. The 1960s were drawing to a close and the state of world cinema was very different to that of 1962 when *Dr No* burst onto the screen. Society, too, had seen many changes. This was the era of the counterculture, and the producers wondered how much of this social revolution should be reflected in the new James Bond. While 007 was never going to swap his tuxedo for a kaftan or put flowers in his hair, a new actor meant a new start, a chance to reinvent the character, and there were several discussions between Broccoli and Saltzman and United Artists whether to go for a younger, more modern personality. In the end the decision was to play safe; change wasn't an option. What they wanted was another Sean Connery.

Early in 1968, the search for the new Bond began in earnest. As Saltzman declared: 'The guy who gets this part will take off. Cubby and I made Sean a millionaire. I don't think any actor has got as rich as he has in recent years. Believe me; playing Bond is better than winning the pools.'[1] Actors' agencies and provincial repertory companies were trawled for suitable talent. Saltzman made it plain what he considered to be the right attributes: 'I look for tremendous virility in an actor, a sexual animal magnetism that makes men identify with my star and women want to kiss him.'[2]

A few 'name' actors were considered. On a trip to London to promote his TV *Batman* series, Adam West recalled meeting with Broccoli over dinner to discuss the possibility of taking over from Connery. Giving the prospect serious thought, West ultimately declined, believing the character should be played by a British actor.[3]

Considered for a second time was Oliver Reed; however, this time it wasn't his age that proved an obstacle, rather his growing public image as a hellraiser, an image that the producers just didn't have the time or patience to remould.

Over dinner at the fashionable White Elephant club in Curzon Street, Saltzman offered the role to Terence Stamp, who recalled: 'Like most English actors, I'd have loved to be 007 because I really know how to wear a suit. But I think my ideas about it put the frighteners on Harry. I didn't get a second call from him.'[4]

Stamp was concerned that with Connery leaving such an indelible mark on the role, any new actor coming in might not be allowed to do it his own way.

> I did have ideas about it and on reflection, because I didn't get to know Saltzman but I heard about him, apparently he was a real egomaniac who would have loved to direct the films himself, so it's possible that the last thing he wanted was an actor with ideas.[5]

The name Roger Moore came up again, and Saltzman personally called the actor: 'Let's talk about you doing Bond.'[6] But it never happened, with Saltzman reasoning that Moore was too identified as The Saint. So, it was going to have to be an unknown, and finding good, undiscovered actors in their late 1920s and early '30s was not too easy.

At 28, Patrick Mower was the right age and physically looked the part, too, though had yet to establish himself on either film or TV. Asked by his agent to go along and see the producers, Mower remembered being almost anatomically scrutinised. 'What's your body like?' asked Saltzman. 'I've never had any complaints,' replied Mower.[7]

Over the next few weeks Mower had several meetings with Saltzman and Broccoli, but confessed that it was his own conceit and sense of humour that robbed him of the role. He'd swan around the Eon office humming the Bond theme and announce, 'The name's Mower… Patrick Mower,' to staff. Then, when he discovered his Bond test at Pinewood also involved ten other actors, Mower was crushed and stayed at home. 'I'd had a part of a lifetime in the palm of my hand, and I had let it slip out. No! I had thrown it away.'[8]

To find their James Bond the producers enlisted the help of a former actor and now casting director, Dyson Lovell, who had just finished working with Franco Zefferelli on *Romeo and Juliet*. When he heard that the Bond people wanted to see him Lovell made his way to South Audley to meet first with Saltzman. He was then instructed to go down to Pinewood and see Broccoli and was shown into the office of Golda Offenheim, an occasional production assistant on the Bonds since *From Russia with Love*. Lovell sat there for quite a considerable time. 'Then Cubby came out of his office and took one look at me and said, "No, no, no, no. No blondes for Bond." And I said, "You don't understand, I'm not here about playing James Bond, I'm here about casting James Bond." That was my introduction to Cubby.'[9]

Lovell was installed in an office a stone's throw away from South Audley. It had been decided there wasn't enough room at Eon's main HQ, so they took over a building across the way on the corner of Tilney Street. 'My office there was the grand conference room on the first floor.'[10] Finding a replacement for Connery was 'a nightmare task', in Lovell's view:

> I was very keen on Timothy Dalton and met with him but he said, 'No, I'm far too young for it.' So, one went through this agonising search to find a Bond and we'd had no luck at all and then an agent called Maggie Abbott called me up and said, 'There's this guy that you should meet, he's not an actor, but he looks really good, you should meet him.'[11]

George Lazenby arrived in London from his native Australia in 1964 and set himself up as a successful car salesman before turning to male modelling. Within a year Lazenby established himself as one of the highest paid models in Europe, selling everything from petrol and cigarettes to cosmetics and paperback books; he even made the break into television, appearing in a series of commercials for Fry's chocolate. It was Maggie Abbott who sought Lazenby out in the belief he could be what the producers were looking for.

In direct contrast to Connery's interview, when he dressed in casual street wear, Lazenby believed if he was going to see the Bond people he really ought to dress for the part. So, after buying one of Connery's old Bond suits from the actor's tailor at Savile Row and having his hair cut at his London barber, Lazenby made his way to South Audley to meet Lovell. 'He looked very good when he arrived,' remembered Lovell. 'I talked to him and then I phoned Harry and said, "Listen there's this guy in my office, he looks good, I don't know anything about him, but I don't want to send him away without somebody seeing him because he does look the part." So, Harry met him.'[12]

Lazenby arrived in Saltzman's office to see him sat behind his desk, on the phone, of course, with his feet on the desk; he wasn't wearing socks. Still talking on the phone, Saltzman motioned for Lazenby to sit down. He thought, 'I'm not sitting down there while your feet are up,' and he looked out the window. Saltzman put down his feet, straightened up and said, 'Have a seat.' Lazenby was sure he'd won the man's respect right there.[13]

The two men chatted for a while before Saltzman asked Lazenby to come back tomorrow afternoon to meet the director. Lazenby couldn't, saying he had to be in Paris for a modelling assignment. 'How much do you earn for a job in Paris?' asked Saltzman.

'£500.'

'Go down and see Stanley Sopel,' ordered Saltzman. 'He'll give you a cheque. Be here at four o'clock tomorrow.'[14]

It was at this meeting that Lazenby met director Peter Hunt for the first time and confessed that he had never acted before in his life, certainly not in front of a movie camera. Far from annoyed, Hunt was impressed. 'And you say you can't act? You've fooled two of the most ruthless men I've ever met in my life. Stick to your story and I'll make you the next James Bond.'[15]

The truth didn't stay secret long, and when Saltzman heard he was incensed. 'Get him out of here. He's a clothes peg. We'll be the laughing stock of the industry if we hire a male model.'[16] Saltzman was also convinced all male models were gay. Lazenby recalled being put up in an apartment and one night a budding film producer by the name of John Daly arrived. 'They sent him around with a girl, a hooker, and to check me out to see if I was gay. That was a good night.'[17] Daly would later form the film company Hemdale and be a successful independent producer of films such as *The Terminator* and *Platoon*.

Maggie Abbott rang Lazenby a few days later to say that the Bond team wanted to go ahead with some tests at Saltzman's country house. Staying over a few nights, Lazenby remembered being awoken early one morning by someone calling out: 'James Bond… James Bond.' He looked out of the window. It was Saltzman calling his two German Shepherds, one he'd called James, the other Bond.[18]

Over the next few weeks, Lazenby got to know the producers on a personal level by going out numerous times to lavish dinners; never in one group, though, always separately, which Lazenby thought especially odd. Harry and Jacqueline would take him out one night, then it would be the turn of Cubby and Dana. 'I couldn't figure out at first why they didn't all go together. But the wives didn't get along.'[19] While working for Saltzman, Andre de Toth also recognised the personal friction that existed between the two women. 'Harry and Jacqueline truly loved each other and both hated the Broccolis. I never found out why, nor did I want to.'[20]

After making a strong impression, a fully-fledged screen test was set up at Pinewood that included a brutal fight with a baddie, played by Russian wrestler Yuri Borienko. As Hunt's camera turned, Lazenby let fly with a massive punch, accidentally breaking Borienko's nose. It was part overenthusiasm and part naïveté, but it did the trick. Watching from the sidelines, Saltzman stepped over the prone Borienko and told Lazenby: 'We're going with you.'[21] Broccoli also later revealed that it was this fight test that clinched it for him.

On 7 October 1968, Lazenby was introduced to the press as the new James Bond during a reception held at the Dorchester Hotel. It was pretty daunting for a guy not used to the pitfalls of showbusiness. The only advice he was given was by Saltzman. 'You know,' the producer said, as Lazenby prepared to enter the press conference. 'These guys in here are all sharks. You're in a pool here and they're going to try and eat you for breakfast if they can. So, no matter what they say to you, don't let it affect you because they make things up just to get you going.'

Lazenby was puzzled. 'Like what?'

Saltzman looked hard at Lazenby. 'Your manhood for instance, they'll attack that. What are you going to say?'

Lazenby thought for a while. 'I'll say, well bend over and I'll show you what sort of man I am.'

Saltzman's face went purple. 'Jesus, don't say that!'[22]

Because Lazenby had never performed or spoken in front of a camera before in his life, the producers enrolled him in an extensive course of acting lessons. And to eradicate his thick Australian accent he was sent to a speech trainer. Saltzman used to say to him, 'How the hell is anyone going to understand you, because I can't!'[23]

Impressed by his potential, and with the backing of United Artists, Broccoli and Saltzman approached Lazenby with the possibility of doing the next five Bond pictures. Lazenby, however, was reluctant to commit, leaving the producers with no choice but to start shooting without their leading man having signed a contract; all they had was a letter of intent from Lazenby. It was an incredible gamble.

For his directorial debut Peter Hunt was delighted the producers had decided to make *On Her Majesty's Secret Service*, which he and many others considered to be Fleming's best novel. After the spectacular excesses of *You Only Live Twice* it was an ideal choice of story to bring Bond back to basics. Even the producers realised the gimmicks had gone too far, and what they wanted now was a strong emotional scenario to place their hero into. Hunt certainly felt a responsibility to the material. 'During the entire shooting schedule, I had a copy of the paperback of the book, where I had written various notes and things, and I was very insistent that we stay with the story of the book.'[24]

Just as important was to surround their new star with recognised and experienced actors, so in came Telly Savalas as the returning Blofeld. 'He was a great friend of Cubby's,' revealed Peter Hunt. 'They enjoyed gambling together and going to the casinos.'[25] On the set, Savalas roped in crew members to take part in big stakes card games. When he tried to take Lazenby to the cleaners, Saltzman quickly moved in and took his place – 'and got my money back! He said, "Now leave my boy alone!" He gave me protection.'[26]

The producers' first choice to play Tracy, the woman Bond ends the story marrying, was Brigitte Bardot. Harry was especially keen and flew to France with Hunt to meet with the famed French actress. Here she calmly announced just signing on to play opposite Sean Connery in *Shalako*. 'Harry and I looked at one another and that was the end of that.'[27] The producers' second choice was Catherine Deneuve, but when she turned them down Diana Rigg became the second actress to graduate from television's *The Avengers* to the world of Bond.

The producers also had to find twelve beautiful international women to fill the roles of the 'Angels of Death', the unwilling carriers of Blofeld's latest plan to unleash germ warfare upon the world. Several names of the future were cast: Julie Ege, Catherine Schell, Jenny Hanley and Joanna Lumley, who recalled the two producers fondly:

> Cubby Broccoli was benign and approachable, always with a kind word for the least of the cast (me) and approval and encouragement to the crew. He came to see us in Switzerland on the mountaintop set and brought with him his small, slightly unruly daughter, Barbara. Harry Saltzman seemed to be more remote, harder to please, slow to smile. I had gone to see him for a part in the film, and we arrived at the front door of Eon Productions in Audley Street at the same time in the early afternoon. Mr Saltzman and I had to walk up three flights to his office as the lift was broken. When he reached his desk he just said 'You have the job' and I skipped out with my heart leaping with joy. I am eternally grateful to them both: they made me forever a Bond girl, a title I would not swap for gold.[28]

Jenny Hanley, spotted by Saltzman in a television commercial, also had vivid memories of visiting the producer at his office:

> It was a very masculine office, with dark furniture and a leather sofa that was so deep if you sat on it and leaned back, your feet were up off the floor like a child. Harry was behind an enormous desk up on a plinth, so he was definitely the King! Harry was very sweet. And Cubby was just as his name suggests, 'Cuddly Cubby'.[29]

Sent on a recce to find a suitable location for Blofeld's new secret lair, Saltzman fixed on using the Maginot Line, the 280-mile-long network of underground fortresses, blockhouses and bunkers constructed along the French border with Germany to prevent invasion during the Second World War, which of course it singularly failed to do. Using his contacts in the French government, Saltzman arranged for some of the buildings to be opened up for him and production designer Syd Cain. When, halfway through their private guided tour, Cain explained it would be cheaper and easier to reproduce it all on a stage back at Pinewood, Saltzman ditched the idea. Next, they went to St Moritz to check out another possible location, only for Cain to report his dissatisfaction at that, too. Finally, Saltzman shouted, 'Find the bloody thing yourself.'[30]

Word reached the production of a revolving restaurant called Piz Gloria under construction atop the Schilthorn mountain in Switzerland, accessible only by cable car. It seemed the ideal location and the producers arranged for filming to be carried out there, provided they undertook the final stages of building work, including putting in a helicopter pad. The final bill came to £60,000, a modest sum compared to the extravagance of Ken Adam's volcano set.[31]

With Bob Simmons unavailable to handle the stunt work, his assistant George Leech took charge and was responsible for some of the most bone-crushing close-quarter fights in the entire series. Leech had been a part of the Bond team since the start, doubling Joseph Wiseman in the reactor pool scrap with Bond in *Dr No*. But his association with Broccoli and Saltzman went back further, having worked on a few Warwick pictures and doubling Albert Finney on a stunt fall in *Saturday Night and Sunday Morning*:

> Cubby I liked. He had an office at the studio and you could go in and see him, and he was always very pleasant to talk to. On the set he wasn't a shout and screamer, he let you get on with it and he would always back you up. Harry was more of a stern and driven man. Coming from a circus background you've got to be tough I guess.[32]

For many, Broccoli was a positive influence on location in Murren, the crew's Swiss base, keen on keeping everyone's spirits as high as possible.

Vic Armstrong,who later worked as second unit director on the Pierce Brosnan Bonds, was a young stuntman then making his way in the business. His first encounter with the Bond producers was inside the volcano set at Pinewood, where he was playing one of the ninjas.'They drove into the massive set in a golf cart which was a real "Hollywood" moment to me in those days. I was just a lowly stunt man watching from afar but they both had a majestic aura around them in those days.'[33]

The next time Armstrong met Cubby was at his office in South Audley, during the search to replace Connery as Bond:

> My father had wangled a meeting through some mutual acquaintances in the horse racing world. Cubby was wonderful and very accommodating and we talked about horses. Cubby was into his horse racing in those days and owned quite a few racehorses. I think Dad was hoping I would get offered the role of Bond, that never happened but funnily enough I did get to play Bond doubling George Lazenby.[34]

By the time Armstrong arrived in Murren, Anthony Squires had just been replaced by John Glen directing the second unit, the lack of snow was holding everything up and there was a palpable sense that everybody was a little deflated:

> Cubby came out to show his support and it had an amazing galvanising effect on everybody. He was at the cable car at 5 a.m. in the morning to send us off to work and was there when we came back down the Schilthorn at night to buy us drinks and hang out with his crew, or rather family, which is what we were to him.[35]

Cubby's bond with his crew has no better example than the story John Glen told about the famous bobsleigh chase climax.The original plan was to shoot at the famous Cresta Run in St Moritz, but when that didn't work out a 2-mile run was built from scratch near Murren. Glen was brought in to film the sequence and was more than a little surprised when Broccoli insisted on being a passenger and road-testing the potentially dangerous circuit himself.[36]

By January 1969, Lazenby had been shooting for nearly three months without having put pen to paper, causing Saltzman and Broccoli mounting concern.'Harry, not Cubby, was offering me money under the counter to sign the goddamn contract,' Lazenby confirmed.'And then United Artists offered me any picture I wanted to do in between each Bond movie.'[37] Saltzman also promised Lazenby the Aston Martin car he drove in the film if he signed.[38]

It sounded like the dream deal, so why did Lazenby turn his back on it? Enter Ronan O'Reilly, a film producer and boss of the famous pirate radio station Radio Caroline, under whose influence Lazenby had fallen hook, line and sinker. Unbelievably, O'Reilly advised Lazenby not to sign the contract, convincing him that with films like *Easy Rider* taking over Hollywood, the character of Bond was in danger of becoming anachronistic, fatal for the actor playing the role.

Lazenby didn't do himself any great favours, either. Believing that the Bond gig was his ticket to stardom, he allowed fame to go to his head. 'He was a bit of a flash character,' recalled George Leech. 'He got into a bit of trouble with Cubby because he bought himself a gun in Switzerland and also drove around on this motorcycle which was thought to be a bit of a hazardous endeavour. Cubby had to put a block on that.'[39]

Nor did Lazenby particularly endear himself to a lot of the crew with his antics. It was Dana who suggested to her husband they throw an impromptu party to cheer everyone up. With just a day to put it together, Cubby organised for food to be brought over from nearby hotels and placed a notice about the party on that morning's call sheet. With everyone having a good time, Lazenby showed up late and stood sulking in a corner. Broccoli went over to him. 'Why don't you come and join us, what's the matter?'

'I should have had a proper invitation to this party,' answered Lazenby. 'I'm the star.'

Broccoli explained that no one had an invite, the party was a spur of the moment thing. 'And just remember, you're not a star till the public makes you one,' and with that Cubby walked off.[40]

This incident is interesting, especially in light of what Peter Hunt confided to his good friend Roger Moore about what Saltzman told Lazenby at the start of shooting: 'You are now a star George. Behave like one.'[41]

At two hours and twenty minutes, *On Her Majesty's Secret Service* was the longest film of the series so far and Hunt confessed to deliberately keeping the producers in the dark about how long it was really going to be. Saltzman kept asking him, 'What's the running time?' and Hunt kept saying, 'Oh, Harry, it's about two hours!' When it came to finally owning up, Hunt was expecting fireworks from Harry, and got them. 'No way!' he yelled. 'You have to lose twenty minutes! We can only get in four showings instead of five per day.'[42] The film was saved by, of all people, the booking manager of the Rank Organisation, George Pinches, who saw the film at South Audley's viewing theatre. Pinches loved it, and before Cubby and Harry could talk to him Hunt seized the moment, 'George, do you think

I should cut the film anywhere? Is it too long?' Pinches was adamant that not a frame should be touched. 'This was said right in front of the producers,' recalled Hunt, 'which ended any controversy over whether the film was going to be re-edited.'[43]

When the film opened in time for the Christmas holiday season of 1969, Lazenby made a decision not to reprise the role and even attended the London premiere sporting long hair and a beard. Cubby had expressly asked the actor not to appear with a beard. 'But it was my way of saying – I'm myself, I'm not James Bond.'[44]

Disappointed that in his estimation the Bond role had not been respected, Broccoli was later complimentary about Lazenby, that for a fledgling actor he gave an effective performance and had the potential to make a good Bond. 'Unfortunately, George ruled himself out of the reckoning by behaving like the superstar he wasn't.'[45]

But as the man instrumental in casting Lazenby, Dyson Lovell believed that the actor was on thin ice right from the start. 'The problem with Lazenby was that Sean had made such an impact in the role that whoever came in next was going to be clobbered.'[46] That was arguably the producers' mistake, by not casting an actor different enough to avoid comparison.

With Lazenby gone, someone else leaving the Bond camp was Peter Hunt, this time for good. While he always remained on favourable terms with the producers and valued their years together, he did not make another film for them. Hunt was asked to do the next one, *Diamonds Are Forever*, but he'd done his bit and it was time for a new challenge. His expertise, especially in the cutting room, was to be sorely missed.

16

A Musical Mishap

While the money pouring in from Bond allowed Saltzman especially the freedom to do the things he wanted to do that he could never do before, it also allowed both men to cater to their own individual vices. For Broccoli that was gambling, mainly craps, chemin de fer and roulette, and he was a distinctive presence around the gambling clubs of London. Back in late 1962 when Terry Southern was working on a script for Eon, Cubby took the writer and his wife on a guided tour of London in his Rolls-Royce, and seemed to take more pride in his young son's ability to recognise and point out various prominent casinos than other more historical landmarks.[1]

One of the more prestigious clubs Broccoli belonged to was the Clermont in Berkeley Square. It was owned by John Aspinall, who described the place as somewhere 'gentlemen could ruin themselves as elegantly and suicidally as did their ancestors 300 years ago.'[2] Cubby spent most evenings with fellow gamblers such as Jimmy Goldsmith and Lord Lucan. Bizarrely, Broccoli at one point even offered Lucan the prospect of becoming James Bond, justifying his choice by saying, 'He had it all – the looks, the breeding, the pride. I seriously wanted to test him for Bond, but all he'd say to that was, "Good heavens!"'[3]

Travelling to world cities for Bond invariably opened up the opportunity to gamble freely. Scouting locations in Macau for *You Only Live Twice*, Broccoli visited one of the famous casinos there and went bust. The management refused to cash a cheque, even after his explanation that he was the producer of the 007 movies. Unperturbed, Cubby managed to raise some money elsewhere, returned to the casino and broke the bank. It wasn't a fortune, just $5,000, but when the management said they didn't have the money and would he take a cheque, Cubby had to laugh. He waited patiently while the money was found.[4]

As for Saltzman, he loved his food and the act of going out to dinner. As Deighton recalled, 'You'd only have to mention a restaurant in Paris and Harry knew a better one.'[5] One of his favourite restaurants in London was the Gay Hussar in Soho, an authentic Hungarian eatery. It was a popular hangout for politicians, where the right-hand side of the dining room was reserved for Tories, and the left for Labour. Harry always sat on the Tory side.[6]

As we know already, Saltzman was a notorious customer, as Roger Moore had fun recalling. 'When the food came out Harry would always find fault. He'd let the waiter know – in no uncertain terms – what he thought of him and the chef, and send it all back. Cubby once quipped that if Harry had been at The Last Supper, he'd have sent it back.'[7]

Saltzman was the scourge of restaurant proprietors across the capital and beyond. La Trattoria Terrazza was one of the most fashionable restaurants in Swinging Sixties London. Situated in Soho, it was run by Mario Cassandro and Franco Lagattolla, and had already been immortalised by Deighton in his novel, *The Ipcress File*. The pair were a great partnership, with Franco taking charge of the food and the kitchens, while Mario was the charming host. Only Franco would always go and hide whenever Saltzman came into the restaurant according to Deighton: 'You couldn't get Franco out of the kitchen. Franco was terrified of him. But Mario wasn't scared of Harry, somebody had not to be terrified of him.'[8]

With this obsession about food, it was no surprise to anyone when Harry opened his own club restaurant in 1969. Situated on the embankment in Pimlico, it seated sixty patrons and served French cuisine prepared by seven chefs. Saltzman was thought to have invested between £50–60,000 into the venture and had gone into partnership with De Vere hotels, although overall control of the restaurant rested with him.[9] Deighton recalled that Harry had lots of grandiose ideas for the place which sadly never materialised. 'Although it was a great location, right on the water looking out over the Thames.'[10]

★

Following *On Her Majesty's Secret Service*, Dyson Lovell remained in the employ of Eon, though over time he became more affiliated with Saltzman, looking for suitable story material for him to option. Lovell got to know Harry as a rough character but liked him enormously. There was one encounter with an agent, a breed Saltzman didn't much care for at the best of times. This agent was coming to his office to discuss compensation for a client's work on one of the producer's numerous projects. Harry offered a cordial greeting and motioned him over to a coffee table laden with tea and biscuits. After a brief piece of conversation – Saltzman didn't do small talk – the agent was asked to quote the figure his client wanted. On hearing it, Harry jumped up into the air spraying the tea and biscuits over the startled agent, who fell off his seat. Not long afterwards a lady agent arrived for a meeting that was along very similar lines. 'Why don't you sit down on the couch,' said Saltzman as she walked in.

'I prefer to sit in the wing chair Mr Saltzman.' As she did so, Lovell noticed the woman hooking both her legs firmly behind the two legs of the chair. He then noticed Saltzman gesturing at him. 'Can you come outside for a minute Dyson.' Both men stood outside the office door. 'Why has that woman got her legs hooked round the chair?' he asked.

'Because she heard about that agent last week who fell off the sofa and she doesn't want the same thing to happen to her.'[11]

For Lovell there was something about working for Broccoli and Saltzman that was reminiscent of old-time Hollywood; they were living like the producers of those bygone golden days. 'They were terrific to me and I liked them both enormously. Harry was particularly generous.'[12] When Lovell became ill with a bleeding ulcer and his doctor urged him to go to the London Clinic, Saltzman insisted that he send all the bills to him.[13]

It was well known amongst the office staff that Sunday was a special day for Saltzman. This is when he did his main entertaining over at his home in Denham. To be invited over to Harry's on a Sunday was a big thing, and the day finally came when Lovell was asked to come over that afternoon. 'I was driving a Ford Capri at the time and Harry came out of the house and said, "Whose car is that?" I said, "It's mine," and Harry said, "Do you mind putting it behind the house."'[14]

Lovell was invited back several times, and there was always a famous face around, a Michael Caine or a Roger Moore. Back when Lovell was ill at the London Clinic, he was sitting idly in bed on a Sunday lunchtime when the door to his room suddenly burst open. 'And there was Harry. I thought, it's a Sunday, what is he doing here. He'd given up his Sunday to drive all the way into town to see if I was doing ok and that everyone was looking after me. I had a real soft spot for Harry.'[15]

Whilst at Eon, Lovell became involved in another Saltzman project called *Toomorrow*, 'a terrible thing',[16] and one that ended up a costly failure.

It began promisingly enough back in February 1969, when America's music and showbiz press were invited to a party at the Rockefeller Centre's Rainbow Grill in New York. The announcement was the creation of a new rock band called Toomorrow, the brainchild of Saltzman and music impresario Don Kirshner, which Saltzman hoped would 'fill a void for 14-year-olds to 30s' left by the break-up of the Beatles; wish-fulfilment for sure.[17]

A lot of people wondered just what Saltzman was doing wasting his time with a prefabricated pop act. As usual with Saltzman, it wasn't quite as simple as that. Toomorrow were to be a 'multi-media' band that was to feature in a series of movies, had just signed to Calendar records, a subsidiary of RCA, and hopefully would be the subject of a huge merchandise campaign featuring a cosmetic range, games and clothing.

The band had been brought together after a six-month worldwide talent hunt and consisted of four young unknowns: Karl Chambers, an R&B drummer from Philadelphia; English pianist Vic Cooper; Ben Thomas, a guitarist from Georgia; and a 20-year-old singer by the name of Olivia Newton-John, who was discovered playing gigs in London clubs.[18] Kirshner thought Olivia had terrific potential and signed her up immediately after a successful audition in Saltzman's office.

Kirshner had a knack for finding and nurturing talent, most notably Neil Diamond and the Monkees. Saltzman's role in this new partnership was, of course, his film experience, and he'd managed to strike a deal for financing with United Artists. It appears this deal went sour, no doubt after *Battle of Britain* laid an egg at the US box office that summer. Instead, Saltzman managed a distribution deal with the Rank Organisation, along with putting a substantial amount of his own money into the project.

Saltzman had an abundance of ideas for the band's debut screen adventure and brought in the novelist David Benedictus to write a draft script. The plot was bizarre to say the least. A group of art students form a band in order to pay their way through college. An alien in disguise living on Earth kidnaps the group and takes them to his home planet, because the sound vibrations coming from their music can save his race from extinction.

Finding the right man to bring all this to the screen was going to be tough. In the end Saltzman chose Val Guest, a highly versatile British director working in all manner of genres, even dinosaur movies and Hammer horrors. Guest had recently worked on the unofficial 007 movie *Casino Royale* and much earlier turned down the chance to make *Dr No*. Saltzman had fun reminding him of this error of judgement when he called him on the phone: 'You could have made a lot of dough from that picture of mine you didn't do, so don't make the same mistake now.'[19] In fact, Guest was about to make one of the biggest mistakes of his career.

When the two men met, Saltzman opened the pitch with, 'How would you like to make the first outer space musical?' Guest later admitted that he should have made his excuses there and then and left, but allowed his curiosity to get the better of him.[20] Saltzman also wanted Guest to rewrite the script after expressing dissatisfaction with the work Benedictus was doing, having read the first thirty pages. 'Don't say anything to him though,' Saltzman advised Guest. 'Let him go on and finish but you start writing the script from scratch now. I'll take care of him.'[21] The problem was that Saltzman didn't, and it was only once production began that Benedictus learnt his script wasn't being used and it was Guest who got the blame. 'As a result, I made a great enemy of Benedictus – he wrote me the most ghastly letter.'[22]

As filming began, Guest discovered that Saltzman's partnership with Kirshner was close to collapse. 'Harry and Don didn't talk to each other, they didn't like each other. It was an absolutely madhouse film.'[23] A stream of daily requests for script alterations would come in from Kirshner's New York office, only for Saltzman to ask Guest to call Kirshner and talk him out of them. After a face-to-face encounter with Kirshner, Guest was of the view that apart from the music and Olivia Newton-John, Kirshner wanted nothing at all to do with the film, and especially Saltzman.[24] Guest really was stuck between a rock and a hard place as production progressed and the problems surrounding Saltzman mounted. 'He was never satisfied; he was always wanting to do a scene or rebuild a set in a different way.'[25]

After filming, Saltzman decided to extend Guest's contract so he could oversee both the editing and the recording of the music soundtrack. However, as things went along the money dried up and Guest was not being paid. When he asked what was going on, Saltzman explained that he didn't have any finance. 'Well, you'd better find it,' Guest's lawyer told the producer in no uncertain fashion. 'Because the film is opening at the London Pavilion next week.'[26]

Nothing did happen, so after a fortnight of the film playing in London's West End during August 1970, Guest was advised to put an injunction on it, which he did and *Toomorrow* was taken off.[27] It wasn't much of a victory; a film Guest had put a lot of work into wasn't being shown and he still didn't get paid. When Guest originally signed on to do the movie his contract was with Sweet Music, Saltzman's newly formed Swiss-based company. It was only later that Guest discovered Sweet Music was in financial trouble. 'We were told that Harry had put up part of his share in the Bond films as collateral for a picture loan, a deal that was forbidden by his partnership with Broccoli. I think that was the beginning of the end for their partnership.'[28]

All this was bad news, of course, for the four young musicians who hoped, indeed had been told by Saltzman and Kirshner, that the film would launch their group into pop orbit. Instead, they were all called into Saltzman's office one afternoon and told the bad news that they were being released from their contracts and that it was all over.[29] The film itself would remain largely unseen by human eyes, save for a few isolated screenings, primarily as a result of Guest's court action and the fact that Kirshner hated it so much and refused to have it released while breath remained in his body. Kirshner died in 2011; a few months later, *Toomorrow* made its belated debut on home video.

The fiasco surrounding the film seemed to do no harm at all to Olivia Newton-John's trajectory course to pop stardom, though it did make her cautious about appearing in more films. It would be eight years before she made another one – *Grease*.

Toomorrow also signalled the end of Dyson Lovell at Eon. His friend Franco Zefferelli had come back into his life and Lovell went to work for him successfully for many years. He still kept tabs on the Bond producers, bumping into them on various occasions; whenever Lovell and Zefferelli were in LA and Cubby was in residence at his Beverly Hills home they'd always invite themselves over and together the three men would cook pasta.[30]

The failure of *Toomorrow* certainly did nothing to curtail Saltzman's film-making activity, with projects galore on the go, none of which ever made it in front of a camera. He hoped to make a comedy with Luis Bunuel in Spain, a film with Peter O'Toole and Michael Caine, a French film starring Jean-Paul Belmondo, and a screen adaptation of crime reporter Andy Logan's book *Against the Evidence*, about police corruption and New York's underworld before Prohibition, to potentially star Lee Marvin.[31]

The project Saltzman was especially interested in concerned Eleanor, the youngest daughter of Karl Marx, a bohemian, socialist and radical intellectual who had a doomed love affair with Edward Aveling, a leading British socialist. 'Harry was terribly keen on that,' recalled Cherry Hughes, whose husband Ken Hughes was slated to direct. 'I did a lot of research on that, Harry would send me off to all these different libraries. I think what drew him to the story so much was the awful way Marx treated his daughter, it gave a different insight into the man, that's what Harry was interested in.'[32]

Working on the project, Cherry and Ken Hughes got to know Saltzman well. 'I liked him tremendously,' said Cherry. 'I always thought Harry was the more interesting of the two Bond producers. He was the intellectual. He was an erudite man, a well-read man. You could sit down at the dinner table with Harry and discuss books, politics, cinema, art, everything.'[33]

It wasn't just films that occupied Saltzman's mind. In the summer of 1970, he made one of the most important financial investments of his life. He'd already headed an English investment group to buy Éclair, the French camera manufacturer. Now he led a group of insurgent stockholders in their bid to wrest control of Technicolor, then the world's largest film processing and printing laboratories, away from the current chairman Patrick J. Frawley Jr. At first Frawley resisted any such takeover, but ultimately he was forced to give up control of the company he'd run for ten years. A new chairman was installed in his place, with Saltzman becoming executive committee chairman.[34]

Like everything Saltzman did, his takeover of Technicolor was carried out with mental precision. 'If Harry was interested in something, he would get all the research and all the books and try to learn everything about it,' said Tom Mankiewicz. 'When he was going to take over Technicolor, Harry knew everything about every member of the board, what they liked and what they didn't like, where they lived. Harry was a very thorough guy when he had his eyes fixed on something.'[35] This time, however, he'd overextended himself and the consequences were to prove ultimately catastrophic. As Steven Saltzman observed, 'My father didn't have the business acumen to be involved in a listed company. He was eaten alive.'[36]

17

Return of the King

With pre-production looming on the latest Bond adventure, *Diamonds Are Forever*, it was now obvious the two producers could no longer work together as before and it was decided they ought to take turns being the operating producer on each new Bond.[1] As Guy Hamilton, returning as director, succinctly put it: 'I can work very happily with Cubby, and I can work very happily with Harry. But working with Cubby and Harry together is a nightmare.'[2] Usually what happened was that the in-fighting tended to slow the production down and ideas, some good ones, wouldn't get through, because if Broccoli liked it Saltzman would reject it on principle.[3]

Diamonds Are Forever would very much be Cubby's film, on hand during the actual shoot, though Harry would look at the rushes and involve himself in pre-production and other creative discussions.

The first thing on the agenda was to find another 007, a search that quickly came to resemble the mad, blind scramble that ended up with Lazenby's casting. The most unqualified of people were approached. How else can you explain the producers' thought patterns behind the potential marquee legend: Michael Gambon is James Bond? Unquestionably a great actor, later knighted by the Queen for services to the industry, but Bond he never was.

At the time Gambon had been enjoying his first real break in the BBC drama serial *The Borderers*, swashbuckling away as a clan chief on the English–Scottish borders in the sixteenth century. It was this series that brought him to the attention of the producers and he was requested to see Broccoli in his office, not knowing what the meeting was about. He was given a smoked salmon sandwich and a glass of champagne before being told they were looking for a new James Bond. Gambon was so flabbergasted he burst out laughing. 'James Bond, me? But I'm bald.' Not a problem, assured Broccoli, so was Connery, a toupee would rectify matters.

'But my teeth are like a horse,' said Gambon.

'We'll take you to Harley Street.'

'But I've got tits like a woman.'

'We'll use ice-packs before the love scenes,' said Broccoli. 'Just like we did with Sean.'

Gambon was encouraged and believed the interview had gone well, but upon leaving the room noticed a parade of other actors waiting to audition. He never heard anything more.[4]

Another hopeful was Simon Oates, best known then as the star of cult TV sci-fi series *Doomwatch*. His agent explained the Bond producers were interested enough in him to have scheduled a screen test over at Pinewood:

> I got a round of applause afterwards from the crew who said, 'Well, that should be you, son, you're all right,' so I thought, that seemed to have gone all right. But then I didn't hear anything back from them, so it never happened for me, but, you know, life goes on.[5]

Actor John Ronane wasn't nearly as charitable after his audition. A member of the Royal Shakespeare Company, Ronane shared the same agent as Connery, Richard Hatton, and it was he who told the actor unexpectedly one day that Saltzman and Broccoli wanted to see him. 'They were both charming but didn't indicate any apparent understanding of the way an actor approaches a part; hence, I suppose, why the Bond role was subsequently played by some of the worst actors ever to carry British Equity cards, in my opinion.'[6]

The real revelation of the meeting came when Saltzman told Ronane that he'd been on his shortlist to play Harry Palmer in *The Ipcress File*. 'I would have dearly loved to have played that character much more than Bond.'[7]

Then there is the case of the man who the *Guinness Book of World Records* would one day acknowledge as 'the greatest living explorer' – Sir Ranulph Fiennes. Certainly, Fiennes had the perfect pedigree to play Bond, being educated at Eton and serving in the British army, including a stint in the SAS. Fiennes was tracked down to an isolated cottage in Inverness, Scotland, where he and his wife were living with very little money and no electricity:

> One day a postman arrived and said that the William Morris agency were on the look-out for a new James Bond. I heard that Mr Lazenby had asked for a certain amount of money for doing a second Bond film and the producers had decided that the answer was to get some actor who wasn't so

keen on being paid too much but who did Bondy type things. They had asked around and someone told them that I might answer that description.[8]

With no acting experience whatsoever, Fiennes was a little baffled by the offer but it had arrived at a propitious moment. Fiennes had heard that the Ministry of Defence were looking for someone with military experience to lead an expedition in British Columbia. Desperate to land the job, Fiennes needed to get to London to see the people in charge. 'But I literally couldn't afford the British Rail ticket from Inverness. So, this Bond interview was a real stroke of luck.'[9]

With his expenses paid, Fiennes found himself in London amongst a host of other Bond contenders. 'There were various types of screen tests and as they went on, I was constantly being surprised about getting through to the next one until I began to start getting stupid thoughts that perhaps the world had gone mad and I actually would be Bond.'[10]

Finally, Fiennes made it through to the very last group where he was going to be vetted by Broccoli himself:

> I went in to see him. He had a big cigar. And he took one look at me and the phrase that he said in front of me, never mind what he might have said after I left the room, was, 'Your hands are too big and you've got a face like a farmer.' He didn't mince his words at all. And obviously I didn't get the role.[11]

All through those Bond tests, Fiennes was secretly sneaking off to the Ministry of Defence to see about the expedition:

> And there were rather fewer contenders for that than there were for Bond. But I wasn't the only contender, so I put in a plan as to how I would do it and ended up organising and leading that particular expedition, which was my first big expedition. So, I'm obviously very grateful for that whole Bond experience happening because it worked out very well for me.[12]

And who knows whether Fiennes' remarkable life of exploring would have happened at all if the Bond producers hadn't paid for that train ticket down to London.

Besides the armed forces, the producers began to scout further afield, settling upon a New Zealander by the name of Roger Green. Then in his early 30s, Green had appeared in a small role in the Dino De Laurentiis movie

Waterloo (1970) and an arthouse BBC2 play. It was Green's agent who decided his client would make a jolly good Bond and sent his photograph to Eon. A few weeks later he was asked to come and meet Broccoli:

> I proceeded to try to impress him with my acting ability by embellishing my very small acting CV. I was well relieved when Broccoli said, 'We are not so concerned with your acting ability. We're more interested in how athletic you are?' This was music to my ears as I had just completed a successful rugby career where I had played for the Junior All Blacks. I told Broccoli of this and the meeting ended with him saying he wanted me to meet his partner Harry Saltzman.[13]

Green's meeting with Saltzman was held around his boardroom table with Guy Hamilton and others present. 'They asked me if I felt I could do this role. Of course, I said yes. They then handed me the script of the forthcoming screen test to be held at Pinewood Studios. I was asked to have a haircut with their favourite barber.'[14]

Green's test, lasting all of ten minutes, featured him romancing actress Imogen Hassel before having to fight an intruder played by stuntman Bob Simmons. Guy Hamilton thought Green had a great chance of getting the part and told him they'd get back in touch soon. 'For this sheep farmer on extended holiday in the UK this was certainly an event to cause me to walk on air for the next three months.'[15] Alas, it was not to be. 'My agent said that Hamilton, Broccoli and Saltzman had wished me to play the role but United Artists said, "Not another unknown antipodean actor, please!"'[16]

After countless weeks of auditions, poring over photographs, talking with agents and getting nowhere, the two producers flew to America to start interviewing likely candidates there. A frontrunner quickly emerged in 40-year-old John Gavin, a former naval intelligence officer with the dark handsome looks of a Rock Hudson. Having worked with the likes of Alfred Hitchcock on *Psycho* (1960) and Stanley Kubrick in *Spartacus* (1960), playing the young Julius Caesar, Gavin had since languished in television, with the odd cinema outing, including a starring role in French Bond spoof *OSS 117 Double Agent* (1968).

Confident in his abilities and after some promising tests, the producers offered Gavin the Bond role. He accepted and signed on the dotted line. Broccoli and Saltzman had their new James Bond.

United Artists were still nervous about introducing another new Bond after the less than stunning box office returns for *On Her Majesty's Secret Service.*

There was only one solution in their minds – bring back Connery. David Picker, now studio president, called the producers to see if there was any chance of making a deal, only to learn that the lines of communication with the actor were severed. 'Their relationship with Connery was essentially non-existent and non-speaking,' said Picker, who had no idea things had got so bad between them.[17] In any case, Broccoli and Saltzman were hesitant about bringing Connery back. In the words of Dana Broccoli, 'They didn't want to beg a reluctant actor to act.'[18]

Picker took charge of the situation personally and flew to London to negotiate a deal with Connery's agent, Richard Hatton. The offer on the table was unprecedented: a fee of £1.2 million (which Connery donated to his own trust fund set up for the artistic development of underprivileged Scots), a healthy share of the profits, and a promise by United Artists to finance, to the tune of $1 million, any two films of Connery's choosing to either appear in or direct. Ultimately only one film was made under the agreement, 1972's *The Offence*.

An additional inducement, given the actor's vocal annoyance at the long shooting schedules of his previous Bonds, was a clause that if the film overran its production schedule, he would receive $10,000 for each additional week. Ironically, shooting was to be completed on time in eighteen weeks. 'It can be done, if there's money at stake,' said Connery, feeling vindicated. 'I've been frigged about too much on other Bond pictures.'[19]

The arrangement was accepted, and after the meeting Picker remembered Hatton saying how much he appreciated United Artists getting involved and that if the producers had dealt with his client in the same way none of these problems would have arisen:

> Basically, he said they treated him like shit. They renegotiated their own deals with UA, but never addressed what Sean had brought to Bond. He was simply, in their minds, an actor lucky to get such a break, and the hell with any reconsideration. He felt used and under-appreciated and he didn't like it one bit.[20]

Broccoli and Saltzman's misgivings about taking Connery back remained, while at the same time neither man could ignore United Artists' insistence, 'nor overlook Sean's strong hold on the world box office,' said Cubby.[21] Yet in all the brouhaha about Connery's return one man was forgotten, the man who had already signed a contract to play 007. Luckily, John Gavin had made a pay-or-play deal and was reportedly compensated with $50,000. 'I don't think he was really disappointed,' said Hamilton. 'He always knew he was in the changing room warming up, but would never play the big game.'[22]

After the back-to-basics scenario of the Lazenby picture, it was to be a return to the fantastical world of James Bond in *Diamonds Are Forever*. Richard Maibaum even produced a draft script that posed Goldfinger's twin brother as a world threat, with the hope that Gert Frobe might play the role.[23] Saltzman's suggestion that some filming could take place in Thailand and India encouraged Maibaum to develop ideas of jungle treks and tiger hunts.[24]

Ditching these ideas, it was decided to bring in a young writer in tune with the new Hollywood. Since much of Fleming's novel took place in the US, he also had to be an American with the ability of being able to write in the British idiom. Picker was sure he'd found the right candidate. Before it closed after just three nights, Picker caught a Broadway musical set in swinging London called *Georgy*. It was written by Tom Mankiewicz, whose father was Joseph L. Mankiewicz, the director of such classics as *All About Eve* and *Cleopatra*. His uncle was Herman Mankiewicz, the writer of *Citizen Kane*. In Hollywood there are few better pedigrees than that.

Following a short meeting with Broccoli, Mankiewicz was hired and put on a two-week guarantee. Delivering the first thirty pages, Cubby called the young writer after reading them and said just two words – 'Keep going.'[25]

Mankiewicz was elated. Here he was, just 27 years old, writing a James Bond movie at a time when 007 was the only real movie event in town. 'There was no *Raiders* yet, no *Superman*, no *Star Wars*, no anything. The world waited for the Bond movie to come out every eighteen months or so. Harry and Cubby really did have the world by the tail.'[26]

It was quite evident to Mankiewicz that the relationship between the two producers had fractured; however, he never witnessed any major arguments on the set during the whole of his three-picture tenure on the Bond series:

> When they were about to blow, it was always done in private. If Guy Hamilton and I were there, it would be, 'Guy, Tom, would you excuse us for a moment.' They did sometimes yell at each other in a creative meeting way, Harry would say, 'It's a great idea,' and Cubby would say, 'No, no, no.' But when there was going to be something serious, that was always done in private.[27]

Far from it being a hindrance, the writer often used the situation to his advantage, playing the two men against each other. If Mankiewicz had a funny line or a certain situation he could say, 'Here's a scene for you to read Cubby.

Harry hates it,' and Cubby would go, 'He does, does he,' and without reading it say, 'Well I love it, it's in Goddamnit.'[28]

On another occasion, Mankiewicz was working in his office when Saltzman came in. 'I understand you're doing a good job, but tell me, what is the threat?'

'The threat is Blofeld's going to destroy the world,' answered Mankiewicz.

Saltzman shook his head disappointedly. 'It's not big enough,' and walked out.[29]

All through his time on the movie, Mankiewicz was making something like $1,250 a week. Prepping the movie in Las Vegas, he was relaxing in the hotel bar with Broccoli one night when Milton Feldman, the production manager, came in. Connery was due to arrive the next day and Cubby wanted to know if all the arrangements had been made. 'How's Sean's suite,? he asked. 'Have you been up there Milton, did you check it?' Feldman said everything was fine. Broccoli turned to Mankiewicz. 'How's your suite?'

'Cubby I don't have a suite, but I'm really happy, I've got a beautiful double room overlooking the strip, everything's fine.'

'Milton, get him a suite.'

'But Cubby.' Feldman looked across at Mankiewicz. 'No offence Tom, but Cubby if we get him a suite that will cost more money than we're paying him.'

'I didn't ask you what it cost Milton,' said Cubby. 'He's writing the fucking movie, get him a suite.'[30]

Mankiewicz was told Connery had tried to get a clause in his contract that he didn't want to see Saltzman anywhere near the Vegas location. 'I don't know why, but Sean had a particular dislike for Harry. In those days Sean and Cubby got along pretty well. Their relationship seemed much better on a day to day basis, although they were both very strong-willed people.'[31]

The first night's shooting was going to be Bond in his red mustang being chased around downtown Vegas, part of an elaborate car chase. The day before, news reached everyone that Saltzman had showed up. 'Oh shit,' was Broccoli's comment when he heard. 'We were all in Sean's motorhome waiting for the first shot,' recalled Mankiewicz:

> Guy Hamilton, Cubby and myself. Suddenly there was a knock on the door, we thought it was an assistant telling us they were ready to shoot. The door opened and there was Harry, and really defiantly, Sean's face lit up with a big grin. 'Harry,' he said, and he walked forward and kissed him on the forehead. Harry left Vegas the next day and never came back. But I think it was Harry

> making his point, which was, this is my film goddammit, as well as Cubby's, and no actor's going to do that to me.[32]

Mankiewicz also had a hand in a key casting decision, that of Plenty O'Toole, Bond's Vegas conquest. Lana Wood, younger sister of Natalie, had just done a heavily publicised *Playboy* pictorial and was a friend of the writer, who put her name forward to Cubby. At her meeting with Broccoli, Lana found him to be 'very charming and very interested in what I had to say'.[33] She got the part.

Other roles went to Charles Gray as Blofeld and Jill St John as Tiffany Case, a vital cog in Bond's investigations into a diamond smuggling racket that turns out to be a SPECTRE-led mission to use large quantities of gems for a laser satellite to hold the world to ransom. There was also a role for an old pal of Cubby's, the veteran actor Bruce Cabot, who had famously appeared in the original *King Kong*. Already suffering from the cancer that would eventually kill him, Broccoli made sure that Cabot was involved in every location so that his role was extended by a further six weeks, along with his pay cheque. *Diamonds* turned out to be his final film role.[34]

Shooting in Vegas was a real eye-opener for Mankiewicz, who described himself as 'very impressionable' at the time. 'There were a lot of questionable people that Cubby knew very well. Sidney Korshak, who was known as the fixer, he was the lawyer for the Teamsters, supposedly one of the few people in the world who knew what happened to Jimmy Hoffa, and Cubby knew all these people.'[35] Korshak was to prove invaluable on the film in smoothing things over with the local unions.

When Mankiewicz needed to go to New York for a couple of days and found there was a paucity of hotel rooms available due to a big convention going on at the United Nations, Korshak made him an offer. 'I have a suite at the Carlyle. It's just sitting there. Take it. I insist.' Mankiewicz thanked him.

Later that evening, Broccoli came over and said, 'Listen, let me give you some advice. Sidney's a great friend of mine, he likes you very much – don't ever let Sidney do you a favour. I'm serious.'

'Cubby there's nothing I can do for Sidney back.'

'Yes there is. It could be a girl you're banging. It could be a lot of different things. All I'm saying is go stay in his suite, because he offered and you said yes, but in the future, don't let Sidney do you a favour.'[36]

Another old friend of Broccoli's proved equally useful to the production. By 1971, Howard Hughes had become an eccentric recluse, living with his entourage of personal aides in the top-floor penthouses of various hotels.

Publicly he was never seen. Cubby, too, hadn't seen Hughes for years, recalling that the last time they ever spoke was during the making of *Thunderball* when the tycoon phoned to ask if he could borrow some 16mm copies of the Bond movies. 'When we asked for the films back,' said Dana, 'they were just run over and over and over. They were almost worn out.'[37]

With Hughes the owner of several top casinos in Vegas, the Bond team were allowed to shoot in places most other film crews would have had zero access to. 'We got the VIP treatment,' revealed Ken Adam. 'And when it became difficult to get permission to shoot somewhere, Cubby used to phone Howard's associate at the penthouse, and we got permission within seconds.'[38]

During their stay in Vegas, Cubby and Dana's room was burgled in the middle of the night, as they lay asleep in bed. For Dana especially, the whole thing was a frightening experience. The following evening, as they returned to their room, two burly men stood outside the door. 'Compliments of Mr Howard Hughes,' one of them said. 'Our orders are to stay here round the clock until you leave.'[39]

Interestingly, during the script process Broccoli must have had his old friend in mind since he awoke one morning having experienced a most vivid dream in which he arrived at Hughes's secluded penthouse, only to discover that he had been replaced by an imposter. It was such a good idea that it was incorporated into the script.

Broccoli was in his element in Vegas and played baccarat every evening; sometimes all night. Ken Adam was his lucky mascot and would invariably sit next to him and play as well. When Adam's own money ran out, Cubby would press $1,000 into his hand to keep on playing.[40] Mankiewicz was often there, too, and saw that Cubby never won or lost less than $10,000 or $15,000 a night, which was a lot of money in 1971. He noticed something else, too. When he left the table after a session, Broccoli always tipped everybody. However, he would always tip more heavily when he lost than when he won:

> I asked him why he did that and he said to me, 'Listen, in your life a lot of things are going to go right and a lot of things are going to go wrong. You're going to have a lot of big success and a lot of big failures, but first you've got to be a gentleman.' And I think he really tried to live that way.[41]

With Connery back, the producers did everything to make the shooting of *Diamonds Are Forever* as pleasurable a return as possible, including arranging for him to play golf at conveniently located courses. 'If this was to be his last Bond film for us,' Broccoli said, 'then we wanted to part as friends.'[42]

The last day of location filming took place on an oil rig off San Diego, and Hamilton, who like Connery was a golf nut, knew of a very fine course nearby. 'Sean and I made a deal with Broccoli that if we finished early, we could go. I think we did sixteen set-ups in about two hours.'[43]

After a long stay in the US, work on *Diamonds Are Forever* was completed on interior sets at Pinewood Studios. Called in to do some second unit shots was Andrew Birkin, who since *Play Dirty* had worked for Saltzman on the ill-fated *Toomorrow*. Birkin was on the Bond set for no more than a week but bumped into Harry a few times. 'He was very warm. Harry was always really sweet to me, I have to say. He did seem to like me, I don't know why. Maybe because I was so enthusiastic.'[44]

Not long afterwards, Birkin was approached about another assignment. Saltzman was contemplating making a film that revolved around the childhood of James Bond. David Puttnam was also involved. 'I was sent out to do some photographic tests on this young boy somebody had found. They didn't have a script at the time, it was just an idea.' The project went no further.[45]

Trading on the nostalgic return of Connery, Shirley Bassey was asked back to perform the seductive title track. John Barry invited the producers and some friends to his London apartment to play them the new song. Barry never had any qualms about Broccoli. 'He was very good about music. He had a good ear and always had very good instincts about the songs. Harry was absolutely tone deaf.'[46] Everyone loved the song except Saltzman, who found Don Black's lyrics – especially the line, 'Touch it, stroke it and undress it' – filthy.[47] Indeed, during the actual recording Barry told Shirley to sing that line as if the diamond were a man's penis.

Barry turned to Saltzman to ask, 'Harry, will you do me one thing? Will you sing me the first two bars of the national anthem?' Flustered, Saltzman let fly with a few swear words and left the room, slamming the door.[48]

Opening in time for the 1971 Christmas holidays, *Diamonds Are Forever* was a worldwide smash. At the Odeon Leicester Square, demand for tickets was so high that it was reported one thwarted patron punched the cinema manager, while another man who couldn't get in threatened to report him to the Director of Public Prosecution.[49] In Italy, the film took more in eleven days than the previous year's top hit, *The Decameron*, did in three months.[50] In interviews, the producers were reluctant to show any guilt about the exorbitant money they were making but did confess it was more than any two people should decently make. 'Mind you,' opined Saltzman. 'We have two very rich partners – the UK and US governments. They cream off about half in taxes.'[51]

Diamonds Are Forever successfully navigated Bond into the 1970s, especially in its more comedic approach that signalled the way the series was headed. It had been Connery who wanted more wit in the film and Broccoli encouraged it. On occasion, when Mankiewicz would say that maybe it was going too far, Cubby would say, 'Don't worry about it, keep writing.'[52]

On the back of the new film's success, Saltzman and Broccoli were now determined to lure Connery back to do *Live and Let Die* and arranged for Tom Mankiewicz, who they knew had a good relationship with the star, to have lunch with him:

> They wanted me to try and get him back! So, we had this lunch and I told him, 'Look Sean, we've got crocodiles, we've got a boat chase, we've got a lot of great stuff going on in case you want to do one more.' And Sean said a really interesting thing, he said, 'I read in the papers sometimes that it's my fucking obligation to play Bond. Well I've done six of them, when does the obligation run out, at ten, twelve, fourteen.' And Sean being very much an actor by then, and he wasn't when he started, meaning he really had become a world star, I think he just couldn't wait to go out and act and play other parts.[53]

Broccoli hoped that he and Connery could part as friends at the end of *Diamonds Are Forever*, but the actor had no intention of holding back on what he thought. His view was that it wasn't just a personal opinion of his own, the two producers themselves were hardly enamoured of each other, 'probably because they're both sitting on $50 million and looking across the desk at each other and thinking: that bugger's got half of what should be all mine.'[54] It was quotes like these that both upset and disappointed Broccoli, since he believed that he had at least tried to maintain a workable and cordial relationship with his star. 'I never had a problem with him until after he left our domain and he started saying terrible things about me. I was the only one he could deal with. He really hated Saltzman.'[55]

18

The Saintly Bond

While *Diamonds Are Forever* was very much Cubby's film, Harry would take the reins on *Live and Let Die*, especially out on location in Jamaica and in the States. 'I don't remember seeing Cubby on that film until we came back to Pinewood,' said Mankiewicz.[1] If anything, their relationship was now even worse than before. This was one of the reasons why Stanley Sopel, a key figure at Eon since *Dr No*, had decided to leave prior to the new Bond going into production. For him the mood around the place had changed since those early days, it had become tense and divisive. 'I knew then that Saltzman and Broccoli were going to divide; it wasn't the same Eon Productions. I enjoyed working with both men, and since I knew they were going to split, I didn't want to be part of that.'[2]

Regardless of the personal problems between the producers, the Bond franchise faced yet another challenge: the search for a new 007. It began early in 1972, with dozens of screen tests. Old Vic and National Theatre alumnus Jeremy Brett was one candidate. So too was another classically trained actor, Julian Glover, who believed his appearance at the time in a BBC espionage series called *Spy Trap* was the reason Broccoli and Saltzman came calling. 'I was in my early 30s and quite presentable looking and I was playing a sort of Bond-style character. I wore a suit and tie and stood up straight and pointed a gun in the right direction.'[3]

When his agent informed him that the Bond producers wanted to set up a screen test, Glover's first reaction was:

> Wow, quite simply, but then, God, I don't stand a chance do I. But my agent was very encouraging, so I went to Pinewood and did the test. Of course, I was absolutely terrified. It was such an outside chance, the idea of me play-

> ing James Bond was almost absurd, that was something that Sean Connery did. I suppose that my test is on the cutting room floor somewhere. I have to say I wouldn't want it to be seen; the shame, the shame.[4]

Of course, Glover would go on to play the double-crossing Kristatos in 1981's *For Your Eyes Only*.

Another candidate emerged after Saltzman's visit to the set of cult TV sci-fi series *UFO* back in 1970. He'd come to the studio to meet with Gerry and Sylvia Anderson and to see footage from the show, as he was planning to follow *Diamonds Are Forever* with *Moonraker* and was looking for someone to handle the special effects. An accomplished casting director in her own right, Sylvia Anderson suggested to Saltzman that Michael Billington, who played Colonel Paul Foster in *UFO*, might be right for Bond. 'When I was spruced up, I did look a little bit Bond-like,' Billington confirmed.[5]

Nothing was heard for a while, then Billington was asked to see Broccoli at South Audley Street:

> I felt the meeting went well and I liked Cubby as a person. I also think I did well on the test for *Live and Let Die* and liked Guy Hamilton, the director. The scene was a specially written one. I heard from my agent that there was going to be an offer made. When it was announced that Roger Moore was going to do it, I was stunned. Getting the Bond role was as close as could be really. I think I was the unanimous choice at one point of both Cubby and Harry and Guy Hamilton; they all at one time or another gave me the seal of approval.[6]

Following *UFO*, Billington appeared in the popular BBC period drama *The Onedin Line*, alongside a young actress called Jane Seymour. When Jane was cast in *Live and Let Die* as the mysterious Solitaire she revealed to Billington that from time to time on the set Saltzman would quiz her about him, probing questions about his sexuality and other intimate details.[7] Was the producer still of a mind to bring Billington into the series at some point? Something about his test also stuck in Broccoli's mind, too, when he later cast Billington as the KGB agent killed by Bond in the famous pre-title ski chase in *The Spy Who Loved Me*.

As the search for a new Bond intensified, United Artists began to lay down the law to Broccoli and Saltzman, insisting that an established actor with solid professional experience be cast this time; in other words, not another George Lazenby. Incredulously, the studio set their sights on Paul Newman and Robert Redford. Even Clint Eastwood was approached, as the actor has revealed. 'I was offered pretty good money to do James Bond. My lawyer represented the Broccolis and he came and said, "They would love to have you." But to me, well, that was somebody else's gig. That's Sean's deal. It didn't feel right for me to be doing it.'[8]

While Broccoli felt that he personally owed something to John Gavin, Hamilton was pushing for Burt Reynolds, with the backing of Saltzman according to Tom Mankiewicz. 'Harry was not averse to casting an American and Burt Reynolds was very seriously considered.'[9] Broccoli also turned to a former client from his agent days, and over an informal dinner talked to Robert Wagner about playing Bond. 'I thought about Cubby's suggestion for about two seconds, but realised it just wasn't a good fit. "I'm too American," I told Cubby. "James Bond has to be English. Roger Moore is your guy."'[10]

At the back of Cubby's mind while all this was going on was someone who had been an option right from the very start of the series: Roger Moore. Though never formally approached to play Bond in *Dr No*, due to his commitments to *The Saint*, Moore was amongst the list of candidates and it's interesting to speculate what the series might have been with him in the role from the outset. Moore wouldn't have looked out of place in *Goldfinger*, for example, but can you visualise him in *From Russia With Love*?

Moore was good friends with both producers, having first met them across the gaming tables of a London casino. Cubby and Harry always made a point of inviting Moore to special previews of the Bond films at their private viewing theatre in South Audley Street. 'We were great social friends and with Harry we would have a poker school probably once a week or play gin.'[11]

Considered once again for *Diamonds Are Forever*, Moore was making another television series, *The Persuaders*. Interestingly, before agreeing to do *The Persuaders* Moore voiced concerns about being saddled long-term to a show and making himself unavailable should the Bond role become free again. 'So, Roger had no contract to do *The Persuaders*,' confirmed the series' creator and producer Robert S. Baker. 'Tony Curtis had a contract, but Roger wouldn't sign, so it just became a gentlemen's agreement.'[12]

Crucially, that left Moore a free agent when TV tycoon Lew Grade was anxious for him to commit to a second season, according to Baker. 'Lew wanted to make more *Persuaders* but Roger didn't. By that time Roger had the offer to play Bond. He was being groomed by Broccoli and Saltzman. At the end of the series we knew Roger was going to be Bond.'[13]

While Moore remained Cubby's choice, United Artists were not fully convinced he was able to make the transition from TV star to film star, since the few films he'd made in between his *Saint* show had not done well. It was something Saltzman was worried about, too; he felt Moore was too identified as The Saint.[14] In the end, Broccoli refused to compromise on his choice and eventually Harry and United Artists went along with it.[15]

It was Saltzman who called Moore up with the good news at the actor's home in Denham. 'Are you alone?' the producer asked first. 'You mustn't talk about this, but Cubby agrees with my thinking in terms of you for the next Bond.'[16]

On 1 August 1972, it was made official: Moore was introduced as the new James Bond at a press conference at the Dorchester Hotel in London. Moore's agent Dennis Van Thal managed to negotiate a very nice three-picture deal, with options to do further films.

Moore's stint on *The Persuaders*, however, with good living on location in the South of France, drinking real champagne on screen, had put something like 20lbs on him. 'The Bond producers kept on saying, "You're too fat, gotta lose some weight." They then declared, "Your hair's too long." I kept having inches cut off. In the end I got so desperate I asked them why didn't they get a bald-headed, thin fella to start with.'[17]

Asked by the press what was going to be different about his 007 from Connery's, Moore replied, 'White teeth!' That one jokey response was the key to Moore's whole approach to playing the role, to chisel off the hard edge surrounding this iconic figure and play the whole thing in a far more tongue-in-cheek way, as though he were sharing the joke with the audience. Mankiewicz certainly recognised that Moore's strong points as an actor were in direct contrast to Connery:

> They were very different people to write for because when Sean walks into a room on screen there's a twinkle in his eye and he looks like a bastard. It looks like violence might happen at any moment. Roger looks like a nice guy. But Roger oddly enough, because I'd read the books, was much closer to Fleming's idea of Bond. Bond was terribly English, not British, English, and I always thought of Fleming's Bond as a slightly more muscular young David Niven and I would have thought that Fleming would have been happier with Roger in the beginning.[18]

So, Roger was in as Bond – or was he? Not so, according to the actor Victor Spinetti, who was enjoying a quiet dinner at home with Sean Connery one evening. Spinetti and Connery were old friends, having first met back in the mid 1950s when the pair shared digs as they toured round the country with the musical *South Pacific*. The phone rang and the mystery caller asked to speak with Connery. Spinetti observed Connery listening intently for several minutes before finally snapping, 'No way! I wouldn't dream of it. Get knotted,' and slamming the phone down:

> I asked Sean, 'What was that about?' He told me that it had been Harry Saltzman. *Live and Let Die* had been shooting for some days, only for them to arrive at the conclusion Roger Moore was hopeless. Would Sean come back? If he did, they would pay off Roger, scrap the footage shot so far, and start again. 'The bastards,' said Sean. 'They won't give him a chance. Now you know what I had to put up with.'[19]

Back on scriptwriting duty, Mankiewicz was delighted the producers had chosen *Live and Let Die* to launch the Moore Bond era. It certainly made commercial sense with the rise of black power in the United States and the recent wave of blaxploitation movies. It was obvious, too, that Fleming's outdated book would need a drastic overhaul. Another problem for Mankiewicz was Saltzman:

> Harry was a volcano of ideas. I always thought the problem with Harry was he would come out with five ideas, two of which were absolutely wonderful and the other three weren't, but he couldn't distinguish between them, as far as he was concerned all five were great ideas. And he never gave up on them.[20]

One obsession of Saltzman's was that Bond should find himself imperilled inside a giant spin dryer. 'What do you mean?' asked Mankiewicz. 'Like the Jolly Green Giant's laundromat.' And Harry would say, 'I don't know, you're the writer.' Saltzman was always trying to get this spin dryer idea into a Bond film. 'And I don't know why,' said Mankiewicz. 'It was a fixation of his.'[21]

On another occasion, when Mankiewicz was near to completing his first draft, Saltzman rang him up with an idea. 'Bond is in bed, you think with Solitaire, and he feels something and he turns around and he's in bed with a crocodile.'

'Harry, if he's asleep why didn't the crocodile eat him?' said Mankiewicz, not unreasonably.

'I don't know, you're the writer.'

Mankiewicz had another question. 'Harry, crocodiles have these little feet, how did he get up on the bed, did he have a plank, because he could never have gotten up there.'

'I don't know, you're the writer!' Needless to say, that scene never made the movie.[22]

While it was Saltzman that regularly came up with these bizarre ideas, Broccoli was always the voice of reason and logic, so far as Mankiewicz was concerned. 'Cubby was the voice of the audience.'[23] There's a good example of this. In *Diamonds Are Forever*, Bond uses the body of a dead baddie to smuggle a cache of diamonds into Los Angeles. Felix Leiter asks Bond where they are, and Mankiewicz came up with this clever riposte: 'Alimentary Dr Leiter.' Cubby didn't get the joke. 'What's that?' he asked.

'The alimentary canal Cubby, it's stuffed up the arse.'

'Nobody's going to know that.'

Guy Hamilton certainly saw the funny side of the line and it was finally kept in. Cut to several months later, and Broccoli and Mankiewicz went down to Grauman's Chinese Theatre where *Diamonds* was playing. It was a packed house, and the line came up, 'Alimentary Dr Leiter,' and two people laughed. Cubby turned to look at Mankiewicz and said, 'Big deal, two doctors.'[24]

With the script almost finished, thoughts turned to casting. Jane Seymour was a young British actress that both producers had asked to come and see them at South Audley without the other knowing. Jane was to recall standing in their office whilst both men engaged in a heated argument as to who had in fact spotted her first. 'Then one of the secretaries pulled me out of there and said, "I think you better come wait out here."'[25]

Nevertheless, she was hired on the spot to play the beautiful fortune teller Solitaire. So elated, Jane recalled leaving the office, getting into her Volkswagen Beetle and accidentally backing into Saltzman's Rolls-Royce.[26]

During shooting, Jane was expressly told by the producers not to read the Fleming novel, only the script. When Saltzman caught her on the set one day with a copy of the book, he snatched it away: 'I'll take that.'[27]

The rest of the cast was filled by prominent American black actors, notably Yaphet Kotto as Mr Big, Bond's latest nemesis whose plan is to corner the world's drug market by flooding it with cheap heroin.

Although Saltzman was to take charge of the shooting itself, Broccoli, along with Mankiewicz, carried out an early location recce in Louisiana. The local sheriff was thrilled that a Bond film was hitting town, but less keen about the number of black actors and crew members. He explained it might upset folks in the neighbourhood to see them driving around in heavy trucks.

'Well sheriff,' said Cubby. 'I guess we'll just have to spend our million dollars in another parish.'

'No, hold on. Okay, but keep it down to a dull roar, will you.'

Broccoli said he would, and as the sheriff walked away Mankiewicz heard Cubby tell the transportation captain, 'I want a black guy behind the wheel of every vehicle.' Then looking at the departing sheriff hissed under his breath, 'Fucking cracker.'[28]

Much of the film was to take place in the United States, principally New York and New Orleans. During production Moore noticed that his relationship with Saltzman had shifted. 'It was no longer one of two friends, but rather that of an employer and employee. It was a subtle difference, but Harry liked me to be aware he was the boss.'[29] Working with Saltzman for the very first time, Moore also came face to face with the producer's notorious temper. 'Harry had a little cuddly bear look about him, but a temper like nobody you could imagine. He really could let fly. But he could be a very generous host.'[30] On the set, the two men engaged in games of gin rummy and poker, in much the same competitive spirit as when Moore would later battle with Broccoli over backgammon on his later Bonds.

There was something else, too, a feeling that Saltzman was overly possessive of the actor, unnecessarily so at times. When the crew were filming in New York, Saltzman refused David Hedison, who played Felix Leiter, to stay in the same hotel as Moore. 'He was jealous of our friendship,' Moore revealed.[31]

Something else Moore couldn't fail but notice was how strained the relationship was between the producers, and how he was often required to 'dodge the crossfire'.[32] Moore had always liked both men, but certainly found it easier to get along with Cubby.

In press interviews, the producers did their best to dispel any rumours of disquiet behind the scenes. 'Friction has to exist in an operation of this size,' offered Broccoli.[33] While Saltzman admitted that yes, the pair of them did engage in rows, 'very healthy rows. Movie making is a volatile business. We'll argue over an actor or interpretations of a script.'[34] The problem was, nobody was buying it any more. Indeed, Peter Lamont recalled that Broccoli was not around very much for the shoot, but he and Dana did come out once to New Orleans and put on a big party because they thought the morale of the unit was low.[35]

New Orleans was the film's big location and Peter Lamont, together with Syd Cain, Guy Hamilton and Saltzman, flew out there on a Pan Am flight. Jacqueline saw off her husband at the airport and Lamont noticed that she passed him a carrier bag. Getting on the plane, Saltzman asked one of the stewards to look after it. The group were flying first class and Saltzman had organised for them all to eat in the dining section. 'We're sitting there,' recalled Lamont. 'And Harry said to the steward, "Can I have my bag." He opened it and inside were tomatoes and other vegetables wrapped in foil from the Saltzmans' garden, and this stewardess turned to me and said, "He's flying first class and he's brought his own food."'[36]

Shooting in and around the city, the crew also made use of the nearby bayous for an elaborate boat chase that became a highlight of the film. Due to time restrictions some bits of business didn't get filmed, including one scene of a golfer on a putting green about to down a two-foot putt when smash, a boat lands in the bunker and he misses. The golfer was going to be played by Ted Moore.[37]

After finishing work in New Orleans, the crew moved to their next location, Jamaica. On the first day of shooting, Saltzman told Moore he would pick him up in the morning and drive him to the set:

> The trouble was Harry drove as if everybody in Jamaica knew that he was the producer of the Bond films and he was very important and they shouldn't be on the road because we would be coming round bends on the wrong side. I was a nervous wreck by the time we got to the location. After that, I said I would much rather drive myself.[38]

That first day almost turned into a mutiny when the crew took their break, opened the lunch boxes provided and discovered inside an apple and an orange on a bed of lettuce along with a sorry looking sandwich. When a delegation led by Peter Lamont and a union official went to complain, all Saltzman could say was, 'Look, I can't help it, all the money was spent in New Orleans.' George Crawford, the catering manager, said to Lamont not to worry, that he'd fix it. 'So, the next day Harry gets his lunch box,' said Lamont. 'And it's limp lettuce, an apple and a sardine tin with no key; and it all changed the next day.'[39]

Conversely, when the crew were filming in Ocho Rios, Saltzman threw a Thanksgiving party for 120 people and flew in the chef from Harry's Bar in Venice.

Back at Pinewood, Syd Cain returned to the Bond team as production designer and got in trouble over the representation of Bond's flat, seen for only the second time in the series. 'What do you call this then?' said Saltzman. Cain was bemused, thinking he'd done a good job. 'You know you're doing a Bond,' Saltzman continued. Cain asked what was wrong. 'Bond is larger than life and the set is too small. I will not shoot on it until you make it bigger.' It was Guy Hamilton who came to the rescue. Overhearing the conversation, he told Saltzman, 'If you make it any bigger, *I* will not shoot on it!' Saltzman backed off.[40]

Live and Let Die had all the familiar Bond elements, save for one curious absence: Desmond Llewelyn's Q. Following his appearance in *Diamonds Are Forever*, Llewelyn undertook his first publicity tour, visiting a host of American cities. It generated so much positive publicity that back at Pinewood, publicist Tom Carlile presented a bulging file of press cuttings onto Saltzman's desk. Glancing over them, Saltzman said, 'H'mm, you can wipe your arse with that lot.' Little wonder Llewelyn dubbed Saltzman 'A pocket Napoleon'.[41] Adding insult to injury, Saltzman decided the new film didn't require Llewelyn's services. The actor was hurt and disappointed when he took his agent's phone call: 'Saltzman wants to do this one differently; he doesn't need you.'[42]

Alongside Moore's debut as Bond, *Live and Let Die* is best known for its classic Paul McCartney theme song. Just how the ex-Beatle came to contribute to a Bond film has much to do with a music publishing company Saltzman owned at the time called Hilary Music, named after his daughter. It was run by two former employees of the Beatles' record label, Apple: American businessman Ron Kass and Tony Bramwell, a childhood friend of the group. Bramwell first met the Bond producers back in 1969 when his girlfriend, actress Julie Ege, was appearing in *On Her Majesty's Secret Service*. Bramwell subsequently bumped into Saltzman at a party and was asked if he would consider starting a music company for him. Bramwell was noncommittal in his reply, but their conversation must have been overheard since a few days later the story made the music and cinema trade papers.[43]

The Apple office was run by the infamous Alan Klein, who had wasted little time firing a large number of the organisation's employees leading to a dismal atmosphere. Bramwell, though, was seen as untouchable, given his personal association with the Beatles. Still, Klein was not best pleased with Bramwell after the Saltzman story broke.

'Tony,' Klein roared. 'I read in *Variety* that you're leaving us for James Bond.'

'Well, there's fuck all to do here, so yes.'[44]

Saltzman gave Bramwell an office on the ground floor of Tilney Street. Although South Audley Street was just a few yards away, Bramwell hardly ever saw Broccoli, and was of the understanding that the two producers were hardly on speaking terms anymore. 'By then there were only a few binding sinews holding them together.'[45]

One of the aims of Hilary Music was to put together soundtracks for films. Bramwell recalls working on the David Puttnam-produced children's drama *Melody* starring Mark Lester and Jack Wild, which employed the music of the

Bee Gees and Crosby, Stills and Nash. Bramwell also managed to get Mary Hopkin to sing the title song to the Michael Caine film *Kidnapped*.

When it came to *Live and Let Die*, given both Bramwell's and Kass's connection with Apple and the Beatles, Paul McCartney seemed an ideal candidate. Bramwell recalled driving out to see McCartney at his London home and asking what his thoughts on it were. 'He said, "Yeah, sure. What's it about?" So, he read the book overnight. I then introduced him to Maurice Binder and together they went through the ideas for the titles and by the weekend Paul had recorded the song and it was ready on the Monday.'[46]

When it came time for Bramwell to play the song to Saltzman, things didn't exactly go to plan. 'Harry said, "Right, now who's going to sing it. We've got B.J. Arnau," who was this Shirley Bassey clone, and I said, "No, Harry, Paul wants his version to be the theme tune, he's sat with Maurice Binder for days working on the title sequence."'[47] It's probably not Saltzman's fault that he didn't have his finger on the pulse of contemporary music and was thinking along the lines of Easy Listening artists like another Bassey or a singer like Matt Munro. Funnily enough, B.J. Arnau did get to perform the song in the film, appearing as a nightclub singer.

If Saltzman was guilty of missing a trick over McCartney, so did Broccoli, when he played the song to Mankiewicz. When the writer professed his enthusiasm for it, Broccoli replied, 'Really. I think it's a pile of crap.' He just wasn't convinced. It wasn't his type of music. 'Cubby liked Sinatra,' said Mankiewicz.[48] In the end, they played it to Jerry Moss, a friend of Mankiewicz who worked at A&M Records. After it finished, Moss turned to Broccoli and said: 'For whatever rights you have to this song, I'll pay you a million dollars, because this song is going to go platinum.' A few days later, Cubby was telling people, 'We have the greatest fucking song you ever heard.'[49]

After *Live and Let Die* opened in July 1973, performing well at the box office, rumours once again surfaced that the two producers were on the verge of splitting up permanently. Saltzman had even begun making public noises that with only five Fleming novels left to film he would probably not stay the course.[50]

This wasn't the first time Saltzman had publicly come out and spoken about his leaving Bond. While he was trying to set up the film of Nijinsky, he gave an interview in which he talked about walking out on the movie business altogether and devoting his time to education, something he had always been passionate about since his days with UNESCO. Saltzman talked about a knowledge explosion and that he hoped to bring his talents and experience in the media to bear upon education.[51] Tony Bramwell recalled that, while working at Tilney Street, he saw Saltzman have a lot of dealings with the Open University, an organisation that had only been up and running a few years. 'There was this guy who was one of the founders and he would be in the office it seems every other day asking for backing and support. And Harry gave him a lot of time.'[52]

But like a magpie, Saltzman couldn't stop himself compulsively hoarding and buying up properties. 'He didn't seem to have any concentration on any one project,' or so it seemed to Tony Bramwell. 'I don't know why he couldn't just be satisfied with James Bond.'[53] Not long after *Live and Let Die* opened, Saltzman bought the film rights to *The Greek*, the bestselling French novel about the super-rich international set by Pierre Rey. Written very much in the style of Harold Robbins, the story revolved around a powerful Greek shipping magnet married to the widow of an assassinated American politician. Obviously, Fey had based his book on the Aristotle Onassis and Jackie Kennedy affair, but that wasn't why Saltzman bought it. 'I simply found it the best social comedy I've ever read, about these super-rich people who live by their own laws, conventions and morals. They are fascinating, and so much larger than life that they make James Bond look like a midget.'[54] Saltzman hoped to interest George C. Scott in playing the lead and start production in the summer of 1974, but first there was the matter of Roger Moore's next Bond.

19

The Last Encore

Keen to capitalise on the success of Moore's first outing as 007, United Artists decreed that the next Bond, *The Man with the Golden Gun*, be raced into production; a little too quickly for Broccoli's liking, who felt this might impact on the quality of the final product.

Work was also hampered by the continuing bad relations between the producers, which United Artist's new president Eric Pleskow felt required his personal intervention:

> I had to go to England several times because they were arguing with each other to such an extent that the production had stopped. I would go over and try to get them to be in the same room together, and one would be sitting at one end of the room and the other would be at the opposite end of the room. They were behaving like children. It was unbelievable.[1]

A combination of diplomacy and knocking heads together would succeed in getting things moving once more. 'Then I'd fly back home,' said Pleskow. 'And ten days later the same problem would happen again and I'd have to fly back.'[2]

As usual, the Bond team looked for a new and deadly threat that 007 could save the world from. There were two possibilities: solar power or weather control. Saltzman felt that a criminal organisation controlling the weather was a bad idea, necessitating a lot of dreadful stock footage of hurricanes and tropical storms.[3] The final plot ended up reflecting the current world energy crisis, and revolved around a device in the hands of a notorious assassin called Scaramanga that can harness the power of the sun.

Mankiewicz resumed scriptwriting duties and did much of his work over at the Tilney Street office. Occasionally, Guy Hamilton would join him to work on the script, 'though we were much more interested in whether Nixon was going to be impeached or not,' said the director. 'But then about five in the evening we would always go over to South Audley and recount what we had cooked up during the day.'[4]

By this time Saltzman was spending most of his time over at Tilney Street, and Mankiewicz observed the vastly different atmosphere that existed in the two camps. 'You could walk into Cubby's office over at South Audley and inside the horse races were always on, Ascot or Epsom, or whatever race was going on, and everybody was on the phone to Ladbrokes making a bet. In Harry's office, shares of companies were being traded. It was a different culture.'[5] It was only when there was going to be a summit meeting or if a bigwig from United Artists was in town that Saltzman would trot round to South Audley because Cubby's was the bigger office. 'They had such different individual pursuits and business interests that of course they couldn't have carried on business from two desks facing each other,' said Mankiewicz:

> They had completely different lives and staff. On Tilney Street Harry had a staff of four or five that worked exclusively for him. I think Harry was very aware too of when he did show up at Audley Street for these big meetings that in a certain way he was on Cubby's turf, because everybody in the outer office worked for Cubby. Harry didn't have anybody working for him over there.[6]

The problem of going with *The Man with the Golden Gun* straight after *Live and Let Die* was that both stories were set in Jamaica, so a search began for a new location. The ancient city of Shiraz in Iran was briefly considered and a small team including Broccoli, Hamilton and Mankiewicz flew out there. In Tehran they booked themselves on a local flight, only for Broccoli to be strip searched at the airport when authorities thought his camera was a gun. Once in the air, there was a dawning realisation that the plane was not heading to Shiraz but to another desert city, Bam, almost 500 miles away. Nevertheless, news had reached the local mayor that the Bond people were coming and a special welcoming committee was hastily organised. 'Forget it,' said Cubby when he was told. 'It's 140 degrees. I'm not sitting here for three hours with the Mayor of Bam.' They turned back and Iran was scrubbed as a location.[7] Instead, focus shifted to the Far East and Hong Kong and Thailand.

As pre-production continued, Mankiewicz decided to leave the project after delivering a first draft, since he felt that he could no longer contribute anything. Mankiewicz was sad to leave the Bond team, and especially Broccoli, whom he had grown very close to and fond of. The two men remained on friendly terms for the rest of their lives. When Connery asked Mankiewicz to write his 1983 Bond comeback *Never Say Never Again*, the American politely declined, feeling that he couldn't do it because Cubby had been so loyal to him. 'Then after the picture was over Sean asked me if I would take a look at it, because they were about to edit it. I called Cubby and asked, "Do you mind if I do that," and he said, "Absolutely not, please do it. Please give any help you can."'[8]

Broccoli asked Richard Maibaum to come in and do a rewrite, but on arriving in London, the veteran writer was surprised to learn that Saltzman was no longer involved in the script development. Maibaum's own relationship with Saltzman was very tenuous by this stage in any case.[9] Having considered his contribution crucial to the early Bonds, he did feel that the producer became disruptive in later years.[10]

With relations between the producers having almost broken down, in the interests of not holding up production Saltzman agreed to allow his partner to get on with things, with the promise that he would be kept informed of progress. 'From then on I was frozen out of all meetings. My relationship with Cubby had reached such a depressing state that it was impossible to get involved.'[11] As for Roger Moore, although he was not privy to all the machinations behind the scenes, he had come to the conclusion that the partnership 'was falling apart',[12] which made things difficult for him on a personal level since he was friends with both men.

In terms of casting, Hollywood bad guy Jack Palance was originally considered for the role of Scaramanga before Christopher Lee, eager to branch out from his Hammer horror roles, was chosen. Lee was actually Ian Fleming's cousin, and back in 1962 the author had wanted him to play Dr No:

> but by the time he got around to remembering to tell the producers, they'd already cast someone else. Unfortunately, Ian wasn't with us when I did Scaramanga, who is not remotely like the character in the book. In Fleming's novel he's just a West Indian thug, but in the film he's charming, elegant, amusing, lethal. I played him like the dark side of Bond.[13]

The thing that most impressed Lee about working on the film was the professionalism of everyone involved and the sheer scope and ambition. 'Money is, literally, no object. I have never seen money spent as it has been on this picture. It's because it's the only film that's made today which is an absolute, 100 per cent certainty before they even make it.'[14]

When news reached Britt Ekland that another Bond film was in production, the actress was determined to be part of it. She immediately went out and bought a copy of the novel and identified the part of Mary Goodnight, Bond's secretary, as the one she wanted to play. Dressing up exactly how she thought secretaries looked in those days, a white fluffy sweater, a white blouse, a grey skirt and her hair up, 'not too sexy', Britt made her way to South Audley, just a few minutes' walk from her own apartment.[15]

Already an international name, Britt had no trouble getting in to see Broccoli, but the producer was rather noncommittal and she left disappointed. A couple of months later, Britt received a call from her agent saying she'd won the part:

> I was told years later that Cubby wanted to cast me after seeing *The Wicker Man*, but of course I was almost four months pregnant when I made that film so had a much fuller figure. I think he was quite surprised when I arrived in Bangkok with a baby rather than big breasts. Although every Saturday night Cubby invited the crew and cast to an Italian restaurant and he made me eat two plates of spaghetti to put weight on![16]

Filming got underway first in Hong Kong and neighbouring Macau, famous for its casinos. At night, after wrapping, many of the crew spent their hard-earned wages freely at the tables, under the watchful and benevolent gaze of Broccoli who would wander around handing out chips to everyone.

Moore's and Broccoli's game was backgammon. They always had a game running throughout each Bond film they made together and would settle up the winnings at the end of the shoot. Often the call would come for Moore to return to the set, and Broccoli would say, 'You can't have him yet – I'm playing him like a banjo.'[17]

Like a lot of rich men, Broccoli couldn't resist a bargain and told Moore about this tailor in Hong Kong he'd found, able to rustle up a couple of suits in twenty-four hours at a good price. When it was time for the unit to leave, Broccoli proudly wore one of the suits to the airport. 'As he was walking up the steps of the plane, the trousers split in two,' recalled Moore. 'Needless to say, he was ribbed mercilessly.'[18]

While Broccoli had taken on the producing chores, Saltzman did undertake an early location recce of Thailand, where he came up with one of his famous ideas. Watching a display of working elephants, he thought it would make for an exciting sequence with Bond and Scaramanga riding these elephants and there's an almighty stampede. Guy Hamilton didn't agree, audiences had seen it before in a million Tarzan pictures. Undeterred, Saltzman looked into the logistics and discovered that these particular elephants wore coverings on their feet to protect them in tough terrain. Months later, Broccoli was in the midst of shooting in Bangkok when he got a call saying, 'Your elephant shoes are ready.' Looking mystified, Broccoli replied, 'What elephant shoes?' Without his knowledge, Saltzman had gone ahead and ordered 300 pairs of elephant shoes for a scene that was not in the movie.[19]

The crew had arrived in Bangkok to face oppressive heat and humidity. To show the crew how much he appreciated the effort they were putting in, Broccoli organised regular big Italian dinners. For Britt, this was indicative of the kind of person he was:

> Cubby was lovely, so friendly and in a way quite fatherly. You could have a private conversation with Cubby, whereas most other producers are pretty distant characters. Harry Saltzman was completely different. I think their relationship had already broken up because I have no memory of Harry being on set in Thailand or in Hong Kong. I never had more than a cordial relationship with Harry.[20]

Paul Tucker, the film's accountant, confirmed that Saltzman was involved in the early pre-production, 'but as soon as it came to the shooting, we never saw Harry on that film'.[21] Having worked under Saltzman on *Live and Let Die*, Tucker found there to be a profound disparity between Broccoli's working methods and his partner. 'Cubby was very hands on and always on the set, every day.'[22] What impressed Tucker most was Broccoli's relationship with his crew. He would know if someone's wife was coming out to the location on a visit and arrange a dinner for them, with him as the host. 'He would make you feel special and that your work was appreciated. Cubby was a charming man.'[23]

Britt Ekland saw that Roger Moore had an equally good relationship with the crew, happy to socialise and not hide away in his trailer on his own:

> I never once saw Roger ill-tempered or moody. And he loved what he did, he loved being James Bond. And there always seemed to be practical jokes going on with Roger. One night he and I got everyone into the pool at the Oriental hotel in Bangkok, including Cubby, with his clothes on. Cubby was later found in his hotel room ironing his dollar bills.[24]

Broccoli wasn't above the odd practical joke, either. On the final day of shooting at Pinewood, Moore was wearing a very nice silk suit for his encounter with a sultry belly dancer and was rather hoping to nab it for himself after it was a wrap. Hamilton set up the cameras and prepared for take one. Moore thought it unusual that Broccoli seemed to be observing matters from halfway up a stepladder. The scene passed off smoothly. Hamilton asked if the cameraman had got it. Yes. 'Print it,' he said. 'That's a wrap.' At that precise moment, Broccoli tipped a bucket of paste on top of Moore, covering both him and his silk suit in a soggy mess.[25]

Moore had developed a close and mutually respectful friendship with Broccoli that was to last for the rest of the producer's life. 'Cubby was completely avuncular as a person. He was large and expansive. When he came on the set nobody was falling over backwards with fear. When Harry came on the set everyone was a little terrified.'[26]

Both men worked well together and Moore valued Cubby's expertise and knowledge of the Bond world. In one scene, Moore was deeply concerned about Bond using rough methods to get information out of a woman. Slapping around a female character just wasn't his scene at all, so Moore went to Broccoli for advice. 'It seems all right to me Roger. After all, the girl is a villain and a liar.' Reassured, Moore went and played the scene.[27]

The film's signature stunt, and one of the most impressive in the entire series, was the corkscrew car jump across a broken bridge in Thailand. Broccoli had seen footage of the stunt performed by New York stock car driver Jay Milligan at a stunt show, and quickly purchased the rights to prevent its appearance in any other film. On the day the stunt was due to be performed, even if they weren't meant to be working, everyone came to watch and lined up along the bank of the river, about 25 yards from where the broken bridge was. 'That was done in one shot,' recalled Paul Tucker. 'He took off, spun the car, went 360 degrees, landed and drove off. When we saw it, it almost looked too good because it worked absolutely perfectly. And I saw Cubby race over to the driver, "Bumps" Willard, and hand him a bonus cheque as a special thank you.'[28]

20

Breaking Up is Hard to Do

As *The Man with the Golden Gun* played round the world, to lower than expected takings, at home Saltzman was facing financial meltdown. Things had gone badly at both Éclair and especially Technicolor, where Saltzman had recently been ousted, in much the same way as he had led a revolt to throw out the previous chairman of the board. The irony of the situation did not compute; indeed, Saltzman complained vehemently about the situation to Tom Mankiewicz. 'Harry said to me, "Those bastards, I just walked in there one day and I'm out the fuckin' door. How can people do something like that?" I thought, Harry, that's just what you did. You fucked the last guy, they're not going to fuck you?'[1]

He faced other financial problems, too: the debacle of his *Toomorrow* movie, the failure of *Battle of Britain*, his ownership of the restaurant on London's Embankment had cost him an estimated £500,000[2] and his music company, Hilary Music, was also falling apart. Tony Bramwell had been given pretty much a free hand at Hilary Music to carry out projects of his own choosing, but it soon became clear that there was a problem with the financing. Bramwell found Saltzman a delight to work for, except when it came to finding the money to do things with, or even to live on. He'd call Harry up, 'Excuse me, I need some money here.' The reply was always the same: speak to Kenneth. Kenneth Richards was the company accountant and based in Switzerland, where all of Saltzman's companies were based. 'So, you had to speak to Switzerland and beg for a few hundred quid.'[3]

Things weren't panning out too well. By this time, Ron Kass had left after he and Saltzman fell out, and Bramwell was feeling pretty much the same. 'In the end I had to give up because of the lack of budgeting for any project you wanted to try and do. There was just fuck all money there to do anything with.'[4]

One afternoon, Bramwell called the Swiss office for some money to be sent over. The phone rang, and rang, and kept on ringing. No one picked up. Sensing something was wrong, Bramwell called round to the other members of the Tilney Street staff and someone was dispatched to Switzerland to see what was going on. 'Kenneth Richards had done a bunk. It turned out to be a very successful bunk. All Harry's money. My accrued royalties in Hilary Music. Ron Kass's royalties. All flown away. Gone.'[5]

Saltzman's entrepreneurial spirit had come back to haunt him. It was something Broccoli had been concerned about for some time:

> Against my advice, Harry had taken on enormous outside ventures and was finding his knees giving way under the weight of it all. He was in up to his neck and floundering. I tried to dissuade him, but he wouldn't listen. There was a constant fight, a struggle to keep him from doing the things which could eventually ruin him.[6]

David Picker over at United Artists had a sense of what was happening, too, and that Saltzman's own worst enemy was often himself:

> Harry changed as the Bond films grew increasingly successful. He felt that he didn't need Cubby to be successful. As Bond's success grew Harry's ego grew as well, and he ventured into businesses he knew little about. His focus was spread, his ego was growing and financial woes started to build up.[7]

Not only were his investments crumbling in front of his eyes, but in the words of Tom Mankiewicz, 'Harry had been caught with his hand in the cookie jar.'[8] In order to buy shares in Technicolor and other acquisitions, Saltzman had taken out loans, including with the Union Bank of Switzerland, pledging his shares in Danjaq as collateral.[9] However, according to his partnership agreement with Broccoli drawn up in 1962, both men agreed never to use Danjaq stock as security for other ventures.[10] Saltzman had patently gone against the by-laws of his own company. 'And Cubby knew about it,' said Mankiewicz, 'and just let Harry keep digging his hole.'[11]

Not only had Saltzman cross-collateralised himself into one big financial mess, running up debts believed to be in the region of $20 million,[12] but the Union Bank of Switzerland was now calling in their loan.[13] That was the killer blow. Saltzman had to bail out. The entire future of the James Bond franchise was in jeopardy.

The only possible way out for Saltzman was to sell his 50 per cent share in Danjaq, which was his major viable asset, and there was no shortage of suitors. There was just one problem: according to the by-laws of Danjaq, if any partner for any reason decided to dissolve the partnership, the remaining partner had the right of approval over who he was going to be partners with. In other words, Cubby had a veto over who Harry could sell his shares to. According to Tom Mankiewicz, the first group that wanted to buy Harry's share was a group headed by the television host, media personality and writer David Frost. 'I don't know who the real money was behind the bid, but it was headed by David Frost, and Cubby said no. I don't want David Frost as my partner.'[14]

Other interested parties included Sir James Hanson, later Lord Hanson, a noted industrialist. Hanson was a friend of Broccoli's and days of meetings took place between their representatives. In the end, Hanson walked, the price of buying out Harry's position deemed too high.[15] Then there was the Saudi Arabian businessman Adnan Kashoggi. This time it was United Artists who voiced their disapproval, Kashoggi was not someone they wanted involved with the Bond franchise.[16] Broccoli felt the same way, too. 'Cubby wanted desperately not to have a partner,' said Mankiewicz:

> I think he intentionally made life a little difficult for Harry by not approving the first two partners that Harry suggested. I think Cubby's plan all along was to wind up in sole control of the Bonds. Doing the Bonds was Cubby's mission in life, he didn't have other interests that way, and he must have thought, my God after all these years and nine pictures, I'm going to have a new guy come in who has never touched Bond before and who is going to have an equal vote to me. Not if I can help it. I think that was very much part of it.[17]

With all this going on, pre-production on the next Bond film, *The Spy Who Loved Me*, was severely hampered. Guy Hamilton, who was slated to direct, left citing his inability to work amidst the acrimonious environment that existed between the two warring producers.[18]

It was at this moment of crisis, a period Broccoli called 'one of the blackest I ever had to face. It threatened to bring down everything I had worked for,'[19] that he turned to the people he trusted the most. Michael G. Wilson, who after graduating from Stanford Law School had worked in leading law firms in New York and Washington, was brought over to England to join Eon as a business affairs advisor. And there was Norman R. Tyre, not only Cubby's Los Angeles-based attorney, and a vastly experienced and knowledgeable expert on film litigation, but also a personal family friend of long standing.

At the same time as all this was going on, Jacqueline Saltzman was fighting for her life having been diagnosed with breast cancer. Suddenly for Harry making movies didn't seem important any more, it was all about spending whatever time he had left with Jacqueline. That's what was driving him at that point more than anything else. 'He was going through hell on both sides,' said Sue St John, Saltzman's assistant for many years. 'Both in business and at home. It wasn't easy for him. It was horrible.'[20] The situation certainly had a profound effect on his 'reasoning and thoughts', according to his son Steven.[21]

Being the tough businessman that he was, it's doubtful Saltzman expected any sympathy. He certainly didn't get any. The loans he'd made went back several years and the Union Bank of Switzerland had not only lost patience, having told Saltzman to reduce his indebtedness as early as 1971,[22] but were making threats about taking over his position in Danjaq. Broccoli and his lawyers sensed that this was a very real possibility and they were going to fight it. Michael G. Wilson characterised the bank's behaviour as 'very hostile',[23] while Broccoli's attorney Norman R. Tyre believed that Saltzman's desperate manoeuvrings to keep his head above water threatened the very existence of Eon and the Bond films' moving forward.[24]

To Broccoli it must have almost felt like a personal attack, even though he never considered Saltzman to have deliberately or consciously set out to bring him down. He was in a mess, plain and simple, 'and he wanted to get out of it by using me and Dana – our money – to pay the banks. There was no way I was ever going to let this happen.'[25]

Of course, the most practical and straightforward solution would have been for Saltzman to personally sell out to his partner, but according to Tyre he was 'implacably opposed to selling his shares to Cubby'.[26] Broccoli was eager to make a deal but Saltzman's son Steven believed that it was Jacqueline who stood in the way of it.[27]

Instead, Saltzman began making overtures to Columbia Pictures, which set alarm bells ringing with Broccoli and at United Artists. The last thing they wanted was another studio taking a slice of the lucrative Bond pie.[28]

A showdown was inevitable. It took place in the luxuriant atmosphere of a five-star Swiss hotel, the Beau-Rivage Palace in Lausanne. A private room was set aside with a long table running almost the entire length. On one side was Broccoli, Michael G. Wilson, a Swiss lawyer and Norman R. Tyre. On the other, Saltzman, representatives of the Union Bank of Switzerland and a battalion of expensive lawyers, including Sargent Shriver, a senior partner with a substantial New York law firm, on $400 an hour and $2,000 a day expenses.[29] Cubby was characteristically blunt about what was riding on these meetings – 'our survival'.[30]

Before proceedings began, Saltzman's side demanded to have everything recorded and brought in their own engineers with the latest hi-tech sound equipment. When they heard of the demand, Broccoli's team did likewise and brought in their own recording devices.[31]

At times, for Broccoli, the whole thing took on the appearance of a black comedy, especially since between the legal hostilities, arguments and shouting the lawyers would all sit down for cordon bleu meals and the finest Alsace wines.

The lawyers acting for Saltzman seemed determined to dissolve the Bond company, bring it into liquidation,[32] and planned to use the sound recordings as evidence that the relationship between the two partners had irrevocably broken down.[33] 'This would mean,' said Broccoli, 'that if it couldn't be settled any other way, the court could order an official dissolution.'[34]

But Broccoli was no pushover, as Tom Mankiewicz related: 'When he was fighting with Harry he would say, "Harry ought to know better than to fuck with me, I'm Calibrasse." Cubby would always joke about, I'm calibrasse, but if you crossed Cubby, he never forgot it.'[35]

By December 1975, Saltzman and United Artists finally agreed a deal of $36 million for the producer's share of Danjaq, minus $10 million from an outstanding debt to the company. This payment was spread over five years so the buyout qualified as a tax-free transaction under Swiss law.[36]

Relieved that it was all over, Saltzman felt a desperate pang of sadness that it had ended this way. 'He was devastated about what happened between him and Cubby,' said his daughter Hilary. 'I don't think he planned on that, but he was desperate.'[37] Still, Saltzman believed that he had been hard done by and sold his Bond shares too cheaply. Ultimately, it took seven years for him to receive the full amount.[38]

Broccoli, too, emerged battered and bruised, if ultimately victorious. When it was all over, he watched the phalanx of lawyers leave the field of battle. With the help and support of Dana he had seen off these wolves and kept his kingdom intact. But of his partner there was no sign. Broccoli left without the two men shaking hands or saying goodbye.[39]

While this skirmish had left Broccoli with new partners in United Artists, he was now the sole producer of James Bond. Tom Mankiewicz for one saw how much Cubby revelled in the fact he was now on his own:

> He specifically said to me, 'In the old days, Harry had a vote, I had a vote, and United Artists had a vote. And now I vote yes, United Artists vote no and I vote yes again.' I think he loved that, that he didn't have to clear anything through Harry.[40]

21

Out on Their Own

It wasn't long before Saltzman was planning his first post-Bond movie project, and typical of the man it was on a mammoth scale, an ambitious multi-million-pound science fiction extravaganza called *The Micronauts*. With a plot that takes place on a future polluted Earth, scientists come up with a solution to combat world food shortages – shrink mankind! A team of scientists are miniaturised and forced to survive in a backyard in a scenario that is part *Fantastic Voyage* and part *Honey I Shrunk the Kids*.

To handle the complex micro-photography, Saltzman drafted in Oxford Scientific Films, a company that produced natural history and documentary programmes. He also planned to take over much of Shepperton Studios to build the vast sets required for some of the film's more technically challenging sequences. Among the props created for the film were blades of grass over 30ft high and a Coca-Cola bottle cap big enough for six people to stand on.[1]

With a filming date commencing at the beginning of 1976, with a planned Christmas release, Gregory Peck and James Mason were mooted to star together under the direction of Don Sharp, but something went wrong. Either the complicated effects photography didn't work, or the projected costs were too high, but the film was delayed so long that cast and crew members left to work on other films. Don Sharp also left the project, and after his experience working with Saltzman was to call him a 'strange man'.[2]

Saltzman replaced Sharp with the young British director Richard Loncraine, and in May *Variety* were reporting *The Micronauts* as, 'Harry Saltzman's $8m comeback picture.' With backing from Columbia, shooting was to begin that autumn, with an estimated $1.8 million having already been spent on pre-production work, mostly on effects equipment and techniques. With such high development costs Saltzman was already talking about a sequel, perhaps a series of films, in order to utilise what would be expensive props and sets.[3]

More delays, however, resulted in Loncraine leaving and when Columbia pulled out no US distributor showed any interest in taking over. Over the next twelve months names such as Charlton Heston and Burt Lancaster were linked to the film. In 1977, Saltzman contacted George Lazenby in Los Angeles. The ex-Bond star had appeared in a TV movie called *Cover Girls* and Saltzman called him from his suite at the Beverly Wilshire to say how much he'd enjoyed it and that he'd come a long way as an actor. He wanted to set up a meeting with Lazenby to talk about *Micronauts* and the possibility of starring him together in the movie with Michael Caine.[4] Sadly, *The Micronauts* would never reach the screen.

It was during Saltzman's thwarted plans for *The Micronauts* that he made public a desire to buy Shepperton Studios, where his film production office was now located. The news was received enthusiastically by a beleaguered native film industry and had the full approval of the National Film Finance Corporation. Certainly, one of the advantages of the plan was Saltzman's ambition to bring American investment back into British film production. With the decline of the pound in recent times, he felt US filmmakers and companies would seek the relatively cheap studio facilities the UK had to offer, as they had done during the film boom of the 1960s.

Shepperton itself had in recent years fallen on hard times, to the extent that its very future was in doubt. If successful, Saltzman's bid could restore the studio to full use again. But the board at Shepperton had other plans, having already entered into an agreement with the local council to sell 14 acres of the site for housing development and a further 20 acres for open space amenity. Saltzman's bid of £8 million was on the condition it was for the entire 60-acre site,[5] and he was convinced the studio would eventually see sense and back him rather than the council. Saltzman was hugely disappointed, and surprised, when his bid was ultimately rejected.[6]

The failure of the Shepperton bid was a personal blow. Saltzman felt unwanted, especially after everything he had given the British film industry. It was a feeling compounded by new restrictive tax laws introduced by the then incumbent Labour Government against resident foreigners that made it impossible for him to stay in the country. Saltzman made a personal appeal to Denis Healey, then the Chancellor of the Exchequer, to stop this punitive measure. 'We're making British films and we're selling Britain,' he told him. 'We are part of a propaganda business and you are closing down that outlet across the world.' It didn't make any difference. 'He looked at me like I was a nut. Healey was wrong.'[7]

It was with a heavy heart that Saltzman and Jacqueline decided to leave Britain early in 1977, going to live permanently at their summer vacation home in St Petersburg, Florida.[8] Pretty much everything he had amassed in the UK was sold, his home, and many of his paintings and antiques were put up for auction at Christie's.[9] Steven Saltzman even recalled his mother having to sell her jewellery, including a 69-carat solitaire diamond.[10] But their friends never deserted them, and people like Michael Caine and Maurice Binder remained close and supportive. Binder especially was very dear to Saltzman. According to Steven Saltzman, it was Binder who acted as a kind of conduit when his father and Broccoli had their problems. 'Maurice was the back-channel between Harry and Cubby throughout the entire period when they didn't get along. And they never didn't get along.'[11] Even George Lazenby called the home once or twice a year to talk to Saltzman, and especially Jacqueline to see how she was faring.[12]

As Saltzman was leaving the UK, Broccoli was about to release *The Spy Who Loved Me*, his first Bond as a solo producer. There had been a gap of almost three years since *The Man with the Golden Gun*, the longest in the series, and Cubby was under enormous pressure, as the film's director Lewis Gilbert remarked:

> For Cubby it was a huge undertaking in the sense that he had to prove something. He was on his own, and if the film were a disaster people would say that he couldn't do it without Harry. I think Cubby was conscious of that and worked very hard on the film, probably more than he did on other films.[13]

And yet at the same time, the film's associate producer William P. Cartlidge saw a man that was totally liberated:

> Although in an odd sort of way, because he didn't have a partner any more, I felt he almost used me as a heavy, in that sense, to do the dirty work. We'd sit there and discuss it all and he'd say, 'Well you'd better tell them we're doing it this way.'[14]

Cartlidge worked on the next Bond, too, 1979's *Moonraker*, and was surprised to see how much bad feeling there still was regarding Saltzman. 'We were getting our film processed at Denham, which was Rank's laboratory, mainly because, apparently, before I came along, we were having nothing to do with Technicolor.'[15] This despite the fact that Saltzman hadn't been anywhere near

Technicolor for years, and yet for Broccoli the association was obviously still there.

Cartlidge had encountered a problem working on the scene where Bond fights Jaws on top of a cable car. Shooting against a blue screen in the studio, Cartlidge knew the only way to get real decent definition in the plate shots for the back projection, since they were shooting in Panavision anamorphic, was to use an old-fashioned system called Vista Vision. Unfortunately, the only people that had the equipment, and indeed could process film that way, were Technicolor. So, Cartlidge told Broccoli they had no option but to use Technicolor.

'No, you're not,' he barked.

'Well, if we don't do that, we can't do it.'

Reluctantly, Broccoli agreed. The work went ahead and the results were excellent, and since Cartlidge had a good relationship with Technicolor, he approached Broccoli and suggested they might as well have the whole film processed there. 'And it was only then that Cubby succumbed and said, "All right, fine, who cares."'[16]

*

In January 1980, Saltzman's world collapsed when his wife Jacqueline succumbed to the cancer she had been fighting bravely for many years. Harry had used his wealth in a desperate search for a cure. 'I know he loved her to pieces,' said Tom Mankiewicz. 'And I know Harry went all over the world trying to help cure her of this cancer.'[17] Peter Lamont remembered bringing over medication from America that Charles Russhon had managed to procure for her.[18]

This may explain Saltzman's involvement with religious spiritualists in the early to mid 1970s. In 1973, Saltzman and Jacqueline travelled to India to meet with the guru, spiritual leader and philanthropist Sathya Sai Baba.[19] Claiming supernatural insight and powers, Baba commanded a huge following of devotees, not just in India but around the world. In his book *The Mystics*, author Aubrey Menen described Saltzman as one of the guru's 'most fervent believers'.[20]

Saltzman was also on the board of directors of the Chakpori Ling Healing Foundation,[21] which was run by a man called Norbu Chen who claimed to be a Tibetan lama. Like Baba, Chen was another controversial figure, whose activities was supported financially by the likes of tobacco heiress Doris Duke, one of the richest women in the world.[22]

It was probably Saltzman's desperation that pushed him towards these men who many people considered to be nothing more than charlatans, which made it all the more tragic when Jacqueline lost her fight for life. 'Jacqueline's death was a tremendous shock to him,' said Dyson Lovell. 'I know he never recovered from that.'[23] Len Deighton recalled that Saltzman was 'devastated' when she died,[24] and that he did fall into a deep depression afterwards.

It wasn't long following the passing of Jacqueline that Saltzman returned to the UK, and Cherry Hughes used to see him around London, sometimes shopping in Fortnum and Mason with his daughter Hilary, which he was fond of doing. They'd say hello and have a coffee and reminisce. 'But he wasn't his old self. When his wife died, he was a shadow of his former self. He was a very sad man. He absolutely adored Jacqueline.'[25]

Saltzman had been lured back to the country by an enticing work opportunity, along with the more advantageous tax laws of a newly installed Conservative government. Saltzman always enjoyed a love affair with the legitimate theatre, and even in the peak days of Bond yearned to own one of the great London theatres such as the Haymarket. When the chance came to buy a controlling interest in the theatrical production company H.M. Tennents and become its new chairman, Saltzman couldn't turn it down. Under the management of theatre impresario Hugh 'Binkie' Beaumont, Tennents dominated the West End and provincial theatres during the 1940s and 1950s but by the time Saltzman arrived it was long past its prime.

He was eager, though, to shake things up by setting the traditional old firm on a new course. The plan was for potential screenplays to be tried out first in the theatre, and if successful turned into a film, with the box office profits ploughed back into stage productions. Saltzman was keen, for example, to return to his idea of doing something about Karl Marx's youngest daughter, Eleanor, and hoped to tempt Glenda Jackson to play the role on stage before attempting any film version.[26] While that never materialised, he did bring Edna O'Brien's play *Virginia*, about the life of Virginia Woolf, to the West End in 1981 with Maggie Smith in the lead, and also produced a play on Broadway in 1982, his first proper theatrical production in the United States. *A Little Family Business* by Jay Presson Allen opened at the Martin Beck Theatre in December, but was poorly received by critics and despite the stellar presence of Angela Lansbury closed after just two weeks.

Tennents' chief executive, Peter Wilson, recalled going to see Saltzman at his suite of offices on the top floor of the Globe, now the Gielgud Theatre. He'd been sent a play which he greatly liked and suggested to Saltzman that Tennents should produce it. 'Harry read it and didn't think it would run. So,

I went ahead and produced it myself.' The play in question was *The Woman in Black*, which recently celebrated thirty years in the West End.[27]

Wilson categorised Saltzman as a forthright and unpredictable character. He recalled when Tennents were producing a musical based on Martin Luther King called *King* that Saltzman asked Wilson to change the title, since it might upset the Royal Family. Saltzman only relented when Wilson pointed out that there was a successful singer called Prince and a highly popular rock band called Queen.[28]

Len Deighton was an occasional visitor to Saltzman's tiny circular rooftop office above the Globe theatre, and there were forays to his 'dimly lit apartment near Victoria Station'.[29] Deighton was to observe a marked difference in his friend. No longer was he the big-shot movie producer moving around in the high society circles he'd been used to. For Deighton, Saltzman was someone who used his wealth well and fitted naturally into that world. 'And to see Harry poor, by his own standards, it really upset me. I hated to see it because if you like someone you don't like to see them like that.'[30]

Dyson Lovell was someone else who recalled trekking all the way up to see his old boss in that tiny office. Lovell didn't know then much about Saltzman's financial situation but it was obvious the great days were behind him and were not coming back. 'There was a sadness there. And yet he was still coming up with these ideas and projects.'[31]

On Deighton's last visit to that Victoria flat, Saltzman was keen to show him his latest endeavour, which was a bit of plastic you put over a TV screen to enlarge the picture. Deighton wasn't impressed. 'My mum and dad used to have one of those in the 1950s, it wasn't new technology. I couldn't see how it was going to be successful, and it shouldn't have been something Harry ought to have been doing.'[32]

On that final visit Deighton was of a mind to do something for his old friend, take him out to a restaurant or have him round to his house for some social occasion, 'because I felt he'd done a lot for me. But the trouble was this with Harry, in all the period I knew him, unless there was business to discuss he couldn't see the point of social gatherings. It was business or it was not business. It was always about making deals.'[33]

As for a return to the cinema, Saltzman was involved in just two films after leaving Bond. In 1980, his long-postponed film of the dancer Nijinsky was finally brought to the screen. He had approached the director Herbert Ross in 1977 after the success of his ballet film *The Turning Point* and Ross cast George De La Pena, a former soloist with the American Ballet Theatre in the title role, with Alan Bates as Diaghilev.

Saltzman also hoped to interest Paul Newman in doing a thriller based on the novel *The Quebec Plot*, in which the American star would play a Canadian journalist investigating a conspiracy that could lead the world to the terrifying brink of a nuclear confrontation. That never worked out, and it wasn't until 1988 that Saltzman earned another film credit, as co-producer on Emir Kusturica's film *Time of The Gypsies*, which told the story of a young Romany boy with telekinetic powers and was shot in Macedonia. This credit was merely a gesture of thanks, however, on the part of Kusturica rather than any deep involvement in the production on Saltzman's part. Early in development Saltzman managed to raise $100,000 as he began a search for a distributor who would give him a large sum of money for the film. When that search failed, he left the project and it was David Puttnam at Columbia that ultimately provided the financing.[34] The film ended up well received by critics and Kusturica won the Palme d'Or at Cannes for Best Director.

One must assume that Saltzman missed the hurly-burly world of 007. In June 1981, along with his children, Saltzman attended the London premiere of *For Your Eyes Only*. It was one of his first public appearances following the death of Jacqueline and had been instigated by the actor Topol, who featured in the film and suggested to Cubby that it might be a good idea to invite his old colleague. 'The two former partners had not split on the most amicable of terms, but they greeted each other as old friends,' recalled Roger Moore. 'I know Harry was touched to be there and to feel he was still a part of Bond. That was a very nice, and a very big gesture from Cubby.'[35]

In 1990, Saltzman left the UK permanently, a decision that must have been a huge emotional wrench for him given how much he had come to regard it as his adopted home. He moved to a village near Versailles, on the far outskirts of Paris.[36] By this time he had also married again, to Adriana Ghinsberg. Like Jacqueline, Adriana was born in Romania and fled Bucharest to France in 1948 when she was only 9 years old. The pair first met in the early 1980s. Adriana spoke of Harry watching each new Bond film as it came out, 'but they were not his style'.[37] He also maintained an active mind, and continued to read books on a variety of subjects, despite ailing health after a series of strokes, the first occurring in 1982.[38] In 1986, he suffered a stroke that left him unable to speak for six weeks.[39] Saltzman also had to cope with another family tragedy when his youngest son, Christopher, died in 1991.[40]

On 28 September 1994, Harry Saltzman died of a heart attack at the American hospital in the Paris suburb of Neuilly-Sur-Seine.[41] His death barely caused a ripple in the media; there were some respectful obituaries in the newspapers and that was about it. The difference when Broccoli died later was startling, as Tom Mankiewicz recalled:

> Harry died almost like a crowned head in exile. Whereas Cubby's was a funeral for Hollywood royalty. They made John Barry and myself honorary pallbearers. And I considered that a huge honour. The problem is, if you're not making successful movies, you're easily forgotten in Hollywood and Harry really did disappear from the showbusiness road map.[42]

★

Having won control of the Bond franchise from Saltzman, and after the enormous success of his first Bond film as a solo producer, *The Spy Who Loved Me*, Broccoli was determined to keep 007 firmly in the family. He'd already brought in Michael G. Wilson as a legal advisor, now he saw fit to move him over to the more creative side of things and by *Moonraker* Wilson was executive producer. The two men would work closely together for many years, right up until *GoldenEye* in 1995. Wilson said that Cubby's guidance on the series was irreplaceable. 'He was my mentor and my dearest friend.'[43]

As early as 1977, Broccoli brought his daughter Barbara into the Bond team, first helping out in Eon's publicity department. Over the years Barbara worked in several capacities, as second assistant director, associate producer and then fully-fledged producer along with Wilson when ill health restricted how much her father could do on the pictures. It was a smart move. Barbara had not just grown up around movies, she'd grown up around James Bond, regularly hanging around the Eon office, and sometimes after school visiting Pinewood Studios where she would be allowed on the set. Most of her time, though, was spent in her father's office at the studio and it was here that Barbara got to see him work first hand. 'So, I began my learning process of producing at a young age.'[44]

One of her most valuable lessons was to trust your instincts. Both Broccoli and Saltzman were risk takers. They knew that in the film business you have to take risks and have the strength of your convictions. Both men were not afraid to make tough decisions, and both stood up for what they believed in. Something that is especially important when you're dealing with a franchise, when you're so often having to think in the long term.

With Michael Wilson and Barbara installed, Broccoli knew the franchise he had helped found and nurture was in the safest hands possible. Indeed, both Wilson and Barbara have often spoken about feeling an obligation, almost a duty, to carry on what is essentially a family business. A family business that had as its head the godfather figure of Cubby Broccoli. For those who worked under him, he earned their devotion and respect. One of Broccoli's most endearing qualities was that he was on the side of his crew. At production meetings he'd listen to all the arguments, the accountants and production managers saying, 'No, you can't afford a crane that big,' then turn to his boys and say, 'Do you need it? You got it.' And if he believed you were right, he would fight on your side to the bitter end.

William P. Cartlidge worked closely with Cubby on two Bond films and recalled that he was always given the freedom to get on with his job:

> The only thing with Cubby was, I used to go in his office at Pinewood at eleven o'clock in the morning and say, 'Right, we've got a bit of a problem.' And he used to say to me, 'Is this a two-finger or a three-finger Jack Daniels job.' He had a bottle of the stuff in the right-hand drawer of his desk. And I used to say, 'Well, it could be a two-finger one, Cubby,' and he said, 'Right,' and he used to get the bottle out at eleven o'clock in the morning.[45]

In the industry, too, he was feted. At the 1982 Academy Awards ceremony, he was bestowed with the Irving G. Thalberg Memorial Award, whose past recipients included David O'Selznick, Walt Disney, Samuel Goldwyn, Jack Warner and Alfred Hitchcock; he was in exulted company, indeed.

Few people had a closer working relationship with Cubby than Peter Lamont, who joined the Eon team back in 1964 and whose final Bond as production designer was Daniel Craig's debut *Casino Royale* in 2006. Lamont was enormously fond of Broccoli, his generosity and the way he conducted himself in life and in business. He recalled being in Egypt shooting *The Spy Who Loved Me* and both of them going into the bar of their hotel with some of the crew:

> And Cubby was always there to buy the first drink, always. And he said to the barman, 'Jack Daniels please,' only to be told they didn't have any. So, Cubby went to his room and brought back a bottle. The barman looked at it and said, 'I can't serve it,' and Cubby said, 'Sell it to me.' That's the type of man he was.[46]

Working on *GoldenEye* out in Puerto Rico, Lamont got a phone call one day and it was from Broccoli, who took enormous delight in poking fun at him reaching the age of 65 and that he was now eligible for a bus pass. Unable to work on the next 007 film, due to having committed to *Titanic* for James Cameron, Lamont was working on that picture when news reached him that Broccoli was desperately ill. 'I rang the Eon office and said, "Is it possible I can go and see Cubby," and they said they'd like me to speak to Mrs Broccoli. And Dana came on the line and said, "Peter, remember him as he was."'[47]

Cubby Broccoli died peacefully at his home in Beverly Hills on 27 June 1996. He was 87. Towards the end of his life there was a rapprochement of sorts between Cubby and the man he helped turn into a star, Sean Connery. 'They acknowledged that what they had done together was very special,' said Barbara.[48] In the aftermath of her husband's passing, Dana received a phone call from the actor to offer his personal condolences.[49]

Right up until the very end, Bond remained an important part of Cubby's life. He had devoted so many years to it and achieved so much. It had made him a rich man and placed him at the pinnacle of his profession. He had helped bring Bond to the screen, and in return it presented him with a life to cherish. 'Cubby's ambition in life,' said Tom Mankiewicz:

> having done all of these different jobs before he and Harry became these wildly successful producers, was very much to live the way he wound up living, with beautiful homes, Rolls-Royces, to be able to gamble, to own race horses, and to really enjoy himself. Harry wanted to take his share and become Howard Hughes.[50]

That was the key difference between Harry and Cubby: one was content with the rewards 007 brought him, the other wasn't. As the former president of United Artists, Eric Pleskow, summed it up: 'If somebody had said to Harry, I can sell you the Eiffel Tower, he would have bought it.'[51]

Harry wanted the world and thought the Bond films would give it to him. Cubby was a more content man, satisfied with what he had created. And it never frustrated him that for most of his career he'd confined himself solely to the Bond franchise. And why should it? 'He was happy to make the Bond films. He loved it,' said Michael G. Wilson. 'He said that he had a tiger by the tail and that he couldn't let it go.'[52]

Bibliography

Adam, Ken, *Ken Adam Designs the Movies: James Bond and Beyond*, Thames and Hudson, 2008
Adler, Tim, *The House of Redgrave*, Aurum Press, 2012
Aldgate, Anthony, *Censorship and The Permissive Society: British Cinema and Theatre, 1955–1965*, Oxford University Press, 1991
Anderson, Lindsay, *The Diaries*, Methuen Drama, 2004
Balio, Tino, *United Artists: The Company That Changed the Film Industry*, University of Wisconsin Press, 1987
Barnes, Alan and Marcus Hearn, *Kiss Kiss Bang! Bang!*, BT Batsford, 2000
Benson, Raymond, *The James Bond Bedside Companion*, Galahad Books, 1986
Box, Betty, *Lifting the Lid: The Autobiography of Film Producer, Betty Box OBE*, Book Guild, 2000
Bradford, Richard, *The Life of a Long-Distance Writer: The Biography of Alan Sillitoe*, Peter Owen Ltd, 2008
Bragg, Melvyn, *Rich: The Life of Richard Burton*, Hodder & Stoughton, 1988
Bramwell, Tony, *Magical Mystery Tours: My Life with the Beatles*, Portico, 2005
Broccoli, Cubby, *When the Snow Melts*, Boxtree, 1998
Brosnan, John, *Future Tense: The Cinema of Science Fiction*, St Martin's Press, 1978
Cain, Syd, *Not Forgetting James Bond: The Autobiography of Production Designer Syd Cain*, GBU Publishing Ltd, 2002
Caine, Michael, *What's it All About*, Century, 1992
Capua, Michelangelo, *Janet Leigh, a Biography*, McFarland & Company, 2013
Carter-Ruck, Peter, *Memoirs of a Libel Lawyer*, Weidenfeld & Nicolson, 1990
Chandler, Charlotte, I *Know Where I'm Going: Katharine Hepburn, A Personal Biography*, Simon & Schuster, 2010
Chester, Lewis, *All My Shows are Great: The Life of Lew Grade*, Aurum, 2010
Cilento, Diane, *My Nine Lives*, Michael Joseph, 2006
Cork, John and Bruce Scivally, *James Bond: The Legacy*, Boxtree, 2002
de Toth, Andre, *Fragments*, Faber & Faber, 1996
de Toth, Andre, *De Toth on De Toth*, Faber & Faber, 1997
Drazin, Charles, *A Bond for Bond: Film Finances and Dr No*, Film Finances, 2011
Duncan, Paul, *The James Bond Archives*, Taschen, 2012

Falk, Quentin, *Cinema's Strangest Moments*, Robson Books, 2003
Farneth, David, *Lenya: The Legend*, Overlook Press, 1998
Fiegel, Eddi, *John Barry: A Sixties Theme: From James Bond to Midnight Cowboy*, Faber & Faber, 2012
Field, Matthew and Ajay Chowdhury, *Some Kind of Hero*, The History Press, 2015
Fleming, Fergus, *The Man with the Golden Typewriter: Ian Fleming's James Bond Letters*, Bloomsbury, 2016
Forbes, Bryan, *Notes for a Life*, HarperCollins, 1974
Forbes, Bryan, *A Divided Life*, William Heinemann, 1992
Frayling, Christopher, *Ken Adam and the Art of Production Design*, Faber & Faber, 2005
Freedland, Michael, *Sean Connery: A Biography*, Weidenfeld & Nicolson, 1994
Gallagher, Elaine, *Candidly Caine*, Robson Books, 1990
Gayson, Eunice, *The First Lady of Bond: My Autobiography*, Titan Books, 2012
Gilbert, Lewis, *All My Flashbacks*, Reynolds & Hearn, 2010
Haining, Peter, *James Bond: A Celebration*, W. H. Allen, 1987
Hall, Sheldon, *Zulu: With Some Guts Behind it: The Making of the Epic Movie*, Tomahawk Press, 2005
Harper, Sue and Vincent Porter, *British Cinema of the 1950s: The Decline of Deference*, Oxford University Press, 2003
Hernu, Sandy, *Q: The Biography of Desmond Llewelyn*, S.B. Publications, 1999
Hill, Lee, *A Grand Guy: The Art and Life of Terry Southern*, Bloomsbury, 2002
Hope, Bob, *The Road to Hollywood*, Doubleday, 1979
Juroe, Charles 'Jerry', *Bond, The Beatles and My Year with Marilyn*, McFarland and Co, 2018
Krantz, Judith, *Sex and Shopping: The Confessions of a Nice Jewish Girl*, St Martins Press, 2000
Kremer, Daniel, *Sidney J. Furie: Life and Films*, University Press of Kentucky, 2015
Lanza, Joseph, *Phallic Frenzy: Ken Russell and his Films*, Aurum, 2008
Linet, Beverly, *Ladd, the Life, the Legend, the Legacy of Alan Ladd*, Arbor House, 1979
Littlewood, Joan, *Joan's Book: The Autobiography of Joan Littlewood*, Methuen, 1993
Luxford, Albert J. and Gareth Owen, *Albert J. Luxford, the Gimmick Man: Memoir of a Special Effects Maestro*, McFarland and Company, 2002
Maasz, Ronnie, *A Cast of Shadows*, Scarecrow Press, 2004
Mankiewicz, Tom, *My Life as a Mankiewicz: An Insider's Journey through Hollywood*, University Press of Kentucky, 2012
McGilligan, Patrick, *Backstory: Interviews with Screenwriters of Hollywood's Golden Age*, University of California Press, 1986
McKay, James, *The Films of Victor Mature*, McFarland & Company, 2013
Meikle, Denis, *A History of Horrors: The Rise and Fall of the House of Hammer*, Scarecrow Press, 2008
Moore, Roger, *My Word is My Bond*, Michael O'Mara Books, 2008
Moore, Roger, *Bond on Bond*, Michael O'Mara Books, 2012
Moore, Roger, *Last Man Standing*, Michael O'Mara Books, 2014
Mosley, Leonard, *The Battle of Britain: The Making of a Film*, Pan, 1969
Murray, Andy, *Into the Unknown: The Fantastic Life of Nigel Kneale*, Headpress, 2006
Osborne, John, *Almost A Gentleman*, Faber & Faber, 1991
Osborne, John, *Looking Back: Never Explain, Never Apologise*, Faber & Faber, 1999
Parrish, Robert, *Hollywood Doesn't Live Here Anymore*, Little Brown, 1989

Passingham, Kenneth, *Sean Connery: a Biography*, Sidgwick and Jackson, 1983
Pettigrew, Terence, *Trevor Howard: A Personal Biography*, Peter Owen Publishers, 2001
Pfeiffer, Lee and Philip Lisa, *The Incredible World of 007, an Authorized Celebration of James Bond*, Boxtree, 1992
Picker, David V., *Musts, Maybes and Nevers*, CreateSpace, 2013
Richardson, Tony, *Long Distance Runner: A Memoir*, Faber & Faber, 1993
Rubin, Steven Jay, *The James Bond Films*, Arlington House, 1981
Rubin, Steven Jay, *The Complete James Bond Encyclopedia*, Contemporary Books, 1990
Sangster, Jimmy, *Do You Want It Good or Tuesday?* Midnight Marquee Press, 2009
Saville, Philip, *They Shoot Directors, Don't They?*, Kaleidoscope Publishing, 2019
Shellard, Dominic, *Kenneth Tynan: Writing for Posterity: A Life*, Yale University Press, 2003
Sherman, Robert B., *Moose: Chapters From my Life*, AuthorHouse, 2013
Sillitoe, Alan, *Life Without Armour*, HarperCollins, 1995
Simmons, Bob, *Nobody Does It Better*, Javelin Books, 1987
Spada, James, *Peter Lawford: The Man Who Kept the Secrets*, Bantam, 1991
Spinetti, Victor, *Up Front…: His Strictly Confidential Autobiography*, Robson Books, 2006
Todd, Richard, *Caught in The Act*, Hutchinson, 1986
Van Dyke, Dick, *My Lucky Life*, John Blake, 2016
Wagner, Robert, *Pieces of my Heart*, Hutchinson, 2009
Wales, Roland, *From Journey's End to the Dam Busters: The Life of R.C. Sherriff*, Pen and Sword books, 2016
Walker, Alexander, *Hollywood, England: the British film industry in the sixties*, Michael Joseph, 1974
Weaver, Tom, *Double Feature Creature Attack*, McFarland & Co, 2002
West, Adam, *Back to the Batcave*, Titan, 1992
Whitebrook, Peter, *John Osborne: 'Anger is not About…'*, Oberon Books Ltd, 2015
Widener, Don, *Lemmon: A Biography*, W. H. Allen, 1977
Wilkerson, W.R., *Hollywood Godfather: The Life and Crimes of Billy Wilkerson*, Chicago Review Press Inc., 2018
Winner, Michael, *Winner Takes All: A Life of Sorts*, Robson Books, 2004
Worrall, Dave, *The Most Famous Car in the World*, Solo Publishing, 1991
Young, Freddie, *Seventy Light Years: An Autobiography*, Faber & Faber, 1999

Notes

Harry and Cubby: An Introduction

1: *Observer*, 16 January 1972
2: Tom Mankiewicz: Author interview, 2007
3: *True, The Man's Magazine*, June 1966
4: Michael Freedland, *Sean Connery: A Biography*, Weidenfeld & Nicolson, 1994, p.127
5: *The Guardian*, 5 October 1976
6: Sir Ken Adam: Author interview, 2006
7: *Everything or Nothing: The Untold Story of 007*, documentary, 2012
8: Paul Duncan, *The James Bond Archives*, Taschen, 2012, p.254
9: *Harry Saltzman: Showman*, documentary, 2000
10: Tom Mankiewicz: Author interview, 2007
11: Paul Tucker: Author interview, 2019
12: Guy Hamilton: Author interview, 2008
13: Paul Duncan, *The James Bond Archives*, Taschen, 2012, p.165
14: George Lazenby interview, International Spy Museum, October 2018
15: *Harry Saltzman: Showman*, documentary, 2000
16: Syd Cain, *Not Forgetting James Bond: The Autobiography of Production Designer Syd Cain*, GBU Publishing Ltd, 2002, p.78

Chapter 1: Cubby

1: Tom Mankiewicz: Author interview, 2007
2: Cubby Broccoli, *When the Snow Melts*, Boxtree, 1998, p.9–10
3: Cubby Broccoli, *When the Snow Melts*, Boxtree, 1998, p.11–12
4: Cubby Broccoli, *When the Snow Melts*, Boxtree, 1998, p.14–15
5: *New York Times*, 1 July 1979
6: *Sunday Telegraph*, 24 June 1979
7: *New York Times*, 1 July 1979
8: Cubby Broccoli, *When the Snow Melts*, Boxtree, 1998, p.22–23
9: *Guardian*, 5 October 1976
10: *Sunday Telegraph*, 24 June 1979
11: *Cubby Broccoli: The Man Behind Bond*, documentary, 2000

12: Cubby Broccoli, *When the Snow Melts*, Boxtree, 1998, p.32
13: Cubby Broccoli, *When the Snow Melts*, Boxtree, 1998, p.35
14: *New York Times*, 1 July 1979
15: Cubby Broccoli, *When the Snow Melts*, Boxtree, 1998, p.50
16: W.R. Wilkerson, *Hollywood Godfather: The Life and Crimes of Billy Wilkerson*, Chicago Review Press Inc., 2018, p.141
17: *Los Angeles magazine*, June 1997
18: Cubby Broccoli, *When the Snow Melts*, Boxtree, 1998, p.66
19: Cubby Broccoli, *When the Snow Melts*, Boxtree, 1998, p.60
20: Cubby Broccoli, *When the Snow Melts*, Boxtree, 1998, p.62
21: *The Times*, 2 April 2009
22: *New York Times*, 15 December 1940
23: AFI.com
24: *Los Angeles Times*, 9 July 1989
25: *New York Times*, 6 July 1946
26: *Kingsport News* (Tennessee), 8 August 1945
27: Cubby Broccoli, *When the Snow Melts*, Boxtree, 1998, p.83–84
28: Cubby Broccoli, *When the Snow Melts*, Boxtree, 1998, p.86–87
29: *Independent*, 27 March 2009
30: *Independent*, 27 March 2009
31: *Los Angeles Times*, 24 September 1958
32: Cubby Broccoli, *When the Snow Melts*, Boxtree, 1998, p.93
33: Richard Todd, *Caught in The Act*, Hutchinson, 1986, p.182
34: Cubby Broccoli, *When the Snow Melts*, Boxtree, 1998, p.100
35: Beverly Linet, *Ladd, the Life, the Legend, the Legacy of Alan Ladd*, Arbor House, 1979, p.161
36: *The Times*, 2 April 2009
37: Cubby Broccoli, *When the Snow Melts*, Boxtree, 1998, p.103
38: W.R. Wilkerson, *Hollywood Godfather: The Life and Crimes of Billy Wilkerson*, Chicago Review Press Inc., 2018, p.143
39: Bob Simmons, *Nobody Does It Better*, Javelin Books, 1987, p.24
40: Syd Cain, *Not Forgetting James Bond: The Autobiography of Production Designer Syd Cain*, GBU Publishing Ltd, 2002, p.38
41: BECTU History Project, August 1988
42: BECTU History Project, August 1988
43: Cubby Broccoli, *When the Snow Melts*, Boxtree, 1998, p.112–13
44: Beverly Linet, *Ladd, the Life, the Legend, the Legacy of Alan Ladd*, Arbor House, 1979, p.175
45: Euan Lloyd: Author interview, 2006
46: Euan Lloyd: Author interview, 2006
47: *Cinema Retro*, No. 1, January 2005
48: *Cinema Retro*, No. 1, January 2005
49: Chris Coppel email correspondence, 2018
50: BAFTA Tribute, 2007
51: Bryan Forbes, *A Divided Life*, William Heinemann, 1992, p.3–4
52: *New York Times*, 26 April, 1959
53: Euan Lloyd: Author interview, 2006
54: Cubby Broccoli, *When the Snow Melts*, Boxtree, 1998, p.104
55: *Hollywood Reporter*, 2 November 1954

56: Roland Wales, *From Journey's End to the Dam Busters: The Life of R.C. Sherriff*, Pen and Sword books, 2016, p.285
57: *Los Angeles Times*, 13 June 1954
58: Terence Pettigrew, *Trevor Howard: A Personal Biography*, Peter Owen Publishers, 2001, p.170
59: Cubby Broccoli, *When the Snow Melts*, Boxtree, 1998, p.123
60: Ronnie Maasz, *A Cast of Shadows*, Scarecrow Press, 2004, p.42
61: *The Washington Post*, 22 November 1955
62: Sue Harper and Vincent Porter, *British Cinema of the 1950s: The Decline of Deference*, Oxford University Press, 2003, p.129
63: Cubby Broccoli, *When the Snow Melts*, Boxtree, 1998, p.125
64: James McKay, *The Films of Victor Mature*, McFarland & Company Inc., 2013, p.19
65: Sue Harper and Vincent Porter, *British Cinema of the 1950s: The Decline of Deference*, Oxford University Press, 2003, p.129
66: Michelangelo Capua, *Janet Leigh: A Biography*, McFarland & Company Inc., 2013, p.77
67: Michelangelo Capua, *Janet Leigh: A Biography*, McFarland & Company Inc., 2013, p.77
68: Cubby Broccoli, *When the Snow Melts*, Boxtree, 1998, p.118
69: Cubby Broccoli, *When the Snow Melts*, Boxtree, 1998, p.119–20
70: Film Finance Archive
71: Film Finance Archive
72: Film Finance Archive
73: *New York Times*, 14 May 1953
74: Ronnie Maasz, *A Cast of Shadows*, Scarecrow Press, 2004, p.40
75: Eunice Gayson, *The First Lady of Bond: My Autobiography*, Titan Books, 2012, p.85–86
76: Sue Harper and Vincent Porter, *British Cinema of the 1950s: The Decline of Deference*, Oxford University Press, 2003, p.129
77: Robert Parrish, *Hollywood Doesn't Live Here Anymore*, Little Brown, 1989, p.105
78: Don Widener, *Lemmon: A Biography*, W. H. Allen, 1977, p.140
79: Cubby Broccoli, *When the Snow Melts*, Boxtree, 1998, p. 124
80: Robert Parrish, *Hollywood Doesn't Live Here Anymore*, Little Brown, 1989, p.107–8
81: Euan Lloyd: Author interview, 2006
82: Euan Lloyd: Author interview, 2006
83: Michael Caine, *What's it All About*, Century, 1992, p.113
84: Robert Sellers, *Don't Let the Bastards Grind You Down*, Preface, 2011, p.223
85: *Kine Weekly*, 31 May 1956
86: Quentin Falk, *Cinema's Strangest Moments*, Robson Books, 2003, p.105
87: *Los Angeles Times*, 16 July 1955
88: *Los Angeles Times*, 15 August 1957
89: James McKay, *The Films of Victor Mature*, McFarland & Company Inc., 2013, p.153
90: *Daily Telegraph*, 26 October 2012
91: John Cork, Bruce Scivally, *James Bond: The Legacy*, Boxtree, 2002, p.22
92: Cubby Broccoli, *When the Snow Melts*, Boxtree, 1998, p.127
93: *Vanity Fair*, October 2012
94: Euan Lloyd: Author interview, 2006
95: Cubby Broccoli, *When the Snow Melts*, Boxtree, 1998, p.127
96: Forestlawn.com
97: Cubby Broccoli, *When the Snow Melts*, Boxtree, 1998, p.133–34
98: Andre de Toth, *Fragments*, Faber & Faber, 1996
99: Cubby Broccoli, *When the Snow Melts*, Boxtree, 1998, p.141

100: *Cubby Broccoli: The Man Behind Bond*, documentary, 2000
101: *Pebble Mill at One*, BBC, November 1995
102: *Pebble Mill at One*, BBC, November 1995
103: IMDB.com
104: Christopher Frayling, *Ken Adam and the Art of Production Design*, Faber & Faber, 2005, p.93
105: *Cinema Retro, Movie Classics, Dr No*, 2012
106: *New York Times*, 1 December 1959
107: Euan Lloyd: Author interview, 2006
108: *Evening Standard*, October 1965
109: Charles Drazin, *A Bond for Bond: Film Finances and Dr No*, Film Finances, 2011, p.16
110: Film Finance Archive
111: Christopher Frayling, *Ken Adam and the Art of Production Design*, Faber & Faber, 2005, p.84
112: Elaine Dundy, *Finch, Bloody Finch: A Biography of Peter Finch*, Michael Joseph, 1980, p.244
113: Cubby Broccoli, *When the Snow Melts*, Boxtree, 1998, p.143
114: Alexander Walker, *Hollywood, England: The British Film Industry in the Sixties*, Michael Joseph, 1974, p.158
115: Cubby Broccoli, *When the Snow Melts*, Boxtree, 1998, p.144
116: Cubby Broccoli, *When the Snow Melts*, Boxtree, 1998, p.145
117: Christopher Frayling, *Ken Adam and the Art of Production Design*, Faber & Faber, 2005, p.84
118: Cubby Broccoli, *When the Snow Melts*, Boxtree, 1998, p.145
119: Euan Lloyd: Author interview, 2006
120: Denis Meikle, *A History of Horrors: The Rise and Fall of the House of Hammer*, Scarecrow Press, 2008, p.49
121: Jimmy Sangster, *Do You Want It Good or Tuesday?* Midnight Marquee Press, 2009, p.43
122: Sheldon Hall, *Zulu: With Some Guts Behind it: The Making of the Epic Movie*, Tomahawk Press, 2005, p.129
123: *Cinema Retro,* No.1, January 2005
124: Web of Stories.com
125: Peter Lamont: Author interview, 2019
126: Peter Lamont: Author interview, 2019
127: Cubby Broccoli, *When the Snow Melts*, Boxtree, 1998, p.146

Chapter 2: Harry

1: *Calgary Herald*, 29 January 1966
2: John Cork, Bruce Scivally, *James Bond: The Legacy*, Boxtree, 2002, p.20
3: *Vanity Fair*, October 2012
4: CBC Radio Canada, 9 December 2015
5: *Harry Saltzman: Showman*, documentary, 2000
6: *Calgary Herald*, 29 January 1966
7: *Daily Telegraph*, 26 October 2012
8: *Le Soleil*, 26 November 2012
9: Leonard Mosley, *The Battle of Britain: The Making of a Film*, Pan, 1969, p.66
10: *Calgary Herald*, 29 January 1966
11: Leonard Mosley, *The Battle of Britain: The Making of a Film*, Pan, 1969, p.19
12: Leonard Mosley, *The Battle of Britain: The Making of a Film*, Pan, 1969, p.67
13: Leonard Mosley, *The Battle of Britain: The Making of a Film*, Pan, 1969, p.70
14: Leonard Mosley, *The Battle of Britain: The Making of a Film*, Pan, 1969, p.70

15: Tony Richardson, *Long Distance Runner: A Memoir*, Faber & Faber, 1993, p.95
16: *True: The Men's Magazine*, June 1966
17: Steven Jay Rubin, *The Complete James Bond Encyclopedia*, Contemporary Books, 1990, p.360
18: 'Harry The Spy' by David Kamp and David Giammarco, *Vanity Fair*, September 2012
19: C.D. Jackson, obituary, *New York Times*, 20 September 1964
20: 'Harry The Spy' by David Kamp and David Giammarco, *Vanity Fair*, September 2012
21: *The Royal Gazette*, 14 January 2013
22: Tom Mankiewicz: Author interview, 2007
23: *Guardian*, 2 December 1972
24: Guy Hamilton: Author interview, 2008
25: *Billboard*, 27 January 1951
26: *Observer*, 21 March 1965
27: Judith Krantz, *Sex and Shopping: The Confessions of a Nice Jewish Girl*, St Martin's Press, 2000, p.134
28: Judith Krantz, *Sex and Shopping: The Confessions of a Nice Jewish Girl*, St Martin's Press, 2000, p.134
29: *Starlog magazine*, November 1983
30: *Starlog magazine*, November 1983
31: *Starlog magazine*, November 1983
32: *Billboard*, 11 September 1954
33: *Calgary Herald*, 29 January 1966
34: Michael Caine, *What's it All About*, Century, 1992, p.173
35: *Billboard*, 11 September, 1954
36: *Billboard*, 26 February 1955
37: Guy Hamilton: Author interview, 2008
38: *Variety*, 4 July 1956
39: *Variety*, 2 January 1957
40: Len Deighton: Author interview, 2007
41: Film Finance archive
42: Ben Hecht archive, Newberry Library, Chicago
43: Ben Hecht archive, Newberry Library, Chicago
44: Betty Box, *Lifting the Lid: The Autobiography of Film Producer, Betty Box*, Book Guild, 2000, p.118
45: Charlotte Chandler, *I Know Where I'm Going: Katharine Hepburn, A Personal Biography*, Simon & Schuster, 2010, p.214
46: Ben Hecht archive, Newberry Library, Chicago
47: Charlotte Chandler, *I Know Where I'm Going: Katharine Hepburn, A Personal Biography*, Simon & Schuster, 2010, p.214
48: *Los Angeles Times*, 8 July 1958
49: Copyright David Lewin, 1975
50: *Hollywood Reporter.com*, 25 October 2012
51: Betty Box, *Lifting the Lid: The Autobiography of Film Producer, Betty Box*, Book Guild, 2000, p.127
52: *New York Film Critics Circle*, November 2012
53: Ben Hecht archive, Newberry Library, Chicago
54: *Los Angeles Times*, 23 August 1956
55: *Billboard*, 16 April 1955

56: Patrick McGilligan and Paul Buhle, *Tender Comrades: A Backstory of the Hollywood Blacklist*, St Martin's Press, 1997, p.19
57: Johanna Harwood: Author interview, 2019
58: Johanna Harwood: Author interview, 2019
59: Johanna Harwood: Author interview, 2019
60: Dominic Shellard, *Kenneth Tynan: Writing for Posterity: A Life*, Yale University Press, 2003, p.96
61: Robert Sellers, *Don't Let the Bastards Grind You Down*, Preface, 2011, p.69
62: Robert Sellers, *Don't Let the Bastards Grind You Down*, Preface, 2011, p.69
63: Anthony Field: Author interview, 2010
64: Michael Caine, *What's it All About*, Century, 1992, p.133
65: John Osborne, *Almost A Gentleman*, Faber & Faber, 1991, p.23
66: John Osborne, *Almost A Gentleman*, Faber & Faber, 1991, p.69
67: John Osborne, *Almost A Gentleman*, Faber & Faber, 1991, p.69
68: Peter Whitebrook, *John Osborne: 'Anger is not About...'*, Oberon Books Ltd, 2015
69: John Osborne, *Almost A Gentleman*, Faber & Faber, 1991, p.69
70: Tony Richardson, *Long Distance Runner: A Memoir*, Faber & Faber, 1993, p.95
71: Tony Richardson, *Long Distance Runner: A Memoir*, Faber & Faber, 1993, p.95
72: John Osborne, *Almost A Gentleman*, Faber & Faber, 1991, p.72
73: John Osborne, *Almost A Gentleman*, Faber & Faber, 1991, p.72
74: Tony Richardson, *Long Distance Runner*: A Memoir, Faber & Faber, 1993, p.96
75: Tony Richardson, *Long Distance Runner*: A Memoir, Faber & Faber, 1993, p.96
76: Tony Richardson, *Long Distance Runner*: A Memoir, Faber & Faber, 1993, p.96
77: Robert Sellers, *Don't Let the Bastards Grind You Down*, Preface, 2011, p.173
78: Walter Lassally: Author interview, 2010
79: *Kine Weekly*, 24 March 1960
80: Andy Murray, *Into the Unknown: The Fantastic Life of Nigel Kneale*, Headpress, 2006, p.96
81: Anthony Aldgate, *Censorship and The Permissive Society: British Cinema and Theatre, 1955–1965*, Oxford University Press, 1991, p.79–80
82: Tony Richardson, *Long Distance Runner: A Memoir*, Faber & Faber, 1993, p.97
83: Tony Richardson, *Long Distance Runner: A Memoir*, Faber & Faber, 1993, p.97
84: Gary Raymond: Author interview, 2010
85: Matthew Field and Ajay Chowdhury, *Some Kind of Hero*, The History Press, 2015, p.38
86: Melvyn Bragg, *Rich: The Life of Richard Burton*, Hodder & Stoughton, 1988, p.125
87: Paul Ferris, *Richard Burton*, Coward Mc Cann, 1981, p.134
88: Tony Richardson, *Long Distance Runner: A Memoir*, Faber & Faber, 1993, p.127
89: *Evening Standard*, 29 October, 1965
90: Anthony Aldgate, *Censorship and The Permissive Society: British Cinema and Theatre, 1955–1965*, Oxford University Press, 1991, p.82
91: John Osborne, *Almost A Gentleman*, Faber & Faber, 1991, p.139
92: John Osborne, *Almost A Gentleman*, Faber & Faber, 1991, p.139
93: *Films and Filming*, April 1960
94: *Films and Filming*, April 1960
95: *Films and Filming*, April 1960
96: Film Finance Archive
97: Tony Richardson, *Long Distance Runner: A Memoir*, Faber & Faber, 1993, p.137
98: John Osborne, *Almost A Gentleman*, Faber & Faber, 1991, p.147
99: Film Finance Archive

100: Film Finance Archive
101: Bectu History Project, October 1990
102: Anthony Aldgate, *Censorship and The Permissive Society: British Cinema and Theatre, 1955–1965*, Oxford University Press, 1991, p.80
103: John Osborne, *Almost A Gentleman*, Faber & Faber, 1991, p.154
104: Johanna Harwood: Author interview, 2019
105: Joan Littlewood, *Joan's Book: The Autobiography of Joan Littlewood*, Methuen, 1993, p.415
106: Johanna Harwood: Author interview, 2019
107: Johanna Harwood: Author interview, 2019
108: Johanna Harwood: Author interview, 2019
109: Johanna Harwood: Author interview, 2019
110: Alan Sillitoe, *Life Without Armour*, HarperCollins, 1995, p.222
111: Alan Sillitoe, *Life Without Armour*, HarperCollins, 1995, p.238
112: Alan Sillitoe, *Life Without Armour*, HarperCollins, 1995, p.257
113: Richard Bradford, *The Life of a Long-Distance Writer: The Biography of Alan Sillitoe*, Peter Owen Ltd, 2008, p.158
114: Anthony Aldgate, *Censorship and The Permissive Society: British Cinema and Theatre, 1955–1965*, Oxford University Press, 1991, p.94
115: Film Finance Archive
116: Film Finance Archive
117: Film Finance Archive
118: Alan Sillitoe, *Life Without Armour*, HarperCollins, 1995, p.262
119: Film Finance Archive
120: Alan Sillitoe, *Life Without Armour*, HarperCollins, 1995, p.262
121: Film Finance Archive
122: Film Finance Archive
123: Film Finance Archive
124: Alan Sillitoe, *Life Without Armour*, HarperCollins, 1995, p.262
125: Richard Bradford, *The Life of a Long-Distance Writer: The Biography of Alan Sillitoe*, Peter Owen Ltd, 2008, p.172–73
126: Tony Richardson, *Long Distance Runner: A Memoir*, Faber & Faber, 1993, p.141
127: Tony Richardson, *Long Distance Runner: A Memoir*, Faber & Faber, 1993, p.141
128: Anthony Aldgate, *Censorship and The Permissive Society: British Cinema and Theatre, 1955–1965*, Oxford University Press, 1991, p.127
129: Tony Richardson, *Long Distance Runner: A Memoir*, Faber & Faber, 1993, p.142
130: Tim Adler, *The House of Redgrave*, Aurum Press, 2012, p.65
131: Richard Bradford, *The Life of a Long-Distance Writer: The Biography of Alan Sillitoe*, Peter Owen Ltd, 2008, p.180
132: Tony Richardson, *Long Distance Runner: A Memoir*, Faber & Faber, 1993, p.142
133: Tim Adler, *The House of Redgrave*, Aurum Press, 2012, p.83
134: John Osborne, *Looking Back: Never Explain, Never Apologise*, Faber & Faber, 1999, p.459
135: John Osborne, *Looking Back: Never Explain, Never Apologise*, Faber & Faber, 1999, p.459
136: Johanna Harwood: Author interview, 2019
137: Alan Sillitoe, *Life Without Armour*, HarperCollins, 1995, p.270

Chapter 3: Everything or Nothing

1: Copyright David Lewin, 1975

2: Betty Box, *Lifting the Lid: The Autobiography of Film Producer, Betty Box*, Book Guild, 2000, p.132
3: Steven Jay Rubin, *The Complete James Bond Encyclopedia*, Contemporary Books, 1990, p.360
4: *True: The Men's Magazine*, June 1966
5: *Vanity Fair*, October 2012
6: Steven Jay Rubin, *The Complete James Bond Encyclopedia*, Contemporary Books, 1990, p.360
7: Tino Balio, *United Artists: The Company That Changed the Film Industry*, University of Wisconsin Press, 1987, p.255
8: *True: The Men's Magazine*, June 1966
9: Angela Huth, *Not the Whole Story: A Memoir*, Constable, 2018
10: Alexander Walker, *Hollywood, England: The British Film Industry in the Sixties*, Michael Joseph, 1974, p.182
11: Alexander Walker, *Hollywood, England: The British Film Industry in the Sixties*, Michael Joseph, 1974, p.182
12: Peter Lamont: Author interview, 2019
13: Michael Freedland, *Sean Connery: A Biography*, Weidenfeld & Nicolson, 1994, p.84
14: Lee Pfeiffer and Philip Lisa, *The Incredible World of 007, An Authorized Celebration of James Bond*, Boxtree, 1992, p.190
15: *True: The Men's Magazine*, June 1966
16: Tom Mankiewicz: Author interview, 2007
17: Charles Jerry Juroe, *Bond, the Beatles and My Moment with Marilyn: 50 Years as a Publicist to the Stars*, McFarland & Co Inc, 2018, p.130
18: Cubby Broccoli, *When the Snow Melts*, Boxtree, 1998, p.150
19: Steven Jay Rubin, *The Complete James Bond Encyclopedia*, Contemporary Books, 1990, p.58
20: Lee Pfeiffer and Philip Lisa, *The Incredible World of 007, An Authorized Celebration of James Bond*, Boxtree, 1992, p.190
21: David V. Picker, *Musts, Maybes and Nevers*, CreateSpace, 2013, p.41
22: David V. Picker, *Musts, Maybes and Nevers*, CreateSpace, 2013, p.39
23: David V. Picker, *Musts, Maybes and Nevers*, CreateSpace, 2013, p.39
24: Cubby Broccoli, *When the Snow Melts*, Boxtree, 1998, p.150
25: David V. Picker, *Musts, Maybes and Nevers*, CreateSpace, 2013, p.42
26: David V. Picker, *Musts, Maybes and Nevers*, CreateSpace, 2013, p.42
27: David V. Picker, *Musts, Maybes and Nevers*, CreateSpace, 2013, p.55
28: David V. Picker, *Musts, Maybes and Nevers*, CreateSpace, 2013, p.56
29: David V. Picker, *Musts, Maybes and Nevers*, CreateSpace, 2013, p.42
30: Lee Pfeiffer and Philip Lisa, *The Incredible World of 007, An Authorized Celebration of James Bond*, Boxtree, 1992, p.190
31: Cubby Broccoli, *When the Snow Melts*, Boxtree, 1998, p.152
32: *Photoplay*, November 1962
33: Len Deighton: Author interview, 2007
34: Tino Balio, *United Artists: The Company That Changed the Film Industry*, University of Wisconsin Press, 1987, p.255
35: Fergus Fleming, *The Man with the Golden Typewriter: Ian Fleming's James Bond Letters*, Bloomsbury, 2016, p.286
36: *Observer*, 16 January 1972
37: Tino Balio, *United Artists: The Company That Changed the Film Industry*, University of Wisconsin Press, 1987, p.259
38: *Dr No* Blu-Ray audio commentary

39: *Bondage* magazine, No.10, 1981
40: Leonard Mosley, *The Battle of Britain: The Making of a Film*, Pan, 1969, p.119
41: William P. Cartlidge: Author interview, 2019
42: *Dr No* Blu-Ray audio commentary

Chapter 4: Just Another Movie

1: Cubby Broccoli, *When the Snow Melts*, Boxtree, 1998, p. 158–59
2: Cubby Broccoli, *When the Snow Melts*, Boxtree, 1998, p. 163
3: Andy Murray, *Into the Unknown: The Fantastic Life of Nigel Kneale*, Headpress, 2006, p.117
4: Guy Hamilton: Author interview, 2008
5: Bryan Forbes, *Notes for a Life*, HarperCollins, 1974, p.354
6: *Saturday Review*, 25 December 1965
7: *Inside Dr No*, documentary, 2000
8: *Daily Telegraph*, 9 May 2000
9: James Spada, *Peter Lawford: The Man Who Kept the Secrets*, Bantam, 1991, p.196
10: *Starlog* magazine, July 1986
11: Michael Craig: Author interview, 2008
12: Gabriel Hershman, *Send in the Clowns – The Yo Yo Life of Ian Hendry*, 2013, p.54
13: *Showtime*, October 1967
14: Museum of Modern Art Lecture, June 1979
15: Robert Sellers, *Sean Connery: A Celebration*, Robert Hale, 1999, p.80
16: Cyril Frankel: Author interview, 2007
17: Cyril Frankel: Author interview, 2007
18: Cyril Frankel: Author interview, 2007
19: *Daily Telegraph*, 9 May 2000
20: Robert Sellers, *Don't Let the Bastards Grind You Down*, Preface, 2011, p.328
21: Kenneth Passingham, *Sean Connery – a Biography*, Sidgwick and Jackson, 1983, p.40
22: Cubby Broccoli, *When the Snow Melts*, Boxtree, 1998, p.168
23: Sheldon Lane, *For Bond Lovers Only*, Panther Books Ltd, 1965, p.161
24: *Saturday Evening Post*, 6 June 1964
25: Philip Saville: Author interview, 2010
26: Michael Freedland, *Sean Connery: A Biography*, Weidenfeld & Nicolson, 1994, p.86
27: Sunday Telegraph, 24 June 1979
28: *Starlog*, March 1983
29: Cubby Broccoli, *When the Snow Melts*, Boxtree, 1998, p.170
30: *Life* magazine, 14 October 1966
31: *Variety*, 13 May 1987
32: John Osborne, *Almost A Gentleman*, Faber & Faber, 1991, p.169
33: *Bondage* magazine, No.10, 1981
34: Johanna Harwood: Author interview, 2019
35: Johanna Harwood: Author interview, 2019
36: Johanna Harwood: Author interview, 2019
37: Lee Pfeiffer and Philip Lisa, *The Incredible World of 007, An Authorized Celebration of James Bond*, Boxtree, 1992, p.204
38: Syd Cain, *Not Forgetting James Bond: The Autobiography of Production Designer Syd Cain*, GBU Publishing Ltd, 2002, p.58
39: *007* magazine, No.27, 1994

40: Steven Jay Rubin, *The James Bond Films*, Arlington House, 1981, p.20
41: Fergus Fleming, *The Man with the Golden Typewriter: Ian Fleming's James Bond Letters*, Bloomsbury, 2016, p.255
42: Earl Cameron: Author interview, 2006
43: Steven Jay Rubin, *The Complete James Bond Encyclopedia*, Contemporary Books, 1990, p.78
44: Robert Baker: Author interview, 2006
45: Steven Jay Rubin, *The Complete James Bond Encyclopedia*, Contemporary Books, 1990, p.78
46: Lee Pfeiffer and Philip Lisa, *The Incredible World of 007, An Authorized Celebration of James Bond*, Boxtree, 1992, p.191
47: Cubby Broccoli, *When the Snow Melts*, Boxtree, 1998, p.172
48: Cubby Broccoli, *When the Snow Melts*, Boxtree, 1998, p.173
49: *Cinema Retro*, *Dr No* special, 2012
50: Monty Norman: Author interview, 2007
51: Monty Norman: Author interview, 2007
52: Monty Norman: Author interview, 2007
53: Monty Norman: Author interview, 2007
54: Monty Norman: Author interview, 2007
55: Cubby Broccoli, *When the Snow Melts*, Boxtree, 1998, p.174
56: Monty Norman: Author interview, 2007
57: Monty Norman: Author interview, 2007
58: Monty Norman: Author interview, 2007
59: Monty Norman: Author interview, 2007
60: Web of Stories.com
61: *Daily Telegraph*, 26 October 2012
62: *Daily Telegraph*, 26 October 2012
63: Christopher Frayling, *Ken Adam and the Art of Production Design*, Faber & Faber, 2005, p.96
64: Steven Jay Rubin, *The James Bond Films*, Arlington House, 1981, p.21
65: Monty Norman: Author interview, 2007
66: Eddi Fiegel, *John Barry: A Sixties Theme: From James Bond to Midnight Cowboy*, Faber & Faber, 2012, p.94
67: *Starlog*, September 1983
68: Sir Roger Moore: Author interview, 2001
69: *Starlog*, September 1983
70: *Variety*, 13 May 1987
71: Norman Wanstall: Author interview, 2015
72: Jeremy Vaughan: Author interview, 2007
73: Johanna Harwood: Author interview, 2019
74: *Sight & Sound*, November 1994
75: *Variety*, 13 May 1987
76: Robert Sellers, *Sean Connery: A Celebration*, Robert Hale, 1999, p.64
77: Cubby Broccoli, *When the Snow Melts*, Boxtree, 1998, p.177

Chapter 5: Calling Mr Hope

1: Cubby Broccoli, *When the Snow Melts*, Boxtree, 1998, p.181
2: Johanna Harwood: Author interview, 2019
3: *Calgary Herald*, 29 January 1966
4: Bob Hope, *The Road to Hollywood*, Doubleday, 1979, p.93–94

5: Bob Hope, *The Road to Hollywood*, Doubleday, 1979, p.93–94
6: Cubby Broccoli, *When the Snow Melts*, Boxtree, 1998, p.182
7: Johanna Harwood: Author interview, 2019
8: Johnny Carson TV show, October 1976
9: Johanna Harwood: Author interview, 2019
10: Johanna Harwood: Author interview, 2019
11: Len Deighton: Author interview, 2007
12: Monty Norman: Author interview, 2007
13: Monty Norman: Author interview, 2007
14: Monty Norman: Author interview, 2007
15: Monty Norman: Author interview, 2007
16: Monty Norman: Author interview, 2007
17: Monty Norman: Author interview, 2007
18: Monty Norman: Author interview, 2007
19: *Variety*, 18 November 1963
20: Lee Hill, *A Grand Guy: The Art and Life of Terry Southern*, Bloomsbury, 2002, p.122
21: Lord Birkett: Author interview, 2011
22: Lord Birkett: Author interview, 2011.

Chapter 6: Turkish Delight

1: Johanna Harwood: Author interview, 2019
2: Johanna Harwood: Author interview, 2019
3: Johanna Harwood: Author interview, 2019
4: Johanna Harwood: Author interview, 2019
5: *Bondage* magazine, No.10, 1981
6: Peter Hunt interview, copyright Edward Gross, 1990
7: Diane Cilento, *My Nine Lives*, Michael Joseph, 2006, p.209
8: Robert Sellers, *Don't Let the Bastards Grind You Down*, Preface, 2011, p.386
9: Paul Duncan, *The James Bond Archives*, Taschen, 2012, p.60
10: David Farneth, *Lenya: The Legend*, Overlook Press, 1998, p.176
11: David Farneth, *Lenya: The Legend*, Overlook Press, 1998, p.176
12: *Fab*, No.8, Fanderson, December 1992
13: *Fab*, No.8, Fanderson, December 1992
14: Steven Jay Rubin, *The James Bond Films*, Arlington House, 1981, p.33
15: Syd Cain, *Not Forgetting James Bond: The Autobiography of Production Designer Syd Cain*, GBU Publishing Ltd, 2002, p.66–67
16: *The Sun*, December 1971
17: Raymond Benson, *The James Bond Bedside Companion*, Galahad Books, 1986, p.173
18: *Bondage* magazine, No.10, 1981
19: Andre de Toth, *De Toth on De Toth*, Faber & Faber, 1997, p.151
20: Guy Hamilton: Author interview, 2008
21: Paul Duncan, *The James Bond Archives*, Taschen, 2012, p.59
22: Tom Mankiewicz: Author interview, 2007
23: *Bondage* magazine, No.10, 1981
24: *Scene by Scene with Sean Connery*, 1997, BBC
25: Sandy Hernu, *Q: The Biography of Desmond Llewelyn*, S.B. Publications, 1999, p.77
26: Paul Duncan, *The James Bond Archives*, Taschen, 2012, p.69
27: Copyright David Lewin, 1975

28: Syd Cain, *Not Forgetting James Bond: The Autobiography of Production Designer Syd Cain*, GBU Publishing Ltd, 2002, p.69
29: *Inside From Russia With Love*, documentary, 2000
30: Syd Cain, *Not Forgetting James Bond: The Autobiography of Production Designer Syd Cain*, GBU Publishing Ltd, 2002, p.68
31: Eddi Fiegel, *John Barry: A Sixties Theme: From James Bond to Midnight Cowboy*, Faber & Faber, 2012, p.106
32: *Observer*, 21 March 1965
33: Robertbrownjohn.com
34: Robertbrownjohn.com
35: *Daily Telegraph*, 21 May, 2009
36: David V. Picker, *Musts, Maybes and Nevers*, CreateSpace, 2013, p.50
37: Tino Balio, *United Artists: The Company That Changed the Film Industry*, University of Wisconsin Press, 1987, p.260
38: *Cinema magazine*, Vol. 1, No. 1, 1963

Chapter 7: All That Glitters

1: Robert Sellers, *The Battle for Bond*, Tomahawk Press, 2007, p.119–20
2: *Bondage* magazine, No.10, 1981
3: Matthew Field and Ajay Chowdhury, *Some Kind of Hero*, The History Press, 2015, p.103
4: Cubby Broccoli, *When the Snow Melts*, Boxtree, 1998, p.189
5: Guy Hamilton: Author interview, 1997
6: Guy Hamilton: Author interview, 2008
7: Guy Hamilton: Author interview, 2008
8: John Cork, Bruce Scivally, *James Bond: The Legacy*, Boxtree, 2002, p.36
9: Guy Hamilton: Author interview, 2008
10: Guy Hamilton: Author interview, 2008
11: *Harry Saltzman: Showman*, documentary, 2000
12: Patrick McGilligan, *Backstory: Interviews with Screenwriters of Hollywood's Golden Age*, University of California Press, 1986, p.285
13: *Esquire*, June 1965
14: *Esquire*, June 1965
15: Cubby Broccoli, *When the Snow Melts*, Boxtree, 1998, p.159
16: *Cubby Broccoli: The Man Behind Bond*, documentary, 2000
17: Monty Norman: Author interview, 2007
18: Guy Hamilton: Author interview, 2008
19: Guy Hamilton: Author interview, 1997
20: Guy Hamilton: Author interview, 1997
21: Honor Blackman: Author interview, 1997
22: Guy Hamilton: Author interview, 1997
23: Cubby Broccoli, *When the Snow Melts*, Boxtree, 1998, p.191
24: Copyright David Lewin, 1975
25: Shirley Eaton: Author interview, 2006
26: Shirley Eaton: Author interview, 1997
27: Shirley Eaton: Author interview, 1997
28: Shirley Eaton: Author interview, 2006
29: *Harry Saltzman: Showman*, documentary, 2000

30: Tania Mallet: Author interview, 1997
31: Guy Hamilton: Author interview, 2008
32: Cubby Broccoli, *When the Snow Melts*, Boxtree, 1998, p.215
33: Copyright David Lewin, 1975
34: Kenneth Passingham, *Sean Connery – a Biography*, Sidgwick and Jackson, 1983, p.61
35: Burt Kwouk: Author interview, 1997
36: Guy Hamilton: Author interview, 1997
37: Matthew Field and Ajay Chowdhury, *Some Kind of Hero*, The History Press, 2015, p.112
38: Matthew Field and Ajay Chowdhury, *Some Kind of Hero*, The History Press, 2015, p.112
39: *The Man with the Golden Gun*, Blu Ray audio commentary
40: *Telescope*, CBC, 9 December 1965
41: Richard Jenkins: Author interview, 2006
42: Ken Adam: Author interview, 1997
43: Ken Adam: Author interview, 1997
44: Ken Adam: Author interview, 1997
45: Peter Lamont: Author interview, 2019
46: Peter Lamont: Author interview, 2019
47: Peter Lamont: Author interview, 2019
48: Ken Adam lecture, Design Museum London, October 2004
49: Dave Worrall, *The Most Famous Car in the World*, Solo Publishing, 1991, p.45
50: Dave Worrall, *The Most Famous Car in the World*, Solo Publishing, 1991, p.45
51: Dave Worrall, *The Most Famous Car in the World*, Solo Publishing, 1991, p.76
52: Director's Guild of America, www.dga.org
53: Guy Hamilton: Author interview, 2008
54: *Goldfinger*, Blu ray audio commentary
55: Matthew Field and Ajay Chowdhury, *Some Kind of Hero*, The History Press, 2015, p.117
56: *Financial Times Weekend* magazine, 12 October 2012
57: Paul Duncan, *The James Bond Archives*, Taschen, 2012, p.99
58: Guy Hamilton: Author interview, 1997
59: Eddi Fiegel, *John Barry: A Sixties Theme: From James Bond to Midnight Cowboy*, Faber & Faber, 2012, p.141
60: Eddi Fiegel, *John Barry: A Sixties Theme: From James Bond to Midnight Cowboy*, Faber & Faber, 2012, p.141
61: Cubby Broccoli, *When the Snow Melts*, Boxtree, 1998, p.197
62: Tania Mallet: Author interview, 1997
63: *The Goldfinger Phenomenon*, documentary, 1995
64: Tino Balio, *United Artists: The Company That Changed the Film Industry*, University of Wisconsin Press, 1987, p.262
65: Peter Hunt interview, copyright Edward Gross 1990
66: *Telescope*, CBC, 9 December 1965
67: *True: The Men's Magazine*, June 1966
68: Christopher Frayling, *Ken Adam and the Art of Production Design*, Faber & Faber, 2005, p.156
69: Ken Adam: Author interview, 2007
70: Paul Duncan, *The James Bond Archives*, Taschen, 2012, p.218
71: Tom Mankiewicz: Author interview, 2007
72: Cubby Broccoli, *When the Snow Melts*, Boxtree, 1998, p.204
73: Roger Moore, *My Word is My Bond*, Michael O'Mara Books, 2008, p.188
74: John Cork, Bruce Scivally, *James Bond: The Legacy*, Boxtree, 2002, p.78

Chapter 8: Kitchen Sink Bond

1: *Sight & Sound*, November 1994
2: *The Times*, 14 May 2008
3: BFI.org.uk
4: John French, *Robert Shaw: The Price of Success*, Nick Hern Books, 1993, p.79
5: John French, *Robert Shaw: The Price of Success*, Nick Hern Books, 1993, p.83–84
6: Cherry Hughes: Author interview, 2019
7: Len Deighton: Author interview, 2007
8: Lindsay Anderson, *The Diaries*, Methuen Drama, 2004, p.86
9: Len Deighton: Author interview, 2007
10: Michael Caine, *What's it All About*, Century, 1992, p.165
11: Michael Caine, *What's it All About*, Century, 1992, p.165
12: Michael Caine, *What's it All About*, Century, 1992, p.165
13: Len Deighton: Author interview, 2007
14: Film Finance Archive
15: Elaine Gallagher, *Candidly Caine*, Robson Books, 1990, p.80
16: The Deighton Dossier blog
17: Len Deighton: Author interview, 2007
18: Web of Stories.com
19: Len Deighton: Author interview, 2007
20: Sidney J. Furie: Author interview, 2010
21: Sidney J. Furie: Author interview, 2010
22: Sidney J. Furie: Author interview, 2010
23: Sidney J. Furie: Author interview, 2010
24: Michael Caine, *What's it All About*, Century, 1992, p.177
25: Michael Caine, *What's it All About*, Century, 1992, p.177
26: Sidney J. Furie: Author interview, 2010
27: Sidney J. Furie: Author interview, 2010
28: Daniel Kremer, *Sidney J. Furie: Life and Films*, University Press of Kentucky, 2015, p.84
29: Sue Lloyd: Author interview, 2006
30: Sue Lloyd: Author interview, 2006
31: Web of Stories.com
32: *Harry Saltzman: Showman*, documentary, 2000
33: *True: The Men's Magazine*, June 1966
34: *Calgary Herald*, 29 January 1966
35: Paul Tucker: Author interview, 2019
36: *True: The Men's Magazine*, June 1966
37: *True: The Men's Magazine*, June 1966
38: Richard Jenkins: Author interview, 2006
39: *True: The Men's Magazine*, June 1966
40: Leonard Mosley, *The Battle of Britain: The Making of a Film*, Pan, 1969, p.192
41: *Harry Saltzman: Showman*, documentary, 2000
42: *Esquire*, June 1965
43: Chaim Topol, *Topol*, Weidenfeld and Nicolson, 1981, p.207
44: William P. Cartlidge: Author interview, 2019
45: William P. Cartlidge: Author interview, 2019
46: BFI

47: *The Observer*, 21 March 1965
48: Film Finance Archive
49: Len Deighton: Author interview, 2007
50: Sidney J. Furie: Author interview, 2010
51: Sidney J. Furie: Author interview, 2010
52: Eddi Fiegel, *John Barry: A Sixties Theme: From James Bond to Midnight Cowboy*, Faber & Faber, 2012, p.170
53: Sidney J. Furie: Author interview, 2010
54: Eddi Fiegel, *John Barry: A Sixties Theme: From James Bond to Midnight Cowboy*, Faber & Faber, 2012, p.172
55: Daniel Kremer, *Sidney J. Furie: Life and Films*, University Press of Kentucky, 2015, p.89
56: Christopher Frayling, *Ken Adam and the Art of Production Design*, Faber & Faber, 2005, p.148
57: *Harry Saltzman: Showman*, documentary, 2000
58: *The Observer*, 21 March 1965
59: *Daily Telegraph*, November 1965
60: Keith Baxter: Author interview, 2018
61: *Ecranlarge.com*, June 2008
62: *Billboard*, 16 July 1955
63: Wellesnet.com
64: Antonio Lázaro-Reboll and Ian Olney, *The Films of Jess Franco*, Wayne State University Press, 2018, p.323
65: *Independent*, 2 October, 2003
66: Keith Baxter: Author interview, 2018
67: Keith Baxter: Author interview, 2018
68: Keith Baxter: Author interview, 2018

Chapter 9: Bond in the Bahamas

1: Robert Sellers, *The Battle for Bond*, Tomahawk Press, 2007, p.125
2: Tino Balio, *United Artists: The Company That Changed the Film Industry*, University of Wisconsin Press, 1987, p.266
3: *New York Times*, 13 December 1964
4: Guy Hamilton: Author interview, 2006
5: Richard Jenkins: Author interview, 2006
6: Peter Haining, *James Bond: A Celebration*, W.H. Allen, 1987, p.167
7: Crawleyscastingcalls.com
8: Crawleyscastingcalls.com
9: Roger Moore, *Bond on Bond*, Michael O'Mara Books, 2012, p.55
10: *Calgary Herald*, 29 January 1966
11: Cubby Broccoli, *When the Snow Melts*, Boxtree, 1998, p.203
12: Copyright David Lewin, 1975
13: Luciana Paluzzi: Author interview, 2006
14: Luciana Paluzzi: Author interview, 2006
15: Matthew Field and Ajay Chowdhury, *Some Kind of Hero*, The History Press, 2015, p.135
16: Mollie Peters: Author interview, 2007
17: Norman Wanstall: Author interview, 2015
18: Albert J. Luxford and Gareth Owen, *Albert J. Luxford, the Gimmick Man: Memoir of a Special Effects Maestro*, McFarland and Company, 2002, p.55

19: Peter Lamont: Author interview, 2019
20: Paul Tucker: Author interview, 2019
21: Guy Hamilton: Author interview, 2008
22: *Observer*, 21 March 1965
23: Matthew Field and Ajay Chowdhury, *Some Kind of Hero*, The History Press, 2015, p.90
24: *Observer*, 21 March 1965
25: *Observer*, 21 March 1965
26: *Calgary Herald*, 29 January 1966
27: Earl Cameron: Author interview, 2006
28: Earl Cameron: Author interview, 2006
29: *Independent*, 29 June 1996
30: Ken Adam: Author interview, 2006
31: Ken Adam: Author interview, 2006
32: *007* magazine, *You Only Live Twice* special, Part 2, 2000
33: Ken Adam: Author interview, 2006
34: Ken Adam: Author interview, 2006
35: Robert Sellers, *The Battle for Bond*, Tomahawk Press, 2007, p.159
36: Steven Jay Rubin, *The James Bond Films*, Arlington House, 1981, p.66
37: Patrick McGilligan, *Backstory: Interviews with Screenwriters of Hollywood's Golden Age*, University of California Press, 1986, p.287
38: Richard Jenkins: Author interview, 2006
39: Copyright David Lewin, 1975
40: Copyright David Lewin, 1975
41: Kenneth Passingham, *Sean Connery – a Biography*, Sidgwick and Jackson, 1983, p.61
42: Michael Freedland, *Sean Connery: A Biography*, Weidenfeld & Nicolson, 1994, p.155
43: *Variety*, March 1965
44: Luciana Paluzzi: Author interview, 2006
45: Mollie Peters: Author interview, 2007
46: Roger Moore, *Last Man Standing*, Michael O'Mara Books, 2014, p.74
47: Peter Carter-Ruck, *Memoirs of a Libel Lawyer*, Weidenfeld & Nicolson, 1990, p.158
48: Peter Carter-Ruck, *Memoirs of a Libel Lawyer*, Weidenfeld & Nicolson, 1990, p.158
49: Ken Adam, *Ken Adam Designs the Movies: James Bond and Beyond*, Thames and Hudson, 2008, p.68
50: Roger Moore, *Bond on Bond*, Michael O'Mara Books, 2012, p.24
51: *Daily Mail*, February 1967
52: John Cork, Bruce Scivally, *James Bond: The Legacy*, Boxtree, 2002, p.300
53: Tino Balio, *United Artists: The Company That Changed the Film Industry*, University of Wisconsin Press, 1987, p.136
54: Eric Pleskow: Author interview, 2019
55: *True: The Men's Magazine*, June 1966
56: *True: The Men's Magazine*, June 1966
57: *Observer*, 16 January 1972
58: *Observer*, 16 January 1972
59: Richard Jenkins: Author interview, 2006
60: Peter Hunt interview, copyright Edward Gross 1990
61: Cubby Broccoli, *When the Snow Melts*, Boxtree, 1998, p.198

Chapter 10: In the Money

1: *True: The Men's Magazine*, June 1966
2: *Harry Saltzman: Showman*, documentary, 2000
3: George Lazenby interview, International Spy Museum, October 2018
4: Matthew Field and Ajay Chowdhury, *Some Kind of Hero*, The History Press, 2015, p.225
5: Andrew Lycett, *Ian Fleming*, Weidenfeld and Nicolson, 1995, p.5
6: Tom Mankiewicz: Author interview, 2007
7: *Illustrated Weekly of Pakistan*, October 1968
8: Tom Mankiewicz: Author interview, 2007
9: *Washington Post*, 4 May 1994
10: Tom Mankiewicz: Author interview, 2007
11: Tony Bramwell, *Magical Mystery Tours: My Life with the Beatles*, Portico, 2005, p.369–70
12: *Sight & Sound*, November 1994
13: Len Deighton: Author interview, 2008
14: *Calgary Herald*, 29 January 1966
15: *Town* magazine, April 1965
16: *Calgary Herald*, 29 January 1966
17: Roger Moore, *Live and Let Die* Diary, Pan Books, 1973, p.134
18: Michael Winner, *Winner Takes All: A Life of Sorts*, Robson Books, 2004, p.122–23
19: Michael Winner, *Winner Takes All: A Life of Sorts*, Robson Books, 2004, p.122–23
20: Leonard Mosley, *The Battle of Britain: The Making of a Film*, Pan, 1969, p.194
21: *Daily Mail*, September 1994
22: Cherry Hughes: Author interview, 2019
23: *Daily Mail*, 15 February 1967
24: *Royal Gazette*, 14 January 2013
25: Comingsoon.net, October 2012
26: Leonard Mosley, *The Battle of Britain: The Making of a Film*, Pan, 1969, p.194
27: *Playboy*, November 1965
28: Raymond Benson, *The James Bond Bedside Companion*, Galahad Books, 1986, p.31
29: Kevin Brownlow, *David Lean*, Faber & Faber, 1997, p.544
30: *Calgary Herald*, 29 January 1966
31: *Daily Telegraph*, November 1965
32: *Daily Telegraph*, November 1965
33: Michael Caine, *What's it All About*, Century, 1992, p.225
34: Peter Lamont: Author interview, 2019
35: *Calgary Herald*, 29 January 1966
36: *Calgary Herald*, 29 January 1966
37: *Calgary Herald*, 29 January 1966
38: Eddi Fiegel, *John Barry: A Sixties Theme: From James Bond to Midnight Cowboy*, Faber & Faber, 2012, p.172
39: Steven Soderbergh, *Getting Away with It*, Faber & Faber, 1999, p.61–62
40: Steven Soderbergh, *Getting Away with It*, Faber & Faber, 1999, p.61–62

Chapter 11: Twice is the Only Way to Live

1: *Whicker's World*, BBC March 1967
2: *007* magazine, No.27, 1994

3: Lee Pfeiffer and Philip Lisa, *The Incredible World of 007, An Authorized Celebration of James Bond*, Boxtree, 1992, p.204
4: Cubby Broccoli's Memorial Service, London, November 1996
5: Cubby Broccoli's Memorial Service, London, November 1996
6: Eddi Fiegel, *John Barry: A Sixties Theme: From James Bond to Midnight Cowboy,* Faber & Faber, 2012, p.199
7: *The Telegraph*, November 1965
8: Peter Haining, *James Bond: A Celebration*, W.H. Allen, 1987, p.92
9: Steven Jay Rubin, *The Complete James Bond Encyclopedia*, Contemporary Books, 1990, p.96
10: *Playboy*, June 1967
11: *Starlog*, August 1991
12: *Starlog*, August 1991
13: *Starlog*, August 1991
14: Freddie Young, *Seventy Light Years: An Autobiography*, Faber & Faber, 1999, p.120–22
15: Lewis Gilbert, *All My Flashbacks*, Reynolds & Hearn, 2010, p.268
16: Christopher Frayling, *Ken Adam and the Art of Production Design*, Faber & Faber, 2005, p.158–59
17: *Inside You Only Live Twice*, documentary, 2000
18: Ken Adam: Author interview, 2001
19: *007* magazine, *You Only Live Twice* special, Part 1, 1999
20: Tino Balio, *United Artists: The Company That Changed the Film Industry*, University of Wisconsin Press, 1987, p.270
21: Tino Balio, *United Artists: The Company That Changed the Film Industry*, University of Wisconsin Press, 1987, p.270
22: Cubby Broccoli, *When the Snow Melts*, Boxtree, 1998, p.205
23: Andre de Toth, *Fragments*, Faber & Faber, 1996, p.398
24: Cubby Broccoli, *When the Snow Melts*, Boxtree, 1998, p.231
25: *GoldenEye* magazine, Spring 1996
26: Matthew Field and Ajay Chowdhury, *Some Kind of Hero*, The History Press, 2015, p.279
27: Ken Adam: Author interview, 2006
28: William P. Cartlidge: Author interview, 2019
29: *Everything or Nothing: The Untold Story of 007*, documentary, 2012
30: William P. Cartlidge: Author interview, 2019
31: Len Deighton: Author interview, 2007
32: Ken Adam: Author interview, 2006
33: William P. Cartlidge: Author interview, 2019
34: Archival interview with Eva Renzi, *The Bird with The Crystal Plumage*, Arrow Video, 2018
35: *Cinema Retro* magazine, Vol 13, Issue 39, 2017
36: William P. Cartlidge: Author interview, 2019
37: William P. Cartlidge: Author interview, 2019
38: William P. Cartlidge: Author interview, 2019
39: Lewis Gilbert: Author interview, 1999
40: *Starlog*, August 1991
41: *Starlog*, August 1991
42: Freddie Young, *Seventy Light Years: An Autobiography*, Faber & Faber, 1999, p.122
43: *007* magazine, *You Only Live Twice* special, Part 1, 1999
44: *Starlog*, June 1995
45: *Guitar Player* magazine, April 1997

46: *Cinema Retro* magazine, Vol. 13, Issue 39, 2017
47: *Cinema Retro* magazine, Vol. 13, Issue 39, 2017
48: Cubby Broccoli, *When the Snow Melts*, Boxtree, 1998, p.200
49: *Showtime* magazine, October 1967
50: *007* magazine, *You Only Live Twice* special, Part 1, 1999
51: Lewis Gilbert: Author interview, 1999
52: John Cork, Bruce Scivally, *James Bond: The Legacy*, Boxtree, 2002, p.93
53: Roger Moore, *Bond on Bond*, Michael O'Mara Books, 2012, p.153
54: Steven Jay Rubin, *The James Bond Films*, Arlington House, 1981, p.74
55: Michael Freedland, *Sean Connery: A Biography*, Weidenfeld & Nicolson, 1994, p.165
56: *True: The Men's Magazine*, June 1966

Chapter 12: Palmer's Last Stand

1: Lewis Chester, *All My Shows are Great: The Life of Lew Grade*, Aurum, 2010, p.165
2: *Evening Standard*, June 1967
3: Ken Russell: Author interview, 2005
4: Web of Stories.com
5: John Baxter, *An Appalling Talent: Ken Russell*, Michael Joseph, 1973, p.156
6: Web of Stories.com
7: Andre de Toth, *Fragments*, Faber & Faber, 1996, p.396
8: Andre de Toth, *Fragments*, Faber & Faber, 1996, p.391
9: Andre de Toth, *Fragments*, Faber & Faber, 1996, p.397–98
10: *The Times*, March 2007
11: TCM.com
12: Ken Russell: Author interview, 2005
13: *Sight & Sound*, November 1994
14: Len Deighton: Author interview, 2007
15: Guardian, 1 November 1969
16: Joseph Lanza, *Phallic Frenzy: Ken Russell and His Films*, Aurum Press, 2008, p.65
17: Ken Russell: Author interview, 2005
18: Ken Russell: Author interview, 2005
19: Ken Russell, *The Lion Roars*, Faber & Faber, 1994, p.43
20: Joseph Lanza, *Phallic Frenzy: Ken Russell and His Films*, Aurum Press, 2008, p.60
21: Joseph Lanza, *Phallic Frenzy: Ken Russell and His Films*, Aurum Press, 2008, p.65
22: *Daily Mail*, September 1994
23: Tim Adler, *The House of Redgrave*, Aurum Press, 2012, p.203
24: Tony Richardson, *Long Distance Runner: A Memoir*, Faber & Faber, 1993, p.279–80

Chapter 13: It's Fantasmagorical

1: *Calgary Herald*, 29 January 1966
2: *True: The Men's Magazine*, June 1966
3: *New York Times*, 1 July 1979
4: Robert B. Sherman, *Moose: Chapters From my Life*, AuthorHouse, 2013, p.401
5: Robert B. Sherman, *Moose: Chapters From my Life*, AuthorHouse, 2013, p.401
6: Robert B. Sherman, *Moose: Chapters From my Life*, AuthorHouse, 2013, p.402
7: Dick Van Dyke, *My Lucky Life*, John Blake, 2016, p.175–76
8: Dick Van Dyke, *My Lucky Life*, John Blake, 2016, p.176

9: Rosie O'Donnell show, Warner Bros Television, October 1998
10: Cherry Hughes: Author interview, 2019
11: *Starlog*, August 1991
12: Dick Van Dyke, My Lucky Life, John Blake, 2016, p.177
13: Dick Van Dyke, *My Lucky Life*, John Blake, 2016, p.180
14: Dick Van Dyke, *My Lucky Life*, John Blake, 2016, p.180
15: Kevin Pollak's Chat Show, August 2013
16: Robert B. Sherman, *Moose: Chapters From my Life*, AuthorHouse, 2013, p.407
17: Robert B. Sherman, *Moose: Chapters From my Life*, AuthorHouse, 2013, p.407
18: Adrian Hall: Author interview, 2019
19: Adrian Hall: Author interview, 2019
20: Graham Hartstone: Author interview, 2018
21: Graham Hartstone: Author interview, 2018
22: Graham Hartstone: Author interview, 2018
23: Cherry Hughes: Author interview, 2019
24: Cherry Hughes: Author interview, 2019
25: Cherry Hughes: Author interview, 2019
26: *Guardian*, 16 July 1970
27: Robert J. Sherman: Author interview, 2019

Chapter 14: Wargames

1: Philip Saville, *They Shoot Directors, Don't They?*, Kaleidoscope Publishing, 2019, p.137
2: Philip Saville, *They Shoot Directors, Don't They?*, Kaleidoscope Publishing, 2019, p.137
3: Philip Saville, *They Shoot Directors, Don't They?*, Kaleidoscope Publishing, 2019, p.138
4: Philip Saville, *They Shoot Directors, Don't They?*, Kaleidoscope Publishing, 2019, p.138
5: Andre de Toth, *De Toth on De Toth*, Faber & Faber, 1997, p.152
6: Andrew Birkin: Author interview, 2018
7: Andrew Birkin: Author interview, 2018
8: Christopher Bray, *Michael Caine: A Class Act*, Faber & Faber, 2005, p.115
9: Andrew Birkin: Author interview, 2018
10: Andrew Birkin: Author interview, 2018
11: Michael Caine, *What's it All About*, Century, 1992, p.247
12: Michael Caine, *What's it All About*, Century, 1992, p.256
13: Andre de Toth, *De Toth on De Toth*, Faber & Faber, 1997, p.151
14: Andre de Toth, *De Toth on De Toth*, Faber & Faber, 1997, p.158
15: Andre de Toth, *Fragments*, Faber & Faber, 1996, p.399
16: Andre de Toth, *De Toth on De Toth*, Faber & Faber, 1997, p.158
17: Leonard Mosley, *The Battle of Britain: The Making of a Film*, Pan, 1969, p.21
18: Tom Mankiewicz: Author interview, 2007
19: Documentary, *Battle of Britain* Special Edition DVD, MGM, 2004
20: Leonard Mosley, *The Battle of Britain: The Making of a Film*, Pan, 1969, p.22
21: *The Times*, March 1967
22: Leonard Mosley, *The Battle of Britain: The Making of a Film*, Pan, 1969, p.28
23: *Film Review*, September 2001
24: Guy Hamilton: Author interview, 2001
25: *Film Review*, September 2001

26: Jonathan Rigby, *Christopher Lee: The Authorised Screen History*, Reynolds & Hearn, 2003, p.163
27: Guy Hamilton: Author interview, 2001
28: Elaine Gallagher, *Candidly Caine*, Robson Books, 1990, p.117
29: Freddie Young, *Seventy Light Years: An Autobiography*, Faber & Faber, 1999, p.123
30: Michael Caine, *What's it All About*, Century, 1992, p.257
31: Nick Alder: Author interview, 2001
32: Leonard Mosley, *The Battle of Britain: The Making of a Film*, Pan, 1969, p.172
33: Tom Mankiewicz; Author interview: 2007
34: *The Times*, December 1987
35: Ron Goodwin: Author interview, 2001
36: Ron Goodwin: Author interview, 2001
37: *Film Review*, September 2001
38: David Picker, email to author, 2018
39: Tom Mankiewicz: Author interview: 2007

Chapter 15: The One Hit Wonder

1: *Daily Mail*, July 1967
2: *Daily Express*, October 1968
3: Adam West, *Back to the Batcave*, Titan Books, 1994, p.186
4: *The Quietus*, August 2018
5: *The Quietus*, August 2018
6: Roger Moore, *Bond on Bond*, Michael O'Mara Books, 2012, p.16
7: Patrick Mower, *My Story*, John Blake Publishing, 2007, p.132
8: Patrick Mower, *My Story*, John Blake Publishing, 2007, p.136
9: Dyson Lovell: Author interview, 2007
10: Dyson Lovell: Author interview, 2007
11: Dyson Lovell: Author interview, 2007
12: Dyson Lovell: Author interview, 2007
13: Paul Duncan, *The James Bond Archives*, Taschen, 2012, p.172
14: Matthew Field and Ajay Chowdhury, *Some Kind of Hero*, The History Press, 2015, p.188
15: Matthew Field and Ajay Chowdhury, *Some Kind of Hero*, The History Press, 2015, p.188
16: Matthew Field and Ajay Chowdhury, *Some Kind of Hero*, The History Press, 2015, p.188–89
17: *American Cinematheque*, June 2011
18: *Harry Saltzman Showman*, documentary, 2000
19: George Lazenby interview, International Spy Museum, October 2018
20: Andre de Toth, *Fragments*, Faber & Faber, 1996, p.400
21: *Inside On Her Majesty's Secret Service*, documentary, 2000
22: 'The Making of *On Her Majesty's Secret Service*' by Philip Masheter, *Movie Collector*, Vol. 2, Issue 2, 1995
23: *Inside On Her Majesty's Secret Service*, documentary, 2000
24: Peter Hunt interview, copyright Edward Gross, 1990
25: *On Her Majesty's Secret Service*, Blu Ray commentary
26: 'The Making of *On Her Majesty's Secret Service*' by Philip Masheter, *Movie Collector*, Vol. 2, Issue 2, 1995

27: 'The Making of *On Her Majesty's Secret Service*' by Philip Masheter, *Movie Collector*, Vol. 2, Issue 2, 1995
28: Joanna Lumley, email to author, 2019
29: Jenny Hanley interview by Mark Cerulli, jamesbond007.se, March 2019
30: Syd Cain, *Not Forgetting James Bond: The Autobiography of Production Designer Syd Cain*, GBU Publishing Ltd, 2002, p.84
31: *007* magazine, No.22 1990
32: George Leech: Author interview, 2007
33: Vic Armstrong: Author interview, 2019
34: Vic Armstrong: Author interview, 2019
35: Vic Armstrong: Author interview, 2019
36: Alan Barnes and Marcus Hearn, *Kiss Kiss Bang! Bang!*, BT Batsford, 2000, p.88
37: 'The Making of *On Her Majesty's Secret Service*' by Philip Masheter, *Movie Collector*, Vol. 2, Issue 2, 1995
38: *Daily Colonist*, 17 March 1970
39: George Leech: Author interview, 2007
40: Sandy Hernu, *Q: The Biography of Desmond Llewelyn*, S.B. Publications, 1999, p.94
41: Roger Moore, *Bond on Bond*, Michael O'Mara Books, 2012, p.23
42: Lee Pfeiffer and Philip Lisa, *The Incredible World of 007, An Authorized Celebration of James Bond*, Boxtree, 1992, p.206
43: Steven Jay Rubin, *The Complete James Bond Encyclopedia*, Contemporary Books, 1990, p.321
44: *007* magazine, No. 9 1981
45: Cubby Broccoli, *When the Snow Melts*, Boxtree, 1998, p.218
46: Dyson Lovell: Author interview, 2007

Chapter 16: A Musical Mishap

1: Lee Hill, *A Grand Guy: The Art and Life of Terry Southern*, Bloomsbury, 2002, p.122
2: *Evening Standard*, 30 November 2007
3: Sally Moore, *Lucan: Not Guilty*, Sidgwick & Jackson, 1987, p.24
4: *True: The Men's Magazine*, June 1966
5: Len Deighton: Author interview, 2007
6: Andre de Toth, *Fragments*, Faber & Faber, 1996, p.395
7: Roger Moore, *My Word is My Bond*, Michael O'Mara Books, 2008, p.175
8: Len Deighton: Author interview, 2007
9: *Observer*, 6 April 1969
10: Len Deighton: Author interview, 2007
11: Dyson Lovell: Author interview, 2007
12: Dyson Lovell: Author interview, 2007
13: Dyson Lovell: Author interview, 2007
14: Dyson Lovell: Author interview, 2007
15: Dyson Lovell: Author interview, 2007
16: Dyson Lovell: Author interview, 2007
17: *Cash Box*, February 1969
18: *Cash Box*, February 1969
19: Val Guest, *So You Want to be in Pictures*, Reynolds & Hearn, 2001, p.163
20: Val Guest, *So You Want to be in Pictures*, Reynolds & Hearn, 2001, p.163

21: John Brosnan, *Future Tense: The Cinema of Science Fiction*, St Martin's Press, 1978, p.192
22: John Brosnan, *Future Tense: The Cinema of Science Fiction*, St Martin's Press, 1978, p.192
23: Tom Weaver, *Double Feature Creature Attack*, McFarland & Co, 2002, p.123
24: Val Guest, *So You Want to be in Pictures*, Reynolds & Hearn, 2001, p.163
25: John Brosnan, *Future Tense: The Cinema of Science Fiction*, St Martin's Press, 1978, p.192
26: Tom Weaver, *Double Feature Creature Attack*, McFarland & Co, 2002, p.123
27: John Brosnan, *Future Tense: The Cinema of Science Fiction*, St Martin's Press, 1978, p.192
28: Val Guest, *So You Want to be in Pictures*, Reynolds & Hearn, 2001, p.164
29: Tim Ewbank, *Olivia: The Biography of Olivia Newton-John*, Piatkus Books, 2008, p.77
30: Dyson Lovell: Author interview, 2007
31: *Films and Filming*, September 1969
32: Cherry Hughes: Author interview, 2019
33: Cherry Hughes: Author interview, 2019
34: *New York Times*, 10 March 1970
35: Tom Mankiewicz: Author interview, 2007
36: *Harry Saltzman Showman*, documentary, 2000

Chapter 17: Return of the King

1: Tino Balio, *United Artists: The Company That Changed the Film Industry*, University of Wisconsin Press, 1987, p.271
2: Roger Moore, *Bond on Bond*, Michael O'Mara Books, 2012, p.177
3: Matthew Field and Ajay Chowdhury, *Some Kind of Hero*, The History Press, 2015, p.255
4: *Observer*, 29 February 2004
5: Simon Oates: Author interview, 2007
6: John Ronane: Author interview, 2007
7: John Ronane: Author interview, 2007
8: Ranulph Fiennes: Author interview, 2007
9: Ranulph Fiennes: Author interview, 2007
10: Ranulph Fiennes: Author interview, 2007
11: Ranulph Fiennes: Author interview, 2007
12: Ranulph Fiennes: Author interview, 2007
13: Roger Green: Author interview, 2007
14: Roger Green: Author interview, 2007
15: Roger Green: Author interview, 2007
16: Roger Green: Author interview, 2007
17: David V. Picker, *Musts, Maybes and Nevers*, CreateSpace, 2013, p.54
18: John Cork, Bruce Scivally, *James Bond: The Legacy*, Boxtree, 2002, p.128
19: *Guardian*, 28 December 1971
20: David V. Picker, *Musts, Maybes and Nevers*, CreateSpace, 2013, p.54
21: Cubby Broccoli, *When the Snow Melts*, Boxtree, 1998, p.222
22: Copyright David Lewin, 1975
23: Steven Jay Rubin, *The James Bond Films*, Arlington House, 1981, p.101
24: Steven Jay Rubin, *The James Bond Films*, Arlington House, 1981, p.102
25: Tom Mankiewicz: Author interview, 2007
26: Tom Mankiewicz, *My Life as a Mankiewicz: An Insider's Journey through Hollywood*, University Press of Kentucky, 2012, p.165–66
27: Tom Mankiewicz: Author interview, 2007

28: Tom Mankiewicz: Author interview, 2007
29: Paul Duncan, *The James Bond Archives*, Taschen, 2012, p.198
30: Tom Mankiewicz: Author interview, 2007
31: Tom Mankiewicz: Author interview, 2007
32: Tom Mankiewicz: Author interview, 2007
33: Matthew Field and Ajay Chowdhury, *Some Kind of Hero*, The History Press, 2015, p.217
34: *Diamonds Are Forever* Blu Ray audio commentary
35: Tom Mankiewicz: Author interview, 2007
36: Tom Mankiewicz: Author interview, 2007
37: John Cork, Bruce Scivally, *James Bond: The Legacy*, Boxtree, 2002, p.127
38: Paul Duncan, *The James Bond Archives*, Taschen, 2012, p.201
39: Cubby Broccoli, *When the Snow Melts*, Boxtree, 1998, p.224
40: Christopher Frayling, *Ken Adam and the Art of Production Design*, Faber & Faber, 2005, p.175
41: Tom Mankiewicz: Author interview, 2007
42: Cubby Broccoli, *When the Snow Melts*, Boxtree, 1998, p.224
43: Guy Hamilton: Author interview, 2001
44: Andrew Birkin: Author interview, 2018
45: Andrew Birkin: Author interview, 2018
46: *Diamonds Are Forever* Blu Ray audio commentary
47: *Nobody Does It Better: The Music of James Bond*, documentary, Channel 4, 1997
48: *Diamonds Are Forever* Blu Ray audio commentary
49: *Observer*, 16 January 1972
50: *Observer*, 16 January 1972
51: *Observer*, 16 January 1972
52: Tom Mankiewicz: Author interview, 2007
53: Tom Mankiewicz: Author interview, 2007
54: *Guardian*, 28 December 1971
55: Lee Pfeiffer and Philip Lisa, *The Incredible World of 007, An Authorized Celebration of James Bond*, Boxtree, 1992, p.190

Chapter 18: The Saintly Bond

1: Tom Mankiewicz: Author interview, 2007
2: *Bondage* magazine, No.10, 1981
3: Julian Glover: Author interview, 2007
4: Julian Glover: Author interview, 2007
5: Michael Billington: Author interview, 2005
6: Michael Billington: Author interview, 2005
7: Michael Billington: Author interview, 2005
8: *Los Angeles Times*, 7 September 2010
9: Tom Mankiewicz: Author interview, 2007
10: Robert Wagner, *Pieces of My Heart: A Life*, Arrow Books, 2010, p.202
11: Matthew Field and Ajay Chowdhury, *Some Kind of Hero*, The History Press, 2015, p.232
12: Robert Baker: Author interview, 2005
13: Robert Baker: Author interview, 2005
14: Cubby Broccoli, *When the Snow Melts*, Boxtree, 1998, p.227
15: Cubby Broccoli, *When the Snow Melts*, Boxtree, 1998, p.228
16: Roger Moore, *Bond on Bond*, Michael O'Mara Books, 2012, p.18–19
17: Sir Roger Moore: Author interview, 2001

18: Tom Mankiewicz: Author interview, 2007
19: Victor Spinetti, *Up Front…: His Strictly Confidential Autobiography*, Robson Books, 2006, p.229
20: Tom Mankiewicz: Author interview, 2007
21: Tom Mankiewicz: Author interview, 2007
22: Tom Mankiewicz: Author interview, 2007
23: Tom Mankiewicz: Author interview, 2007
24: Tom Mankiewicz: Author interview, 2007
25: David Giammarco, *For Your Eyes Only: Behind the Scenes of the James Bond Films*, ECW Press, 2002, p.135
26: *Live and Let Die*, Blu Ray audio commentary
27: *Observer*, 4 July 1973
28: Tom Mankiewicz, *My Life as a Mankiewicz: An Insider's Journey through Hollywood*, University Press of Kentucky, 2012, p.153–54
29: Roger Moore, *My Word is My Bond*, Michael O'Mara Books, 2008, p.175
30: *Live and Let Die*, Blu Ray audio commentary
31: Roger Moore, *Last Man Standing: Tales from Tinseltown*, Michael O'Mara Books, 2014, p.249
32: Roger Moore, *Bond on Bond*, Michael O'Mara Books, 2012, p.177
33: *Daily Mail*, June 1973
34: *Daily Mail*, June 1973
35: Peter Lamont: Author interview, 2019
36: Peter Lamont: Author interview, 2019
37: Peter Lamont: Author interview, 2019
38: *Live and Let Die*, Blu Ray audio commentary
39: Peter Lamont: Author interview, 2019
40: *007* magazine, No.22, 1990
41: Sandy Hernu, *Q: The Biography of Desmond Llewelyn*, S.B. Publications, 1999, p.98
42: Sandy Hernu, *Q: The Biography of Desmond Llewelyn*, S.B. Publications, 1999, p.99
43: Tony Bramwell: Author interview, 2018
44: Tony Bramwell: Author interview, 2018
45: Tony Bramwell: Author interview, 2018
46: Tony Bramwell: Author interview, 2018
47: Tony Bramwell: Author interview, 2018
48: Tom Mankiewicz, *My Life as a Mankiewicz: An Insider's Journey through Hollywood*, University Press of Kentucky, 2012, p.159
49: Tom Mankiewicz, *My Life as a Mankiewicz: An Insider's Journey through Hollywood*, University Press of Kentucky, 2012, p.158–59
50: *Daily Mail*, June 1973
51: *Daily Mail*, July 1969
52: Tony Bramwell: Author interview, 2018
53: Tony Bramwell: Author interview, 2018
54: *New York Times*, 6 January 1974

Chapter 19: The Last Encore

1: Eric Pleskow: Author interview, 2019
2: Eric Pleskow: Author interview, 2019

3: Steven Jay Rubin, *The Complete James Bond Encyclopedia*, Contemporary Books, 1990, p.383
4: Guy Hamilton: Author interview, 2008
5: Tom Mankiewicz: Author interview, 2007
6: Tom Mankiewicz: Author interview, 2007
7: Paul Duncan, *The James Bond Archives*, Taschen, 2012, p.240
8: Tom Mankiewicz: Author interview, 2007
9: Steven Jay Rubin, *The James Bond Films*, Arlington House, 1981, p.128
10: Steven Jay Rubin, *The James Bond Films*, Arlington House, 1981, p.125
11: Paul Duncan, *The James Bond Archives*, Taschen, 2012, p.243
12: *The Man with the Golden Gun*, Blu Ray commentary
13: Sir Christopher Lee: Author interview, 2005
14: *Cinefantastique*, Spring 1975
15: Britt Ekland: Author interview, 2019
16: Britt Ekland: Author interview, 2019
17: Roger Moore, *My Word is My Bond*, Michael O'Mara Books, 2008, p.189
18: Roger Moore, *My Word is My Bond*, Michael O'Mara Books, 2008, p.190
19: *Bondage* magazine, No.8, 1980
20: Britt Ekland: Author interview, 2019
21: Paul Tucker: Author interview, 2019
22: Paul Tucker: Author interview, 2019
23: Paul Tucker: Author interview, 2019
24: Britt Ekland: Author interview, 2019
25: Roger Moore, *My Word is My Bond*, Michael O'Mara Books, 2008, p.193
26: *The Man with the Golden Gun*, Blu Ray commentary
27: Copyright David Lewin, 1975
28: Paul Tucker: Author interview, 2019

Chapter 20: Breaking Up is Hard to Do

1: Tom Mankiewicz, *My Life as a Mankiewicz: An Insider's Journey through Hollywood*, University Press of Kentucky, 2012, p.137
2: Alan Barnes and Marcus Hearn, *Kiss Kiss Bang! Bang!*, BT Batsford, 2000, p.117
3: Tony Bramwell: Author interview, 2018
4: Tony Bramwell: Author interview, 2018
5: Tony Bramwell, *Magical Mystery Tours: My Life with the Beatles*, Portico, 2005, p.369
6: Cubby Broccoli, *When the Snow Melts*, Boxtree, 1998, p.231
7: David V. Picker, *Musts, Maybes and Nevers*, CreateSpace, 2013, p.56–7
8: Tom Mankiewicz: Author interview, 2007
9: John Cork, Bruce Scivally, *James Bond: The Legacy*, Boxtree, 2002, p.164
10: Roger Moore, *My Word is My Bond*, Michael O'Mara Books, 2008, p.196
11: Tom Mankiewicz, *My Life as a Mankiewicz: An Insider's Journey through Hollywood*, University Press of Kentucky, 2012, p.165
12: Cubby Broccoli, *When the Snow Melts*, Boxtree, 1998, p.237
13: Paul Duncan, *The James Bond Archives*, Taschen, 2012, p.254
14: Tom Mankiewicz: Author interview, 2007
15: Cubby Broccoli, *When the Snow Melts*, Boxtree, 1998, p.241
16: John Cork, Bruce Scivally, *James Bond: The Legacy*, Boxtree, 2002, p.164
17: Tom Mankiewicz: Author interview, 2007

18: Cubby Broccoli, *When the Snow Melts*, Boxtree, 1998, p.235
19: Cubby Broccoli, *When the Snow Melts*, Boxtree, 1998, p.231
20: John Cork, Bruce Scivally, *James Bond: The Legacy*, Boxtree, 2002, p.164
21: Paul Duncan, *The James Bond Archives*, Taschen, 2012, p.254
22: *Variety*, August 1972
23: John Cork, Bruce Scivally, *James Bond: The Legacy*, Boxtree, 2002, p.164
24: *Sunday Telegraph*, September 1998
25: Cubby Broccoli, *When the Snow Melts*, Boxtree, 1998, p.231–32
26: Cubby Broccoli, *When the Snow Melts*, Boxtree, 1998, p.241
27: Matthew Field and Ajay Chowdhury, *Some Kind of Hero*, The History Press, 2015, p.282
28: Alan Barnes and Marcus Hearn, *Kiss Kiss Bang! Bang!*, BT Batsford, 2000, p.117
29: *Sunday Telegraph*, September 1998
30: Cubby Broccoli, *When the Snow Melts*, Boxtree, 1998, p.235
31: *Sunday Telegraph*, September 1998
32: John Cork, Bruce Scivally, *James Bond: The Legacy*, Boxtree, 2002, p.164
33: *Sunday Telegraph*, September 1998
34: Cubby Broccoli, *When the Snow Melts*, Boxtree, 1998, p.239
35: Tom Mankiewicz: Author interview, 2007
36: Tino Balio, *United Artists: The Company That Changed the Film Industry*, University of Wisconsin Press, 1987, p.273
37: whatculture.com, January 2013
38: Matthew Field and Ajay Chowdhury, *Some Kind of Hero*, The History Press, 2015, p.285
39: Cubby Broccoli, *When the Snow Melts*, Boxtree, 1998, p.242
40: Tom Mankiewicz: Author interview, 2007

Chapter 21: Out on Their Own

1: *Science Fiction Monthly*, November 1975
2: *Cinema Retro*, January 2012
3: *House of Hammer*, December 1976
4: *007* magazine, No.10, 1982
5: Derek Threadgall, *Shepperton Studios: An Independent View*, BFI Publishing, 1994, p.146–47
6: Gareth Owen, *The Shepperton Story*, The History Press, 2009, p.231
7: *Evening News*, June 1980
8: *St Petersburg Independent*, 17 December 1977
9: *The Times*, June 1977
10: Matthew Field and Ajay Chowdhury, *Some Kind of Hero*, The History Press, 2015, p.286
11: Matthew Field and Ajay Chowdhury, *Some Kind of Hero*, The History Press, 2015, p.282
12: *Harry Saltzman Showman*, documentary, 2000
13: Roy Moseley, *Roger Moore: A Biography*, New English Library, 1985, p.188
14: William P. Cartlidge: Author interview, 2019
15: William P. Cartlidge: Author interview, 2019
16: William P. Cartlidge: Author interview, 2019
17: Tom Mankiewicz: Author interview, 2007
18: Peter Lamont: Author interview, 2019
19: *Screen India*, April 1973
20: Aubrey Menen, *The Mystics*, Dial Press, 1971, p.192
21: *Fate* magazine, August 1974

22: Elmar R. Gruber, *From the Heart of Tibet*, Shambhala Publications, 2010, p.176
23: Dyson Lovell: Author interview, 2007
24: Len Deighton: Author interview, 2007
25: Cherry Hughes: Author interview, 2019
26: *Evening News*, June 1980
27: *The Stage*, 16 September 2016
28: *The Stage*, 16 September 2016
29: Len Deighton: Author interview, 2007
30: Len Deighton: Author interview, 2007
31: Dyson Lovell: Author interview, 2007
32: Len Deighton: Author interview, 2007
33: Len Deighton: Author interview, 2007
34: *Positif: Revue De Cinema*, November 1989
35: Roger Moore, *My Word is My Bond*, Michael O'Mara Books, 2008, p.244
36: *GoldenEye* magazine, Issue 4, Vol. 1, 1996
37: Matthew Field and Ajay Chowdhury, *Some Kind of Hero*, The History Press, 2015, p.470
38: Matthew Field and Ajay Chowdhury, *Some Kind of Hero*, The History Press, 2015, p.470
39: *GoldenEye* magazine, Issue 4, Vol. 1, 1996
40: Matthew Field and Ajay Chowdhury, *Some Kind of Hero*, The History Press, 2015, p.470
41: *GoldenEye* magazine, Issue 4, Vol. 1, 1996
42: Tom Mankiewicz: Author interview, 2007
43: *Cinefantastique*, January 1998
44: Steven Prigge, *Movie Moguls Speak: Interviews with Top Film Producers*, McFarland & Co, 2005, p.19
45: William P. Cartlidge: Author interview, 2019
46: Peter Lamont: Author interview, 2019
47: Peter Lamont: Author interview, 2019
48: *The Guardian*, September 2012
49: *Daily Telegraph*, 9 May 2000
50: Tom Mankiewicz: Author interview, 2007
51: Eric Pleskow: Author interview, 2019
52: *The Guardian*, September 2012

Index